TAKING HAWAII

Taking Hawaii

How Thirteen Honolulu Businessmen Overthrew the Hawaiian Monarchy

in 1893, with a Bluff

Stephen Dando-Collins

OPEN ROAD

INTEGRATED MEDIA

NEW YORK

Copyright © 2012 by Stephen Dando-Collins

ISBN 978-1-4976-3808-2

This edition published in 2014 by Open Road Integrated Media, Inc.
345 Hudson Street
New York, NY 10014
www.openroadmedia.com

CONTENTS

ACKNOWLEDGMENTS

The author extends his grateful thanks to the many people in Hawaii who provided assistance during the research for this book. In particular, Louise Storm and a number of other diligent staff at the Hawaii State Library's Hawaii and Pacific Section; many patient and helpful staff at the Hawaii State Archives; Corine Chun Fujimoto, Curator of Washington Place, and her staff; numerous personnel at the Hamilton Library, University of Hawaii at Manoa, especially Map Technician Ross R. Togashi; Kamehameha Schools archivist Janet Zisk; Juria Kyoya and historian Tony Bennes at the Moana Surfrider Hotel, Waikiki; Frank S. Haines of the American Institute of Architects, Honolulu; and, at the Iolani Palace, Collections Manager Malia Van Heukelem, docent Dolores Leguinecke Oates, and Curator Stuart Ching.

Special thanks go to the Reverend Rod Waterhouse of Hobart, Tasmania, for sharing invaluable family information on John T. Waterhouse and Henry Waterhouse. And to William Kaihe'ekai Maioho, Curator of the Royal Mausoleum, Mauna 'Ala, Hawaii, for conducting my wife and myself through the mausoleum chapel and the royal crypt. To David Waipa Parker, I wish to extend most grateful thanks and profound respect for sharing his family's history. And to Francis K. W. Ching, I record my sincere gratitude for his patient guidance over several years, and for his valued friendship.

This book came together as a result of the unstinting encouragement and knowledgeable input of my New York City literary agent Richard Curtis. And most of all, this book would not have been possible without the dedicated involvement and sustaining support of my wife Louise, the power behind my throne.

'There are only three places that are of value enough to be taken that are not continental. One is Hawaii, and the others are Cuba and Porto Rico (sic). Cuba and Porto Rico (sic) are not now imminent and will not be for a generation. Hawaii may come up for decision at any unexpected hour, and I hope we shall be prepared to decide in the affirmative.'

US Secretary of State James G. Blaine,
to President Benjamin Harrison,
August 10, 1891.

'As regards Hawaii…we should take the islands.'

Theodore Roosevelt, when US
Assistant Secretary of the Navy,
to Captain Alfred T. Mahan,
May 3, 1897.

INTRODUCTION

THE KEY WAS AS BIG AS A MAN'S HAND. AND NOW Bill Maioho, Curator of the Royal Mausoleum at Mauna 'Ala, placed that massive piece of iron in the keyhole and turned it. The heavy black wrought iron gate, richly decorated with six gold seals bearing the coat of arms of Hawaii's kings and queens, swung open at the Curator's hefty push. Bill turned to my wife Louise and myself, and gestured for us to enter the crypt, the burial place of men and women whose names had become familiar to me over years of research.

For a moment, I paused, looking around. There, sitting beneath the palm trees, was the Gothic-style Royal Chapel that Bill had just guided us through. Nearby, the Hawaiian flag fluttered on a flagpole in the warm morning breeze. This 2.7-acre plot at Mauna 'Ala overlooking Honolulu on Oahu is the only place in Hawaii where the US flag does not fly beside the Hawaiian flag. This is sacred Hawaiian land, and long has been.

With a smile, Bill, who occupies his post as Curator here at the pleasure of the Governor of Hawaii, urged us to proceed. Louise and I walked down the steep stone steps and entered the underground space. The interior of the Kalakaua Crypt is not large. The white marble walls are inscribed in gold leaf with the names and dates of birth and death of twenty-one members of the Hawaiian royal family, whose remains are interred on the other side of the marble. I had come to see the final resting place of one former royal in particular–Queen Liliuokalani, last ruler of the Kingdom of Hawaii.

There, high in the left-hand corner, was Liliuokalani's name inscribed in gold. Looking at it with respect and reverence, I felt that I knew her a little. I had read her autobiography. I had read her intimate diary entries covering her strife-torn life. I had read countless accounts of her by people who had known her, in books, newspaper articles, letters and official reports. I am not Hawaiian. I have been to Hawaii a number of times, but I am only a *haole*, a foreigner. To be brought down here into the sacred crypt at Mauna 'Ala was a huge honor for a haole. So, it was quite a presumption to think I might know, and understand, Hawaii's last queen. Silently, I asked Liliuokalani's forgiveness for this intrusion. Sometimes, when I visit a grave or a memorial, I feel a connection with the person who lies buried or is commemorated there. Yet, here I was not feeling any link whatsoever.

We emerged from the crypt, and Bill used his heavy key to lock the gate behind us. As we climbed back to the top of the steps, we saw a gardener waving urgently to us, then pointing to the sedan in which we had arrived. That sedan belonged to Francis Ching, our patient Native Hawaiian host here in the islands. As we hurried to the car, we saw that a rear window had been smashed. Louise gasped; she had left a travel bag on the back seat, thinking that here, in this holy place, it would have been safe. She was proven wrong. The bag had been snatched.

The police were called. Within minutes, a pair of blue and white Honolulu Police Department cruisers arrived. As we described our loss to the policemen, one of the Native Hawaiian officers shook his head, angry that a crime had been committed here, of all places. "The ancestors will not be pleased," he said with a scowl.

Later, a local told us that if Native Hawaiians caught the people responsible for this–a band of Filipinos with a track record in this sort of robbery was immediately suspected by the police–they would be torn limb from limb. Bill, on behalf of his people, apologized profusely for the robbery, but we assured him he had nothing to apologize for, and thanked him for his kindness that morning. I was feeling for our host Francis, whose window had been smashed; but at least his car insurance covered the repair.

A few hours later, Louise and I were at the Iolani Palace, Queen Liliuokalani's former residence in Honolulu, trying to forget the stolen bag and the hassle of replacing its contents. Few visitors to Hawaii know this palace exists. Many longtime residents of Hawaii are equally ignorant of its existence, and it's significance. It is not as if the building is hidden away. The Iolani Palace is in the heart of downtown Honolulu. Cars, taxis, buses stream past it, day and night. But ask a Native Hawaiian, and they will unerringly direct you here. The Friends of the Iolani Palace, a community group, saved the palace from destruction at the last minute in the 1960s, and slowly, painstakingly, proudly restored it, returning it to much as it had been when Liliuokalani lived and ruled here, at the same time retrieving looted palace objects from throughout the United States. Though grand in appearance, the Iolani Palace is the size of a gatehouse at many European palaces. It's a palace in miniature.

Louise and I joined a regular guided tour of the palace conducted by a volunteer docent, or guide, Dolores Leguinecke Oates. Reverently, the dozen or so tour members removed their shoes and donned special slippers designed to preserve the palace's flooring and carpets. From room to room we went, on the first floor: the grand throne room, the dining room, the reception room, where the drama of Queen Liliuokalani's overthrow had been played out a little over a century before. Upstairs, to the former royal study and four bedrooms. Finally, we came to the bedroom where Queen Liliuokalani was kept a prisoner for a year, in her own palace, by the rebels who overthrew her. The decor of the queen's improvised cell was just as it had been back then, with just a few sticks of furniture including the hard single bed her captors had given her to sleep in.

As Dolores told the visitors about what had taken place in this room over a century before, I noticed that the air in here was cold. Icy cold. Outside, it was a typically warm Hawaii day, in the 80s Fahrenheit, and, with no air conditioning in the building, even the large vestibule outside the bedroom was warm, despite the high ceilings. Yet, in here, in the bedroom that had served as the queen's prison cell, it was so cold that goose bumps stood out on my arms. Standing at the back of the group, and sensing someone beside me, I turned to my right. No one was there. Yet, there was a brooding presence here, right beside me.

Later in the palace's basement, after the other visitors had departed, Louise and I chatted with docent Dolores, and I revealed that I was researching a book about the overthrow of the queen.

Louise then said to me, "Did you feel how cold it was in the queen's bedroom?" When I agreed, Louise, looking at Dolores, said, "She was there, wasn't she? The spirit of Queen Liliuokalani is in that room."

Dolores nodded. "You noticed it, too? I always feel her

presence when I go into that room. One or two others, like yourself, do too. I don't think she's very happy."

Who would have been happy, dethroned in a military coup, imprisoned in one of her own bedrooms while she was tried for treason—with a death sentence hanging over her head. Treated as an equal by the crowned heads of Europe up that point, Hawaii's queen must have equated her predicament with that of other ill-fated queens such as Mary Queen of Scots, Anne Boleyn and Marie-Antoinette.

Once we were outside and walking toward the Royal Hawaiian Band, which was giving a recital in the palace grounds, a Native Hawaiian docent hurried after us, calling for us to wait. Dolores had mentioned us to this lady, who said, once she had overtaken us in her flowing floral caftan. "I hear you're writing a book about the overthrow of Queen Liliuokalani." Taking my hand, she smiled warmly, and said, "I want to wish every success. It is a story that should be told."

As Louise and I rode a bus back to Waikiki and our hotel, I was deep in thought about Liliuokalani. The bus passed Fort De Russy, and I remembered that it sits on land once occupied by the Waikiki beach house of John T. Waterhouse, father of the Australian-born man who, I now knew from my research, had led Liliuokalani's overthrow. And I knew, in that moment, that, no matter how long it took, I must tell the true and complete story of how Liliuokalani had lost her throne. Many accounts of the overthrow had been written previously, but most had been colored by bias, from both sides of the spectrum, or more often from lack of all relevant information. Information which I had managed to unearth on several continents.

The telling of that tale—the full, warts-and-all tale—would at least set the record straight, and might perhaps let Liliuokalani rest peacefully at last.

1.

THE FIRST SHOT

DEPENDING ON WHO WRITES THE HISTORY BOOKS, a failed revolution is an act of treason, while a successful revolution is a turning point in history. On the afternoon of Tuesday, January 17, 1893, tough-minded American adventurer John Good was determined that the revolution of which he was a part would make history for its success rather than its failure. And to that end he was prepared to shed blood if need be.

Good had been appointed ordnance officer of the rebel forces by the revolutionary leaders. During the late morning, he had supervised the unpacking of Springfield rifles and crates of ammunition that had been illicitly shipped into Honolulu, capital of the Kingdom of Hawaii, from the United States. Disguised as general merchandise, the shipment had been received by the importing firm of E. O. Hall and Sons, whose L-shaped hardware store occupied the south-eastern corner of Fort and King Streets in downtown Honolulu. In the back of the Hall and Sons store, Good and several companions had filled scores of leather bandoleers with rifle rounds. Then, in the yard behind the store, they loaded rifles and bandoleers onto a horse-drawn wagon.

The Hawaiian authorities were aware that the proprietors of Hall and Sons had previously been engaged in the illegal receipt of arms, so Good would not have been surprised to see a uniformed Honolulu policeman lounging in the Fort Street shadows nearby as 2.00 p.m. came and went. The policeman, like all members of the local constabulary, was a native Hawaiian. His uniform was dark blue, buttoned to the neck. The badge on his left breast and blue slouch hat bore the crown of the Hawaiian monarchy. Sure enough, the constable, who was unarmed, had been posted to keep an eye on Hall's store in case suspected rebels were using it as an arms depot.

John Good knew that the revolution was scheduled to start at 3.00 p.m., and it was his task to transfer the rifles and ammunition to the former Armory of the Honolulu Rifles Association on Beretania Street. Companies of rebel volunteers had been secretly ordered to assemble there prior to going into action against the Government Building near Palace Square at 3.00.

At 2.20, John Good and three companions climbed up onto the loaded wagon in Hall and Sons' yard. To drive the wagon, Good had chosen Ed Benner, a mature and experienced driver for Honolulu merchants Castle and Cooke. For guards, Good had selected Edwin Paris, an American, and Fritz Rowald, a German, and both were now toting loaded Springfield rifles as they seated themselves on the back of the wagon. At the same time, rebel Oscar White, another American, who was secretary and treasurer of Hall and Sons, drew back the gates that opened onto Fort Street from the Hall and Sons yard. Good, who sat on the bench seat on the driver's right, patted Benner on the back and ordered him to drive like the wind. The driver lashed his whip along the backs of his two horses. The horses jumped forward. And the wagon rolled toward the gate.

Good's timing was poor. Just as the wagon came through the gateway, the horse-drawn Fort Street trolley car appeared opposite the gate, having just crossed the King Street intersection. A dray was beside it, going in the other direction. The way was completely blocked. At this same moment, the watching policeman came hurrying up, and grabbed at the wagon's reins.

"Halt!" the policeman ordered.[1]

Benner was forced to rein in his horses. Beside him, John Good drew a revolver from his belt. Seeing this, the constable blew his police whistle. Four more uniformed Hawaiian police officers, all of them big men, had been stationed a little further along Fort Street, watching the law offices of William O. Smith, a suspected rebel. Summoned by the whistle, all four came at the run. The first cop to arrive grabbed the bit of the nearest horse. The next officer began climbing up beside the driver to take over the reins; Benner immediately reacted by lashing him with his whip, sending the policeman sprawling back onto the roadway on his back. Two policemen who ran to the rear of the wagon found themselves staring down the barrels of rifles leveled at them by Paris and Rowald. In the face of the guns, these two cops backed off.

As coincidence would have it, two more rebels stood on the rear platform of the small, open Fort Street trolley car, heading for the rebel meeting place just down the street at the Smith law offices. American-born and thirty-five years old, John A. McCandless had lived in Hawaii for twelve years, where, together with his two brothers, he had made a small fortune drilling artesian wells. His trolley car companion was a tailor by the name of Martin. The tailor promptly drew a pistol from his belt and brazenly aimed it at the policeman who had grabbed the horse bit. This officer fearfully let go of the bit and raised his hands.

At this moment, McCandless, on the street car, and Oscar White at the Hall and Sons gates, both yelled warnings to John Good. Prompted by their warnings, Good turned to his right in time to see another policeman running determinedly toward him down Fort Street from the King Street intersection. Good would later claim that he saw this policeman reach behind him as he ran, as if going to draw a pistol from his belt. Without hesitation, Good quickly took a bead on the officer with his revolver, and fired. The cop, who, like his fellow officers, proved to be unarmed, went down.

That shot was heard across downtown Honolulu.

It was heard by the US Marine Corps' Lieutenant Herbert. L. Draper, in charge of a detachment of marines stationed a block away at the American Consulate on the corner of Fort and Merchant Streets. Draper immediately hurried to use the telephone at the consulate to report to Captain Gilbert C. Wiltse, commander of the cruiser USS *Boston*, which lay at anchor in the harbor, that a shot had been fired.

The shot was also heard at the Honolulu Police Station House on Merchant Street. There, behind sandbags, more than a hundred policemen and Hawaiian Household Guard reservists armed with rifles and a pair of Gatling machineguns had been waiting tensely all day for something like this to happen. Charles B. Wilson, Marshal of the Kingdom of Hawaii and commander of Hawaii's police, promptly ordered all remaining policemen in the city to retreat to the station house. At the same time, Wilson rang Major Sam Nowlein, commander of the troops of the Household Guard protecting the Queen of Hawaii two blocks away at her royal residence, the Iolani Palace, to be ready to defend her with their lives and repel a rebel assault.

The shot was likewise heard at the Fort Street legal offices of William O. Smith. There, eighteen wealthy and influential local businessmen had been gathered since earlier in the day to finalize arrangements for the overthrow of the queen. Most of these men were American, or of American descent. Several were British and German. One, thirty-six-year-old Henry Waterhouse, had been born in Tasmania, Australia, and in Hawaii had the nickname of 'the Tasmanian'. Waterhouse, a deacon of the Central Union Church, had for the past few years been running the extensive Hawaiian business interests of his wealthy father, John T. Waterhouse, who, as a leading Honolulu capitalist, now devoted his time to promoting major new enterprises such as the Pacific telegraph cable. If it had not been for Henry Waterhouse, this coup would have fizzled like a damp firecracker in the preceding days, when the leading lights of the revolutionary movement had lost their courage and slunk away.

Now, the coup leaders who had joined Waterhouse at Smith's legal office puzzled over the meaning of the shot they had just heard; it didn't figure in their plans at all. Before long, their colleague John McCandless arrived by trolley car from the scene of the shooting just down the street, and solved the mystery for them. McCandless brought the breathless report: "Good has shot a policeman."[2]

The rebel leaders all looked at each other in shock and surprise. It quickly dawned on them that the police could arrive at any moment to arrest them. Yet the revolt wasn't due to start for another thirty minutes. At least Good's shot had the advantage of drawing off the police who had been watching the Smith law offices from across the street. Fred McChesney, the California-born manager of the Honolulu branch of his father's San Francisco import-export business, spoke the thought that was in all their minds: "Now is the time to go," he said.[3]

With those words, the Hawaiian revolution was launched.

Henry Waterhouse, voicing his agreement, jumped to his feet. He and the seventeen other revolutionary leaders hurried out the door. Fred McChesney hailed a passing horse-drawn taxi–a light, four-wheeled hackney carriage, or a 'hack' as it was known– and dashed to his nearby home to fetch his pistol. English-born John H. Soper, a former Marshal of the Kingdom who had been appointed commander of all rebel forces by the revolutionary leaders, was dispatched by Waterhouse to the Armory to collect those armed men who had already assembled there, then lead them to the Government Building. The other members of the rebel leadership decided to proceed directly to the Government Building without delay. Splitting into two groups, they hurried on foot via Merchant Street and Queen Street toward Palace Square.

Meanwhile, John Good and his wagonload of rifles and ammunition had completed their escape from the Hall and Sons store. Good's pistol shot had scared the wagon's horses into motion, just as, fortuitously, the trolley car and dray in their path had parted and opened the way for them. As the wagon charged up Fort Street a crowd quickly gathered around the downed policeman, with people coming from all directions. At the same time, the two unarmed cops who had gone to the rear of the wagon commandeered a hack, and gave chase to Good and his load.

Maintaining a respectful distance between their hack and the speeding wagon–for rebel guard Edmund Paris kept his rifle pointed at them all the way–the two policemen followed the wagon as it dashed along Fort Street then turned into School Street. From there, wagon and pursuers sped along Punchbowl Street to the former Armory on Beretania. Ever since the Honolulu Rifles militia had been forcibly disbanded by the Hawaiian Government, the Armory had been used as a bicycle repair shop. As the wagon careered around the corner from Punchbowl Street, a group of men stood formed up in neat ranks outside the Armory. These were all immigrants of German birth, led by Charles Ziegler. As soon as the wagon came to a halt, the Germans hurried to it and opened the boxes it contained. Taking out the rifles brought by Good, they loaded them, and strapped on the leather ammunition bandoleers.

The pair of shadowing policemen, seeing the mass of armed men ahead when they reached the Beretania Street intersection, turned their taxi away. Returning to the police station downtown, the pair reported to Marshal Wilson that they had observed men arming themselves at the Armory. When Wilson asked how many men were involved, his officers calculated they only numbered fifteen or twenty.

Marshal Wilson now prepared to fight. The combined force of Hawaiian police and soldiers, all men who had sworn to defend their queen to their last drop of blood, vastly outnumbered the known rebel forces. But a question nagged at Wilson. The previous evening, one hundred-and-sixty-two US Marines and sailors had been landed from the *Boston* and had taken up strategic positions in the city center, uninvited by the Hawaiian Government. The US force was well armed, not only with rifles and side-arms but with a cannon and a Gatling machinegun. The question was, would those US troops take part in the revolution, on the rebel side? In which case, the Hawaiians would not only be fighting home-grown rebels–American, British, German, Portuguese, and Australian residents of the Kingdom of Hawaii–they would also find themselves at war with the United States of America!

2.

THE HAWAIIAN
MONARCHY

To FULLY UNDERSTAND THE OVERTHROW OF HAWAII'S monarchy, it is first necessary to understand the nature of that monarchy. By 1893, the concept of a monarch ruling over all of the Hawaiian Islands was not even a century old.

The original Maori residents of Hawaii had come across the Pacific to the islands in seagoing canoes. Anthropologists believe that these first Polynesian immigrants came around A.D. 400, about the same time that their cousins made their way to Aotearoa (New Zealand) from the Tahitian islands, by way of the Cook Islands and the Marquesas. There would have been intermittent migration to Hawaii from the other Polynesian islands over the next 600 years or so, but another major migration from Tahiti is believed to have taken place between the 10th and 13th centuries.

In their sturdy canoes, the original settlers brought their wives, their children, chickens, hogs, and the taro plant. The first settlers also brought a common Maori language and customs.[4] From Hawaii to Easter Island, Tahiti to Aotearoa, all Polynesian peoples including Hawaiians are believed to have come from the same roots. Once upon a time, the Hawaiians, like their cousins the Maori of New Zealand, greeted one another by rubbing noses. This custom is not so much about the touching of skin as the exchange of breath, which is seen by Polynesians as an exchange of *mana*, or life force.

Over the centuries, the native society of Hawaii developed along caste lines, brought from east central Polynesia. Hawaiian society was very structured. There were several castes–the most superior being the ali'i, (pronounced ah-lee). The ali'i, who were both male and female, in turn consisted of eleven classes.[5] Four major professions were practiced by the ali'i. The lani profession, (whose members were known as the kalani), was broken up into eleven major classes, headed by the ali'i nui.[6] These kalani were the experts in managing the resources of the land, ocean and people.

Members of the huna profession, (the kahuna), comprised the medical practitioners, the seers, the astronomers, the truth seekers, the canoe builders, the navigators, the feather workers, to name a few. The most senior and revered kahuna was the kanuna nui. The third profession, that of the lawaia, consisted of the master fishermen, and their branch was in turn divided into numerous sub-professions connected with fishing and the sea. The last of the major professions practiced by the ali'i, the mahiai, were the master farmers, and they too had a number of sub-professions.

Immediately below the ali'i caste came the noa caste, which consisted of four classes.[7] Last of all came the kauwa, the caste of no status, made up of slaves, prisoners of war, and outcasts. As in India to this day, you were born into your Hawaiian caste and nothing you did could ever elevate you to a higher caste. If you took a member of a lower class as a partner, your children took their caste.

The members of the upper class, the ali'i, provided what Westerners would call the chiefs and sub-chiefs of the islands. There was no concept of land ownership among the Hawaiian people. The ali'i considered themselves the islands' resource management stewards, acting on behalf of their ancestors. The Hawaiians believed that people lived in three different plains of existence–the plain in which you and I live, the plain in which the ancestors lived, and the plain in which gods lived. The people who lived on our plain of existence all worked for the ancestors–the real rulers or chiefs. It was the ancestors who were the landowners, and the lawgivers.

There were ali'i ancestors governing every aspect of existence. The kahuna–which included both men and women–oversaw the worship of a pantheon of heavenly gods such as Ku the war god, who was also the ancestor who looked after tall trees, and Pele, goddess of fire and the volcano. Likewise, there was a kahuna for every part of Hawaiian life. The fishing kahuna advised the people on the best time to fish, and where. An agricultural kahuna was the expert on the growing of taro and other crops. There was a kahuna in charge of the capture and release of the rare birds that provided the feathers used in the making of the cloaks and capes of senior ali'i for use on special occasions and during times of war–the oo bird for dull yellow feathers as well as black ones, the mamo bird for golden yellow and black, the i'iwi for dark red, the apapane for bright red. Other birds furnished green and white feathers.

A particular kahuna selected the trees that would be made into canoes, led the prayers of thanks to the tree for sacrificing itself to become a canoe, then supervised canoe construction. There was a kahuna for the hula, a ritual dance performed at important Hawaiian ceremonies. A kahuna supervised the training in chanting; individual young ali'i who showed aptitude for this art were expected to master this traditional means of telling the ancestry of his or her family back into the mists of time, and chants could last for hours. An ali'i who made a mistake in a chant could face the death penalty. There were many individual kahuna, and they could all be called on for help by any ali'i. Some kahuna worked directly for the 'chief', especially those kahuna trained in healing, using both herbal and spiritual remedies.

Westerners would later equate the latter kahuna with the witch doctors of Africa, especially when it became known that they could cast curses of death over unfortunate native victims–who invariably died. This was the kahuna anaana. His job was to discover the truth regarding an alleged crime, and to punish the person responsible. It was believed that if the kahuna anaana made a mistake, the death curse would come back and kill *him*.

On leaving an audience with a ruling ali'i, his people were required to back away, never turning their backs on the ali'i. Members of the lower castes had little to do with the ali'i. It was the ali'i who made all the decisions, and who did all the fighting. No one questioned these social mores, just as no one questioned the right of a senior ali'i to have as many female partners as he liked–there was no formal Hawaiian marriage ceremony. Only those of ali'i nui rank, of the senior family lines, had many 'wives', and these unions were for political purposes, to cement families to that ali'i through any resulting children. Such children were raised by the family of the mother.

Down through the centuries, numerous senior ali'i controlled various parts of the eight inhabited islands of the Hawaiian chain, and occasionally one would control an entire island. But no one ali'i controlled all the islands of Hawaii. Control came via military conquest, and few were the years that passed without a battle on one island or another, despite the otherwise gentle, easy-going nature of the Hawaiian people. Hawaiian men were typically tall and powerfully built. Warriors of seven feet in height are recorded.

Hawaiian weapons were the wooden spear, daggers, slings and sling stones, and the war club. There was also unarmed fighting. Gord masks, described as 'helmets' by Westerners, were used by a kahuna who was keeper of the ku kii–feathered and non feathered images. These keepers would transport a small feather image of Ku during the time of Lono–as captured in an eighteenth century sketch by Captain James Cook's shipboard artist. Ali'i nui, and pukaua–war leaders–wore wicker helmets with feather crests to set them apart during times of war, just as Roman centurions had feathered crests on their helmets in early times. And, just as a general of ancient Rome wore a scarlet cloak and a Roman commander in chief wore a purple cloak, the cloaks and capes of Hawaiian war leaders were designed to enable their warriors to easily distinguish them on the battlefield.

Often, the champion of one chief would fight the champion of another, but most fighting involved all warriors. After an initial exchange of spears, combatants would charge in for bloody hand-to-hand combat, with the object of killing the pukaua and taking control of his body, or killing the ali'i nui. Once that was achieved, the battle was over. They were not fighting for land or territory as such; fighting was over the right to manage the natural and human resources.

In January 1778, the Hawaiian people had their first recorded encounter with the European world, when British navigator Captain James Cook's two vessels HMS *Resolution* and HMS *Discovery* arrived off Kauai. Cook gave the name Sandwich Islands to the island group, in honor of his patron back in England, the Earl of Sandwich. When Cook returned to the islands ten months later, after exploring the Pacific, and anchored at Kealakekua Bay on the Kona coast of the island of Hawaii, or the Big Island as it is known, he was once again welcomed by the Hawaiians, who considered him the reincarnation of Lono, their god of the harvest. But things soon turned sour.

On the night of February 13-14, 1779, one of the *Discovery*'s boats, a 'painter,' which was tied up alongside, was stolen. The Hawaiian thieves' intent was to dismantle the boat for the long iron nails used in its construction, which they converted into tools and weapons. Cook, furious at the theft, landed early that morning with ten armed marines, intending to kidnap Kalaniopuu, the elderly senior ali'i ruling the island of Hawaii, and ransom him for the return of the stolen boat. Kalaniopuu's warriors massed. Cook himself fired two pistols, killing a warrior with one shot, and a melee at the water's edge ensued. Cook and four marines were killed.

Kalaniopuu's party included his twenty-year-old nephew, a six feet-plus, handsome, well-built ali'i by the name of Kamehameha–pronounced ka-mayha-mayha. According to legend, this strapping warrior, who had previously proven a worthy champion for his uncle in battle, took possession of the dead Captain Cook's hair. The hair of ancestors was treated with great reverence by Hawaiians. On ceremonial occasions, leading ali'i, male and female, wore necklaces woven from the hair of their ancestors. Among the Hawaiians, Cook's hair added greatly to Kamehameha's mana and prestige.

After old Kalaniopuu died in 1782, his nephew Kamehameha went to war with the chief's sons, his heir and a younger brother. During years of bloody conflict, Kamehameha gained control of the Big Island, then fought the ali'i of the other islands. Building an army of 16,000 warriors, and aided by two British sailors, John Young and Isaac Davis, prisoners of Kamehameha who subsequently trained his warriors to use captured American muskets and cannon, by 1796 Kamehameha controlled all the Hawaiian islands except Kauai. That island seemed destined to remain beyond his control, for every time he was about to launch an invasion of Kauai he was prevented by storm or plague.

Kamehameha had long believed that he was destined to rule over all the Hawaiian Islands. When he was born, a fiery light had been seen in the sky–later historians suggest it was Halley's Comet. A kahuna had told Alapai, the ali'i then reigning over much of the Big Island, that this fiery light would herald the birth of 'a killer of ali'i.' Fearful for his own life, Alapai had ordered the death of the child, but Kamehameha had been smuggled away and raised in secret. When Kamehameha was five, Alapai had mellowed and allowed the child to be returned and raised in his court. There was another, even stronger reason for Kamehameha to believe in his destiny. Just as Sir Galahad had plucked the sword Excalibur from a stone, at age fourteen Kamehameha had been the first to lift Hawaii's Naha Stone. Hawaiian legend had it that he who lifted the Naha Stone, which can be seen at Hilo to this day, would rule over all the islands.

In 1810, Captain Nathan Winslip, a visiting American trader, brought Kamehameha the friendly greetings of his cousin Kaumuali'i, the ruling ali'i of Kauai. Winslip and other Westerners would misconstrue this to mean that Kaumuali'i would henceforth acknowledge Kamehameha as his sovereign while Kaumuali'i himself continued to rule on Kauai. But Kauai did not effectively come under the control of the ruler of the other Hawaiian islands until the reign of Kamehameha III, decades later. So adamant were the native people of Kauai that Kamehameha never gained control of their island that, when, late in the nineteenth century, the central government at Honolulu proposed to erect a statue of Kamehameha on Kauai, the people of Kauai refused to accept it.

As far as the outside world was concerned, Kamehameha had established his total control of all the islands, and, as far as the Europeans were concerned, he established an all-powerful Hawaiian monarchy of the kind that they were familiar with in Europe. Kamehameha founded the first Hawaiian ruling dynasty, in the same way that Augustus became the founder of the first imperial dynasty of Rome. And, in the same way that the Caesar name would be adopted by Augustus Caesar's early successors, so four successors to Kamehameha would take his name–Kamehameha II through V–while the original sovereign of the islands came to be known as Kamehameha the Great.

When Kamehameha died in 1819, he left behind close to one hundred female partners, and as many as sixty children. The highest-ranking of his partners was his niece Keopuolani, and her twenty-two-year-old son Liholiho was Kamehameha's heir apparent. In succeeding his father, Liholiho took the title Kamehameha II.

The new ruler was installed wearing a scarlet, gold-trimmed jacket in the style of a British army officer, evidencing the strong influence of the European residents of, and visitors to, the islands, by that time. Overhead flew the flag which Kamehameha had created for himself. In the top left-hand corner it featured the British ensign, the so-called Union Jack, based on a 'red ensign' given to Kamehameha by the British navy's Captain George Vancouver as a gift. Kamehameha's flag was dominated by eight horizontal stripes in red, white and blue, representing the eight main islands of Hawaii. This flag, the flag of the sovereign nation of Hawaii, still flies in the islands to this day, as the state flag of Hawaii.

Foreign trading vessels regularly called at the islands, particularly at Oahu's capital of Honolulu, which offered a safe deep-water anchorage. Since 1811, the islands' sandalwood trees had attracted increasing numbers of foreign traders determined to make their fortune selling sandalwood to China, where it was in big demand. Within several decades these foreign traders would greedily denude Hawaii of sandalwood. There were other more visible signs of change. Ever since John Young had built the first frame house in the islands, at Kawaihai on the Big Island, other substantial buildings had been erected, although the large grass huts of the natives were still everywhere to be seen.

Another great change came over Hawaii and its people with the ascension of Kamehameha II. The new king's installation ceremony was presided over by one of Kamehameha the Great's female partners, Kaahumanu, who took the position of kuhina nui, or governor. For the rest of her days, Kaahumanu would control Hawaii's council of ali'i, or Council of Chiefs as Westerners called it, serving as the kingdom's *de facto* 'queen.' Kamehameha II, known as king to the outside world, used the title of ali'i nui within his kingdom. The female kuhina nui soon shook up Hawaiian society, bringing resistance from some senior ali'i, who rose in revolt, only to be put down by the ali'i nui's superior forces.

These changes came at precisely the time that the brig *Thaddeus* sailed from Boston, Massachusetts carrying a party of Christian missionaries from the Congregational Church. The Boston missionaries had as their mission the Christianizing of the natives of the Hawaiian Islands. Led by two ordained ministers, Hiram Bingham and Asa Thurston, the party included a doctor, teachers, a farmer, a printer complete with a printing press, and their wives. These were the forerunners of more than one hundred missionaries, mostly American, who would come to the Hawaiian Islands over the next few decades.

The *Thaddeus* dropped anchor off Kohala, on the Big Island, in March, 1820. When a number of native canoes came out to trade, members of the missionary party were horrified by the sight of near-naked men and bare-breasted women. Some of the puritanical New Englanders, in tears, could not bring themselves to continue looking at this 'depraved' scene.

Permitted to remain in the kingdom by Kamehameha II, the New England party set out to convert the locals to Christianity, taking no interest in Hawaiian culture or beliefs, which they considered barbaric. Taught to read and write by the missionaries, many Hawaiians did indeed become Christians. But there was a price for their literacy–the missionaries imposed bans on Hawaiian customs such as the hula, the meaning-rich, hip-swinging dance which the prim New Englanders saw as lewd. Intoxicating drinks were banned, and the missionaries also determinedly set out to eradicate the promiscuity that they associated with the polygamous customs of senior Hawaiian ali'i.

The missionaries also 'reduced to written form' the Hawaiian language, so that they could print an Hawaiian language bible. Much of this work was done by William Ellis, a British clergyman who arrived from Sydney, New South Wales, in 1822 and spent two years in the islands. Ellis had previously served in Tahiti, and had become familiar with the native tongue there. In putting the language of the Hawaiians into written form, Ellis and the missionaries bastardized the language, discarding some sounds which they considered too close to others. They kept the 'k' but did away with 't,' for instance, and retained the 'l' but discarded the rolling 'r' used by the Hawaiians.

King Kamehameha II, meanwhile, had been made intensely curious about the outside world by all he saw and heard from the *haoles*, or foreigners, who visited his kingdom or resided there. In late 1823, he and his favorite wife, Queen Kamamalu, sailed for England to visit King George IV, aboard the chartered whaler *L'Aigle*, accompanied by a party of ali'i. But, in England, the party came down with measles, against which they had no natural resistance. First the queen died. A week later, the grief-stricken king also passed away.

Kamehameha II's twelve-year-old brother Kauikeaouli was inaugurated as Kamehameha III, with the all-powerful kuhina nui Kaahumanu acting as his regent. The real reins of power remained where they had lain since the death of Kamehameha the Great, in the hands of his capable widow. Kaahumanu continued to wield power up until her death, at the age of sixty-four, in 1832. By that time, nineteen-year-old Kamehameha III, now with a western education, had become dashingly handsome and debonair, and was a wearer of smart military uniforms of the kind favored by European royalty. With the death of the kuhina nui, the young king tried, unsuccessfully, to exercise sole control of the kingdom. To keep him in check, the council of ali'i appointed a new kuhina nui, another female, the king's sister; her successor would also be a woman.

Kamehameha III, after kicking against the traces of Christianity and trying to wrest power from his sister and the council of ali'i, had by 1835 resigned himself to a life essentially of a royal figurehead. Yet in 1839 he surprised many by promulgating a Declaration of Rights for his people which came to be known as the 'Hawaiian Magna Carta.' He followed this the next year with Hawaii's first written Constitution, which created a bicameral legislature for the kingdom based on the Westminster system. With one house appointed and the other elected, it emulated the system used by Great Britain in all her major colonies, such as those in Australia, and in the province of Canada.

Three years later, in 1843, an event shook Hawaii which had little lasting effect at the time but which was to have great influence half a century later in 1893 when armed rebellion threatened the Hawaiian throne. For years, the British consul in Honolulu, Richard Charlton, had been in dispute with the Hawaiian Government concerning a piece of waterfront land over which he claimed to hold a lease. In late 1842, Charlton set off for England on business, leaving Alexander Simpson as acting British consul. The Hawaiian authorities refused to accept Simpson as acting consul, for he had been appointed by Charlton, not by the British Government. Before long, Simpson found himself in court in Honolulu representing Charlton in a suit launched by an English firm that involved a decade-old case.

The Honolulu court found against the absent Charlton, to the amount of almost $10,000, and an order was issued against the consul's Oahu property in lieu of payment. In response, his fill-in, Simpson, sent a dispatch to a British consul in Mexico asking for a British naval vessel to be sent to Hawaii to protect the interests of British subjects. In response, Rear Admiral Richard Thomas, commander of the British navy's Pacific Squadron, dispatched the frigate HMS *Carysfort*, commanded by Captain Lord George Paulet, to Hawaii.

When the *Carysfort* arrived at Honolulu in February, 1843, Lord Paulet acted haughtily, and King Kamehameha III reciprocated with equal haughtiness. Over several weeks the pair exchanged written demands, until Paulet issued an ultimatum that had western residents of the now sprawling town of Honolulu packing up and taking refuge on ships in the harbor, convinced that Paulet would bombard the town. By this time, Hawaii no longer possessed an army or a navy as it had in Kamehameha the Great's time, and all the great Hawaiian military commanders of Kamehameha's era were long gone. Under the threat of the *Carysfort*'s guns, Hawaii's young king backed down, acknowledged Simpson as acting consul, and granted Consul Charlton a 299-year lease on the disputed waterfront property.

Pompous Paulet did not stop there. He insisted that the verdict in the Charlton court case be overturned, and pressed a claim for some $100,000 in damages. Kamehameha III and his principal adviser, American missionary physician Dr. Gerrit P. Judd, realized that the unreasonable Paulet wanted nothing less than control of the kingdom. They knew that, in any contest, the British gunners aboard the *Carysfort* would easily outgun the old cannon and inexperienced gun crews at Honolulu's two forts. Honolulu could be destroyed and thousands killed. Deciding that, to avoid bloodshed, he must back down, the king begrudgingly agreed to settle the dispute by provisionally ceding the Hawaiian Islands to Great Britain until the matter could be resolved by cooler heads in London.

On February 25, a formal handing over ceremony took place on the parade ground of the coral fort built on Honolulu's shore by Isaac Davis for Kamehameha the Great. The deed of cession was read aloud, the Hawaiian flag was lowered, and the Union Jack run up. A twenty-one gun salute was fired by the *Carysfort*, and answered by the aged guns at the fort, and the frigate's band played the British national anthem. Under threat of violence, Hawaii had overnight become a British possession. Lord Paulet allowed the king and his counselors to continue in their posts, but to oversee government affairs he set up a commission consisting of himself, two British residents, and Kamehameha III. Before long, Paulet, through the commission and supported by his frigate's guns, was running roughshod over the government of the islands.

Hawaiians had been increasingly incensed by Paulet by the

time that, on July 26, HMS *Dublin* dropped anchor at Honolulu carrying Admiral Thomas, Paulet's superior. The admiral was unimpressed with the way that Paulet had handled things, and, once he had obtained a guarantee from the king that safeguarded the future rights of all British subjects in the kingdom, he announced that he would immediately terminate the cession agreement.

Admiral Thomas formally ceded control of the Hawaiian Islands back to their king on July 31. At the Honolulu fort, the British flag came down and the Hawaiian flag was once more run up the staff. All the ships in the harbor boomed a fresh salute, which was answered by the guns at the coral fort and the Hawaiian battery established on top of Punchbowl Hill by Kamehameha the Great. In a speech, King Kamehameha III said "Ua mau ke ea o ka ain I ka pono"–the life of the land is preserved by righteousness. This became Hawaii's official motto.[8]

Ten days of joyous festivities followed, as the Hawaiian people celebrated the return of their independence. The wise and fair Admiral Thomas remained in the island for six months, ensuring that the restoration was not upset by fractious Britons. He only departed when a new British consul arrived from London. Following this event, the Hawaiian Government was able to obtain guarantees of its sovereignty and independence from the governments of Britain, France and the United States.

Several lessons came out of the Paulet affair. The Hawaiian people would always remember that the unfair seizure of control of the islands had been reversed by a senior representative of a foreign power. It taught them to believe that good men could always be relied upon to help them in their time of need. But Paulet's forced cession of the islands to British control, as brief as it had been, had also taught the world that it would only take a small display of military might for the islands to be seized in future.

The concept of personal land ownership was alien to the Hawaiian people. Consequently, the idea of allocating control of land by means of a piece of paper, and of buying and selling land, was laughable to them. This encouraged the missionaries in the islands to pressure King Kamehameha III into looking at ways of dividing up the land in western style. When, by the end of 1847, the king could not come to agreement with the two hundred and forty-five 'chiefs' of the islands, the most senior ali'i, American lawyer William Little Lee suggested a formula for land division. Lee had landed in Honolulu the previous year when the ship on which he was traveling to Oregon was forced into harbor by a storm. Just twenty-six years of age, Lee, a New Yorker, was only the second qualified lawyer in a town whose inhabitants included six hundred foreigners. In 1848, Lee, who would die young from tuberculosis, became Hawaii's chief justice.

The Lee plan established a four-member commission to which all chiefs were required to submit their land claims. Claims recognized by the commission were entered into the Mahele Book. All missionaries and foreigners in the kingdom also laid claim to the lands which they were occupying throughout the islands, and they were granted title in fee simple to those lands. Young Chief Justice Lee was himself granted title to 2500 acres of prime agricultural land, much of which he soon planted with sugar cane. The American missionaries of the Congregational and Presbyterian Churches claimed many thousands of rural acres during this Great Mahele, as the land grab became known. They also invested in sugar cane plantations, saying that the missions needed to be self-sufficient in their incomes.

Two Boston missionaries, Samuel Castle and Amos Cooke, gave up missionary work altogether in 1851 and established the Castle and Cooke department store in Honolulu. They would invest heavily in sugar plantations. By the 1890's, Castle and Cooke would be one of Hawaii's 'Big Five' companies, with vast land holdings–on the island of Lanai alone they would own ninety-five percent of the arable land. None of this would have been possible without the Great Mahele. With ideal growing conditions and cheap labor, Hawaiian sugar production rapidly expanded in the 1850s, creating a major export trade that made a select few foreigners such as Castle and Cooke very rich men. Come the 1870s, one third of Hawaii's sugar would be going to Australia, with two-thirds exported to the United States. By the 1890's, with Queensland in Australia developing its own sugar industry, almost all Hawaiian sugar would be going to the US.

In 1851, too, an enterprising new arrival to Hawaii from Australia set up in business in Honolulu not far from the Castle and Cook store. The arrival of thirty-four-year-old Englishman John T. Waterhouse on May 1 of that year would in fact spell the end of the Hawaiian monarchy forty-two years later, although, of course, no one could know that in 1851. Born at Reading, Berkshire in England, John Thomas Waterhouse was the eldest son of the Reverend John Waterhouse. In 1832, when he was just sixteen, John T. journeyed to the United States, taking along a stock of toys and cheap jewelry, which he sold at a profit. In Sullivan County in upstate New York, young John T. went into partnership with a local, hunting wolves for the $40 bounty being offered on their scalps. But it was John's partner who proved the greatest wolf, cheating the youth out of his share of their profits. To survive, John T. became a teacher and part-time fur trader.

After six years in the US, John T. rejoined his family in England, where, in 1838, he married Eleanor Dickenson. The couple promptly joined the remainder of the Waterhouse family boarding ship for Van Diemen's Land, (renamed Tasmania in 1856), where John T.'s father took up an appointment as Wesleyan minister at Hobart Town in February, 1839. Members of the large Waterhouse clan would, in time, spread throughout Australia and New Zealand, becoming prominent in business and government. Young John T. promptly opened a Hobart ironmongery at 48 Elizabeth Street, later finding a business partner and opening the chandlery business of Waterhouse and Whitney at Hobart's New Wharf. Their two-story store was filled with goods imported from Britain, and John T. quickly prospered, purchasing the 123 ton schooner *Timbo* to transport grain. John T. was perfectly happy raising a young family in Hobart, and he would have been there to his dying day, would have played no part in Hawaiian history, had it not been for a chance event one winter's night in 1850.

John T. had taken a lease on a farm at Cornelian Bay, on Hobart's then northern outskirts, and he, Eleanour and their six children lived in the farmhouse there. Late one night, he was awoken by a gunshot and then female screams from nearby. Rushing out into the frosty night in just his nightshirt, John T. found that his neighbor, a Mr. Shoobridge, had spotted several women digging up potatoes from his potato patch and had fired a warning shot into the air. But what goes up must come down, and the ball had fallen and pierced the skull of one of the unfortunate women. John T. was unable to do anything for the woman, who died shortly after, but he himself caught such a severe chill that he almost died. On recovering, and on the advice of his doctor, John T. began to think about moving to a warmer clime before the next winter arrived. Taking out a map of the Pacific, John T. decided to move the family to the Sandwich Islands, as Hawaii was called by the British.

In January, 1851, a massive auction sale took place at the two-story Waterhouse and Whitney Hobart store, as the business disposed of its entire stock. The sale catalogue, which ran to thirty-five pages, contained everything from cannon to cutlery. Once the sale was over, and he had also sold the *Timbo*, John T. sailed for Hawaii, taking eldest son, nine-year-old John Thomas Jr., with him. Wife Eleanour was left to tidy up the remainder of the family's business interests; she arrived in Honolulu in October, via San Francisco, bringing the remaining children, including six-year-old Henry.

Fortuitously for John T. Waterhouse, he had chosen to emigrate to the Kingdom of Hawaii in the wake of the Great Mahele, the great distribution of Hawaiian land ownership. During the Great Mahele's first phase, few native Hawaiians had come forward to lay claim to the land they and their families had been living on for centuries. Not only was the concept of individual land ownership alien to Hawaiians, members of the lower castes had always considered themselves vassals of the ali'i, and it would have been seen as a colossal and unforgivable insult to the ali'i had lower castes attempted to put themselves on an equal footing with them as landowners. As a consequence, in 1850 a portion of Crown land was set aside for division between all the native families in the kingdom, with each to be granted a kuleana, or title, to a small plot. But because Hawaiians were expected to apply for their own land to facilitate this grant of title, many failed to do so.

The missionaries claimed that the Great Mahele ended the old Hawaiian feudal system of lord and master, and made all Hawaiians equal. What it actually did was put vast tracts of prime Hawaiian land into the hands of foreigners, primarily the missionaries and their descendants, and the likes of haoles such as John T. Waterhouse. Arriving in Hawaii in 1851 cashed up, John T. was able to buy extensive parcels of land from the government, throughout the Hawaiian Islands, at bargain prices. The Great Mahele, which facilitated the makings of what would become the Waterhouse business empire, marked the end of traditional Hawaiian society and set the scene for the loss of Hawaiian independence and identity that would come to a head with the military coup of 1893.

* * *

By 1853, the United States was in an expansionist frame of mind. Between 1845 and 1848 the US had annexed Texas, taken California, and won the Mexican War. In 1853, new secretary of state William L. Marcy had secured the Gadsden Purchase, which, for ten million dollars, acquired 30,000 square miles of territory from Mexico to add to the states of Arizona and New Mexico.

Soon after taking office, Marcy began receiving confidential reports from the US consul in Honolulu, David L. Gregg, which indicated that the government of the Kingdom of Hawaii was very interested in allowing Hawaii to be annexed by the US. Gregg's enthusiastic annexation reports were fueled by his conversations with Dr. Gerrit Judd, influential ex-missionary minister of the Hawaiian Government. Judd was of the opinion that the Hawaiian native race was dying out. As a result of the introduction of devastating foreign diseases such as smallpox and leprosy that had previously been unknown in the islands, the native population had decreased from an estimated 300,000 at the time of Captain Cook to some 40,000. Judd was convinced that Hawaii's future lay in the hands of her foreign residents, as a territory of the United States.

The Hawaiian Government had recently been in dispute with the French Government, and Judd was able to persuade King Kamehameha III to consider US annexation of the kingdom to prevent foreign domination. Consul Gregg, in a February 7, 1854 dispatch, led Secretary Marcy to believe that 'the ruling authorities of the Hawaiian Government have been convinced of their inability to sustain themselves any longer as an independent state.' Gregg also assured the secretary of state that, if the United States did not act, it was likely that Hawaii would 'seek a less desirable connection elsewhere,' and Hawaii would be made a protectorate by France or Britain.[9]

On that basis, Marcy authorized Gregg to undertake annexation negotiations on behalf of the US. Marcy was a cautious man, but he did not want Hawaii to fall into French or British hands 'in view of the large American interests there,' and also taking into account Hawaii's strategically important location in the Pacific. Marcy wrote to Gregg: 'It might well be regarded as the duty of this Government to prevent these islands from becoming the appendage of any other foreign power.'[10]

As it was now revealed, Consul Gregg had misrepresented the true feeling of the Hawaiian king. At best, Kamehameha III seems to have been interested in temporary US protection. All that he warily authorized his officials to do, in a signed order of February 6, was ascertain Washington's views on annexation and to learn on what terms such an annexation might proceed. But the very next day Consul Gregg was writing to his secretary of state falsely claiming that the Hawaiians had acknowledged that they were incapable of governing themselves.

Secretary Marcy stressed to the consul that US President Franklin D. Pierce was not interested in merely making Hawaii a protectorate. In that situation, said Marcy, Hawaii would retain its sovereignty, and its monarch, while the US would assume all the burdens of a protector, for no gain. The only form of Hawaiian annexation that Marcy was interested in discussing was that of the total and permanent surrender of Hawaii's sovereignty and territory.

American annexation supporters in Hawaii now also found themselves confronted by a very able opponent–twenty-year-old Prince Alexander Liholiho, heir apparent to Kamehameha III's throne. The son of the late kuhina nui, the prince was a grandson of Kamehameha the Great. Alexander had formed a dislike for Americans after facing naked racial prejudice in San Francisco and New York on his way to Europe with Gerrit Judd on a diplomatic mission. In England, by comparison, he had been treated as an equal by the British royal family. The prince now led a number of leading ali'i in vocally opposing American annexation, and he succeeded in convincing his uncle to dismiss Gerrit Judd from cabinet office.

Undaunted by the prince's vocal opposition, Consul Gregg proceeded to draw up an annexation treaty for the king and his heir to authorize. Prince Alexander absented himself from Honolulu as much as possible through 1854 so that treaty drafts failed to reach him, and this tactic neatly stalled the treaty. When Kamehameha III died in December, 1854 after a brief illness, aged just forty-one, the treaty was still unsigned. Prince Alexander became the new King of Hawaii, with the title of Kamehameha IV, and one of his first acts was the official termination of annexation discussions with the US Government's representative.

Just the same, an annexation movement had been given life in Hawaii by Consul Gregg's determination to see the US take the kingdom, and that movement was not going to die.

In 1856, Kamehameha IV married his childhood sweetheart Emma Naea Rooke. She was the granddaughter of John Young and his Hawaiian ali'i wife, and, via her mother, a great grandniece of Kamehameha the Great. Queen Emma, as she became known, was one of the most beloved members of the Hawaiian royal family. A considerable beauty, Emma was highly intelligent and had received a sound education at the Royal School, which had been set up to educate the children of high-ranking ali'i. By this time, Hawaiian society attached no stigma to the children of mixed marriages. Now, as long as one parent was ali'i, the child took that parent's ali'i rank.

Kamehameha IV was determined to modernize his little kingdom, and to take its destiny out of the hands of the select few Protestant missionaries who had come to feel that the islands were their own private fiefdom. With whaling and trading now making Honolulu one of the busiest ports in the Pacific, the young king had Honolulu's coral fort knocked down in 1857 to make way for new wharves and warehouses. But the king's independent streak troubled the *haole* residents of Honolulu, and in 1858 they established a white volunteer militia, the Honolulu Rifles, ostensibly to 'assist' the government. A subscription among businesspeople raised the money to equip the Rifles and to build a long, single-story building on Beretania Street as a drill hall and storage place for the militia's equipment. The self-appointed officers of the Honolulu Rifles called this drill hall the Armory.

In 1859, the king had gaslight introduced to the growing city of Honolulu. The first Hawaiian ruler to take just one wife, Kamehameha IV also invited the Anglican Church (the later Episcopal Church) to set up in Hawaii, even paying the Anglican bishop's salary. The islands' Congregationalist, Presbyterian, Mormon and Catholic missionaries all took great umbrage at the arrival of the rival denomination, which initially went by the name of the Hawaiian Reformed Catholic Church, and to the king's support of it. Protestant missionaries actively competed with the

English churchmen for the minds and souls of Hawaiians, and strove to reassert their influence over the kingdom's government.

Kamehameha IV, meanwhile, became intensely jealous of his American private secretary Henry Neilson. Believing a rumor that Neilson and Queen Emma were having an affair, the king took a pistol and shot Neilson in the chest. Neilson survived, and the shooting was swept under the carpet, but Kamehameha was mortified by what he had done. Queen Emma had borne the king a son, Prince Albert Edward Kauikeaouli. The prince was angelic in looks, but not in temperament, and in August, 1862, the exasperated king put his impish four-year-old's head under a faucet to cool him down after a tantrum. Within days, the little prince had come down with what his doctor could only describe as a disease of the brain. On August 27, Prince Albert Edward, whose godmother, by proxy, was Britain's Queen Victoria, passed away.

The shocked people of the kingdom went into deep mourning. Because of the mourning period, a wedding scheduled for September 2 between a member of the royal family and an American resident of the kingdom had to be postponed. The groom was John Dominis, a Honolulu-based American whose father had made a small fortune trading between the islands and China. A former sea captain himself, the younger Dominis now served on the staff of the king. The teenaged bride, Liliu Kamakaeha, known as Lydia, was the daughter of a senior Hawaiian ali'i related to the king. Neither Lydia nor anyone else had the slightest inkling that thirty-five years later she would become Queen of Hawaii. September 2 was Lydia's nineteenth birthday, but, because of the death of the prince, the planned dual celebration of birthday and wedding was not to be. At the request of the king, Lydia's marriage was delayed until September 16.

Blaming himself for his son's demise, Kamehameha IV drank heavily. Moody and ill-tempered, he became increasingly reclusive. At the same time, asthma that had troubled him as a child began to flare. On November 30, 1863, the king experienced a serious asthma attack and collapsed. Despite Queen Emma's desperate attempts to breathe life into her husband, King Kamehameha IV died, after a reign of nine years. He was just twenty-nine years of age.

The late king's brother and designated heir, Prince Lot, was proclaimed Hawaii's new sovereign, as King Kamehameha V. Thirty-five years of age, a tall but solid man, Lot was in many ways different from his dashing, handsome predecessor. But in several things he and his late brother were alike–both possessed a strong independent streak and a desire to shape Hawaii's future. Having served as his late brother's Minister of the Interior, Kamehameha V was well versed in the intricacies of government.

The new king began his rule by refusing to take an oath to support the amended Constitution of 1852, which he felt had diluted the powers of Hawaii's monarchs. The king called a constitutional convention, composed of both houses of the Hawaiian legislature, to put together a new constitution. After several months, he terminated the convention when its members would not approve the constitution he wanted, announcing that he would give the nation a new constitution.

On August 20, 1864, Kamehameha V signed into law his new constitution, and took an oath to abide by it. He expressed the view that the nation's constitution was a gift of the monarchy, because the first constitution had been created and introduced by the then king. Therefore, he said, he, as current king, had the right to change the current constitution. It was an argument which no one could or would dispute, and the 1864 Constitution became law. Among other things, this new constitution abolished the office of kuhina nui and strengthened the power of the monarch and his cabinet.

The Hawaiian sugar industry meanwhile, was booming to such an extent that there were insufficient workers for the ever-expanding, labor-intensive sugar plantations. So Kamehameha V's government authorized sugar planters to import contract laborers. This initiative would dramatically change the ethnicity of the Hawaiian population within two generations. Most of these foreign laborers came from Japan, China, and Korea. Many thousands also came from the Portugal's North Atlantic islands of Madeira and the Azores. Most were illiterate, and few could speak English. The first shipload of Japanese workers would arrive in 1873, on contracts of three to five years in length. The plantation owners provided basic accommodation and meals and paid their contract employees a few dollars a month, but worked them so mercilessly that, once their contracts expired, a number left the islands. This only created the need for even more imported labor.

Still, many Chinese did stay on, opening their own businesses, and a bustling China Town developed in downtown Honolulu. Several enterprising Chinese merchants grew extremely wealthy. Before long, intermarriage between Asian immigrants and Hawaiians became widespread. The Portuguese workers, on the other hand, were the least likely to integrate. Looked down on by all classes of society, the Portuguese at least introduced native Hawaiians to the guitar and the Portuguese sausage, both of which became part of the Hawaiian way of life.

King Kamehameha V also fostered a building boom. In 1872, the swank new Hawaiian Hotel, later called the Royal Hawaiian, (not today's Royal Hawaiian at Waikiki), opened in downtown Honolulu. Under the king's direction, a range of other new government buildings sprang up in and around Honolulu–schools, a prison, an insane asylum, the Royal Mausoleum, a quarantine building, and the handsome Hale Koa, or 'Warrior's House,' a barracks to house the troops of the small Royal Household Guard, the king's bodyguard.

Back in 1868, Kamehameha IV had authorized construction of a new royal palace in Honolulu to replace his Iolani Palace, which was then a modest two-story residence. The design of Thomas Rowe, a Sydney, New South Wales architect, was accepted, but construction did not begin until the reign of Kamehameha V. Australian craftsmen were shipped in to construct the handsome building in shaped concrete blocks.

But Kamehameha V's cabinet did not see the need for a grand new palace, and Rowe's blueprint for a palatial interior was replaced by a design that allowed for a meeting chamber for the two houses of the legislature, the supreme court chamber, offices of the members of the cabinet, the national treasury, and the national archives. This building still stands today, and is familiar to millions worldwide as the (fictional) headquarters of the task force featured in the revived Hawaii Five-O television series.

Within twenty-years, the grand structure, called the Ali'iolani Hale, literally 'House of the Heavenly Chiefs,' and always referred to as a palace by Hawaiians while generally known among the white community as the Government Building, was to play a crucial role in the monarchy's future, come a tumultuous day in January, 1893.

3.

THE ROYAL ELECTION RIOT

KAMEHAMEHA V GREW SO ENORMOUSLY OBESE that by the end of his life he could not even stand. Remaining a bachelor, he named his sister Princess Victoria to succeed him, but she died in 1866. As Kamehameha lay on his death bed in December, 1872, he reluctantly acceded to the wishes of his counselors and named the senior ali'i Bernice Pauahi, a.k.a. Mrs. Charles Reed Bishop, to succeed him.[11] But she declined the nomination, so that when the king died on December 11, his forty-second birthday, the succession was left up in the air.

The Constitution provided for the legislature to determine the next monarch in the current circumstances, but there was strong public pressure for the entire electorate to be involved. Cabinet considered four potential candidates to replace Kamehameha V, but in the end decided that the choice came down to just two. In terms of ali'i bloodline, William Lunalilo had the best claim to the throne. A cousin of Kamehameha V, he was the grandson of a half-brother of Kamehameha the Great. Well-educated, intelligent, and popular, Lunalilo was known throughout the islands as 'Prince Bill.' The late king had little time for Prince Bill, considering him a frivolous heavy drinker who did not take life seriously enough. The alternative was David Kalakaua, a descendant of senior Big Island ali'i who had fought for Kamehameha the Great. Kalakaua was widely viewed as a refined gentleman, and had served for some years in the legislature. But Kamehameha V had thought him a fool.

Both Prince Bill Lunalilo and David Kalakaua put their cases for election to the people, and on January 1, 1873, voters went to the polls. Under the Constitution, the result of this special election, called by the cabinet to appease the general public, could not, legally, be recognized–it was still up to the legislature to appoint the kingdom's next monarch. But it would be a foolish legislator who would go against the expressed will of the people. The popular vote proved to be overwhelmingly in favor of Lunalilo.

On January 3, the legislature met to fulfill its constitutional duty to choose the next monarch, serving in this instance somewhat like the electoral college in the United States. Not surprisingly, all but one vote in the legislature was cast for the man who had received the majority of the popular vote. The legislature announced that Lunalilo had been duly elected, to great popular approval. On January 8, just three weeks short of his thirty-eighth birthday, Prince Bill officially ascended the throne, as King William Lunalilo.

Within eight months, the new king faced a mutiny by his small army. The sixty Hawaiian men who comprised the standing companies of the Royal Household Guard demanded the removal of their sadistic Hungarian drillmaster and American adjutant general, and took over their barracks. The king sent John Dominis, whom he had appointed Governor of Oahu, to command the troops to return to the authority of their officers, but only the members of the Royal Hawaiian Band and a dozen infantrymen marched out of the barracks as a result. With the remaining regular troops occupying their barracks, two volunteer reserve companies were called out to guard the king.

Many Hawaiians supported the mutineers, and, to the infuriation of the king, the men of one of the reserve units, the Cavalry Company, sat down with the rebels to dine on poi. After several days of negotiations, the king abruptly dissolved the Household Guard, retaining just the military band. He subsequently increased the size of the police force, and relied on the promise of the white Honolulu Rifles militia to support the Crown in an emergency.

In August, the king was diagnosed with tuberculosis. By November he was increasingly unwell, and went to Kailua on the Big Island hoping to rest and regain his strength. But when he returned to Honolulu the following January he had to be carried ashore. On February 3, 1874, just over a year after taking the throne, King William Lunalilo died. Barely into his thirty-ninth year, he followed the tragic tradition where so many members of Hawaiian royalty died young.

Like his predecessor, Lunalilo had not married and had not named a successor. For the second time in a little over a year, it would fall to the legislature to elect a new monarch. Once again, David Kalakaua, the unsuccessful candidate in the last royal election, put up his hand as a candidate. He had just one opponent. This was none other than the Queen Dowager, Emma, much loved young widow of King Kamehameha IV, who declared that the late king would have wanted her to rule in his place because, like him, she was of the Kamehameha bloodline.

Both candidates campaigned aggressively. Kalakaua had the support of the English-language press and the local business community, which felt that Emma, like her late royal husband, leaned too far toward Britain and away from the United States. But Emma had wide grass roots support. Deprived of the influential newspapers as a propaganda vehicle, she circulated handbills and placards throughout the islands. This time, the cabinet chose not to bother to waste time or money on a general election, and merely set the matter down for a decision by the legislature, as the Constitution required, on February 12.

The failure to call a general election caused considerable unrest, particularly among Emma's supporters, and as the day of the legislature's decision approached, the tension was high in the streets of Honolulu. At noon on February 12, the forty-five members of the House of Nobles and the Legislative Assembly, the vast majority of them men of Hawaiian native blood, met at Honolulu's courthouse. After the legislators cast their ballots to determine the next monarch of Hawaii, thirty-nine votes were counted for David Kalakaua, and six for Emma.

This outcome was quickly relayed to the large crowd that had gathered outside the courthouse, bringing both cheers and boos. Among this seething crowd were teenaged white schoolboys playing truant from Honolulu's Punahou School. Founded by Congregationalist missionaries in 1841, this is the same school that would one day be attended by the first Hawaiian-born President of the United States, Barack Obama.[12] One of these schoolboys in the crowd was fifteen-year-old Lorrin A. Thurston, Hawaiian-born grandson of Asa Thurston, one of the two clergymen who had headed up the first Boston missionary party to land in the islands back in 1820.

As five legislators delegated by their colleagues to inform David Kalakaua of his success in the legislative election climbed into a carriage at the courthouse door, angry supporters of Queen Emma surged forward and attacked them. Bruised and battered, the shocked legislators retreated back indoors, as a full-scale riot now broke out. The legislators' carriage was demolished, and, using pieces of wood from it, the rioters went on the rampage. There were policemen outside the courthouse, both white men and native Hawaiians, but they did nothing to stop the riot. Either sympathetic to Emma, or fearful for their own hides, or both, the police hid their badges and melted away. Gaining entry to the rear of the courthouse, the rioters surged inside. Furniture, books and papers were destroyed as rioters rampaged through the building. Cringing legislators were set on and mercilessly beaten; more than a dozen had to be treated in hospital for their injuries. One legislator discovered by rioters in a second floor room was thrown from the window; he later died from his injuries.

David Kalakaua was waiting for the election results with two of his sisters in a city house once owned by King Lunalilo. One of the sisters with the new king was Lydia Dominis, wife of John Dominis, governor of Oahu. The other sister was Miriam Likelike–pronounced Leekay-leekay. On David Kalakaua's official ascension to the throne, Miriam would take the title of Princess Likelike, and Lydia would become Princess Liliuokalani–pronounced Lilly-oo-oh-kallarney–and which means 'High in the heavens.'

Breathless members of the late king's cabinet soon arrived, congratulating Kalakaua on his election and bringing him the worrying news of the riot at the courthouse and of the ineffectiveness of the police. After King Lunalilo abolished the Household Guard the previous year, Kalakaua had formed the Hawaiian Guard, a volunteer militia of men of Hawaiian ali'i blood, which he personally equipped and trained. It was suggested that he now call out the Hawaiian Guard to put down the riot, but Kalakaua suspected that too many of the members of the Guard would be sympathetic to Emma and would only join the rioters–if they had not already done so.

There were currently three foreign warships in the harbor, two American and one British. The royal counselors now decided that, if law and order was to be restored, the foreign navies should be requested to land troops to aid the Hawaiian Government. A written request along those lines was quickly drafted and signed by the king elect, as well as by the Minister of Foreign Relations and head of cabinet, Charles Bishop, and by John Dominis as Governor of Oahu. This request, addressed to Henry A. Pierce, the US Minister–as the post of US ambassador was then called– was hurriedly carried across town to the American Consulate.

Ambassador Pierce reacted swiftly to the request. In the late afternoon, 150 armed US marines and sailors landed from the USS *Portsmouth* and USS *Tuscarora*. These troops, under Commanders George Belknap and Joseph Skerrett, hurriedly marched into the center of Honolulu and took possession of the courthouse, and the square where it stood. As soon as the US marines and blue jackets arrived on the scene, the rioters quickly dispersed.

A similar request for assistance was also sent to the British ambassador, James Wodehouse, and, as a result, seventy British marines and sailors landed from HMS *Tenedos* and quickly took possession of the deserted military barracks, considered the best defensive position in the town, and also set up a guard outside the Iolani Palace, where the body of the late king was lying in state prior to his funeral. The British and American troops would remain in Honolulu for eight days. Only when the Hawaiian authorities felt confident that they had the situation under control were the troops returned to their ships.

On February 13, 1873, King David Kalakaua was sworn in at the wrecked Honolulu courthouse, becoming Hawaii's seventh monarch. At that moment, the foreign warships in the harbor boomed out twenty-one-gun salutes. Emma, meanwhile, acknowledged the legitimacy of her rival's election, and instructed her followers to accept him as their king.

Kalakaua, the second elected monarch of Hawaii, quickly named his younger brother Prince William Pitt Leleiohoku as his successor, and appointed a cosmopolitan cabinet which included an Hawaiian, an American, an Englishman, and a German. With a long-held love of military matters, the new king reconstituted the Household Guard, giving it one fulltime standing company plus five volunteer reserve companies covering infantry, cavalry, and artillery. Men and officers of the new Guard would all be of ali'i blood, and would swear to fight to their last breath to defend their king. At the same time, Kalakaua ordered the disbanding of the *haole* Honolulu Rifles militia.

Under the new king, the police force, too became almost entirely staffed by men of Hawaiian or part Hawaiian blood. Kalakaua would also recreate the first Hawaiian navy since the days of Kamehameha the Great, purchasing and arming a British steamer and renaming it the *Kaimiloa*, or 'Far Seeker.' These measures, in which the king quite consciously reclaimed Hawaiian control of her military and police, bred discontent and unease among the white missionaries and businessmen of the kingdom

Yet King Kalakaua agreed with the island's American sugar interests who advocated a treaty of reciprocity, or free trade, with the United States. In late 1874, the king, heading a formal Hawaiian Reciprocity Commission, sailed to San Francisco, becoming the first monarch from any nation to pay an official visit to the United States. After an official reception, the royal party traveled by train to Washington DC. President Ulysses S. Grant hosted a state dinner at the White House for the king and his party, and Congress threw a reception for them. After leaving Washington, the king also visited New York City, Boston and other New England cities, and stopped off at several other centers along his rail route back to San Francisco, from there, he sailed home to Honolulu.

In Washington, despite earning White House support, the draft reciprocity treaty promoted by the king was to face a tortuous path through both houses of Congress. In Hawaii, the proposed treaty, the king's part in it, and the slow passage through the US Congress combined to generate accusations of a conspiracy. Some Hawaiians feared that such a treaty would threaten the independence of their little nation, and several vocal opponents of the monarch were voted into the lower house at the next election.

The US-Hawaii reciprocity treaty was finally signed into law by President Grant on September 9, 1876. This treaty, as amended by Congress, prevented Hawaii from signing a similar treaty with any other nation during its seven year duration. It gave Hawaiian sugar growers unrestricted access to the American market, and as a result sponsored a massive expansion of the sugar industry in the islands. The amount of Hawaiian land sown to sugar cane increased tenfold over the next decade, and sugar mills, including the largest, most modern steam-powered sugar mill in the world, soon sprang up on the islands. This surge of development in turn created a huge demand for capital, much of which came from San Francisco, and for even more imported labor.

Several months after this treaty came into effect, the kingdom was rocked by the news that Prince William, the twenty-two-year-old heir apparent, had died. Once again, a prominent member of the Hawaiian royal family had been taken at an early age. On April 10, 1877, the king named a new heir to his throne–his thirty-eight-year-old sister, Princess Liliuokalani, the former Lydia Dominis.

4.

AT THE BAYONET'S POINT

KING DAVID KALAKAUA AND HIS WIFE QUEEN
Kapiolani went on an 1881 world tour that took in many
countries in Asia and Europe. The last leg involved visits to
numerous US cities including Washington DC, where they were
entertained by President Chester Arthur. Wherever they went, the
royal couple and their entourage were hosted by queens, kings,
emperors, princes and presidents. In the king's absence, his sister
and heir Princess Liliuokalani served as regent of Hawaii, with all
the powers of the monarch, which gave her valuable experience
as head of state.

After their return to Honolulu in 1882, the king and queen
moved into the new Iolani Palace. Built on the site of the original
Iolani Palace, this solid, ornate structure in Renaissance Revival
style was built of brick faced with stucco. As palaces go, it was
modest, reflecting Hawaii's status as a kingdom in miniature.
The basement contained staff offices, the first floor a throne room,
formal dining room and reception room, and the top floor, four
bedrooms, a study, and a living area.

But King Kalakaua spared no expense on the interior detail
or furnishings. The palace was the first residence in Hawaii to
be equipped with newfangled flush toilets. In the US, the king
had met Thomas Edison, and, inspired by the great inventor, he
also made sure that his modern new palace was equipped with
telephones and electric light. Curiously, the palace's lighting
was centrally controlled, with no individual light switches in
its rooms. Under the king's sponsorship, downtown Honolulu
was also equipped with electric light. And by the 1890s the city

would have the highest per capita distribution of telephones of any metropolis in the world.

The Iolani Palace's domestic servants were liveried in uniforms of royal blue velvet with silver trim, designed by the king. Those servants all came from ali'i families. King Kalakaua also designed his own uniforms, and those of his four staff officers, along lines then popular in Europe. For his troops of the Royal Household Guard he replaced the scarlet tunics used by the earlier Household Guard with a smart all-white dress uniform and an 'undress' uniform of blue tunics and white pants. For formal occasions, Kalakaua's Guards wore smart white leather Prussian-style *Pickelhaube* helmets; at other times they wore peaked caps of US Army pattern.

To inaugurate his new palace, and to introduce his people to some of the pageantry he had experienced in Europe, the king announced that he would celebrate a formal coronation. Two jewel-encrusted crowns were ordered from Europe, and an eight-sided Coronation Pavilion was erected in the palace garden and surrounded by bleachers. The $50,000 cost of the coronation and its two weeks of celebrations including luaus and balls throughout the islands incensed conservative whites, who saw it as a massive waste of money, but the coronation was hugely popular with those of Hawaiian blood.

King Kalakaua particularly outraged the Christian clergy by ordering the hula danced at his coronation. And after he placed the crown on his own head in the February 12, 1883 coronation ceremony in the Pavilion, watched by thousands of his subjects, his haole critics accused the king of grandiosely emulating the Emperor Napoleon of France. With king and queen crowned, the Royal Hawaiian Band played the new national anthem, 'Hawaii Ponoi,' whose lyrics had been written by the king. The Hawaiian battery on Punchbowl Hill sounded a twenty-one-gun salute, which was echoed by guns on foreign warships in the harbor. And the Hawaiians in the bleachers cheered.

But the westerners in the community were not happy with the king, with his policies, or with his cabinet, whose ministers approved Kalakaua's heavy borrowing to sustain his government programs and royal lifestyle. One of the most controversial policies during the king's reign was an Opium Bill, which, for a fee paid to the Treasury, would license a member of the Chinese community to import and sell opium in the kingdom. This bill, opposed by the churches, was designed to end the smuggling of opium into Hawaii, which had resulted in hundreds of convictions in the past year, and to regulate its distribution and sale to the Chinese community.

Kalakaua particularly blotted his copybook when it was revealed that he had taken $71,000 in cash from a Chinese rice planter Tong Kee, better known as Aki, who expected to receive the opium license. The license subsequently went to another Chinese, Chun Lung, for $80,000. Aki, who had paid what could only be termed a bribe, demanded his money back, but King Kalakaua responded by claiming that the money had been a gift, and refused to remit it. Despite this scandal, Hawaiians of native blood still revered their king, which only infuriated Kalakaua's western opponents even more.

The westerners also opposed the king's plan to mint a million dollars of Hawaiian silver dollars in San Francisco. The measure passed the legislature in 1884, but three Honolulu lawyers sought a court injunction to prevent the project going ahead, on the basis that the middle man in the coinage program, San Francisco banker Claus Spreckels, would be making a tidy commission on the deal. One of the major beet sugar producers in the US, on which his fortune was based, the astute German-born Spreckels had become the largest investor in the Hawaiian cane sugar industry. The Californian's influence on Hawaii's economy and government was resented by the local white business community, whose members wanted to be the sole purveyors of power and influence in the islands.

The three lawyers who sought the injunction against the coinage program were Sanford B. Dole, who had been elected to the lower house of the legislature that year as a candidate of the new Reform Party, as well as William R. Castle and William O. Smith. All three men were the descendants of missionaries, and had attended Honolulu's Punahou School–Dole's father had been the school's first principal. The case was dismissed by the court, and the coins were duly minted and went into circulation in the kingdom, but the three lawyers who had opposed the king were to before long figure prominently in Hawaii's history.

In 1886, Sanford Dole was reelected to the legislature, along with several other candidates of the Reform Party, which openly opposed the king. This was the strongest showing of the Reform Party to date. One of the other successful Reform candidates in this election was Lorrin Thurston, who, as a teenaged schoolboy had been in the crowd outside the courthouse on the tumultuous day that the legislature had elected David Kalakaua king of Hawaii.

Since leaving school, Thurston had worked as clerk to the little nation's attorney general for a year, and in 1880-81 attended the Columbia Law School in New York, after which he had returned to Honolulu and was admitted to the bar of the Supreme Court of Hawaii. Ever since, he had practiced as an attorney. Through his family's money and influence, Thurston was one of the owners of the Haleakala Ranch Co., was secretary and director of another cattle company, of the Hawaiian Fruit Packing Company, of a plantation company, and of a company which operated a hotel on the Big Island. Thurston had served as editor of the Honolulu *Daily Bulletin* in 1884, during which time he had written scathing editorials attacking king and cabinet. This editorial role, above all, had given Thurston the audience and the prominence he craved among the leading white men of the kingdom, and had guaranteed his election to the legislature at the age of just twenty-seven.

One day in late 1886, Lorrin Thurston bumped into Reform Party leader Sanford Dole in the Honolulu street. Physically, the two men could not have been more dissimilar. Young Thurston was of average height and build. His dark hair was already thinning, his jet-black beard was closely trimmed in the fashion of European royalty. His hooded eyes gave him the look of a bull frog about to snap up an unsuspecting fly. Forty-two-year-old Dole, meanwhile, stood six feet two inches tall. His thick hair and beard were gray. That long, forked beard, in the style favored by an earlier generation and giving him the look of an ancient philosopher, was so thick a bird could have nested in it.

"Dr. Tucker has urged upon me the importance of organizing," said Thurston.[13]

"Indeed?" said the softly-spoken, cautious Dole. He knew that the doctor to whom Thurston was referring was S. G. Tucker, Superintendent of the Honolulu Insane Asylum who, like them, was of American stock. Dole also knew what Thurston was talking about organizing: 'A protest,' Dole was later to write, 'backed by sufficient organized force to go farther, if necessary.' By 'farther,' Dole meant armed insurrection.[14]

"It should be done without delay," Thurston urged.[15]

Dole agreed, and suggested a meeting at his Honolulu home with gentlemen of like mind. That meeting took place one evening several days later. In addition to Dole and Thurston, it was attended by Dr. Tucker and by thirty-six-year-old lawyer William R. Castle, a fellow Reform Party member of the legislature, Columbia Law School graduate, and close friend of Thurston.[16] At their meeting, this quartet put together a framework for a secret organization. Called, innocuously, the Hawaiian League, it would have cells throughout the islands, with agents going from place to place to recruit new members from among Westerners in the kingdom. More than just protest against the king, the Hawaiian League would set out to bend him to its will, by force.

Before long, the Hawaiian authorities came to hear that there was a secret organization in existence which had as its goal the overthrow of the government, and the police began to pay close attention to the activities of men who were chiefly suspected of being behind this organization. To counter this, the League's covert meetings were disguised as social gatherings and were rarely held at the same house twice in succession.

As Hawaiian League membership grew to number around four hundred Westerners, the League's founders formed a management committee, calling it the Directorate, in emulation of the leadership of the French Revolution a century earlier. The Directorate decided that it was time to arm their members in preparation for a move against the government. Under the Hawaiian penal code it was illegal for anyone other than the Household Guard and sailors of the kingdom's little navy to bear arms in the street. Even the police normally went about their duties unarmed.

Hawaiian League members were able to buy a few pistols, hunting rifles and shotguns in Honolulu hardware stores such as Hall and Sons, but, to counter the government's supremacy in arms, the League resorted to secretly and illegally importing Springfield rifles and ammunition. This shipment, described as anything but arms on its consignment note, was held up by the customs house, as the authorities queried the boxes' contents. The lawyers among the League's members quickly went to court and received a court order in their favor. This forced the Department of Customs to release the shipment, and the rifles were quickly distributed to League members around Honolulu.

In 1884, after persistent requests from Westerners in the

community, the king had given permission for the Honolulu Rifles militia to be reformed. Despite placing limits on the Rifles' weaponry and activities, reinstatement of the white militia was to prove a major error on Kalakaua's part. The colonel of the reformed Rifles was Volney V. Ashford. A theatrical English attorney with an ostentatiously large mustache, he had previously served in the Canadian military and the US Army. Under Ashford, and based around the Rifles, an enlarged militia of two hundred Hawaiian League members was secretly created. This force, the Hawaiian League intended, would form the basis of a citizen's army that would change the face of Hawaiian government.

At one point in early 1887, assassination of King Kalakaua was even contemplated by the Directorate. According to a tale told later, the plot went forward, and Volney Ashford, Sanford Dole and three others drew straws to determine who would go to the palace and shoot the king. Sanford Dole drew the short straw, and was given a pistol to execute the deed. But Dole's courage deserted him; he failed to go through with the murder, and the assassination plot fell to pieces.[17]

5.

CASTRATING THE KING

KING KALAKAUA'S SISTER AND HEIR APPARENT Princess Liliuokalani was out of the country for much of 1887. She and the king's wife, Queen Kapiolani, had been invited to attend the jubilee of Queen Victoria, and in April they sailed off to England for the celebrations. Had Liliuokalani been in Hawaii during the most crucial months, things may have turned out differently. For Liliuokalani was not afraid to stand up to her brother when he buckled to pressure from others. Once, when Kalakaua was talked into giving several posts held by her husband John Dominis to someone else, Liliuokalani had protested vehemently. The king had countered, "Well, say that I have made my appointments, what is there remaining that I can do for you, my sister?" Standing her ground, Liliuokalani was able to convince Kalakaua to give Dominis several other prestigious appointments, in compensation for the posts the king was taking off him and giving to others.[18]

The dissatisfaction of the Hawaiian League with the king grew in early 1887 as Kalakaua attempted to develop a concept that had long been in his mind, of a confederation of the island states of the Pacific. In December, 1886, around the time that Thurston and Dole established their subversive Hawaiian League, King Kalakaua dispatched a Hawaiian delegation to Samoa to bring Samoa, and if possible, Tonga too, into an alliance of Polynesian states with Hawaii. The Hawaiian Government delegation was welcomed by Samoa's King Malieto, who, in February, 1887, gladly signed a confederation agreement allying his little country to Hawaii. In May, Kalakaua sent the kingdom's lone warship, the *Kaimiloa*, to Samoa to show the Hawaiian flag.

This all incensed the leaders of the Hawaiian League. The Samoan confederation affair was made farcical by a mutiny of the crew of the *Kaimiloa*, and the Hawaiian League's leadership railed against what they considered the unwarranted costs involved in Kalakaua's Polynesian empire-building. They blamed the cabinet for giving the king unlimited access to the nation's purse strings, and accused Kalakaua of being totally out of financial control. As an example, they pointed to $30,000 which the king expended on the state funeral of his thirty-six-year-old sister Princess Miriam Likelike, who died unexpectedly that February after a short illness.

Most importantly, Kalakaua's desire to strengthen ties with other Polynesian states went completely against the goal of many American residents of Hawaii, who saw Hawaii ultimately not as part of the Pacific but as part of the United States. For these men, annexation of Hawaii by the US was the only future they were prepared to consider. Their only disagreement was over the means by which that annexation was achieved. Growing dissatisfaction with the king among members of the Hawaiian League through the first half of 1887 led to a heated meeting of the leadership one evening in June. Sanford Dole, who was present, was to say that there was a strong undercurrent of anxiety in the community generally by this time. There was, he said, 'a vague expectation that something serious impended,' although no one knew what. In the ranks of the Hawaiian League, there was, said Dole, 'a vigorous sentiment, in favor of overthrowing the monarchy by force.'[19]

Dole now resigned from the Directorate. He was not alone. Another member of the Directorate, a forty-eight-year-old Peter C. Jones, also now quit the League. Born in Boston, Jones had come to Hawaii in 1858, married a local woman, and became managing partner of C. Brewster & Company–one of Hawaii's 'Big Five' companies, a large importer with widespread sugar plantation holdings. A 'crisis in league affairs' had been reached, said Dole, 'because of the policy of the radical wing.'[20] That radical wing, led by Thurston, was pushing for military action against the throne. Despite pulling out of the League leadership, both Dole and Jones would before long play prominent roles in Hawaii's changing political history.

Fully aware of the unrest in the foreign community, and well informed of the existence of the Hawaiian League, the king ordered the Household Guard to prepare to defend the Iolani Palace and other government buildings. Overnight, sandbags, Gatling guns and field pieces made their appearance. But instead of settling the prevailing mood of anxiety, this only provoked fears and stoked anger in the *haole* community.

The head of Kalakaua's cabinet, with the courtesy title of Premier, was Walter Murray Gibson, an aging, ailing American who was fluent in Hawaiian and had long championed the rights of native Hawaiians and been many times elected to the legislature by a strong native vote. At one time, Gibson was one of only three white men in the legislature. The colorful Gibson also owned two Honolulu newspapers, the *Pacific Commercial Advertiser* and another, printed in Hawaiian, which between them gave him great public influence. He had great influence with the king, too, who trusted him implicitly. That influence, and his pro-Hawaiian and anti *haole* views, made Premier Gibson despised by the Hawaiian League.

Gibson and the king had hoped to ride out the political storm, but as the Western community became increasingly agitated, the pair realized that the Crown would have to make concessions. On June 28, on Gibson's advice, King Kalakaua called on his cabinet to resign. For the sake of the monarchy, and the country, Gibson was the first to fall on his sword, followed by his colleagues, all native Hawaiians. The cabinet's resignation *en masse* was announced in the press the next day, but as the editorial writer of the English-language Honolulu *Daily Bulletin* of June 29 made patently clear, this did not go far enough in the opinion of the Hawaiian League: 'The king must be prepared to take his own proper place, and be content to reign without ruling.' The League would not be satisfied until the king was a mere figurehead, with the true power resting in their hands.

Now the Hawaiian League settled on a compromise plan, one which would give the king the opportunity to retain his throne, if he acceded to the League's demands. They called a mass meeting of League members and other interested parties for Thursday, June 30. By early afternoon that day, business in downtown Honolulu had come to a standstill as stores and offices closed. The meeting, attended by several hundred merchants, mechanics and professional men, took place in the former Armory building on Beretania Street. Peter Jones was in the audience, and was prevailed upon to chair the meeting. Jones, a stout, shabby figure, began by saying, "We have assembled here this afternoon, in a constitutional manner, resolved to ask the king for good government, something which we have not had."[21]

A score of leading men then spoke in quick succession, among them Thurston and Dole. Most spoke in favor of reforming government and constitution, but a minority spoke against it. Local English-language newspapers which supported the League's stance would only report the speeches that advocated drastic change. One of the most influential of the speeches came from Charles R. Bishop. As founder of Hawaii's largest bank, the husband of Princess Bernice Pauali, and a member of the House of Nobles and the king's Privy Council, he was a man with feet in both camps–money and the monarchy. "I came here in 1846, became naturalized (as a Hawaiian citizen) in 1849, and have lived under five kings," Bishop told the crowded Armory. "We thought we had a liberal constitution, because those kings did not encroach upon the rights of their subjects. But we have found out within the last few years that our constitution is defective, partly on account of bad advice to the king, but largely on *his own* account."[22]

Bishop did not spell out exactly how the king had 'encroached upon the rights' of his subjects. Kalakaua had in fact implemented policies that were widely popular among his native Hawaiian subjects. It was only the white minority business community that was unhappy with him. What irked them most was Kalakaua's refusal to fall into line with their wishes. Bishop did not favor removing the king. But he did want change–change that reined in the monarch's powers. "I believe it means either a new constitution, or one with material reforms," he said.[23]

Bishop read out a letter he had received from His Majesty that morning. King Kalakaua informed Bishop that he was inviting William L. Green to form a new government. Green was a London-born merchant who had previously served in the Hawaiian cabinet. He was a member of the Hawaiian League and was at the Armory meeting. Stepping up to the dais, Green declared to the gathering, "If it should happen that I should head a Ministry, I shall conduct it not only for His Majesty, but for the country."[24] Green, a moderate, was not the Directorate's first choice to head the government, but they would settle for him if the other cabinet posts were filled by Hawaiian League men of their choice.

Lorrin Thurston, addressing the meeting for a second time, said, "I am reminded of a story. I remember reading somewhere of a man who was going to shoot a coon, and the coon said, 'Don't shoot, I'll come down.' The king is the coon, and this meeting is the gun!" Thurston's naked racial prejudice generated a gale of laughter and thunderous applause. Thurston then proceeded to read out a list of the Directorate's demands upon the king, demands which received unanimous approval from the white audience.[25]

The Directorate's plan had been for the League's militia to come onto the streets under arms and take control of Honolulu, to prevent Kalakaua's military and police from intervening on behalf of the palace when the Directorate's demands were pressed. But the palace proved to be fully aware of what was going on, and beat the League to the punch. For, while the Armory meeting was taking place, Volney Ashford received a hand-delivered note from the palace. As the nation's military nominally included the reconstituted Honolulu Rifles militia, Lieutenant Colonel Ashford was ordered by the king to bring all members of the Honolulu Rifles onto the streets in their companies, supposedly to help keep order. Ashford duly complied, and, with bayonets fixed, the Rifles joined the Household Guard and police patrolling Honolulu over the next few tense days. In effect, martial law prevailed. Ostensibly answering to the government, the Rifles were in reality following the commands of the Directorate, and, despite the façade of joint action, both sides knew it.

The Armory meeting broke with a deputation setting off for the palace to deliver the list of demands to the king. Kalakaua received the deputation, and read the demands. Those demands called on the king to appoint a new cabinet which would oversee the drafting of a new constitution for the country. He was also required to repay the $71,000 'gift' associated with the opium license scandal, and dismiss the Hawaiian government official who had negotiated it. And he had to give his word to keep out of politics and not interfere with the administration of his cabinet.

Once he had read through the demands, the king looked up, and said that he was prepared to agree to them all, at once. This surprised the delegates, who responded that the meeting at the Armory had resolved to give him twenty-four hours in which to respond, which he was required to do in writing. They then withdrew. Overnight, pressed by advisers to think again, and to seek the support of foreign governments, Kalakaua called in the senior diplomatic representatives in Honolulu. But they all advised him to accept the Hawaiian League's demands.

On the morning of July 1, King Kalakaua agreed in writing to the demands. That afternoon, William Green presented his new cabinet. Green himself would serve as premier and finance minister. His interior minister would be none other than Lorrin Thurston, whose determination to reshape the kingdom had taken him from law student to cabinet minister in just six years. Privately, Thurston was overjoyed. He and his fellow 'missionary boys,' as he called the sons and grandsons of the Protestant missionaries, had achieved a bloodless revolution in Hawaii.[26] Two Englishmen who were also members of the Hawaiian League would fill the other cabinet posts–Godfrey Brown in the foreign affairs portfolio, and, as attorney general, lawyer Clarence Ashford, brother of the Honolulu Rifles' Volney Ashford.

The Hawaiian League immediately set to work drafting a new constitution for the Green cabinet to present to the king. Meanwhile, the new cabinet ordered the arrest of former premier Walter Gibson and his son in law, on trumped up charges of embezzling public funds. But not before Lorrin Thurston had freed them from the clutches of a mob led by Volney Ashford, who was threatening to hang Gibson from the yardarm of a ship in port. When the humiliated pair was arraigned several days later, the prosecution had no evidence of embezzlement to present against them. The charges were dropped, and the pair set free. The Green cabinet promptly decreed that Gibson be sent into exile. Escorted to the docks, Gibson was put on a ship which set sail on July 12 for San Francisco. Gibson was to die there, of tuberculosis, just six months later. His family would have to seek cabinet approval for his body to be returned to Hawaii for burial. Even Sanford Dole was to describe Walter Gibson as 'visionary.'[27] But Gibson's vision was for a sovereign Kingdom of Hawaii, and that did not fit with the vision that many other Americans had for Hawaii.[28]

The work of drafting the new constitution rapidly progressed. The final document was based partly on the previous Constitution of Hawaii and partly on the constitutions of several American states. Thurston, Dole and the other Hawaiian League legal brains who worked on the new constitution knew that Kalakaua would not like it, but they did not care. 'If he doesn't accept it, he will be promptly attacked, and a republic probably declared,' Dole wrote to his brother George on Kauai.[29]

The new constitution removed the monarch's power to appoint members of the House of Nobles; from now on, they would be elected. It allowed the king's previous power of veto over legislation to be overridden by a two-thirds majority in the legislature. Power to organize the military was taken from the king and vested in the legislature. The king could still appoint the members of the cabinet, but could not remove them; that could only be done by a successful vote in the legislature of 'no confidence' in a cabinet minister. And, the Constitution could only in future be altered by the legislature.

Most drastically of all, the voting laws were changed. Voters now had to be male taxpayers who could read and write Hawaiian, English, or a European language such as Portuguese; this totally disenfranchised many Hawaiians and virtually all residents of Asian background. Voters also had to take an oath to support the new Constitution, and a number of Hawaiians would refused to do this. Hawaiian Chief Justice Albert F. Judd later said of Thurston and the others who drafted the new constitution: 'They didn't want the Hawaiians to vote at all. And the reason that the Portuguese were allowed to vote was to balance the native vote.'[30]

In the case of upper house elections, eligible voters had to meet property and income qualifications. All candidates for both houses also had to own property of a certain minimum value, and to have an income not less than the limit set by the new Constitution. This ruled out many Hawaiians. The new constitution also gave all foreigners living in the kingdom who met these new requirements the right to vote and stand for the legislature, even if they were the citizens of other countries–few foreigners living in Hawaii had bothered to take out Hawaiian citizenship. These changes ensured that, in the main, only wealthy, educated whites, who made up just three percent of the population of ninety thousand people, could stand for election. Not surprisingly, at the first elections held under the new Constitution, that September, white Reform Party candidates won most seats, and dominated the nation's legislature and government.

Late in the evening of Wednesday, July 5, once the new constitution had been agreed by Thurston and the others who had drafted it, Sanford Dole walked with it to a second floor printing house on Merchant Street. It was almost midnight when Dole handed the document to the printer, who was waiting to set it in type and run it off. Outside, the streets of Honolulu, bathed in moonlight, were as quiet as Dole could ever remember. The entire city was breathlessly awaiting the next developments in the latest political drama.

On July 6, Lorrin Thurston and the other three members of the new cabinet arrived at the Iolani Palace with the freshly printed constitution, and were shown into the Blue Room, an intimate reception room immediately to the left of the main entrance. There, they took seats beneath a huge portrait of Louis Philippe, King of the French, an 1848 gift to Kamehameha III from Louis himself. Ironically, the portrait had arrived in Honolulu just nine days before the French king abdicated his throne.

King Kalakaua kept the cabinet waiting some time before he finally made his entrance. Premier Green then handed the document to the king. Kalakaua read it carefully. There was then a long, pregnant pause. Green asked if His Majesty accepted the new constitution. His Majesty replied that he certainly did not. There followed hours of discussion, as Kalakaua argued every point. Receiving an articulate riposte for each question he raised, he would stare into space for a long time, then return his attention to the document and pose a fresh objection. This went on right through the afternoon.

The cabinet would not budge on a single point. The document had been released to the press, they declared, and could not be changed. Kalakaua had to sign the new Constitution, or face the consequences. With armed Hawaiian League men on the streets, and without the counsel of his once strong right arm, Walter Gibson, who was at that time behind bars awaiting the trial that never eventuated, the king caved in. The sun had set when he surprised the cabinet members by producing a resigned smile and agreeing to sign the new Constitution into law. Chief Justice Judd was immediately summoned to the palace, to witness the signing and administer an oath to Kalakaua that he would uphold the new Constitution.

When the Chief Justice arrived, the king looked unhappily at him, and asked, in Hawaiian, "Had I better sign it, or not?"

"You must follow the advice of your responsible ministers, Your Majesty," Judd replied.[31]

The king signed the Constitution, then, hand on Holy Bible, took the oath to observe it. Sanford Dole was to comment, 'The king was never enthusiastic about the new Constitution; among his friends there was a good deal of irritation.'[32] Because of the way it was forced on the king, this document became known as the Bayonet Constitution. Similarly, the Green cabinet which Kalakaua was forced to appoint by the Hawaiian League became known as the Bayonet Cabinet.

In the name of cost cutting, this Bayonet Cabinet wasted no time making drastic changes to projects that Kalakaua had championed or which were slanted toward the interests of Native Hawaiians. Hawaii's little navy was abolished; the *Kaimiloa* was decommissioned and its Hawaiian crew dismissed. The standing company of the Royal Household Guard was renamed the King's Guard, and the Honolulu Rifles were officially constituted as the nation's principal military reserve unit. The Hawaiian mission to Samoa was recalled. The cabinet terminated the Kalakaua Studies Abroad program, which had sent several promising young male ali'i, and one female, to England and Italy to improve their education at government expense; these young people were called home. Funds previously allocated by the legislature to a board for Hawaiian ethnological research into the genealogy of the ali'i, a matter close to the heart of many Hawaiians, were immediately stopped. The native Hawaiian Board of Health was also abolished.

To cement their control of the military, the Bayonet Cabinet created the new official government post of Colonel of Volunteers, and appointed Volney Ashford to fill it. To increase their influence within the judiciary, they had the king appoint Hawaiian League co-founder Sanford Dole one of the three justices of the Supreme Court. The Bayonet Cabinet also set in motion steps to form closer official ties with the United States, ties that had grown weak during Kalakaua's reign. The first step was to reaffirm the kingdom's reciprocity treaty with the US. The term of the original treaty had lapsed several years before, and the treaty had been continued on a year to year basis since. Negotiations between Honolulu and Washington shaped a new treaty, which, while containing similar free trade provisions to the last, also ceded Pearl Harbor to the United States for use as a naval base. The Bayonet Cabinet would make the humbled, hobbled Kalakaua sign the final version of the new treaty before year's end.

That fall, the king's wife and sister arrived back from England. While in England, they had been stunned to learn of the death of Liliuokalani's sister Princess Likelike in February. Now, when the queen and the heir apparent arrived back in the kingdom, they were equally stunned to find that, in their absence, the white money men of Hawaii had castrated the monarchy and taken power out of the hands of native Hawaiians and placed it in the hands of Lorrin Thurston and his colleagues. The king was now nothing more than a puppet with a crown.

Princess Liliuokalani would have to reign under the terms of the new constitution once she succeeded her brother to the throne, and she was livid with Kalakaua for caving in to the Hawaiian League. Not only was Liliuokalani furious at the way that Kalakaua had given away Hawaiians' control of their own affairs, she could not forgive the handing over of sovereign Hawaiian territory to a foreign power. She wrote in her diary, about the cession of Pearl Harbor to the US: 'It should not have been done.'[33]

6.

WILCOX THE ASSASSIN

Many Hawaiians disapproved of the way their king had buckled to the *haoles*. Robert William Kalanihiapo Wilcox was one of them. The actions of the Bayonet Cabinet changed his life. His father was William Wilcox, a whaling captain from Newport, Rhode Island, his mother a high-ranking ali'i of the island of Maui. Robert Wilcox had been one of the young ali'i sent to Italy under the Studies Abroad Program. After serving a one-year term in the Hawaiian legislature, in 1881 he had commenced studies at the Royal Military Academy in Turin. By the time that he was recalled to Hawaii by the Bayonet Cabinet in 1887, Wilcox had reached the rank of lieutenant in the Italian army and had married Gina Sobrero, a beautiful young Italian baroness from Naples.

On October 5, Wilcox and his bride arrived in Honolulu aboard the steamer *San Pablo*. Robert Wilcox was a fine figure of a man, over six feet tall, dashingly handsome, with a well-groomed mustache and flashing dark eyes. To add to his good looks, he wore his smart Italian army uniform at every formal opportunity. His wife, a tempestuous, head-turning, raven-haired beauty, was pregnant with their first child when they reached Honolulu. As the couple was ferried ashore, their launch was surrounded by small boats filled with scantily clad Hawaiians. Robert had told his wife that he was the son of a Hawaiian princess, which had led Gina to conjure expectations of a royal lifestyle once they arrived in the kingdom. And, as the son of a high ranking ali'i, the locals gave him and his Neapolitan wife a welcome fit for royalty when they stepped ashore.

Gina Wilcox was charmed by the local women who swarmed around them on the dock, draping flower leis around their necks and smiling warm alohas as they chattered away to her in Hawaiian. But after the heady dockside welcome, Gina's expectations received a blow. A carriage deposited the couple at the modest, single-story, wooden Honolulu home of Wilcox's cousin, Samuel Nowlein, on King Street. Nowlein, like Wilcox, an ali'i of mixed blood, had been born and raised on Maui. Gina had met Sam before–he had attended the Wilcox's wedding in Turin accompanied by his daughter, Elizabeth Maile. The lone woman on King Kalakaua's Studies Abroad Program, Elizabeth had been studying Italian art at the time.

Sam Nowlein and his wife Lucy made young Mr. and Mrs. Wilcox welcome in the warm, open, Hawaiian manner, but their cramped suburban house, an abode of 'the most primitive of Kanaka families,' as Gina would describe them in her diary, was not the palatial residence that she had been expecting prior to her arrival. And, to her horror, the Nowleins had not a single servant. Lucy Nowlein was the product of a Chinese father and an Hawaiian mother, and Gina thought her hostess looked like 'a monkey.' Lucy wore unfashionable, loose-fitting clothes, and went about the house barefoot. The Hawaiians bathed in the open, and ate their food, which was unfamiliar and unappetizing to Gina, with their fingers. In time, Gina grew to appreciate and like Lucy Nowlein, but she never became accustomed to Hawaiian food or eating habits.[34]

When the baroness demanded that Robert put them up at the Hawaiian Hotel, with its airy rooms, excellent cooks, and white guests, her husband had to confess that he couldn't afford it. He didn't have a penny to his name. Wilcox had lavished money on his bride in Italy, but now he was stony broke. His government allowance had been stopped by the Bayonet Cabinet, and his expectation of a plum job in Hawaiian government service had been dashed–the post of Hawaiian consul in San Francisco had previously been mentioned, but it was never conferred on Wilcox.

Gina produced such tantrums and crying fits that Robert sought and was granted an audience with the king, where he asked for help. As a result, for three weeks King Kalakaua paid for the couple to stay at the Arlington Hotel, formerly a gracious mansion that had once been the childhood home of the king and his sisters. To Gina's delight, the Arlington was filled with genial European travelers and wives of American and British naval officers whose ships spent months at a time anchored at Honolulu. Her social life quickly blossomed, and she became a regular visitor to the homes of the Italian and French consuls.

Robert also took his bride to Maui, where he had grown up, to meet his family. There, the couple was treated like gods by the local people. In contrast, Robert's father William Wilcox– tall, rigid, dried up, and as deaf as a post–showed no pleasure in seeing his son for the first time in more than six years. On being introduced to his new Italian daughter-in-law, old Captain Wilcox blankly looked Gina up and down, then said, "Italy, Italy! Oh, yes, beautiful country."[35]

On the couple's return to Honolulu, Princess Liliuokalani offered a cost-free solution to the Wilcox's accommodation problem. The princess's Honolulu residence, Washington Place, a grand mansion on Beretania Street, was her husband's family home; Liliuokalani's ailing mother-in-law, with whom she did not get on, still lived there. Liliuokalani herself owned several suburban houses, including one at Waikiki and another at Palama. She was virtually estranged from her indifferent husband; 'First time in a year that John was attentive,' the princess confided to her diary on November 20.[36] Theirs had been a loveless, arranged marriage. Liliuokalani always felt more comfortable at her own residences, where she stayed as often as possible. She had room to spare at her Palama house, so, 'in pity for their situation,' Liliuokalani herself was to write of Robert and Gina, 'I offered them quarters under my roof until they could provide for themselves.'[37]

Wilcox, telling his wife that it could be to his advantage to live under the same roof as the princess, accepted the offer, and in the middle of December the couple moved out to Palama and took up residence in a long building attached to the main house. There, Gina was thrilled to have a spacious bedroom, a parlor of her own, and a magnificent garden in which to walk. Gina was expected to dine in the main house with the princess, but at least here knives and forks were used, and there was a fulltime cook and servants to clean and serve the meals, just like in Gina's grand family home back in Italy. Liliuokalani even allocated Gina a personal maid, a cheery little Japanese girl, and gave Gina a mare and buggy for her own use.

To further help Robert, Liliuokalani asked her friend Charles

B. Wilson to try to find him a job. Wilson, whose father was English and mother Tahitian, had started out as a blacksmith before becoming an engineer. Currently Superintendent of the Honolulu Water Works, Wilson would soon receive the additional appointment of Chief Engineer of the Honolulu Fire Department from Interior Minister Lorrin Thurston. At the princess's request, Wilson spoke to his colleague Surveyor General W. D. Alexander. A year earlier, Honolulu's Chinatown had been razed by fire, making six thousand Chinese residents homeless, and there was still much rebuilding work to be done. So Alexander was able to offer Robert Wilcox a post as a surveyor. Wilcox accepted the job, but only begrudgingly.

Meanwhile, Wilcox sympathized with the many Native Hawaiians who blamed Kalakaua for surrendering his rights, and their rights, meekly to the Hawaiian League. They believed that Liliuokalani was made of sterner stuff, that she would make a far better monarch than her brother, and would overturn the Bayonet Constitution if she took the throne.

On the other hand, few whites sympathized with the sense of loss and outrage felt by native Hawaiians as a result of the Bayonet Constitution. A bemused Admiral L. A. Kimberly, commander of the US Navy's Pacific Station, told the secretary of the navy, from Honolulu, 'The natives seem to have an uneasy feeling as to their rights being usurped by the whites' as a result of the 'present constitution, which, to their ideas, circumscribes too much of the kingly power.' Admiral Kimberly's reaction to this 'uneasy feeling' was to ask for more US forces to be stationed at Hawaii.[38]

With Kalakaua in his job for life, the only way to empty the throne for his successor was with his removal, one way or another. Robert Wilcox began to neglect his new wife and his new job as he threw himself into a lead role in a new movement agitating to take back the political ground stolen from Native Hawaiians by the Hawaiian League. Performing his surveyor's job perfunctorily during the day, Wilcox spent all his spare time writing articles for the Hawaiian newspapers, chairing meetings at the Palama house and elsewhere, organizing a shooting club, and preparing speeches and delivering them at various gatherings.

Wilcox was accompanied by wife Gina to one of these political meetings. Held in the Armory, the very same hall that the Hawaiian League had used for its inflammatory all-male meetings, it was packed with Hawaiian men, and their wives. Gina was amazed to see that her Robert was a powerful speaker who stirred passions and quickly won the support of the crowd. Hawaiian womenfolk at the meeting crowded around Gina, showering her with flowers and kissing her hands. But she had no desire to share her husband's political stage. Perceiving that the other side in this political argument had most of the money, and therefore most of the power, she was certain that Robert's political ambitions were doomed to be disappointed. 'The Kanakas have true right on their side,' she conceded, writing in her diary, but, believing that might would overcome right, she chose to be an indifferent spectator to the unfolding drama.[39]

Princess Liliuokalani, Mr. and Mrs. Wilcox' host, was now spending much of her time at the Palama house with the couple. She said that she could more easily write music in the peaceful surroundings there. Liliuokalani was the talented composer of more than two hundred songs including Hawaii's first national anthem and, later, the haunting 'Aloha Oe.' She could play numerous instruments, including the piano, and her favorite, the zither. But Gina believed that the princess had another motive for living at the Palama house. Within weeks of moving in there, Gina came to suspect that Robert and the princess were plotting together.

Young Mrs. Wilcox may have been temperamental, but she was also intelligent and perceptive. She wrote of Liliuokalani, in a December diary notation, 'She has taken seriously her role as a royal princess, has her ladies, her court, her party, nourishes a queenly scorn for her brother (King Kalakaua) whose weakness and lack of capacity she understands, and she actually aspires nonetheless to rob him of the throne and put herself in his place.' Gina was convinced that Liliuokalani was using Robert. 'My husband, who is basically a big boy, does not realize that he is only an instrument of this woman's ambition, and he follows her advice.'[40]

Yet, for all her suspicions about Liliuokalani, Gina felt able to confide to the princess, on December 26, that she wished she had not married Robert.[41] As only her diary knew, Gina was by this time having romantic thoughts about a handsome Italian physician, Dr. Mario de Lungo, whom she and Robert had met on the steamer out to Hawaii. Appointed King Kalakaua's personal physician, Dr. De Lungo called on Gina several times, always acting the perfect gentleman. Just after Christmas, De Lungo was sent by the king to Kauai, to help the staff at a leper facility. The handsome doctor soon wrote to Gina from Kauai, allowing her to cherish secret hopes of a romance.

While Gina Wilcox was dreaming of running off with the Italian doctor, she missed the nuances of the political struggle that was going on right under her nose. In November, Princess Liliuokalani had been approached by her brother the king to join him in signing away the kingdom's Crown Lands, so that he could raise a million dollars to pay off his personal debts, incurred from a life of drinking, gambling and traveling that had gained him the title 'the Merry Monarch' from his *haole* detractors. Twice in the one day, Kalakaua came to his sister with the same request. She, determined to preserve the Crown Lands for the people, sent him away disappointed on both occasions. As Kalakaua departed the second time, he bitterly declared Liliuokalani a *kipi*, or traitor. This shook her. When, on December 11, the day before Robert and Gina Wilcox moved in with her, Liliuokalani was told by her friend Charles Wilson that he could raise a company of young ali'i to put her on the throne, she told him not to do anything of the sort–she would not be a *kipi*.[42]

Nine days later, when a member of the legislature told Liliuokalani that the people wanted her to be queen, she told him that she would take the throne, but only if her brother abdicated. Then, on December 23, she was visited by Hawaiian League co-founder William Castle. With the king refusing to sign into law bills that had been passed by the legislature, Castle asked the princess, on behalf of the League, if she would influence Kalakaua to sign the bills, or take the throne herself.

"I would not sit on the throne where violence was used to my brother," Liliuokalani informed Castle in response to his question, before sending him away.[43]

When the king held his New Year's Ball at the palace, prominent Hawaiian League members including Castle, Dole, Jones and Thurston boycotted the event. The stalemate between king and League was continuing when, a week later, Princess Liliuokalani was visited by ali'i Robert Boyd. Like Wilcox, Boyd had been undergoing military training in Italy until recalled by the Bayonet Cabinet. 'Boyd seems to think it will be well to have a revolution,' Liliuokalani wrote in her diary.[44] But she quickly dismissed the idea. When a delegation of leading ali'i came to the princess on

January 14, asking if she would take the throne, 'I gave them the same answer as I gave to the League,' she recorded. 'That is, I would take it when he abdicated, not otherwise.'[45]

Gina Wilcox noticed that in January the private meetings between the princess and her husband were becoming more frequent. Robert told his wife nothing of what transpired in these meetings. Gina was unaware that, on January 16, her husband joined with Charles Wilson in making an approach to the king. In this meeting, Wilcox and Wilson asked King Kalakaua to abdicate in his sister's favor. Kalakaua replied that he 'would think it over.' To give her brother time, Liliuokalani told Wilcox to 'wait a while.'[46] Wait for what, she did not say.

A January 21 mass meeting of Robert Wilcox's supporters appointed a committee of five, which, in an audience with the king two days later, asked if he would abdicate. Kalakaua refused to give them an answer. The following day, the Reverend J. Waiamau told Liliuokalani, "The people are very much against the king's weaknesses." When the princess reiterated that she would only accept the throne if the king abdicated, the clergyman said his group would call a public meeting to demand Kalakaua's abdication.[47]

But the patience of Robert Wilcox and his more radical followers was running out. Wilcox was coming home later with each passing night, but would not tell his wife what he was up to. As January came to an end, Gina was one morning strolling in the Palama garden when she was approached by a diminutive native who furtively thrust a note into her hand. On opening the note, Gina found that it was from her husband's married sister Caroline Sharratt. The sisters-in-law had grown fond of each other, and in the note Caroline warned Gina that she must not fail to go to the house of French consul Georges Bouliech that evening, for her by now weekly visit to the Bouliech family, 'Because the revolution would break out and the king would be killed.' The consul's house was on the other side of the island, well away from Honolulu and away from danger. Caroline added that Gina must not tell Robert that she had passed on this warning, as he would never forgive her.[48]

Gina dined with Princess Liliuokalani that evening as usual. Neither woman said a word that indicated they knew what might occur at the palace a little later. After Gina informed Robert of her sudden plan to visit the Bouliech family, he told Gina he would collect her from their home late that evening. Following dinner with Liliuokalani, Gina drove her buggy out to the Bouliech house. There, her socialite lady-friends saw immediately by the look on the Gina's face that something was amiss, and when they pressed her she blurted out the secret. Once they had overcome the shock, the ladies began chattering, about anything, to distract their friend. Discreetly checking the time every now and then, they waited out the hours in growing tension.

A little before midnight, a carriage came crunching up the Bouliech drive. The entire party rushed out to greet it, with Gina suddenly fearful that it was bringing news of Robert's death. But it was Robert who stepped down from the carriage. There was an embarrassed smile on his face. Calmly, he told his wife that the plotters had met, his name had been drawn from a hat, and he had been armed with a knife–to kill the king. But when he had entered the palace bedroom where King Kalakaua was sleeping, he could not bring himself to plunge the dagger into the sleeping monarch's chest.

Robert and Gina drove back to the Palama house in silence. Gina, writing about the night's events in her diary, said that she was filled with a mixture of horror and contempt. To her mind, Robert was just as guilty as if he had actually gone through with the murder. Now, he also had the mantle of failure to bear. At dinner next evening, as Robert sat at the table silent and depressed after failing to carry out the deed that would have set the princess on the throne, Liliuokalani was particularly frosty toward him. In contrast, the princess was friendlier to Gina Wilcox than she had been in weeks. Gina, for her part, acted as if she was unaware of the previous night's murderous affair.

The story of a failed attempt to overthrow the king soon swept the kingdom. The English language press reported that a group of young ali'i had bailed up the king in an Iolani Palace room and attempted to force him to sign his abdication. Kalakaua, said the reports, had refused, and the police were investigating the whole affair. No mention was made of an attempt on the king's life. It is likely that, after Kalakaua's refusal to sign the abdication document, Wilcox had hidden in the palace, and when certain the king was asleep, had made his aborted assassination bid. The king slept through it, blissfully unaware of how close he came to death.

Several days later, Gina Wilcox was sitting, writing, in her

sun-drenched parlor at Liliuokalani's Palama house when her
Japanese maid announced that Hawaii's Minister for Foreign
Affairs had arrived to see her. Gina immediately thought that the
visit heralded a government offer to her husband of the lucrative
and prestigious post of consul in San Francisco that had once
been promised him. With her eyes shining with expectation, she
asked for the Minister to be shown in. Jonathan 'Jona' Austin
had taken up the Foreign Affairs portfolio just six weeks before.
A 'huge' man in Gina's estimation, Austin waddled into the
Palama parlor. The glum look on his face was enough to swiftly
dispel Gina's hopes of good tidings.

"Madam," said Minister Austin, "it is only through concern
for your unfortunate condition, (she was by now very obviously
pregnant again), that we are warning you that the Government
has decreed the death of your husband."[49]

Gina looked at Foreign Minister Austin in shock. Yet, she was
to say, she didn't faint, her hair didn't turn white, and neither did
she cry.[50] She should have been expecting something like this, but
in her naiveté she had thought that the affair at the palace several
nights before would simply be forgotten in this laid-back little
country. But the attempt by her husband and his associates to
force the king to abdicate was an act of treason.

"If he does not leave the islands forever and give up his political
intrigues," Minister Austin went on, "he will be imprisoned and
executed."[51]

Gina went cold from head to toe. With a firm voice, she thanked
'His Excellency,' and promised to do all in her power to convince
her husband that they should leave the kingdom at once.[52] As soon
as Austin had departed, Gina prepared to go out. An hour later,
she arrived at the Nuuanu Valley house of the Italian consular
representative in Hawaii, German-born Frederick Shaeffer, who
ran the Melchers and Company trading concern. Pushing a bag
containing her jewels into Shaeffer's hands, she begged him for a
cash advance that would permit Robert and herself to flee Hawaii.
Shaeffer duly provided the Wilcoxes with the money to leave.
Lorrin Thurston would claim that Gina Wilcox went to him and
begged him to have the charges against her husband dropped if
she promised that they would leave the kingdom.[53] Gina's diary
made no mention of any such meeting, and it seems to have been
an invention of Thurston, who would soon display a talent for
exaggeration and distortion on a grand scale.

Robert and Gina Wilcox departed Honolulu for San Francisco aboard the SS *Alameda* on February 11. The day before they sailed, Gina received news from Kauai that Dr. Mario de Lungo, the handsome young Italian doctor who had inspired her romantic notions, had been found dead in his bed. He had died from a brain aneurysm. In a matter of just a few days, every aspect of Gina's life had been turned upside down, and all her hopes and dreams destroyed.

7.

THE REDSHIRT REBELLION

CAPTAIN ROBERT PARKER WAIPA, ADJUTANT OF the King's Guard, was a descendant of John Palmer Parker, a native of Newton, Massachusetts whose ancestors in turn hailed from Essex in England. As a young seaman, in 1815, John Parker had left his ship in Hawaii, and, with the support of John Young, had been permitted by Kamehameha the Great to settle in the islands. Parker married Kipikane, daughter of one of Kamehameha's senior ali'i, and with their three children began the Parker dynasty. Captain George Vancouver had given Kamehameha the Great several head of cattle, and these beasts became the foundation of a ranch developed on the Big Island by the Parker family. Today it is one of the largest individually-owned cattle ranches in the United States.

Robert Parker Waipa was born on the Parker Ranch, and he grew up there among the pianiolas, as Hawaiian cowboys were called–after the Big Island's early Mexican cowhands. Of medium height and build, but lithe and fit, Robert proved to be a natural in the saddle, and with a gun–a crack shot, throughout his life he would win prizes for his marksmanship. He was particularly renowned among the pianiolas for being able to ride at speed and lean over and shoot, with dead-eye accuracy, beneath the belly and through the legs of his galloping horse.

One of Robert's closest boyhood friends had been a fellow ali'i, Crown Prince Leleiohoku, the younger brother and original heir of King David Kalakaua. After Robert's mother initially refused her permission for Robert to move to Honolulu at the invitation of his friend the prince, she relented, and as a young man Robert joined the King's Guard. In 1884, when he was twenty-seven, Robert Parker, as he was known in the white community, received a commission as a third lieutenant in the Guard. Robert also became a crewman of the king's prestigious racing canoe. With his shooting and riding abilities, and displaying total loyalty and reliability, Robert swiftly rose through the ranks of the Guard. Promoted to second lieutenant in 1885 and first lieutenant a year later, in October, 1886, Robert was made a captain. The following January, he was appointed the Guard's adjutant and day to day commander.

On the night of July 29-30, 1889, the young captain's loyalty and reliability were put to the test, after he received an unexpected order to report to King Kalakaua. Of the commander of the Guard, Captain John Paul Kahalewai, there was no sign, as mustachioed Adjutant Parker Waipa came to attention in front of the king. Possessing a prominent mustache and side whiskers, Kalakaua was a solid man, and tall–like all the adult male members of the Hawaiian royal family, Kalakaua was over six feet in height. Putting his hands on the young adjutant's shoulders, the king looked down into his eyes, and informed Parker Waipa that a band of insurgents led by Robert Wilcox would, in the early hours of next morning, attempt to seize the palace.

"Captain Waipa," King Kalakaua then said, "you and your men will defend the palace to your last drop of blood."

"Yes, my king," Robert returned.[54]

Accompanied by the majority of the sixty men of the King's Guard, the king hurriedly departed the Iolani Palace and made his way through the night to the Royal Boathouse several blocks away at the waterfront. The Boathouse was a large, two-story building where the royal barge and the king's racing canoes were kept. Kalakaua sometimes slept at the Boathouse, and held grand luaus there, especially for visiting guests such as Scottish author Robert Louis Stevenson of 'Treasure Island' and 'Dr. Jekyll and Mr. Hyde' fame, who spent six months of 1888 in Hawaii before settling in Samoa.

Captain Parker Waipa was left with twelve men, including two sergeants and a corporal, and these he posted at the four palace gates. Parker Waipa himself made up a bed for himself on the floor of the palace, giving his men orders to wake him the moment that there was any sign of trouble, from Robert Wilcox or anyone else.

The captain knew fellow ali'i Wilcox well. Who didn't in Hawaii? Wilcox and his temperamental Italian wife Gina had separated not long after they arrived in San Francisco in 1888. Gina gave birth to a daughter, and soon fled back to Italy with the child. There, Gina's family approached Pope Leo XIII, who, despite the fact that Gina had given birth to Robert Wilcox's child, had granted her an annulment of her marriage. In the spring of 1889, after receiving assurances from contacts in Hawaii that the government would forgive him his past sins if he kept out of politics, Wilcox had returned to Honolulu.

Princess Liliuokalani's mother-in-law had died in April, after which the princess had moved into Washington Place in the city with her husband. So, on Wilcox's return, Liliuokalani had allowed him to move back into the quarters he and Gina had occupied at the Palama house. There, behind closed shutters, Wilcox had conducted secret meetings with his political allies. On the afternoon of July 29, Liliuokalani had driven out to the Palama house for the first time in months–to check out the garden, she would later assert.[55]

By coincidence, Liliuokalani was to claim, she ran into Wilcox at the Palama house, and he told her that come that very evening he would be leading a bid to 'release the king from that hated thralldom under which he had been oppressed.' When Liliuokalani asked him if the king was aware of his intentions, Wilcox said that he was not.[56] Liliuokalani then returned to Washington Place, now aware of Wilcox's plans to stage a *coup d'état* of sorts. But she made no attempt to warn her brother the king. Perhaps she suspected that Kalakaua did in fact know what was going on, and had sanctioned Wilcox's planned 'coup.' Either that, or Liliuokalani wanted Wilcox to succeed.

During the three months that Wilcox had been back in the country, he had put together an eclectic coalition of disaffected Hawaiians, Westerners, and several wealthy Chinese merchants. They had assembled a tidy little fighting force; Sanford Dole would many years later write that this numbered 'several hundred' men, but the indications are that Wilcox had no more than eighty men under arms on the morning of July 30. Wilcox, an admirer of Giuseppe Garibaldi, the Italian patriot who had led his Redshirts in aid of Italian democracy half a century earlier, similarly outfitted his little force in red shirts. Their arms were a mixture of rifles, pistols, and scatterguns used by the Chinese to keep their paddy fields free of birds. Among his rebel officers were Robert Boyd, and George Markham, who, like Wilcox and Boyd, had been recalled from training with Italy's Royal Military College by the Bayonet Cabinet's termination of the Studies Abroad program.

The revolutionaries rendezvoused in the suburbs at 3.00 a.m. Just before dawn, Wilcox, wearing his handsome Italian military uniform, marched his little band into downtown Honolulu through deserted streets. Not long before 6.00 a.m., they were on King Street outside the Iolani Palace's Kauikeaouli Gate and the eight-foot-high masonry wall that surrounded the eleven-acre palace garden. There, Wilcox divided his force. First, he sent B. H. Kahananui with twelve men to the Government Building, today's Judiciary Building, with orders to seize and hold it. On the far side of the street, this was home to the parliament and government.

B. H. Kahananui and his men trotted up the drive past the statue of Kamehameha the Great standing in front of the Government Building, and reached the front doors to find that the building's janitors had just started work for the day. Kahananui sent the janitors away, allowing them to lock the doors, then ordered his men to take up defensive positions around the building. Before long, Justice Lawrence McCully arrived, driving up to the front door to commence work for the day, but he was warned away by Kahananui. Around the back, Kahananui's men refused entry to Chief Justice Judd when he arrived.

Across the street, Captain Parker Waipa was woken by one of his men with the news that Wilcox was at the Kauikeaouli Gate with a body of armed men, and demanding that the gates be opened. The captain promptly had his men withdraw from all the gates, to the palace itself, leaving the gates barred. Soon, in the low early morning light, Parker Waipa saw several of Wilcox's redshirts climb over the wooden gates from King Street and open them from the inside. Wilcox then marched his men in through the gateway and up the drive, forming them up in a line in front of the palace in full view of the guardsmen stationed there. Captain Waipa Parker estimated the insurgents with Wilcox to number sixty or so. With his men watching from the front door and windows, the King's Guard captain drew his sword, came out onto the palace veranda, and purposefully walked down the cast iron steps to confront Wilcox.

"I order you to surrender your sword," Wilcox said to him, "and the palace enclosure."

Parker Waipa shook his head. "No," he firmly replied, before telling Wilcox to withdraw.

When Wilcox refused to leave, the captain turned and retraced his steps. This astonished and infuriated Wilcox, who'd been certain that the men of the Guard, fellow ali'i, would not stand in his way. Wilcox drew his pistol from its holster, and strode after Waipa Parker, who would later tell the Hawaiian-language press that all the time he was climbing the steps with his back to Wilcox he hoped that he would not become a dead man.[57]

When Wilcox was half way up the steps, he had a change of heart, stopped, then trotted back down again and returned to his waiting line of men, issuing orders as he went. In response, Boyd, Markham and a bunch of redshirts went trotting away. Skirting around the side of the palace, they headed in the direction of the barracks. Shortly after, Wilcox again climbed to the top of the steps, where Captain Waipa Parker now stood.

"Where are the cannon carts?" Wilcox demanded, referring to the ammunition caissons of the Guard's artillery pieces.

"I don't know," the captain lied.

Cursing, Wilcox again went back down the steps. Shortly after, two of the four small brass, breech-loading cannon kept at the barracks armory were being rolled into the enclosure at the front of the palace by Wilcox's men. The two field pieces were positioned on the lawns south of the palace, one to the west, the other to the east, in the open. The ease with which Wilcox's subordinates acquired these guns from the barracks would later be the subject of much discussion in the English-language press, and it would emerge that men of the King Guard's artillery reserve company had been recruited by Wilcox for his redshirt army.

Captain Waipa Parker now slipped out the Iolani Palace's back door and hurried to the barracks, where the commander of the Guard, Captain Kahalewai, had his quarters. There, he found Kahalewai, informed him of the situation, and asked for orders.

"Return to the palace," Captain Kahalewai instructed his deputy, as he himself apparently made preparations to depart, "and allow no one to enter it."

Captain Waipa Parker saluted, then slid back into the palace. He arrived to find Wilcox on the front veranda, and calling for him. Opening one of the two tall glass front doors a little way, the captain asked Wilcox what he wanted now.

"I again call on you to surrender the palace," said Wilcox impatiently. "I want to place my cannon on the upper floor." That would allow the guns, which had a relatively flat trajectory, to fire over the palace walls.

"I will not surrender the palace," said Waipa Parker adamantly. And when Wilcox responded that, in that case, he would take it from him, the captain declared, "I will fight to the last man."

Again denied, the frustrated Wilcox once more retreated to his men. But, highly agitated, he soon returned to the palace door, this time to demand to know where the small arms were being kept. Once more, Waipa Parker feigned ignorance.[58]

The delay caused by the captain's defiance provided time for more government forces to be summoned. The alarm had already been raised in Honolulu after the two judges had been turned away from the Government Building by redshirts. Lorrin Thurston was now serving as Premier of Hawaii, having replaced William Green as the head of the cabinet. Once Thurstson received a telephone call from one of the judges conveying the news of the events at the palace and Government Building, he gave orders for the men of the Honolulu Rifles militia to be called to arms. Tellingly, the Hawaiians of the four reserve companies of the King's Guard were not called out; Thurston and his colleagues were concerned that those units might join with Wilcox's rebels, as the artillery men had already done. Telephones were soon jangling across Honolulu as the white militiamen of the Honolulu Rifles were summoned to assemble at the old Armory on Beretania Street.

Also on Beretania, Princess Liliuokalani had spent the night at Washington Place. She always rose early, but, knowing that Wilcox planned to launch his coup attempt in the early hours of July 30, by the time that events had begun at the palace the princess was up, dressed, and in the Washington Place garden, in sight of the palace, waiting to see how those events unfolded. Soon, she saw a ragged line of men of the Honolulu Rifles running along Beretania Street toward Punchbowl Street, making for the Armory. Some men were wearing their uniforms, others were trying to dress as they ran. Hurrying to the gate, Liliuokalani recognized one of the passing men, a youngster by the name of Harry Auld who worked at the Custom House.

"Mr. Auld," she called to him, "what is the meaning of the commotion at this early hour?"

"Mr. Wilcox has taken possession of the palace, Your Highness, and is supported there by a company of soldiers," Auld replied, before continuing on.[59]

Liliuokalani would have smiled inwardly; it seemed, from Auld's information, that Wilcox was well on his way to achieving his objective. But Auld's information was faulty. Wilcox and his men had taken possession of the palace grounds, but Captain Parker Waipa and the Guard still stubbornly held the palace. And Wilcox, stymied by the Guard commander, was not sure what to do next.

Soon, Volney Ashford was leading lines of men of the Honolulu Rifles companies down to the palace from the Armory, at the double. Setting up his headquarters at the Hawaiian Hotel, Ashford stationed some of his men at the corner of Punchbowl and Queen streets, behind the Government Building. The remaining men of the Rifles, commanded by 'Major' John H. Soper, who, the previous year, had served his second stint as marshal of the kingdom, took over the upper floor of the Kamehameha V Opera House, a thousand-seat music hall right next door to the Government Building. From there, Soper's men could direct fire both at B. K. Kahananui's rebel detachment at the Government Building and at Wilcox's redshirts in the palace grounds. Seeing this threatening activity close by, Boyd and Markham swung their two cannon around and aimed them at the Opera House.

Several local men and visitors to the city who were not members of the Honolulu Rifles–described as 'outside men' by Sanford Dole–were quick to volunteer their services to Volney Ashford, and the marksmen among them were given rifles.[60] One 'outside' group was stationed in a two-story house on Richards Street, to cover the palace's northwestern Kinau Gate, the tradesmen's entrance. Another group of civilian sharpshooters took positions in the tower of the Kawaiahao Church, which offered an ideal sniping position south of the palace grounds. Several other 'outside men' went scuttling along Likelike Street east of the palace to cover the northern entrance, but as they were passing the Likelike Gate it suddenly opened. Several of Wilcox's red-shirted men dashed out, grabbed an 'outside' man, disarmed him, then dragged him back into the palace grounds, making him their prisoner.

Wilcox may have ringed the palace–and Captain Parker Waipa's King's Guard men inside it–but the Honolulu Rifles, the 'outside men,' and the Honolulu police had formed a broader encirclement in the surrounding streets, trapping the revolutionaries at the Government Building and palace grounds. The drama dragged on into the middle of the morning, as the standoff at the palace paralyzed all downtown Honolulu, whose streets remained deserted apart from the armed men.

A little before 10.00 a.m., forty-four-year-old Honolulu banker Sam Damon, who had recently joined Lorrin Thurston's cabinet, replacing Godfrey Brown as Minister of Finance, attempted to negotiate with Robert Wilcox. The locally-born Damon, son of Massachusetts missionary Samuel C. Damon and a product of the Punahou School, had the look of a leprechaun about him. Diminutive, bald, with large eyes, protruding ears, and equipped with a luxuriant mustache that linked with his side-whiskers in the fashion then current in Europe, Damon went to the Kauikeaouli Gate on King Street and called to those on the other side of the wall. Damon said that he wished to come inside the palace compound and talk with Wilcox. But the revolutionaries refused to let him in.

In the 'mule yard' behind the Government Building, red-shirted B. H. Kahananui had come across five Hawaiian 'trusties,' low security prisoners from Oahu Prison, which was nicknamed 'the Reef'. The trusties had been ferried over from the Reef that morning to work in the building's grounds. "Do you favor the doings of today?" Kahananui asked them. "Will you go over into the palace yard?"[61]

The prisoners all volunteered to join the revolt and join Wilcox's men in the palace grounds. So, as 10.00 o'clock approached and all was quiet on the opposing lines, Kahananui led the trusties from the Government Building, dashing across King Street, and then heading quickly up Likelike Street. Kahananui figured that the palace's northeastern Hakaleleponi Gate, on Palace Walk, modern-day Hotel Mall, would be the safest to approach with his new recruits. There may also have been an element of reverence in the revolutionary's choice of entrance–custom held that the Hakaleleponi Gate was also the only palace gate that could be used by retainers of the Crown.

But when Kahananui and his unarmed followers turned into Palace Walk, they saw two men of the Honolulu Rifles and an armed policeman loitering on the corner of Punchbowl Street to their right. Those three spotted them and immediately brought up with their rifles, forcing Kahananui and the trusties to duck back into Likelike Street. Kahananui began to hurriedly retrace his steps. As he did, he and his party met Finance Minister Sam Damon coming the other way after his failed negotiation bid at the King Street gate. Damon was pleased to see a redshirt, despite the rifle in Kahananui's hands, and struck up a conversation with him, hoping that the revolutionary might take him to Wilcox. As they were talking, a rifle shot rang out nearby.

The shot had been fired from the Opera House, toward Wilcox's position in the palace grounds. Three or four redshirt rifles crackled in reply, and then Wilcox's two cannon boomed a more frightening response. One shell struck the outside wall of the Opera House, showering it with shrapnel. The other passed through a second floor Opera House window and detonated inside. Miraculously, no one in the Opera House was injured. Now, all hell broke loose, as every gun on both sides opened fire.

At the two cannon, standing exposed in the palace grounds, their red-shirted crews frantically loaded fresh shells into the breeches to fire again. But the sharpshooters in elevated positions all around the western and southern perimeters of the palace had clear shots at them. Bullets whined all around the gun crews. At one gun, Robert Boyd took a bullet, and fell, wounded. At the other, George Markham was also hit, and had to be carried away. The gunner of the westernmost gun dropped, dead, with the lanyard in his hand, as he was about to fire.

Seeking cover, Wilcox and his revolutionaries dispersed in all directions. Abandoning the two cannon, some men ran to the wall fronting King Street, where they were safe from fire from the south. Wilcox and the majority of his men ran to a pink building to the northwest of the palace called the Haleakala. Better known as the Backyard Bungalow, this two-story structure was surrounded on all sides by verandas enclosed by ornate latticework. This latticework, which gave the building the appearance of a Cairo bazaar, made the Bungalow both private and cool in summer, and it was a favorite retreat for the king and queen on Honolulu's most languid summer nights. Meanwhile, another group of a dozen or so redshirts ran toward the palace, firing as they came.

With his hand resting on the hilt of his sheathed sword, the Guard's Captain Robert Parker Waipa was standing on the palace's front veranda when the firing began. Almost immediately, a bullet hit him in the left shoulder; passing through his body, it continued on and slammed into the palace wall behind him. Without flinching, the captain directed his men to open fire on the advancing revolutionaries. Several red-shirted men in this group were hit, but most managed to tumble into the small, open concrete moat that surrounded the palace, and, via that, enter the palace basement.

At Washington Place, stray bullets were zipping by, and Princess Liliuokalani, her curiosity suddenly dampened, grabbed up her skirts and quickly withdrew inside the house and closed the door. In Likelike Street, revolutionary commander Kahananui abruptly terminated his conversation with Finance Minister Damon, who, looking 'excited' in the Hawaiian's opinion, rapidly took cover beside the palace garden wall. Kahananui set off in a crouching run to return to his men at the Government Building. When he started out, the five terrified trusties were right behind him.

Somehow, Kahananui was able to cross King Street unscathed despite bullets flying all around him. When he reached the Government Building's drive, he looked around to see that just one of the trusties, and man named Kelelua, remained with him; the other four had fled. As bullets came flying from the Opera House, Kelelua flattened himself against the slender trunk of a palm tree. This only offered minimal cover, and Kahananui urged Kelelua to follow him to the Government Building just a hundred feet away, but the terrified prisoner would not budge. Kahananui ran on, and reached the Government Building's front verandah, where three of his redshirts were crouched. Gratefully, he threw himself behind the cover provided by the concrete balustrade. Incoming Government fire was rapid, and as bullets chipped the concrete all around him, Kahananui saw the trusty Kelelua take a bullet and fall, without a sound, from behind his palm tree. The unarmed Kelelua was dead by the time he hit the ground.

In the palace grounds, the incoming fire was so intense that the redshirts skulking at the wall scampered from their hiding place to the Bungalow and joined Wilcox. Revolutionaries now occupied the Bungalow, controlled the Government Building, and occupied the palace basement. But these assets were soon to be whittled away from them. At the palace, Captain Parker Waipa was not happy to have rebels under his feet. With several of his best men of the King's Guard and sword in hand, he charged down the stairs from the first floor and took the revolutionaries by surprise–at the sight of his naked sword and the bayonets of his men, the rebels in the palace basement surrendered to the captain without a fight.

By 11.00 a.m., B. K. Kahananui was alone on the Government Building verandah, having been deserted by all his men after Kelelua the trusty had been killed before their eyes. Deciding that it was pointless staying around any longer, Kahananui made his way to the east side of the building. With bullets plowing into the dirt all around him, he reached Queen Street. From there, he was able to make his escape. With Kahananui's retreat, Government forces moved in to occupy the Government Building. Wilcox and his remaining men were now bottled up in the Bungalow.

Sanford Dole, who had been serving as one of the three judges of the Hawaiian Supreme Court for the past twenty-two months, departed his house on Emma Street around 10.00 that morning, and reached the Opera House not long after the two cannon fired on it. He would remain at the Opera House for the rest of the day. Around midday, with all shooting now ceased and an uneasy calm hanging over downtown Honolulu, Dole noticed, from an Opera House upper window, that a white-clad figure had left the palace and was walking calmly toward the Likelike Street gate carrying something.

Government marksmen opened up on the man, but none hit him as he continued to blithely walk through the storm of bullets that he attracted. At the Opera House, orders rang out from John Soper for a cease-fire as it became obvious that the man was a non combatant. Even as the firing petered away, the man turned about and retraced his steps to the palace basement. Later, Dole learned that the man was King Kalakaua's steward, and that he had been loyally trying to take the king's lunch to him at the Boathouse.

Inside the Iolani Palace, using the palace telephone, Captain Parker Waipa asked the operator to connect him with Volney Ashford. Once he was put through to the Hawaiian Hotel, the Guard commander informed Ashford that he had secured the palace basement, and asked what he should do with his prisoners. Ashford instructed him to send them out to the street, one at a time. The red-shirted prisoners were soon trotting out from the palace, with hands raised and looking all about them in fear of being shot. Once collected in the street, they were marched off to the police station and lodged in its basement cells.

The stalemate dragged on well into the afternoon. At the Hawaiian Hotel, the main concern was that, once night fell, Wilcox's men would be able to use the darkness to reclaim the cannon that now stood deserted in the palace yard, then use the guns to devastating effect against government forces. Among the volunteers congregated at the hotel was Hay Wodehouse, son of James Wodehouse, long-time British ambassador to Hawaii. Young Wodehouse had grown up in the islands, and had joined a local baseball team, becoming an accomplished catcher. He suggested that hand-bombs be made using dynamite, which he would lob over the palace wall onto the Bungalow.

The idea was enthusiastically taken up, and a small collection of bombs was soon made, each consisting of a stick of dynamite strapped to an iron spike–for added weight. Arthur Turton, purser of the Oceanic Line steamer SS *Australia*, which was in port en route from San Francisco to Sydney, volunteered to act as Wodehouse's bombing assistant, and in the late afternoon the pair carefully made their way to the Richards Street wall on the northern side of the palace garden, carrying a collection of the home-made bombs.

Skulking beside the wall, Turton lit a fuse, then handed a bomb to Wodehouse. The young Englishman heaved the bomb over the fence. With a clunk, the bomb landed on the corrugated iron roof of the bungalow. Long seconds passed, and then the silence was rent by an almighty explosion. Grinning with boyish glee, the pair repeated the act. Another bomb went flying over the wall. Another explosion. They kept this up until they had used every one of their improvised explosive devices.

The explosions ripped off part of the Bungalow roof, did considerable damage to the Bungalow's interior and its valuable antique furniture, and killed and wounded several of the revolutionaries. Wilcox's already dispirited men now lost all heart, and several rushed out behind a white flag. Wilcox had no choice but send a message that he, too, was prepared to surrender. The Honolulu Rifles company that had been at the Hawaiian Hotel marched in through the Richards Street gate and formally took the surrender of the red-shirted revolutionaries including twelve wounded men, among them Boyd and Markham, and released their lone Honolulu Rifles prisoner. Seven men had been killed during the day's fighting–six redshirts and Kelelua the unarmed trusty. No one on the government side was killed, and only a few, including Captain Robert Parker Waipa, were injured. The key role of Waipa Parker and his Hawaiians of the King's Guard in sending Wilcox's Redshirt Revolt off the rails would not be mentioned by many later histories.

In the middle of the day, the Hawaiian Government had given permission for a company of marines to be landed from an American warship then in port, the USS *Adams,* to protect the US consulate and legation. At the same time, the *Adams* sent ashore 10,000 rounds of rifle ammunition for the use of Hawaiian Government forces. Later in the day, at the request of Foreign Affairs Minister Jona Austin, an additional party of armed sailors came ashore from the *Adams* to help the Government forces in maintaining order. The marines and the sailors would all return to the *Adams* the following day.

Wilcox, the last revolutionary to emerge from the Bungalow and be placed under arrest, was found to be carrying a draft for a new Hawaiian constitution in his pocket. Based on the 1864 constitution, this document, had it been signed into law by the king, would have restored all the powers of the monarchy removed by the Bayonet Constitution. No abdication document was found on Wilcox, so he apparently had no intention of attempting to force the king to step down.

The previous afternoon, when he had told Liliuokalani of his plans, Wilcox had assured her that he would gladly lay down his life *for* the king. Later, when brought to trial for staging his little revolution, he would claim that everything he had done was *for* his king, leading some to suspect that the king was complicit in Wilcox's coup attempt. Kalakaua certainly had been forewarned, by someone, that Wilcox was going to storm the palace. And Kalakaua despised the Bayonet Constitution.

Yet, if the king had believed that Wilcox was acting in his interests, it would have paid him to have allowed himself to fall into the hands of the revolutionaries and signed the new constitution carried by Wilcox, a constitution which would have allowed him to have immediately dismissed Lorrin Thurston and his cabinet. Instead, the king removed himself from the palace and ordered Captain Parker Waipa to defend the empty building to his last drop of blood–as if the monarch were inside. This suggests that Kalakaua suspected that his sister Liliuokalani was a *kipi*, as he had previously accused her of being, and that he believed Wilcox to be planning to depose or assassinate him and put Liliuokalani on his throne, with his sister's knowledge.

Liliuokalani herself revealed, years later, that she had certainly been aware of Wilcox's planned coup the day before he attempted it. Immediately after the event she was disgusted with Wilcox—for failing, a second time, to do what he had set out to do in support of the Hawaiian monarchy. His Redshirt Rebellion was, in Liliuokalani's words, 'foolish and ill-organized.'[62] Wilcox's former wife Gina had described him as 'a big boy,' and it was his boyish enthusiasm that led him into his dangerous schemes. 'His enthusiasm was great,' Liliuokalani was to say of him, 'but was not supported by good judgment or proper discretion.'[63] She obviously believed that Wilcox had used poor judgment and lack of discretion in revealing the latest plot to someone who had subsequently forewarned the king. Liliuokalani was not to know that Robert Wilcox would yet play an important part in her future.

As Wilcox was conveyed to Oahu Prison to await trial for raising a riot, Captain Robert Parker Waipa went to the spot in the Iolani Palace wall where the bullet that passed clean through his shoulder on July 30 had lodged. Using a knife, he dug out the slug. He attached the bullet to his watch chain, and would wear it there as a lucky charm for the rest of his days.

On August 5, King Kalakaua removed Captain John Kahalewai from command of the King's Guard, suspecting him of complicity in Wilcox's rebellion for being absent from his post during the rebellion. In Kahalewai's place as Commander of the Guard, the king appointed his loyal and fearless adjutant Robert Parker Waipa. Like Robert Wilcox, Parker Waipa was fated to play a key hand in the future of his nation's monarchy before much more time had passed.

8.

LONG LIVE THE QUEEN

In the second half of 1889, Robert Wilcox was one of three men brought to trial for staging the Redshirt Rebellion. Despite the damning evidence against him, he was acquitted of all charges by a jury of his peers. Realizing that no Hawaiian jury would convict the other native revolutionaries, the Thurston cabinet didn't bother pressing further charges; all imprisoned members of Wilcox's band were set free.

Wilcox was now a hero to many Hawaiians. Two books about him became big sellers in the kingdom. Hailed as 'Hawaii's Garibaldi' and 'Hawaii's Iron Duke,' Wilcox promptly turned to politics via the Hui Kalaiaina, the Hawaiian Political Association. He teamed up with John E. Bush, a mixed blood ali'i who had been Kamehameha V's ambassador to Samoa during the failed Pacific confederation episode and later served as both Hawaiian Foreign Minister and Interior Minister. Bush now owned an influential Hawaiian-language newspaper, which he swung behind Wilcox and the Hui Kalaiaina. As 1890's general election approached, the Hui Kalaiaina established an alliance with the Mechanics' and Workingmen's Political Protective Union. These odd political bedfellows jointly formed the National Reform Party, (quite separate from and opposed to the Reform Party). This new political entity attracted a vast following of native Hawaiians, unionists, and even disaffected Hawaiian League members.

The Hawaiian League, meanwhile, was being torn apart from within. Extreme radicals such as Volney Ashford, emboldened by the way that Wilcox's rebellion had been crushed, were all for doing away with the monarchy by force. Others, such as young premier Lorrin Thurston, focused on strengthening ties with the United States. Thurston had reshaped his Reform Party cabinet, eliminating Green and Brown and bringing in Sam Damon and Jona Austin, Hawaiian League men he could control. And, following the Wilcox affair, Thurston tightened security to prevent an uprising by the likes of Ashford. All arms in the kingdom other than those of the King's Guard were collected and stored at police headquarters, and the volunteer King's Guard artillery company that had provided men for Wilcox's doomed military adventure was abolished. So that the eight-foot-high wall around the palace could not shelter insurgents in future, the cabinet ordered it reduced to three and one half feet, and topped by an iron railing, ignoring the king's strenuous objections–this deprived him of privacy, he complained, to no avail.

But by the time the election of February, 1890 arrived, the Reform Party had become fractured by its internal dissension, and Thurston's control of it was less assured. In this election, Wilcox, Bush and their new National Reform Party won a number of seats from the Reform Party, gaining the most seats in the legislature. By June, 1890, a majority in both houses had passed votes of 'no confidence' in Thurston and his cabinet. This allowed King Kalakaua to dismiss the Bayonet Cabinet from office under the terms of the Bayonet Constitution which they themselves had written, and under which they must have been confident guaranteed they would never lose office. A shocked Thurston was out of power.

A new cabinet was sworn in, headed by sugar planter and National Reform Party man John A. Cummins, an ali'i and close friend of the king. The rest of the cabinet was made up of another National Reform man and two conservative Reform Party ministers. To the delight of the non white population, the new cabinet ordered the disbanding of the Honolulu Rifles, and abolished the post of Colonel of Volunteers, taking military power out of the hands of the Hawaiian League and putting the spluttering Volney Ashford out of a job. The Rifles' Armory building on Beretania Street became a bicycle riding school and repair shop called the Honolulu Cyclery, whose proprietors R. G. Wootten and W. H. Bromley promised 'first-class work and charges to suit the times.'[64]

To complete the turnaround, volatile Volney Ashford, who would not take the abolition of his beloved Honolulu Rifles lying down, was arrested for seditious activities and thrown in prison. This was in June, the same month that Thurston and his cabinet were thrown out. Ashford would escape from Oahu Prison in November, with the authorities turning a blind eye when he stowed away on a ship bound for the US–for, this conveniently removed him from the kingdom.

King Kalakaua now authorized former redshirt leaders Robert Wilcox and Robert Boyd to head a committee that would organize a constitutional convention to be attended by all legislators. The objective of the convention was the drafting of a new constitution that would replace the Bayonet Constitution with a document that more closely resembled the constitution of 1864 and restored the monarch's prerogatives. Wilcox and Boyd, who, less than a year before had been behind bars for leading a failed revolution, were achieving by democratic means more than they had ever achieved with a gun.

But Kalakaua's constitutional convention failed to materialize, as other matters became the focus of national attention. In October, 1890, the US Congress passed the protectionist McKinley Tariff Act, which levied a punitively high import duty on most imported goods. Some agricultural imports were exempted, sugar among them–to the great relief of the Hawaiian sugar industry, which now depended entirely on the US market. But by way of compensation, the McKinley Tariff provided for a bounty of two cents a pound to American sugar producers. The Hawaiian sugar men, including Premier Cummins and San Francisco banker Claus Spreckels–who would be receiving the two cent bounty for his American-grown beet sugar–pressured the king to demand the same bounty for them, under the US-Hawaii Reciprocity Treaty.

King Kalakaua's health had not been great of late and he played a reduced role in public affairs in 1890, traveling around the islands and rarely staying in Honolulu. Drinking more heavily than usual, he was living up to his nickname of 'the merry monarch.' When the sugar men asked him to put a case for them to the US Government, the king saw an opportunity to make a trip to the United States. Leaving Princess Liliuokalani again in charge as regent of the kingdom, on November 25 the king and a small entourage steamed out of Honolulu Harbor aboard the USS *Charleston*, which had been provided for the journey to San Francisco by Rear Admiral George Brown.

Through December, the king traveled extensively in Southern

California and northern Mexico, being feted wherever he went. Early in January, while in Santa Barbara, California, he suffered a mild stroke. After he returned to San Francisco, Kalakaua's health declined rapidly, and on January 18, appropriately at the Palace Hotel, he lapsed into a coma. Two days later, at the age of fifty-four, King David Kalakaua passed away in his San Francisco hotel bedroom. The official diagnosis of the US Navy physicians who attended him was that Kalakaua had died from Bright's Disease–inflammation of the kidneys. This did not prevent a rumor soon springing up back in Hawaii, a rumor that persists to this day, that the king was poisoned.

Kalakaua, seventh monarch of Hawaii, was dead. Under the twenty-second article of the Constitution of Hawaii, his sister Liliuokalani was now Queen of Hawaii.

On assuming office, Queen Liliuokalani took an oath to abide by the nation's constitution; this was the Bayonet Convention of 1887, which was still in force. She would later claim that she was railroaded into taking that oath by Premier Cummins and his colleagues of the last cabinet of Kalakaua's reign, who thought they could control the nation's first female monarch. After Chief Justice Judd swore in the queen, he took her aside and advised her to say 'yes' to everything that the cabinet put before her. Not only did Liliuokalani not say 'yes' to what the cabinet wanted, she said 'no' to the cabinet, asking for their resignations. Cummins and his colleagues refused, pointing out that, under the Bayonet Constitution, cabinet members could only be removed by a majority vote of the legislature.

"You ought to understand the situation and accept it," said Attorney General Arthur Peterson, a doe-eyed man with the look of a scolding missionary, to the Queen.[65]

Liliuokalani did understand the situation. Perfectly. She had taken private legal advice, and was sure of her ground. With her cabinet refusing to budge, the new queen put the matter before Hawaii's Supreme Court, where, in February, Chief Justice Judd ruled in her favor, saying that on the death of King Kalakaua the commissions of his ministers had expired. Entitled to now appoint ministers of her choice, Liliuokalani reappointed one cabinet member, Interior Minister Charles Spencer, but made new appointments to the other portfolios. Hermann H. Widemann, an elderly German planter with a native Hawaiian wife, had served as a judge and in one of King Kalakaua's cabinets; he now took the Finance ministry. American-born lawyer William Whiting became Attorney General. And, as Foreign Minister and Premier, the queen appointed Samuel Parker. An amiable and widely popular ali'i from the Parker Ranch on the Big Island, he was also a cousin of commander of the Guard, Robert Parker Waipa. None of the members of the new cabinet were descendants of missionaries.

Having cemented her authority and created a cabinet of her choosing, Queen Liliuokalani began her reign with a reputation as a strong woman. Among the Hawaiians, she was hailed as *hanai*, the mother of her people. Among the kingdom's white residents, particularly Americans, who had no experience of, or desire for, being ruled over by a woman, there was an undercurrent of disquiet, even of disrespect. This became all too evident to Liliuokalani when she granted an audience to the American ambassador to Hawaii since 1889, John L. Stevens.

While most foreign diplomatic representatives in Honolulu came to the Iolani Palace to pay their respects to the new sovereign, in contrast, Chauvinistic, seventy-year-old Stevens, ambassador to Hawaii for the past two years, came to lecture. Not long after taking up his post, Stevens had publicly declared that all monarchies were backward and detestable. Now he informed the Queen of Hawaii that he expected her to be a constitutional monarch who took a back seat and permitted her cabinet to administer the laws. He added insult to injury, at the start of the interview, by ignoring protocol and good manners in taking his seat before the queen sat down.

But Queen Liliuokalani was not going to be held back by the likes of Stevens. Supported by her new cabinet, she made a number of announcements. One of the most significant was the appointment of Charles B. Wilson as Marshal of the Kingdom to replace Hawaiian League member John L. Soper. Liliuokalani had the dynamite-damaged Bungalow repaired, and allowed Wilson and his wife Eveline to take up residence in a room there, appointing Mrs. Wilson one of her ladies in waiting. It was widely rumored that Charles Wilson was the queen's lover, and had been for years, even though he was a married man. Whether or not this was true, the handsome, courageous Wilson in 1891 certainly enjoyed Liliuokalani's utmost confidence, and was to become her closest confident and most trusted adviser over the next few years.

The queen's opponents would be rabid and unstinting in their criticism of Marshal Wilson, and of Liliuokalani's use of him, but they could not escape the fact that he had enjoyed the utmost confidence of Lorrin Thurston when he was Premier during the Bayonet Cabinet years. During Thurston's premiership, Wilson had been, concurrently, Superintendent of the Water Works, Chief Engineer of the Fire Department, and Clerk of Market. Thurston was on close personal terms with Wilson, calling him 'Charlie.' What was more, Thurston was to publicly declare Wilson the most capable man in Liliuokalani's government.[66]

The queen also appointed her own choice as commander of the King's Guard, Sam Nowlein. A cousin of Robert Wilcox. Nowlein had been made a lieutenant with the part-time King's Own reserve company back in 1883. Now, given the rank of captain, Nowlein had the fulltime task of leading the queen's bodyguard. Like Wilson, Nowlein would faithfully serve Liliuokalani for years to come. The queen also taking the fulltime King's Guard increased from sixty men to eighty, and restored the unit's original title of the Royal Household Guard. The enlarged royal bodyguard also took over responsibility for the four cannon that had previously been manned by reservists.

To make way for Nowlein, the queen removed Captain Robert Parker Waipa entirely from her service, discharging him from the Guard and leaving the career soldier unemployed. Parker Waipa was never given a reason for his dismissal by Liliuokalani, and was to tell his family that he believed it was because of his unstinting loyalty to the late king, and because he had been instrumental in foiling Robert Wilcox's 1889 coup attempt. Parker Waipa initially found a new job as a government fisheries inspector, but Marshal Wilson, recognizing his abilities, and ignoring the queen's dislike of him, soon recruited him into the police force, giving him the rank of senior captain. This made Parker Waipa the nation's highest ranking police officer after the marshal and deputy marshal of the kingdom.

The queen's marriage with John Dominis had been childless, meaning she had no child and heir. So, in March, she announced that her heir apparent would be her fifteen-year-old niece, Princess Victoria Kaiulani, daughter of Scottish-born Honolulu merchant Archie Cleghorn and Liliuokalani's late, lamented sister Princess Miriam Likelike. This young beauty Kaiulani, pronounced Kay-oo-lar-nee, who was known as Vicki within the family, (she signed herself 'Vike'), was currently attending school in England. She had charmed everyone in the kingdom as she grew to womanhood, and the announcement that she would eventually succeed her Aunt Lydia on the Hawaiian throne received widespread approval.

But one or two of the queen's native subjects were unhappy. Many ali'i had audiences with the queen in the early days of her reign, to congratulate her, and to seek favors and appointments. Among them were Robert Wilcox and John Bush. These founders of the National Reform Party sought a joint audience and asked the queen to appoint them to her new cabinet, with Wilcox no doubt expecting the top job as premier. Over the coming years Liliuokalani was to demonstrate that she had a long memory. Twice in the past, Robert Wilcox had failed her, and she was not going to give him a third opportunity to disappoint her. And Bush had written damning newspaper articles about the late king. Doubting the loyalty and reliability of both men, the Queen declined to offer either Wilcox or Bush any official post. They were furious, and didn't mind letting her know it before they withdrew from Liliuokalani's presence. In a diary notation on February 3, following this meeting, Liliuokalani was to describe the pair as 'two sore-heads who are angry because I did not make them Ministers.'

In the past, Liliuokalani had paid the price for trusting Wilcox. Now, he was determined to make her pay for rejecting him. Wilcox and Boyd went out and founded a radical new political party, the Liberal Party, taking a number of the supporters of the National Reform Party with them. The principal plank of their Liberal Party platform was the abolition of the Hawaiian monarchy and the creation of a republic in its place. Wilcox now had visions of ruling the little nation himself, as president.

Seven months after Liliuokalani ascended the throne, her husband John Dominis died at Washington Place after a long illness. In many ways Dominis' passing was a release for Liliuokalani. Now, she had no personal distractions as she pursued her political agenda. That agenda saw her at odds with the legislature, where, after the election of 1892, seats were divided between twenty-one Liberal members, fourteen Reform members, nine National Reform members, and four independents, with no single party able to command a majority or anchor a coalition. Seven times during 1891-92, motions of 'no confidence' would be moved against the cabinet by the legislature. Four of these were successful, forcing the queen to dismiss her cabinet and appoint a new one each time, although Premier Sam Parker remained a fixture through much of this period.

This political instability came at a time when the country was experiencing an economic downturn as a result of the McKinley Tariff, creating an undercurrent of dissatisfaction with the government on which Robert Wilcox and John Bush thrived. Wilcox's personal disdain for the queen who had rejected him fueled his politics. 'I do not wish to be governed by dolls!" he would declare in one speech. 'I believe no woman ought to reign. They have no brains!'[67] Meanwhile, Liberal Party colleague Bush railed in his newspaper against the queen's closest advisers, Marshal Wilson and Premier Parker–'A half-Tahitian blacksmith and a half-caste cowboy,' he called them.[68] These personal attacks, on ali'i by ali'i, and on the nation's ruler, were damaging to Liliuokalani personally and to the monarchy in general.

Wilcox also created another organization, the shadowy Hawaiian Patriotic League, which attracted the most radical agitators with its catch-cry of 'Hawaii for Hawaiians' and talk of establishing a Hawaiian republic by force of arms. Most radical of all was Volney Ashford, who had been pardoned for his last crime and permitted to return home to Hawaii. Ironically, the former commander of the Honolulu Rifles, the man who had headed the military response to Wilcox's 1889 redshirt rebellion, now joined ranks with Wilcox.

Marshal Wilson soon learned of the Hawaiian Patriotic League's suspicious activities and inserted spies into the organization. Convinced that he had enough evidence of a treasonous conspiracy against the Crown, in May, 1892, Marshal Wilson had Wilcox, Ashford and sixteen other Patriotic League members arrested. In Lorrin Thurston's opinion, Wilcox and his colleagues were their own worst enemies: 'They overreached themselves by talking too much before they were ready to act.'[69] But few of the conspirators were brought to trial. A dozen of Wilcox's fellow accused were soon released for lack of evidence, and, in a snub to the queen, Reform Party Attorney General William Whiting ignored Marshal Wilson's recommendation to try Wilcox for treason. The others were acquitted by friendly juries.

Just the same, the marshal's prompt action had been a telling blow to the Patriotic League. Chief troublemaker Volney Ashford, aware now that he was under police scrutiny, made another hurried departure from the kingdom, bound for California and self-exile, and this, said Lorrin Thurston, 'disconcerted and disheartened those who had been working with him.'[70] Disenchanted Patriotic League members walked away from the organization in droves, and Robert Wilcox was left to devise a new strategy.

Wilcox's vitriolic friend John Bush suggested in his newspaper that, if a Hawaiian republic was not achievable, anything was better than rule by a queen, even annexation by the US, Britain, or France. But the treason scandal, and Marshal Wilson's swift intervention in the Patriotic League's activities, had worked in Liliuokalani's favor. Said Lorrin Thurston, several months later: 'The result of the whole was a swinging of the pendulum against annexation and in favor of the queen.'[71]

Liliuokalani was now confident that she was on track to achieve her greatest wish, and that of her late brother–the replacement of the Bayonet Constitution of 1887 with a more liberal constitution along the lines of the 1864 document. But the queen could only count on the support of National Reform Party legislators now that Wilcox's Liberal Party had muddied the political mix, and National Reform were in the minority. Before Liliuokalani could change the constitution, she would have to bide her time, to wait for an opportunity to present itself, and then act swiftly and decisively.

Urged by Marshal Wilson and Commander of the Guard Sam Nowlein, in the second half of 1891 the queen conducted a series of secret conferences with a small circle of men whom she considered her most faithful supporters. Held at Muolaulani, Liliuokalani's country house at Kapalama, north of the city, these conferences produced two drafts for a new constitution. Following the general election of February, 1892, the queen received petitions signed by two thirds of the nation's registered voters calling on her to promulgate a new constitution. One of those petitions came via the Hui Kalaiaina; the queen subsequently suggested that the Association also provide a constitutional draft.

Liliuokalani was certain that when the time came to act she would have all the ammunition and input she needed for her new constitution. That time was not far off.

9.

CEMENTING
WASHINGTON'S SUPPORT

Lorrin Thurston had enjoyed the heady days of the apparently unstoppable rise of the Hawaiian League, and for three years he had tasted power as a cabinet minister, sitting as premier for one of those years. Now, the Hawaiian League had imploded, and the Reform Party was in the minority in the legislature, with Thurston sitting in the ineffectual House of Nobles. Infamous as an architect of the Bayonet Constitution, Thurston knew that there was absolutely no possibility that Liliuokalani would invite him to join any cabinet of hers. While she was queen, Thurston would be relegated to the political sidelines. He was back to being a small-time attorney, working from a single, second-floor room at 119 Merchant Street, above the then chambers of the Bishop and Co. Bank.

Thurston saw just one way to reverse his fortunes–the annexation of Hawaii to the United States. In one fell swoop, annexation would do away with the monarchy and eliminate the damage being done to the Hawaiian economy by the McKinley Tariff, which had reduced Hawaiian sugar exports to the US and impacted the local economy. Thurston believed that if he took a prominent though secret role in the kingdom's annexation by the US, he could manipulate power in the islands. If his three years as a cabinet minister had taught him anything, it was that it is difficult to achieve a secret agenda in the spotlight. Government office demands scrutiny, and transparency. On the other hand, the man who remains in the shadows can potentially get away with just about anything. Secrecy was the key.

It was with these thoughts in his mind that, one day in late February, 1892, following the latest election for the legislature, Thurston walked out the door of his Merchant Street building and bumped into fellow lawyer Henry E. Cooper. A young real estate attorney with a jet black beard and intense eyes, Cooper had just the previous year moved his family to Hawaii from San Diego, California. The pair began discussing local politics. News of the mass petitions to the queen for a new constitution was then dominating the Honolulu newspapers, and Cooper was also receiving inside information on the queen's plans via contacts in the government.

Said Cooper, "Thurston, if Liliuokalani attempts to subvert the Constitution of 1887, what do you intend to do about it?"

"I'll oppose her," said Thurston emphatically.

"Who else in the community thinks as you do?" Cooper asked.

Thurston could think of a dozen or so men, among them several of his fellow founders of the Hawaiian League, who shared his views on the queen.

"Conditions have gone so far," Cooper went on, "that the only effective remedy is annexation to the United States."[72]

Thurston must have smiled. He later wrote that he 'reluctantly' agreed with newcomer Cooper. Within days, Thurston, Cooper, and ten other leading Honolulu businessmen met secretly in Thurston's office. 'Our object was not to promote annexation,' Thurston wrote, 'but to be ready to act quickly and intelligently, should Liliuokalani precipitate the necessity by some move against the constitution.' The twelve men agreed to form a secret organization–the Annexation Club. In its initial form, the Club would number just seventeen members, representing leading business interests in Hawaii. "The organization should be small, but it should be thorough," Thurston told his colleagues.[73]

Thurston had another reason for keeping the Club secret–his pocket. The Hawaiian Government had decided to stage an exhibit at the 1893 World's Columbian Exposition in Chicago. Thurston had joined the board of commissioners formed by the Hawaiian Government to organize its exhibit. What was more, Thurston had convinced Premier Sam Parker that the exhibit should take the form of a cyclorama featuring a working model of the Kilauea Volcano, Hawaii's premier tourist attraction. It just so happened that Thurston was a director of the Kilauea Volcano House Company, which operated a hotel beside the volcano. In addition, because of his knowledge of the site, Thurston had been appointed by Premier Parker as one of two special commissioners who would be sent by the Hawaiian Government, at its expense, to Chicago that March to make preliminary arrangements for the exhibit. If it were to be revealed that Thurston was part of a secret organization whose object was the surrender of the sovereignty of the Kingdom of Hawaii, he could kiss goodbye to the government-paid opportunity to promote his own business interests in Chicago.

Thurston meanwhile told his fellow Annexation Club members that this Chicago trip would give him the perfect opportunity to sound out annexation supporters in the United States, particularly among government and congressional leaders in Washington DC. Club members agreed, and contributed funds to allow Thurston to make covert side trips to Washington during the months that he would be working in Chicago for the Hawaiian Government. In his memoirs, Thurston, a lawyer who liked to paint himself as a man who strictly observed the law in all he did, would give the (incorrect) impression that the Club paid the entire cost of his US trip. He did this to cover the embarrassing fact that he was prepared to accept his own government's money to make a trip on which he worked assiduously and illegally to subvert that very government.

On March 29, Thurston and fellow Exposition special commissioner Edward Walsh sailed from Honolulu for San Francisco aboard the SS *Australia*, on the first leg of the journey to Chicago. By April they were in Chicago, and, by May, Thurston was in Washington on a secretive Annexation Club side trip, knocking on influential doors. Thurston knew from John L. Stevens, US ambassador to Hawaii, that Stevens' close friend Secretary of State James G. Blaine strongly supported the idea of US annexation of Hawaii, as did Stevens himself. Blaine and Stevens had previously been partners in a newspaper in Maine.

But Blaine was ill when Thurston called at the State Department, so Thurston's first meeting was on Senator Cushman Davis, a Republican member of the Senate Foreign Relations Committee. Thurston followed this with a visit to Representative James H. Blount. A Georgia Democrat nearing retirement after eighteen years in the House, Blount was chairman of the powerful House of Representatives Foreign Relations Committee.

The meeting with Congressman Blount, a handsome, clean-shaven, white-haired man, took place in a committee room on Capitol Hill. Two years later, Blount would recall that this meeting was only brief.[74] Thurston would claim that it lasted 'about a half-hour.' Thurston would also write that Blount correctly and quickly surmised that he wanted to find out what the reaction would be in the House 'in case action becomes necessary in Honolulu.'[75]

Blount, who considered Thurston 'a pretty uppish sort of person,' remembered the conversation differently. According to him, Thurston came straight out with his object, bluntly declaring, "I am a member of the legislature, and I mean to endeavor to bring about the annexation of the islands."[76]

"I don't know very much about this subject," replied the courtly, cautious Blount, who had a background as an attorney. "But I can tell you this–if the question does come up, it will treated as a national one, and not as a Democratic one. I advise you to see Mr. Blaine, secretary of state, and see what he thinks."

"I intend to see Mr. Blaine, but he is ill," Thurston replied. "I haven't seen him, although I hope to meet him soon."

"All right," said Blount. "You do so, and let me know what he says."

"I will, sir," Thurston responded.[77]

With that, the interview ended. The following year, both men would play vital opposing roles in the future of Hawaii and that of Queen Liliuokalani.

Several days after the short meeting with Blount, Thurston finally met with Secretary Blaine at the State Department. Blaine, his long face accentuated by a pointed gray beard, was a gaunt figure. Suffering from a terminal illness, he would be dead within ten months. Presenting Blaine with a letter of introduction from Blaine's old friend Ambassador Stevens in Hawaii, Thurston explained that he and his colleagues back in Honolulu were prepared to act against the queen if she tried to introduce a new constitution, after which they would seek annexation–provided the US would entertain the proposal.

Blaine was more than ready to entertain the proposal. The previous August, based on assurances that he'd received from his friend Ambassador Stevens, the secretary of state had written to

US President Benjamin Harrison to say that Hawaii would soon be ready for 'taking' by the United States.[78] Just weeks prior to Thurston's visit to Washington, Blaine had received a dispatch from Stevens in Honolulu in which the ambassador had said, 'The great lack here now is an intelligent and efficient executive, which it is impossible to have with the existing monarchy. For twenty years the palace has been the center of corruption and scandal, and is likely to remain so as long as the Hawaiian native monarchy exists.'[79]

"Have you talked to anyone else in Washington on this subject?" Blaine asked Thurston.

"I have," Thurston replied. "To Senator Davis and Mr. James Blount."

Blaine, a Republican, was displeased to hear the name of Blount, a Democrat. "I consider this subject of the utmost importance, Mr. Thurston," he said gravely. "I am somewhat unwell, but I wish you would call on B.F. Tracy, secretary of the navy, and tell him what you have told me. And say to him that I think you should see the President."

"Yes, sir," Thurston beamed.

"Do not see Mr. Blount again," Blaine added sourly. "I will attend to him." The pair came to their feet and shook hands. "Come to me after you have seen President Harrison," Blaine instructed.[80]

Thurston went directly to the nearby Navy Department building, where the navy secretary saw him at once. Benjamin Franklin Tracy, winner of the Medal of Honor during the Civil War, was in the process of creating America's new 'blue water navy' of powerful battleships and fast cruisers. The prospect of a permanent base in Hawaii for the US Navy's Pacific Squadron fitted neatly into his plans. Sixty-two-years-old, bald, with a neatly trimmed gray beard that hugged his face like a glove, Secretary Tracy eyed the young man from Hawaii thoughtfully as they sat in high-backed leather easy chairs beside the secretary's cluttered desk.

"I don't know whether you had better see the President or not," said Tracy once Thurston had told him about the Annexation Club and its objectives. He drew himself to his feet. "But come with me, and we will learn what he thinks."[81]

To Thurston's astonishment, Secretary Tracy led him from the Navy Department building and then walked him the few hundred yards to the Executive Mansion, as the White House was known. After depositing Thurston in an anteroom, Tracy was able to walk right on into the president's office, off the Cabinet Room–the Oval Office did not exist at that time–and meet with President Benjamin Harrison without an appointment. After thirty minutes, Tracy emerged. As he kept walking, toward the exit, Tracy beckoned for the bewildered Thurston to join him, and together they proceeded out into the spring sunshine.

"I have explained fully to the President what you have said to me, and have this to say to you," Tracy began once they were outside. "The President does not think he should see you." Had the President of the United States personally interviewed a foreign national who had stated that he was planning to overthrow a friendly head of state, one whose country had a treaty with the US, such an act would have had so many international law implications that Benjamin Harrison could not afford to even contemplate it. "But he authorizes me to say to you that, if conditions in Hawaii compel you people to act as you have indicated, and you come to Washington with an annexation proposition, you will find an exceedingly sympathetic administration here."[82]

Thurston smiled wide, like a man who had just won a lottery, and said, "That is all I wanted to know."[83]

Before Thurston left Washington, he attempted to again see Secretary of State Blaine, to report the outcome of his meeting with Tracy, but Blaine's declining health prevented it. Within several months Blaine would resign from his post, and, just five months after that, Thurston would be reading the secretary's obituary. As Blaine suggested, Thurston avoided another meeting with James Blount. He set off on his way back to Hawaii in high spirits. On June 4, he stepped ashore from the SS *Mariposa* back in Honolulu.

Newspaper reports from the US began to circulate in Hawaii over the coming weeks that the matter of Hawaiian annexation had again raised its head in Washington and was the subject of discussion in the House Foreign Relations Committee. There was no mention in the press of Thurston's role in the revival of that discussion, but it seems that word reached Foreign Minister Sam Parker that Thurston had been up to no good while he was supposed to be in the US working for the Hawaiian Government.

Parker, it seems, had been advised of Thurston's subversive

activities by the Hawaiian ambassador to Washington, Dr. John Mott-Smith. Thurston had used Mott-Smith for his initial introductions to Senator Davis and Congressman Blount, apparently believing that Mott-Smith was warm to annexation. The ambassador had been present during both those initial meetings. Later, Thurston would warn his Annexation Club colleagues: 'Dr. Smith is not the man at Washington who should be there to properly forward our interests, more particularly in the line of annexation.'[84]

The upshot of the information received by Parker was that the Hawaiian Government now cancelled its exhibit at the Chicago Exposition and put Thurston out of a job. Instead, it was announced that the Royal Hawaiian Band would be sent to Chicago to represent the kingdom, at a cost of $12,000. The events of 1893 would see even that compromise measure canceled. As for Thurston, in August he set up the Hawaiian Information Bureau, Hawaii's first tourism promotion body, and pushed ahead with his Kilauea Volcano cyclorama for the Chicago Exposition as a private enterprise, in the hope of making a handsome profit. Both projects showed typical Thurston initiative. And both projects would prove to be financial failures.

With Queen Liliuokalani's government now alerted to the threat posed by Thurston, Marshal Wilson employed spies to learn what he could about Thurston's pro-annexation activities. The Annexation Club, meanwhile, secretly made its plans and preparations, as Thurston the bullfrog waited patiently to snare Liliuokalani the fly. All Thurston needed was for Liliuokalani to make a misstep that would trigger his plot to remove her, and subsequently enable him to deliver the Hawaiian Islands over to the United States of America.

10.

THE CRUISE OF THE BOSTON

THE ATLANTA CLASS 'PROTECTED' CRUISER *BOSTON*, fifth US Navy ship to bear that name, was one of the most modern vessels in the Navy. Less than five years old in January, 1893, she was only the second all-steel warship to fly the star spangled banner. Displacing 3,189 tons, and with a crew of 284, she had arrived in the Pacific in the summer of 1892 after sailing around Cape Horn, and dropped anchor off Honolulu on August 27. It had become the habit of the US Navy to station at least one warship at Honolulu on a semi-permanent basis. British warships also frequently anchored at Honolulu. The Hawaiian Government welcomed the presence of these foreign warships; local merchants profited from supplying them, and the ships' off-duty crews spent plenty of money ashore. So it was that Honolulu became temporary 'home' port for the *Boston* in 1892-93.

The wives of married *Boston* officers came out from the States and lived at the Arlington Hotel to be close to their husbands, and all the officers, married and single, joined the vibrant Honolulu social circle. Balls and dinners; parties at the residences of the white community and leading Hawaiians; official functions at the palace, the US consulate, and aboard the *Boston* itself; lunches at the swank Pacific Club, which occupied a downtown mansion; luaus at the Waikiki beach-houses of wealthy locals; horserace meetings at Kapiolani Park; there were always plenty of diversions for the American officers.

Lieutenant Lucien Young, gunnery officer with the *Boston* and a native of Lexington, Kentucky, particularly enjoyed shore life in Hawaii. He came to take a proprietary interest in the islands, making copious notes about Hawaii and her people during the fourteen months he was there. Young befriended a number of influential local figures. 'Within a few weeks after my arrival I was upon terms of more or less friendly intimacy with nearly all of the leading men of all parties,' he was to say. Among them was Sam Parker, until recently a minister of the government, 'of whom I was fond,' Young was to note, 'and from whom I had been the recipient of many acts of friendly hospitality.'[85]

On the morning of Wednesday, January 4, 1893, short, slight Lieutenant Young, whose face was dominated by a drooping walrus mustache of the kind then all the rage in the Navy, rode through the streets of Honolulu in an open carriage with Sam Parker, heading back to his ship. Parker, handsome, six feet tall, with a neat mustache and sparkling eyes, was a widely popular man with eight adoring children. Wealthy as a sugar planter and inheritor of the Parker Ranch, he was a much respected ali'i, with, in his own words, blood that was seven-eighths native Hawaiian. Parker had been deposed as premier the previous November when the legislature passed the latest 'no confidence' motion in a cabinet of Queen Liliuokalani. To appease her critics, the queen had appointed a new cabinet made up entirely of conservative Reform Party men including Peter Jones and Cecil Brown, both of them Hawaiian League founders.

Yet Parker was in good spirits this January morning as the carriage made its way through busy Honolulu streets alive with businessmen in white linen suits and flat boater hats. Parker waved to languid, laughing barefoot Hawaiians, as Chinese in coolie hats and mandarin jackets scurried from the carriage's path. Uniformed foreign sailors and not a few European tourists watched the carriage pass as it rolled by carrying the impressive-looking Hawaiian and the US Navy officer.

Several times, Parker had the driver stop the carriage to allow him to talk with passersby, who, Lieutenant Young realized, were Hawaiian members of the legislature. Young listened with interest to what passed between Parker and the legislators; 'I became convinced that a movement was under way to oust the cabinet,' he was to say, referring to the Reform Party cabinet headed by George Wilcox, (no relation to Robert Wilcox), which had come to power the previous November.[86]

At the docks, Young alighted, thanking Parker for the ride, then climbed into a waiting launch that took him out to the *Boston*. The cruiser, gleaming in her all-white peacetime paintwork, lay at anchor half a mile offshore with smoke curling from her two funnels, and with crewmen busying themselves on deck as the ship prepared to get under way. Often, there would be a collection of white warships from a variety of nations lying side by side out here, with just a hundred yards separating one from the next.

It was not long after Young boarded the *Boston* and reported for duty that the ship's commander, Captain Gilbert C. Wiltse, ordered the anchor raised and the engines full ahead, then pointed the ship seaward. The cruiser was heading off on a ten-day cruise to the Big Island, where it would undertake gunnery practice off Hilo. Coming along for the ride as official guests of the captain were US ambassador John L. Stevens, and his daughter Grace, who served as the ambassador's secretary in Honolulu. Over dinner in the wardroom that evening as the cruiser steamed north, Lieutenant Young remarked to Stevens that, from what he'd heard in the street, the Wilcox cabinet would be voted out.

Stevens, who would soon turn seventy-three and had become increasingly frail over recent months, disagreed. Shaking his craggy, white-bearded head, he declared, "The Wilcox cabinet has come to stay."

Lieutenant Young felt sure that his instincts had served him correctly. But the ambassador was a combative, self-opinionated man. 'He was talking confidently, and with manifest sincerity,' Young was to note.[87]

That very afternoon, as the American warship sailed away, the Hawaiian legislature sat in the Government Building, and as Young suspected, a motion of 'no confidence' in the Wilcox cabinet was put. The motion was defeated. The Wilcox cabinet remained in power. Stevens was right. But not for long. Eight days later, a fresh motion of 'no confidence' was moved against the Wilcox cabinet, and this time a majority of legislators voted for it, with accusations being later made that money had changed hands to ensure the cabinet was voted out. Premier Wilcox and his ministers had no choice but tender their resignations to Queen Liliuokalani.

The following morning, the queen appointed another cabinet from the small pool of available elected legislators. The new Premier and Minister for Foreign Affairs was Lieutenant Young's friend Sam Parker, a National Reform man, making a return to the job after a brief break. The queen's most loyal supporter in the legislature, Parker was also rumored to be, along with Charles Wilson, one of the queen's lovers. Of the remaining cabinet ministers, Reform Party men John F. Colburn and William H. 'Billy' Cornwell became Interior Minister and Finance Minister respectively. Liliuokalani's choice for Attorney General, Arthur Peterson, was a National Reform man.

Those aboard the *Boston* knew nothing of this change of cabinet until January 13, when they were anchored off Laihana. An inter-island steamer arrived and dropped anchor alongside the cruiser, before a small boat pulled away from the steamer and brought the vessel's purser across to the *Boston*. The purser was a friend of Lieutenant Young, to whom he gave the latest Honolulu newspapers, and related the news, with some excitement, that the Wilcox cabinet had been voted out and replaced by another. Young promptly went in search of his captain. Finding Wiltse and ambassador Stevens together, the lieutenant passed on the news.

'They both expressed much surprise and asked which of the white members of the legislature had joined the vote,' Young would later report.[88] Neither the purser nor the newspapers could answer that question. Captain Wiltse gave orders for the *Boston* to raise steam and prepare to get under way at midnight, for an immediate return to Honolulu.

At midnight, the cruiser hauled in its anchor and set a course for Honolulu. Steaming at speed through the early morning hours it made good time. As the sun came up on Saturday, January 14, the coast of Oahu came in sight. When the warship was off Diamond Head, a crewman's pet dog fell overboard. The *Boston* spent more than an hour looking for the dog before giving it up for lost. By 10.00 a.m., the cruiser was easing into her regular mooring position in Honolulu Harbor.

As soon as the ship was anchored, mail came aboard. Shortly after, Captain Wiltse sent for Lieutenant Young. Wiltse was fifty-five years old, portly, with thin gray hair and pendulous gray side-whiskers that were so ostentatiously long they could have endangered his life and limb had they become caught in machinery. He had graduated from the US Naval Academy just in time to take part in the famous 1862 battle with the Confederate ironclad *Merrimack*, in which his wooden Union Navy ship was sunk. After a varied naval career on the oceans of the world,

Wiltse had come to the *Boston* in 1889 after commanding a training ship.

Captain Wiltse now read Lieutenant Young a note from new Hawaiian Premier and Foreign Affairs Minister Sam Parker, inviting Wiltse and his officers to be present at the official prorogation, or adjournment, of the legislature that same day. Ordered by the captain to represent the *Boston* at the prorogation, Young hurriedly donned his US Navy dress uniform, complete with sword, then went ashore to the US consulate in downtown Honolulu. From the consulate, Young and US consul general H. W. Severance, deputy to ambassador Stevens, took a carriage to the Government Building. The carriage rolled up the circular drive, passing the prominent statue of Kamehameha the Great which still graces its center, and the palm tree where the trusty Kelelua had been shot dead thirty months earlier during the Redshirt Rebellion.

As Young and the consul general alighted at the foot of the building's front steps, a figure emerged from the crowd and took the lieutenant aside. Young later described this figure as 'a very prominent citizen.'[89] This was almost certainly Alfred Hartwell, a Harvard-educated native of Massachusetts who had served as an Hawaiian supreme court justice and also as attorney general under Kamehameha V. Hartwell was friendly with Lorrin Thurston, and is likely to have been a member of the secret Annexation Club. Lieutenant Young, allowing the consul general to go on ahead of him up the Government Building steps, tarried to listen to what Hartwell had to say.

"The queen, immediately after the adjournment of the legislature, is going to proclaim a new constitution from the palace," the man said. "A constitution that would abrogate the rights and privileges of all foreigners in favor of native rule and autocratic power."

Young looked at him in disbelief.

"The danger is imminent, Young," Hartwell said impatiently. "I wish you would return to your ship at once and inform Captain Wiltse."

Young laughed. "I place no credence in your report, sir," he said.

"I have it from the very best authority, one of the cabinet ministers," his informant countered. The cabinet minister to whom he referred was Interior Minister John Colburn. "I urge you to inform your commanding officer," Hartwell said anxiously.

Still Young would not believe him. He shook his head. "I cannot do that."[90] The lieutenant pushed on by, and once he had topped the steps and entered the Government Building's marble-floored entrance hall he rejoined the consul general. As the pair stood waiting with a crowd of dignitaries in the entrance hall, Young passed onto Severance what he'd just been told.

Consul General Severance, an elderly man who had spent many years in the Hawaiian Islands, smiled. "The gentleman who informed you of this is of a rather nervous disposition," he advised. "I place no credence in his statement. Nor do I believe the queen contemplates any such movement."[91]

Young agreed with him. But both Young and the consul general were wrong. Very wrong.

11.

THE TIME HAS ARRIVED

A LITTLE BEFORE 10.00 A.M. THAT MORNING OF January 14, just as the *Boston* was easing into her anchorage in the harbor after the dash from Hilo, Premier Sam Parker and the members of his cabinet arrived at the Iolani Palace, having been summoned by the queen. The ministers knew that Her Majesty would be officially ending the current session of the kingdom's legislature with a brief prorogation ceremony at midday, and two of them believed that this summons to the palace was a mere formality connected with that event. Premier Parker and Finance Minister Cornwell knew different; on appointing them to the cabinet several days earlier, the queen had confided that she intended introducing a new constitution after she had prorogued the legislature. And both men had assured her of their support when the time came.

Premier Parker arrived at the palace first, and was ushered into the Blue Room, where Queen Liliuokalani was waiting, seated on the largest of the regal blue satin chairs which gave the room its name. Her Majesty began by discussing arrangements for the prorogation ceremony, then added, almost as a throwaway, "It is my intention to promulgate a new constitution, here, in the throne room, following the ceremony."

Parker, standing, frowned. "Your Majesty, we have not seen the new constitution."[92]

"It will be time enough, when you come here," Liliuokalani responded impatiently. "I will show it to you and your colleagues. Be here soon after the prorogation of the legislature."[93]

The other ministers, Colburn, Peterson and Cornwell, then

arrived, and the queen said she wanted to discuss the matter of signing the new constitution with them all.

"Your Majesty, we have no time," Parker interjected. "We have to be at the legislature now." He was not at all happy with the queen's plan to push through a new constitution without the cabinet having scrutinized it in detail. Looking at his bemused colleagues, he said, "We have to go right over to the hall."[94]

With that excuse, Parker shepherded the cabinet from the Blue Room and from the palace. As the quartet walked toward the Government Building, the premier revealed that the queen expected them all to counter-sign a new constitution in a ceremony at the palace following the noon prorogation of the legislature. John Colburn's jaw dropped. Attorney General Peterson looked disconcerted. Cornwell shook his head.

"I haven't seen it," Parker told the others. "I told her we could not do anything until we have first read it."[95] They all knew, after all the petitions for a new constitution that had come to the palace the previous year, that any new constitution produced by Liliuokalani would be aimed at rolling back the changes introduced by the Bayonet Constitution, and that was sure to lead to resistance from the white community.

Looking worried, the four of them went their own separate ways, to follow their own separate agendas.

Toward 10.30 a.m., Lorrin Thurston was in his neglected law office on Merchant Street, sorting through legal papers. The office door opened. Thurston looked up, and was surprised to see new Interior Minister John Colburn walk in, 'looking much excited,' in Thurston's opinion.[96] Colburn, a timorous man with a neat mustache, was a 'missionary boy' and old friend of Thurston—they had gone to school together at the Punahou School. Colburn may also have been one of the four original members of the Annexation Club who would never be identified by Thurston.

"Lorrin, we've been having a hell of a time up at the palace, and I've come to tell you about it," Colburn blurted.

Thurston listened as Colburn explained what Parker told the cabinet. The lawyer then asked, "Have you talked to anyone else about this?"

"No," the flush-faced Colburn replied, "I've come directly to your office from the palace."[97]

This was not entirely accurate. Colburn had originally sought out his good friend Henry Waterhouse. Although Henry was only John T. Waterhouse's second son, John T. had found him a much better businessman than eldest son John Jr., and had handed the running of the Waterhouse business enterprises over to him several years before this, so that he himself could concentrate on grander schemes such as the Pacific telegraph cable. The well-connected Henry Waterhouse possessed great influence. He had gone to school with many leading white members of Honolulu society, and had married into the Dimonds, one of Hawaii's elite American missionary families, who had made a fortune in sugar. Meanwhile, Henry's sister Mary had married William Hyde Rice, a member of the Rice missionary clan; William was currently serving as Governor of Kauai, an appointment he had received from Queen Liliuokalani.

In the past, John Colburn had passed confidential information onto Henry Waterhouse, when Henry was a Reform Party politician in the Hawaiian parliament, keeping him abreast of what was happening within cabinet and at the palace. When Colburn had hurried this morning to Henry's office above the Waterhouse department store on Queen Street, he was told that Henry was absent. When Colburn couldn't locate Waterhouse, he had instead come around to Merchant Street in search of Thurston.

"We should see Judge Hartwell," Thurston suggested, and, grabbing his hat, led Colburn out the door.[98]

Together, Thurston and the cabinet minister hurried the short distance to 'Judge' Albert Hartwell's upstairs law office on the south-side corner of Fort and Merchant Streets. Once the former supreme court justice had been appraised of the situation, he suggested that another attorney, William O. Smith, also be consulted, and they all went to Smith's premises, which were a little way along Fort Street, on the ground floor.

Slender, mustachioed, forty-four-year-old Smith, known to his friends as 'W. O.,' was, like Thurston, the son of a missionary–Dr. James Smith. W. O. was also a Punahou School graduate and a leading member of the Annexation Club. In addition to his legal practice, he had extensive sugar plantation interests and had served several terms in the legislature as a Reform Party politician. Now, his three visitors filled him in on the situation regarding the queen's intended new constitution.

After considerable discussion, all three lawyers advised Colburn that he should refuse to approve the new constitution. The legal trio agreed to raise support for Colburn 'among the men downtown,' in a stand against the queen, with Hartwell in particular promising to 'get into immediate touch with some of the businessmen.'[99] They all knew that, for starters, Attorney General Arthur Peterson thought the same way as Colburn. So, with the four of them agreeing to meet up at the Attorney General's office at the Government Building following the prorogation of parliament, at the time when the queen expected the cabinet to co-sign her new constitution, the meeting broke up. While the others set off to round up support, Colburn hurried away to dress for the formal midday prorogation ceremony.

It would have been not long after this that 'Judge' Hartwell spied Lieutenant Young outside the Government Building and took him aside to urge him to warn Captain Wiltse of what the queen was planning.

A little before noon, together with the American consul general, other foreign diplomatic representatives and invited guests, Lieutenant Young was escorted into the Legislative Hall and shown to his seat in the public gallery, which was filling with Hawaiians and part-Hawaiians, both men and women.

The Speaker's desk sat on a platform at one end of the sixty feet by thirty feet room, with a semicircle of clerks' desks nestling before it. The legislators' benches spread across the room, and these began to fill with members of both houses of the legislature in their finery. To Lieutenant Young's surprise, all the members in attendance were colored; no Reform Party member of either the Nobles or Legislative Assembly put in an appearance. The white members had been warned by Thurston, Smith and Hartwell, and were obviously staying away quite deliberately, and it now dawned on Lieutenant Young that perhaps the warning that he had dismissed only minutes before had credence; perhaps the queen was up to something after all.[100]

A Hawaiian member of the House of Nobles sitting in front of Young turned to the lieutenant, and smiled in greeting. Above the general hubbub of many voices, the noble, who was 'on quite intimate terms' with Young, leaned closer to the lieutenant, and said, "We have them at last! Wait until we leave the hall and you will see something. Come over to the palace when you go out."

"What do you mean?" said Young.

"Never mind," the noble replied. "But come over to the palace."[101]

Young then asked if the Hawaiian was referring to the rumored new constitution, to which the gentleman merely smiled serenely. Their conversation was cut short by the commencement of proceedings. The queen's brother-in-law, Archie Cleghorn, Governor of Oahu, entered the hall, wearing a flash uniform covered with gold braid and royal decorations, and took up a position to one side of the Speaker's platform. He arrival was the signal for all the audience members to come to their feet.

The Chamberlain of the Household, James Robertson, then made his entrance from a side door, leading the royal procession. With a Scottish father and an ali'i mother, Robertson, a trim, bearded man in his thirties, had married one of Archie Cleghorn's daughters. Privately, the queen called Robertson 'Jimmie.' In his hands, the uniformed chamberlain carried the rolled speech that the queen was to deliver. In his wake came the queen's three honorary aides-de-camp, James Boyd, John Holt and Henry Bertelmann. All were mixed blood ali'i, all sported mustaches and bore the honorary rank of colonel, and all wore dress uniforms modeled on that of the US Army, and carried swords. Next came the bearers of the royal *kahilis*. These cylindrical clusters of feathers on long poles were the venerated traditional standards of ruling Hawaiian ali'i. As far as Lieutenant Young was concerned, they were 'the emblems of savage royalty.'[102] At the funeral of a high ranking ali'i, the ali'i bearers of the kahilis were expected to hold them aloft for twenty-four hours without a break.

Her Majesty Queen Liliuokalani then appeared. Wearing a lavender silk dress with a long train, and followed closely by four pages in royal blue livery and buckle shoes, the queen made her way slowly and regally to the platform and the Speaker's desk, where Chamberlain Robertson had laid out her speech. Lucien Young, born and raised in the American South, managed to conceal his contempt for colored people while he was in the Hawaiian islands, but it would come out later when he wrote a book about his time there. In that book, he would describe the fifty-four-year-old Hawaiian queen as having a 'dark complexion and negro-like features.' Liliuokalani's ladies in waiting, who followed the queen in the Legislative Hall procession, were, according to Young, 'dressed in the loud colors so much admired by all dark-colored races.'[103]

The queen's two adult nephews by marriage, Princes David Kawanakoa and Jonah Kuhio Kalanianaole, followed the ladies in waiting, both also resplendent in tailored uniforms and the decorations of royal orders. They preceded the cabinet ministers–Parker, Cornwell, Peterson, and Colburn–with the three current Supreme Court justices, Albert Judd, R. F. Bickerton, and Sanford Dole, bringing up the rear. In the bigoted opinion of Lieutenant Young, the three white judges were 'dignified' men 'whose manly bearing and intellectual appearance gave a relief to what had preceded.'[104]

From the platform, the queen read the prorogation speech, in both Hawaiian and English. Lieutenant Young considered all the royal pomp surrounding this 'semi-savage queen,' as he described her, to be 'a comedy compared with which *Pinafore* and *The Mikado* would be considered Shakespearean.' Young would also later claim that the queen displayed anger, mental strain, and nervousness as she read.[105] Judge Sanford Dole, on the other hand, was to describe the day's prorogation ceremony very differently: 'It was an impressive function,' he said. And, of the queen's part in it, he wrote, 'With great dignity, she read the address of prorogation.'[106]

The queen then withdrew to the adjoining office of the Minister of the Interior, followed by her entourage. The invited guests began filing into the room to be received by the queen, but the American consul general whispered to Young that he would not go in, and left Young to represent the United States. When Young entered the room, he found the cabinet ministers and court officials standing behind a chair in which Liliuokalani was seated. Governor Archie Leghorn was by the door, and the Scotsman briefly engaged the lieutenant in conversation before Young took his turn in approaching the queen. Saluting Her Majesty, the lieutenant congratulated her and told her she had made an excellent speech.

Liliuokalani clearly did not believe that he was genuine. According to Young, she eyed him coldly. Young was to later claim he was certain that the queen was under the influence of alcohol. It was a claim not supported by any other participant in, or chronicler of, the day's events. 'I paid no attention to her conduct toward me,' Young was to write of the queen.[107] He then moved along the receiving line to chat with his friend Sam Parker, who had regained the premiership since they had parted company at the Honolulu docks ten days before. Not long after this, the lieutenant left the Government Building. Young missed an announcement by Chamberlain Robertson, made once all guests had paid their respects to the queen, that a meeting of special significance was to be held that afternoon at 2.00 in the palace's Throne Room, and all present were invited to attend.

Outside, Lieutenant Young found a large crowd, made up mostly of excited Hawaiians, with a few small clusters of whites among them. Hawaiian troops of the Household Guard in their smart white uniforms and Germanic helmets, and with rifles on their left shoulders, formed two lines along the drive and over King Street to the open Kauikeaouli Gate. Young could also see great numbers of Hawaiians streaming into the palace grounds.

A local politician now appeared beside Young. It was the charismatic Robert Wilcox, one-time redshirt revolutionary, now leader of the Liberal Party and now, too, a vocal opponent of the queen. Wilcox passed on the now stale news that the queen intended proclaiming a new constitution that afternoon. When Young replied that he had heard that elsewhere, Wilcox declared theatrically, "I will have nothing to with it!"[108]

Wilcox went on to say that, in anticipation of resistance to the new constitution from white members of the community, Household Guard commander Major Sam Nowlein had installed four cannon on the top floor of the palace, one on each veranda, covering all approaches. Wilcox claimed that, the previous evening, the queen had sent for him and offered him command of those guns, but he had declined. Had Wilcox accepted, he would have been answerable to his cousin Sam Nowlein, and to Marshal Wilson, a man he despised for his influence with the monarch. Wilcox also assured Lieutenant Young that a pair of Gatling machineguns had been installed at the police headquarters, and additional police had been called in by Marshal Wilson.[109]

Aware of Wilcox's excitable nature, and of his reputation for being a man who was 'generally mixed up in every revolution that takes place,' Lieutenant Young didn't take him too seriously. But when the lieutenant crossed the road and walked up the drive toward the palace, he saw the snout of a cannon poking out from the upper veranda. Now beginning to think that Wilcox had been telling the truth, Young turned around and headed to the docks. From there, he took a launch out to his ship.[110]

Back aboard the *Boston*, Lieutenant Young reported directly to Captain Wiltse and detailed all he had seen and heard ashore. Wiltse was surprised, although he had received a message a little earlier which had said much the same thing–from 'Judge' Hartwell. The captain had taken no notice of Hartwell's message, but now Young's news unsettled him.

"You had best find out all you can, Young," said Captain Wiltse, before ordering the lieutenant to change into civilian clothes and return ashore to learn as much as he could, as discreetly as he could, about what was really going on in Honolulu.[111]

As Young hurried away to carry out his mission, Captain Wiltse issued orders for all shore liberty for the *Boston*'s enlisted men to be canceled forthwith, and for any officers going ashore to be ready to return to the ship immediately should they hear a signal gun fired from the cruiser.

As Queen Liliuokalani emerged from the front door of the Government Building, the Punchbowl battery of old muzzle-loading cannon to the east of the little city began booming out a royal twenty-one-gun salute. Manned today by Household Guard reservists, during the time of Kamehameha the Great this battery had been commanded by Liliuokalani's great-grandfather, Aikanaka.

From the Government Building, the queen returned the short distance to the palace in a carriage, after which she climbed the steps and passed in through the front doors. Turning left, she made for the Blue Room. Mustachioed Marshal Charles Wilson stood by the door, tall, handsome, wearing his double-breasted royal blue uniform, gold belt, and sword, and with his blue slouch hat set at a rakish angle. Liliuokalani stopped when she drew abreast of him, and asked, "Is all ready, Marshal?"

"Yes, my queen," Wilson responded firmly.[112]

At the beginning of January, Liliuokalani had informed Wilson and Major Nowlein of the Guard of her intention to promulgate a new constitution, and had instructed them 'to prepare themselves

to quell any riot or outbreak from the opposition.'[113] Her plan
had been to do this once the cabinet had been changed following
a successful vote of 'no confidence' on the afternoon of January 4.
It is almost certain that she chose that date knowing that the USS
Boston would be sailing for its gunnery cruise on the morning of
January 4, taking US ambassador Stevens with it.

Since late 1892, the queen had been receiving written
information from an unidentified informant inside, or linked to,
the Annexation Club; information which had forewarned her that
Stevens was in league with the annexationists. Having decided
that the time had come to introduce a constitution that reformed
Lorrin Thurston's Bayonet Constitution, Liliuokalani was astute
enough to make her move when Stevens and the US Navy were
out of town, so that they could not support the annexationists
against her. After the January 4 'no confidence' vote had failed,
Liliuokalani knew that she had a ten day window before the
return of the *Boston* in which to try again, and by January 12 she
had convinced a majority of legislators of the need to throw out
George Wilcox's cabinet to allow her to install another; the 'no
confidence' motion of that day had succeeded accordingly.

The queen would write that, when she had told Wilson and
Nowlein to prepare for the worst, 'they had assured me that they
would be ready; and I gave strict injunctions of secrecy.' When
the queen had entered the Legislative Hall at noon on January
14, she had noticed that the Reform Party legislators were not
present. To her, 'this looked ominous of some coming trouble.'[114]
Someone had let the cat out of the bag. Only much later would
Liliuokalani learn that it was Interior Minister John Colburn
who had rushed to inform Lorrin Thurston and the Reform Party
leadership of her intent to promulgate her constitution that day–
after she had informed Premier Parker of her plans at 10.00 a.m.

Now the queen looked at Marshal Wilson, and said, "You will
have to be brave today," then moved on into the Blue Room.[115]
She was also talking about herself. Liliuokalani, the kingdom's
first female monarch, would also have to be brave if she was to
successfully negotiate the day and overcome the many men who
were opposed to her and what she wanted to do. Her personal
motto was *kulia kanuu* –'Strive for the summit'–and she was
determined to do just that. Taking her seat in the Blue Room, the
queen allowed her attendants to adjust the train of her dress then
back from the room.

Now, with the chamberlain at the front door and the marshal stationed at the Blue Room door, and with invited guests filing into the Throne Room across the hall, Liliuokalani began a wait. The cabinet ministers had been instructed to report to her here immediately following the prorogation of the legislature. But as the minutes ticked away and the queen sat waiting, alone, there was no sign of any of them.

Thirty minutes later, the four ministers finally trooped into the room, looking sheepish.

"Everything in the Throne Room is ready," the far from pleased queen told them, coming to her feet. "The guests are awaiting our presence. We must not keep them waiting."[116]

Those guests included members of the diplomatic corps, Governor Cleghorn, Princes Kuhio and Kawanakoa, Hawaiian members of the now prorogued legislature, and Justices Judd and Bickerton. The third supreme court judge, Sanford Dole, had chosen not to be present. 'I did not attend the afternoon meeting, feeling that events were likely to occur which I could not countenance,' Dole was to write. 'So I spent the afternoon in giving a boat trip off the harbor to a party of schoolboys, to whom I had promised the treat.'[117]

Also waiting in the large white Throne Room, which occupied the entire eastern side of the palace's first floor, were thirty members of the committee of the Hui Kalaiaina patriotic association. All were dressed in evening clothes and top hats, and many were quite elderly. Following a blueprint for the ceremony drawn up by the queen herself, the Hui Kalaiaina committeemen had formed two neat lines to the low dais which supported the room's two thrones. On a blue silk cushion, the president of the association bore a document, the new constitution which the queen intended promulgating.

Premier Sam Parker now said to the queen, "Your Majesty, we have not read the constitution. But before we read it, you must know it is a revolutionary act. It cannot be done."

"Read it," the queen implored. "See what it is."

"Your Majesty, your ministers do not think it advisable for you to take such a step," said another of her ministers, either Colburn or Peterson. "They think there is a danger of an uprising..."[118]

"An uprising!" the queen boomed, quite astonished. From all she had seen, her people were right behind a new constitution. She cast her steely gaze around the faces of Parker's quaking cabinet. "I would not have taken such a step if you gentlemen had not encouraged me."[119]

She was to later insist that both Parker and Cornwell had known, before she appointed them to their ministries, that she intended bringing in a new constitution, and they had given her assurances of their support. A third cabinet member, Peterson, had known of her intention since the previous October, she said. And, while she had said nothing about a new constitution to Colburn, whom, she knew, was close to Lorrin Thurston, she had assumed that Peterson would have told him about it.

"You have led me to the edge of a precipice, and are now leaving me to take the step alone," the queen went on. At this moment, she later wrote, she felt humiliated. But she would not back down, and was fully prepared to take that solo step. "Why not give the people the constitution," she now suggested, "and I will bear the brunt of all the blame afterwards."

To this, Attorney General Peterson protested, "We have not read the constitution, Your Majesty."

"Mr. Peterson, you had it in your possession a whole month!" Liliuokalani raged.

The previous October, once she had finalized a draft with which she was happy, the queen had given it to the attorney general to look over, asking him to correct it and to strike out any defects he might find, and to add any clauses that 'would be good for the people and for the country.' A month later, in November, 1892, Peterson had returned the document to her. 'To my knowledge he consulted many lawyers and others in regard to many points of interest in the document,' she later wrote. 'When it was returned I looked it over and found no changes had been made, so I concluded that it was all right.' Later, in early January, the queen had also asked Peterson to prepare a preamble for the new constitution, but to date he had not provided her with one.[120]

The queen now looked 'pretty excited,' Premier Parker would recall. He said to her, "We advise you to give it up–not to think about it anymore."[121]

According to one account, Liliuokalani thumped her fist down on a table in her frustration.[122]

"If you insist upon it," said either Colburn or Peterson, "we will resign," and one or more of the others agreed.[123]

But Parker had no intention of letting the cabinet resign–that would leave his queen even more exposed. "Now, gentlemen," he said, "if you will walk into the next room, I will have a few words with Her Majesty."[124]

Peterson took this opportunity to say that he and his colleagues would like to withdraw to his office for fifteen minutes to consult over the matter. At first, Liliuokalani refused them permission, but after Parker supported them she begrudgingly agreed to give them the requested fifteen minutes.[125] Leaving Premier Parker to speak privately with the queen, the three ministers backed from the room, and out of the discussion.

Once he and Liliuokalani were alone, Parker asked the queen why she was so determined to stir up trouble by unilaterally introducing a new constitution. Liliuokalani looked with sad eyes to her loyal premier, and replied, "It is the people's wish, Sam. So many thousand signatures have been sent in. I have thought the matter over carefully, and think that I ought to give them a new constitution."[126]

Parker shook his head. "I will not, and my colleagues will not, agree to it."[127] He understood Liliuokalani's motives well enough, and sympathized with them. In his view, Kalakaua should never have signed the Bayonet Convention. But this was not the way to correct that error. The nation had progressed beyond the days when the monarch's will was law. By all means, change the existing unfair constitution, give the people back their voting rights. But not like this. Even weak King Kalakaua had seen the wisdom of setting up a constitutional convention to write a new constitution.

Liliuokalani glared at her stubborn chief minister. "Why don't you resign?" she said.

"I will not resign unless it is according to law," he retorted. In other words, he would only go if the legislature voted him out in a vote of 'no confidence,' as the existing Constitution provided.[128]

With the atmosphere between them now extremely strained, Parker sought and received the queen's permission to withdraw.

Lorrin Thurston and fellow lawyer and Annexation Club member William Smith lunched together that day. They then made their way to the attorney general's office in the Government Building. They were waiting there when Peterson, Colburn and Cornwell arrived from the palace after their brief confrontation with the queen. Several other unidentified men were present–all

Annexation Club members. The three ministers confirmed to the small gathering that the queen was insistent that the cabinet co-sign a new constitution.

"We only have the vaguest idea of what it contains," added one of them, almost certainly Peterson.[129]

"There is no use us trying to argue her out of her position," said Colburn, who was looking increasingly stressed by the affair.[130]

All three ministers denied having any prior knowledge of the contents of this new constitution, and said that the first they had known of the queen's intent to promulgate it was when she informed them at 10.00 o'clock that morning. If the queen was to be believed, Peterson, for one, was lying.

"I advise that the cabinet counters upon the queen," said attorney W. O. Smith, who had the look of a harassed bank teller. "Declare her in revolution against the government and the constitution, declare the throne vacant by reason of her treasonable attitude, and call upon the people to sustain you."[131]

Thurston supported Smith's idea. But the three cabinet members were horrified by the suggestion. 'They were in a blue funk as to their course,' Thurston was to record. At this point, the door opened, and Premier Sam Parker walked in, having followed the ministers across the road from the palace. His cabinet colleagues gushed out their concerns to him, and relayed what Smith and Thurston had suggested. According to Thurston, Parker didn't say much, but was 'practically of the same mind as the other ministers.'[132] Just the same, Parker would not support the idea of dethroning the queen, to whom he was both close and loyal.

Thurston pushed the ministers to make a declaration along the lines that Smith had suggested, but 'they did not agree to make the declaration,' he was to write. Nonetheless, he kept hammering away at them until 'they assented to my suggestion of drafting it.'[133] Thurston promptly sat down at the attorney general's desk, took pen and paper, and began writing. Moments later, a messenger arrived from the Iolani Palace and passed on a demand from the impatient queen that the members of the cabinet proceed at once back to the palace so her ceremony could begin.

"I'm not going!" a quaking John Colburn declared. "I don't consider my life safe at the palace. I was at a meeting last night, and something of the character of this proposed new constitution was discussed, and I heard Kaluna (a Hawaiian member of the legislature from Maui) say that he would die happy if he could secure the adoption of the new constitution, and had the blood of a few white men on his hands." He vehemently shook his head. "I'm not going back!"[134]

Peterson and Cornwell, although not quite as panicky as Colburn, also said that they would not go to the palace for the constitution's promulgation. It seems that they were as much afraid of the imperious queen herself as of any attempt to harm them by her supporters.

But Premier Parker said, "I'm not afraid. I'll go to the palace and see what the queen wants us to do." Then he added, as if to say they had nothing to fear while he was around, "You might as well go over with me."[135] He then departed and walked quickly back across the street and up the drive to the palace.

As soon as Parker had gone, Thurston, seeing what he perceived as a golden opportunity to overthrow the monarchy slipping through his fingers, said from behind the desk, "I suggest that the cabinet officially request John L. Stevens, United States minister, to land forces from the USS *Boston* in order to prevent violence on the part of Liliuokalani."[136]

The landing of US troops from the cruiser when the time had come for the annexationists to move against the queen was something which Thurston and the Annexation Club had secretly agreed with ambassador Stevens the previous year, following Thurston's visit to Washington. Both Peterson and Colburn now said that they certainly did fear violence on the part of the queen. The sight of cannon on the palace balconies was enough to frighten anyone. Thurston was now able to wring approval from Peterson, Colburn, and Cornwell to draft a suitable request to ambassador Stevens to land US troops, a step that would change Hawaii's destiny.

Laying aside the first document that he had been working on, Thurston quickly scribbled a suitable letter, in several brief, to the point paragraphs. After reading it aloud to the ministers, he gave the letter to Peterson, who handed it out to a typist in the adjoining office. A few minutes later, the typed document was handed back in. Thurston was to later claim that he successfully pressed all three ministers to sign it, but Lieutenant Young of the *Boston* wrote that only Peterson and Colburn signed, and this aligns with other indications that it was only those two who were most definitely opposed to the queen at this point. Gleefully grabbing up the signed request, Thurston headed for the door. But as he opened the door, Peterson called him back.

"I think you had better give me that request," said the attorney general, after having had second thoughts, holding out his hand. "I'll deliver it to Minister Stevens myself."[137]

Thurston didn't believe him. Worried that Peterson had lost his courage, Thurston argued for personally making the delivery. But Peterson, a lawyer by training, was clearly having serious doubts about the legality of the document. For, in the hands of Marshal Wilson, it could be said to be a treasonous document, and the signatories could find themselves charged, thrown in jail, and looking at the hangman's rope. Peterson insisted that Thurston surrender the letter, which, reluctantly, he did. 'I have never seen it since,' Thurston was to write of the letter, 'and Peterson did not deliver it to Minister Stevens.'[138]

Peterson's cabinet colleague Billy Cornwell now decided to return to the palace to join Parker, leaving Peterson and Colburn fretting about what they should do next. Before long, Peterson and Colburn decided that they had better go back to the palace, too, to join the others and do their best to talk the queen out of pressing forward with her new constitution. With some trepidation, the duo tramped back across the street to continue this game of political see-saw.

Thurston had been so close to setting his revolution in motion, but the timid attorney general had stymied him at the last moment. Now, Thurston and Smith were forced to retreat to Smith's law offices on Fort Street to rethink their strategy. Once they reached the offices, they found that other members of the Annexation Club had gathered there, and had been joined by leading members of the white community. These gentlemen had heard any number of startling rumors, so now listened intently as Thurston and Smith told of the queen's determination to introduce her new constitution and of how the cabinet ministers had shrunk from the brink of revolution against her at the last moment.

"That's a very good thing," said shipping company owner William C. Wilder, a fifty-eight-year-old with a gray goatee beard, when he heard about the queen's plan to promulgate a new constitution. "A splendid opportunity to get rid of the whole old rotten government concern and now get to annexation to the United States."[139]

This remark brought laughter and a chorus of agreement.

But at least one of their number looked a little alarmed. Paul Neumann, a German-born attorney and former cabinet minister, was not in favor of the queen changing the constitution. But, he told the others, as for overthrowing the queen and seeking annexation, "That might be going a little far."[140]

Sitting next to Neumann was Henry Waterhouse. Fine-boned, and with a walrus mustache, Waterhouse was wearing a prim, high starched collar that made him look like a clergyman. 'The Tasmanian' was an Annexation Club member, and having been an early member of the Hawaiian League and prominent in pushing through the Bayonet Constitution, Waterhouse was not ready to see Queen Liliuokalani water it down with a new version. 'We were all very much excited, feeling that our rights were being taken away from us,' Waterhouse was later to recall of this meeting, 'and we decided then and there that we would not submit to it.'[141]

Waterhouse, like his father, a devout Wesleyan, was the kind of man who tended to act first and think about the repercussions later. Henry's boundless energy, enthusiasm and habit of taking on big challenges and driving through to a conclusion while overcoming all obstacles had convinced his father that he was the man to run the business empire he had founded. In the same way, Henry's ability to translate visions into concrete reality made him a leader in the church and in the development of Hawaii's YMCA. With an infectious laugh, he was not known for a temper, or for violence, although he was a crack shot with a rifle.

Only once had Henry's rosy demeanor been known to fracture in public, when, in a Honolulu street one day in 1884, he had come across his father John T. and premier Walter Murray Gibson arguing. In the heat of the exchange, John T. had raised his walking stick, and Gibson had told him that he would only continue with their conversation when the elder Waterhouse lowered the stick. Young Henry had rashly pushed the frail Gibson away, sending the unwell man crashing to his knees, an act for which Gibson's *Advertiser* would castigate both Waterhouses.

Most of all, Henry Waterhouse was a man who would not back down, and he now urged Lorrin Thurston and the others not to give in to the Queen's maneuver. Thurston duly sat down and drafted the document that he had originally wanted to press on the cabinet ministers. Once he had dashed it off, he read it aloud to the others. In essence, the document declared that, as Liliuokalani had announced her intention of subverting the constitution and arbitrarily promulgating a new one, the undersigned declared her to be in attempted revolution against the constitution and government, and pledged their support to the cabinet in resisting her.

At this point, Thurston quite deliberately made no mention, in writing or verbally, of overthrowing the monarchy and seeking annexation by the United States. He knew that, apart from the seventeen members of the Annexation Club, few others in the room wanted to go that far. That step could come later. As a result, Thurston was able to gain signatures on this document from most of the men present. But not all.

Paul Neumann, along with several others, undertook to supervise the document, which lay on Smith's desk for the rest of the day while various men came to the office to add their signatures. Thurston was to claim that by day's end it had been signed by 'nearly a hundred leading businessmen.' Considering the comparatively small number of American, British, and German businessmen then in Honolulu, this is likely to have been another of Thurston's exaggerations. The actual number who signed can never be known, for the document disappeared that same day, and was never seen again. Thurston came to suspect Neumann of destroying it before the queen's opponents could use it.[142] For, Neumann would soon show his colors as a supporter of the queen.

At every turn, Thurston and his little band of subversives were being thwarted. Lucien Young had been quick to ridicule the pomp and circumstance with which the Queen of Hawaii surrounded herself, but it was Lorrin Thurston's revolution that was turning into a comic opera.

As Captain Wiltse had instructed, Lieutenant Young had changed into civilian clothes then had taken a ship's boat from the anchored cruiser back to the Honolulu docks. When he stepped ashore, beaming native boatmen congregated at the landing were quick to tell him that the queen was going to make a new constitution and that there was much excitement at the palace and uptown.

Young had only just started to make his way toward the center of town when he met an American hurrying the other way. This was former California attorney and Annexation Club member Henry Cooper, who was on his way to the *Boston* to inform Captain Wiltse that Queen Liliuokalani had commanded her ministers to countersign the constitution, and that they had refused. "In consequence of which, she threatened their lives!" Cooper dramatically declared to Young.[143]

Whether Cooper had genuinely been told of this so-called threat, or had invented it, is unclear. Either way, it was untrue; no such threat against the lives of the cabinet members had been made by the queen. Cooper also informed the lieutenant that the members of the cabinet had appealed to the leading men of the community to 'protect and sustain them.' Cooper went on to say that a large number of prominent men were holding a meeting at William Smith's offices on Fort Street.[144]

Lieutenant Young left Cooper to continue on his way to report to the commander of the *Boston*. Cooper would deliver a verbal request to Captain Wiltse for US troops to be landed to protect the Hawaiian cabinet from violence by their own head of state. With a quickened step, the lieutenant and made his way up Fort Street, which, like most of the streets of downtown Honolulu, was just wide enough to permit two wagons to pass each other, while the narrow sidewalks could accommodate just two pedestrians side by side.

Young soon reached the Smith law office. Inside, he found the two rooms of the street-level premises crowded with what he described as 'the best men of the city.' All seemed to be talking at once. 'Some excitement was exhibited on the part of a few, and much uneasiness by all,' Young was to write. At this stage, the only sentiment the lieutenant heard expressed was one of 'condemnation of the queen's act as unconstitutional, and threatening the business interests of the kingdom'–in taking power back from Hawaii's few hundred white businessmen and vesting it once more in the hands of the native majority.[145]

Seeing nothing being accomplished at Smith's office, Lieutenant Young withdrew and quickly walked several blocks along King Street to the palace grounds, which were thronging with thousands of people, mostly Hawaiians and part-Hawaiians. A festival atmosphere was prevailing; the people were 'unconcerned and quiet,' Young was to observe, as they waited patiently for their queen to appear on a palace balcony to make an expected announcement concerning a new constitution for the kingdom. Meanwhile, the white-uniformed troops of the Household Guard

were drawn up in a neat line from the palace to the Kauikeaouli
Gate, standing rigidly in the sun with their rifles on their shoulders.
Young had heard a rumor that those rifles were loaded, but there
was no way to confirm that.[146]

To gauge the mood elsewhere in the city, Lieutenant Young set
off, on foot still, to do a circuit of downtown Honolulu.

At the palace, the four cabinet ministers had returned to the Blue
Room.

"I sent for you, gentlemen," the queen said, looking and
sounding like a scolding schoolmarm. "I was requested by my
people to promulgate a new constitution. I want you gentlemen
to sign it or to consent to it."[147] She then gave them a copy of the
constitution which she meant to introduce by decree next door in
the Throne Room.

By the time that each member of the cabinet had read through
the lengthy document, it was well into the middle of the afternoon.
The ministers then all looked at Parker, who again informed the
queen that they could not sign it.

"What do you see that is injurious in the document,"
Liliuokalani asked with frustration.

"There are some points which I believe are not exactly suited,
Your Majesty," said Attorney General Peterson.

"The legislature could make the amendments," said the
queen.[148]

Peterson looked pained. "Your Majesty," he returned, "I beg
you to wait for two weeks. In the meantime, we will be ready to
present the document to you."[149]

Liliuokalani looked at each of the men seated opposite her.
All of them, including her faithful Sam Parker, nodded their
agreement with Peterson. "Two weeks?" she repeated. Under
article 78 of the Bayonet Constitution, the monarch was bound
to act with the consent and support of her cabinet. Liliuokalani
had been banking on that consent and support to give legitimacy
to her revised constitution. Without it, she considered herself
up the proverbial creek without a paddle. "Very well," the
queen conceded with a heavy heart, yielding to their concerted
opposition.

Coming to her feet, the queen led the way into the Throne
Room, where the guests who had been kept waiting for hours

came to their feet. From the dais, Liliuokalani explained to the gathering that she had asked them all to the Throne Room to witness her promulgate a new constitution at the request of her people. "The Constitution of 1887 is imperfect and full of defects," she added. Turning to the Chief Justice, she said, "Is that not so, Mr. Judd?"[150]

Caught unprepared, Chief Justice Albert Judd replied, "Er, yes, Your Majesty."

"Under the advice of my ministers," Liliuokalani went on, "I yielded. For they have promised that on some future day I can give you a new constitution. Now, return to your homes and keep the peace."[151]

Lieutenant Young was just returning to the palace after walking around the city center. Apart from the gathering at William Smith's office and loud talk from some whites in bars denouncing the queen–'the intelligent people' of Honolulu, was how Young described these men–the lieutenant had found the city going about its business as normal.[152] He had just reached the open palace gates on King Street when a carriage came down the drive carrying Chief Justice Judd. Recognizing Young, the chief justice ordered his driver to pull up alongside him.

When Young asked what had transpired at the palace, Judd sourly replied, "After hours of argument and persuasion, the queen has been induced to defer her coup d'état. But she has announced her determination to promulgate the new constitution in a few days." After Young wondered precisely how long Liliuokalani would hold off, Judd said, "I think she will attempt it again on Monday. Such is her stubbornness and determination, Young, we will have the whole affair to go through with again!"[153]

Ordering his driver to proceed, the unhappy chief justice drove off, leaving the lieutenant to join the crowd waiting outside the palace. He was just in time to see Queen Liliuokalani emerge onto the palace's first floor veranda, outside the Throne Room. From there, she delivered a short speech, which, Young was later told, was much along the same lines as the one she had delivered in the Throne Room. Young was surprised to see no cheering or evidence of enthusiasm or anger on the part of the crowd. But he was looking at the Hawaiians through Western eyes. The queen had told the crowd to go home and keep the peace, and that was what the people would do; their ruler had spoken. Besides, according to Hawaiian custom, to cheer a ruling ali'i was simply not done.

As Liliuokalani was leaving the balcony, two natives began to harangue the crowd. Young said that this pair climbed right up onto the palace balcony with the queen to address the crowd in her support, 'and appealed to them to rise and kill those opposing her.'[154] But this would have been physically impossible–the moat separating the palace from the grounds meant that the only way to reach the balcony was via the front steps, atop which stood Household Guards.

Judge Sanford Dole gave a more accurate and less theatrical account of this episode. 'Two of them made inflammatory speeches *from the steps of the palace*.' And, Dole was to say, these speakers didn't call on anyone to rise up and kill the queen's opponents; they limited their call to 'threatening the ministers with punishment' if they defied their head of state.[155] According to Young's account, these two speakers were swiftly removed by other, more moderately minded, Hawaiians, who hustled the pair away.[156] The crowd now began to disperse. But, said Sanford Dole, some leading native Hawaiians were 'sorely cast down at the failure of the movement' to introduce a new constitution.[157]

Meanwhile, Marshal Wilson had reportedly spoken with the queen prior to the return of all the members of the cabinet and attempted to convince her to diffuse the confrontation with her new cabinet by not proceeding with her attempt to promulgate the new constitution. According to Lucien Young, the queen obdurately refused to change her plans, after which Wilson gave up his attempt to dissuade her. Assuring Liliuokalani of his loyal support if she persisted, the marshal left the palace and returned to his office at Honolulu police headquarters.

From there, Wilson alerted his network of informants around the city to keep their eyes and ears open for any suspicious acts by Lorrin Thurston and his friends. Wilson could sense trouble brewing; not at the palace, but downtown, in the law office of William Smith. And he was determined to stamp it out. 'The marshal deserves great credit for his course during this exciting period,' Lucien Young was to write. In the lieutenant's estimation, Wilson 'was loyal to his mistress and displayed more judgment and genuine pluck than all of her other followers put together.'[158]

* * *

As Sanford Dole came ashore after taking his party of schoolboys on the promised sailboat outing, he found Hawaiians at the docks all talking about what had been taking place at the palace, and he hurried up Fort Street to William Smith's office, where he knew that the members of the Annexation Club would be gathered. Dole was quite unsurprised by what he found going on. Businessmen and several senior white civil servants milled about the two crowded rooms and spilled out onto the sidewalk. The atmosphere here was 'earnest and intense,' Dole was to write. Many of those present were impatient with the queen's rule, and a few made it clear that they wanted 'to have done with it.'[159]

As Dole arrived, Charles Cooke, forty-three-year-old head of Lewers and Cooke, a firm with interests in shipping, sugar, and lumber, was being urged to sign the declaration drawn up earlier by Thurston condemning the queen and supporting the cabinet. In Lorrin Thurston's opinion, Cooke was 'one of the most conservative and careful of men,' but nonetheless had no time for Hawaii's monarchy, and for a female monarch in particular. "Does it mean no more queen?" Cooke inquired. When assured that would be the case, Cooke gladly added his signature to the list.[160]

The cabinet members, after convincing the queen to wait to allow them to consider her new constitution, had left the palace, and between 3.00 and 4.00 p.m., ministers Colburn and Peterson arrived at William Smith's office, where they informed Smith, Thurston and the other businessmen gathered there of the delay they had forced on the queen. This did not suit Thurston and his Annexation Club colleagues at all. They had hoped to push the Hawaiian monarchy over a precipice, and here the cabinet had brought the movement against her to a shuddering halt at the brink.

Once the two ministers had left, Thurston turned to Henry Cooper, and said, "I think the time has come for the Annexation Club to act."[161]

Cooper agreed, and Thurston set the ball rolling. Thurston was to say, 'I stated to the gathering that a "committee of safety" should be appointed to devise ways and means to deal with the situation.'[162] Just like the Directorate, the leadership body created for the now defunct Hawaiian League, the concept and title of 'committee of safety' had been originated in France more than a century earlier. It would seem that Thurston was the student of the French Revolution behind both Hawaiian revolutionary innovations.

The 'situation' that Thurston was referring to was the failure of the cabinet to force Queen Liliuokalani into a confrontation, or, preferably, as far as the annexationists were concerned, to generate arrests and a violent crackdown by Marshal Wilson. That situation would have allowed the annexationists to call on the US ambassador to land American forces from the *Boston* to supposedly protect American interests in Hawaii. With those troops on shore, the annexationists would be able to embolden their own supporters and intimidate Liliuokalani's loyalists.

Numerous voices heartily concurred with Thurston's suggestion, and, on his recommendation, Henry Cooper, who had by this time returned from the *Boston*, was elected the meeting's chairman. Cooper then nominated fourteen of those present, including Thurston and himself, to make up the Citizens' Committee of Safety. Thirteen of the fourteen were members of the Annexation Club. Those who had not been elected to the Committee of Safety now left the room. Once committee members were alone, Thurston moved a resolution: "That it is the sense of this committee that in view of the present unsatisfactory state of affairs, the proper course to pursue is to abolish the monarchy and apply for annexation to the United States."[163]

Thirteen committeemen voted for the resolution. One, the only man present who was not a member of the Annexation Club, voted against it. That odd man out was Albert Wilcox, the premier removed from office just two days before. He excused himself by saying that he not had time to consider the proposal. Next day, Wilcox would resign from the Committee of Safety. Wilcox may have been unhappy with the queen after losing his premiership, but he wanted nothing to do with the overthrow of the monarchy.

Of the thirteen members of the Committee of Safety who remained, four were US citizens, one had been born in the US but had become a Hawaiian citizen, four had been born in Hawaii to American parents, two were Germans—with one of this pair retaining German citizenship and the other having become a naturalized Hawaiian citizen—one committee member was a Scotsman, and one, Henry Waterhouse, was Australian-born.

With the sun setting beyond the harbor and the downtown area's street lighting coming to electric life, the committee adjourned. They agreed to reconvene next morning at 10.00 at the home of William Castle. As the two rooms were clearing, Thurston took aside several men, some of them members of the committee and some not, and invited them to come around to his home that evening after dinner for a 'sub-meeting.'

That night, at Thurston's house on Judd Street, this sub group met to discuss the way ahead. Not all those invited by Thurston turned up, but the six who did had several things in common. All were American by birth or parentage, and all were connected with the law. Four were, like Thurston, attorneys–William Smith, William Castle, Charles Carter, and 'Judge' Alfred Hartwell. The fifth was a sitting supreme court justice, Sanford Dole, and the sixth was the Clerk of the Supreme Court, forty-year-old Fred Wundenberg.

At this meeting, Thurston explained that he was not pleased with the 'tentative action' of the Committee of Safety. He explained that ' I had called this sub-meeting to consider means of bringing about the contemplated action, and particularly to ascertain the military force at our disposal.'[164] Sanford Dole would recall that Thurston's 'contemplated action' that night involved using force to overthrow the monarchy. Differences of opinion soon emerged, with 'Judge' Hartwell and several others expressing doubts 'as to whether we were strong enough to carry out such a program.' This was despite the fact, Dole would say, that 'we knew that the United States minister was in sympathy with us.'[165]

Thurston assured the others that they did indeed have sufficient men and arms to carry out the queen's overthrow. He was one of the few people in the kingdom who knew that an illegal shipment of rifles and ammunition was at that moment sitting in the storeroom at Hall and Sons' hardware store, waiting to be collected by the Annexation Club. To reassure the faint-hearted, Thurston recommended that Fred Wundenberg report on the number of rifles and amount of ammunition available. This idea was endorsed, and, said Dole, 'the feeling in favor of using force against the queen finally prevailed.'[166]

Although both Hartwell and Dole were in favor of dethroning Liliuokalani, they had yet to be convinced that the monarchy itself should be abolished. As the meeting broke up, both were thinking about replacing Liliuokalani with her named successor, young Princess Kaiulani, and no conclusion was reached by the meeting about how far this action against the queen should go. A legal case might be put together to show that the queen was acting unconstitutionally and was therefore liable to removal, but the overthrow of the monarchy would itself be unconstitutional, as both the judge and ex judge well knew.

The conspirators were unaware that, even before this meeting began, Marshal Wilson, across town at police headquarters, knew from one of his informants that the meeting was taking place. His informant also told him where it was held, and precisely who was present. Wilson's objective now was to collect evidence of the seditious nature of the discussion that took place at this meeting, after which he could build cases against every single participant and lay charges of conspiracy to commit treason. A capital crime.

It was midnight by the time that Lieutenant Young, still dressed in civilian clothes, wearily climbed the gangway steps up the side of the cruiser *Boston* after spending half the day ashore on his spying mission. He reported at once to Captain Wiltse in his quarters.

'I made a detailed statement of the situation,' he later wrote of his meeting with the *Boston*'s commander, 'and expressed the opinion that nothing would happen that night, but that, from the state of feeling of the people, serious trouble would come as soon as the counter-revolutionists could organize.'[167] These 'counter-revolutionists' to whom Young referred were Thurston and his seditionist colleagues of the Committee of Safety–in the coming days, the Committee would push the propaganda line that the queen had attempted a revolution by trying to introduce a new constitution, and that they were attempting to counter her revolution. Young had quickly embraced their line.

The most telling thing about Young's report to Captain Wiltse was his statement that trouble would come as soon as the Committee of Safety could organize. On this basis, should the Committee fail to organize then there would be no trouble for Captain Wiltse to counter. The dice, and the future of Hawaii, were in the hands of Lorrin Thurston and the Annexation Club.

12.

SUNDAY: THE MAKING
OF A COUP

Aᴛ 6.00 ɪɴ ᴛʜᴇ ᴍᴏʀɴɪɴɢ ᴏꜰ Sᴜɴᴅᴀʏ, Jᴀɴᴜᴀʀʏ 15, Lorrin Thurston dismounted from a horse outside the Kinau Street home of cabinet minister John Colburn. Rapping on Colburn's door, Thurston woke the household, and was invited inside. After Thurston had brought the bleary-eyed Colburn up to date on the formation of the Committee of Safety and the plan to go forward with the dethroning of Liliuokalani, Colburn said they should immediately inform Attorney General Peterson of this development.

As soon as Colburn had dressed, he and Thurston rode to Peterson's house on Pensacola Street, arriving at 6.30. Thurston now revealed to both ministers that the full plan was to declare the queen in revolution against the government and the throne vacant and monarchy abrogated, with a provisional government set up to replace Liliuokalani. Thurston added that the Committee of Safety favored then seeking annexation to the US. Peterson was to later state, 'He (Thurston) said that Stevens would land his troops and support the movement, if a proclamation to that effect (declaring the queen overthrown) was issued from any building in town. He then asked Mr. Colburn and me if we would, without consulting with our colleagues, take control of the situation, and in our own names ask the American minister to assist in carrying out their proclamation.'[168]

To let the two cabinet ministers see that there was strong backing for the plan from some of the best legal minds in the country, Thurston was able to reel off the names of the men who had met at his house the previous evening. Still, the two ministers were overwhelmed by the enormity of the plot. Seeing this, Thurston added, "If the ministers will lead, the Committee will back them. Otherwise, the Committee will act alone." It was a thinly veiled threat–either lead the overthrow of the monarchy, or stand aside while Thurston and his cabal carried out the coup themselves. 'Both Colburn and Peterson said that they were not ready to answer then,' Thurston was to write, 'but would consider.'[169]

Peterson remembered it differently: "We declined," he very pointedly declared just months after the event.[170]

As Thurston left Peterson's house, the rebel-rouser knew that the Annexation Club still had plenty of work to do, and that they would have to do it without the cooperation of members of the queen's cabinet.

At 10.00 a.m., the Committee of Safety met at William Castle's house on Kinau Street. After Thurston informed his twelve colleagues of what had transpired at his house the previous evening and then during his meeting with Colburn and Peterson earlier that morning, they all agreed that they must ignore the cabinet and arrange a major public demonstration of support for action against the queen. It was resolved to hire the old Honolulu Rifles Armory, with its memories of the Hawaiian League's past glories, for a public meeting next day.

As this gathering at Castle's house was wrapping up, Fred Wundenberg and John Soper arrived, despondent, after conducting a survey of men and arms available to the Committee. William Smith would recollect: 'They reported that the prospect of arms was very discouraging,' and that they had only been able to locate sixty rifles in all of Honolulu apart from the cache at Hall and Sons.[171] This news was not well received by some of those present, who suddenly seemed to lose their enthusiasm for an armed insurrection. But Henry Waterhouse, Smith, Cooper and a handful of others vowed that they had no intention of being deterred.

The Armory was duly hired by the Committee of Safety from Cyclery operators Wootten and Bromley, for twenty dollars. Chairs for attendees and a table for the speakers were hired from a furniture store. An advertisement announcing the meeting would be placed in Monday morning's editions of the Honolulu press, and five hundred dodgers and posters were run off by the Hawaiian Gazette Company. Advertisements, dodgers and posters all stated, in official-sounding tones: 'A mass meeting of citizens will be held at the Beretania Street armory on Monday, January 16, at 2 p.m., to consider the present critical situation. Let all business places be closed. PER ORDER OF THE COMMITTEE OF SAFETY.'[172]

After the meeting at the Castle house broke up, a sub-committee of Thurston, close friend William Smith, and shipping company owner William Wilder traveled out to the American Legation, the home of US ambassador John L. Stevens, on Nuuanu Avenue near the School Street corner. There, the trio briefed Stevens on all that had taken place and was expected to take place. The possibility of Liliuokalani's overthrow had been discussed with Stevens for months past, and he now assured Thurston and Smith that in the event of an uprising he would authorize the landing of US troops from the *Boston* to protect American lives and property. But, he emphasized, he could not recognize any revolutionary government until it was actually established, 'and repeated that the United States forces, if landed, would not take sides with any party, but would protect Americans.'[173]

This was good enough for Thurston, Smith and Wilder, who went on to discuss with Stevens what grounds he would use to recognize a revolutionary government. Stevens told them that he would recognize a revolutionary government if he was confident that it controlled the country's legislature, treasury, and archives. The members of the trio looked at each other and smiled. They knew, as Stevens well knew, that in Honolulu the legislature, treasury and archives were all contained within a single building, the Government Building. Stevens was telling them that if they could take control of the Government Building–not the palace, not the military barracks, not the police headquarters–he would recognize them as the legitimate government of the nation of Hawaii.

But what if the Hawaiian Government should move against the plotters? Attorneys Thurston and Smith knew that they were already guilty of conspiracy under Hawaiian law. William Smith was to say of this meeting with Stevens, 'Among other things we talked over with him what had better be done in case of our being arrested, or extreme or violent measures were taken by the monarchy in regard to us.' Smith said that, in response, 'Mr. Stevens gave assurance of his earnest purpose to afford all the protection that was in his power.'[174]

Thurston, Smith and Wilder left this meeting assured that all they had to do was take possession of the Government Building to receive US Government recognition, and that, in the event that they were arrested, ambassador Stevens would step in to help them.

By the middle of the day on Sunday, cabinet ministers Peterson and Colburn had reconciled with their fellow minister Cornwell and Premier Parker, even though Colburn had been calling Parker 'a treacherous liar.'[175] The early morning visit from Lorrin Thurston, and his threatening attitude in that meeting, had jolted Peterson and Colburn into realizing that what he was proposing was much too radical a step. They decided to try to dampen down the situation by convincing Queen Liliuokalani to issue a proclamation that would remove the grounds for an uprising from beneath Thurston and his fellow radicals.

At noon, at the suggestion of Colburn, a group of politically moderate 'conservative businessmen' secretly met with the cabinet in the premier's office at the Government Building. Their aim was to help the queen out of the tight corner into which she had painted herself. The annexationists would claim that all the leading lights in the Hawaiian business community at this point supported their cause against the queen, but the men who came together in the premier's office this afternoon to support and provide friendly counsel to the queen were all heavy hitters in Hawaiian commerce.

These were former finance minister Sam Damon, who headed up Bishop's Bank, Hawaii's largest bank; German merchant and Italian consul Frederick Shaeffer of Shaeffer and Company; Joseph. O. Carter, son of an American sea captain and for the past two years head of Brewer and Company, one Hawaii's 'Big Five' corporations; S. C. Allen, from Allen and Robinson, Hawaii's oldest lumber company; W. M. Giffard, manager in Hawaii for powerful Californian sugar baron and banker Claus Spreckels; former cabinet minister Edward C. Macfarlane, principal of G. W. Macfarlane and Company, shipping agents and wholesale merchants, forty years old and born in Hawaii to American parents; and German-born former judge and cabinet minister, the seventy-year-old Hermann Widemann, who had a made a fortune from sugar and had recently introduced coffee beans from Guatemala that would become the foundation of Hawaii's famous Kona coffee plantations.

'Some thought we ought have the committee of thirteen (the Committee of Safety) arrested,' Sam Parker was later to say. 'But I thought it was not necessary.'[176] In hindsight, how different subsequent events might have turned out had the members of the Committee of Safety been arrested that Sunday as suggested. Instead, Parker proposed that the members of this influential loyalist group gathered in his office draft a proclamation which he would take to the queen, for signature by her and the members of the cabinet. The men at this meeting, hoping this would end the unrest in annexationist quarters, all agreed, and they labored for several hours over the wording of just such a proclamation.

At 7.30 that evening, Premier Parker and Attorney General Peterson called on US ambassador Stevens at the American Legation. They told Stevens of the difficulties they had experienced with the queen that day, even of the offer of several cabinet members to resign, before assuring the ambassador that they were confident that Liliuokalani would sign the statement they had prepared that afternoon, which, in their opinion, was sure to diffuse the situation. The intent of this meeting with Stevens, Peterson was to write, was to find out what stand the ambassador would take in the event of an armed insurrection in the kingdom. Before Stevens answered, the two Hawaiian ministers hastened to point out that the Hawaiian Government was 'perfectly capable of dealing with the situation.'

"I desire to protect the government," Steven replied, untruthfully. "And I advise Her Majesty's Government not to resign."

"So, the government can rely upon your assistance, if we ask for it, Mr. Stevens?" Peterson pointedly asked.

To which Stevens replied, "I do not see how I can assist the government as long as C. R. Wilson remains Marshal of the Kingdom. The man is a scoundrel!"[177]

Peterson and Parker must have looked at each other. Stevens had never hidden his contempt for Charles Wilson. But it was in his confidential dispatches to the US secretary of state in Washington that Stevens revealed an absolute loathing of Wilson, continually referring to him as 'the Tahitian half-caste favorite of the queen, the marshal of the little kingdom.'[178] And he'd had no hesitation in repeating, in these dispatches, the rumors that Wilson and Liliuokalani were lovers.

When Peterson now asked what Stevens had against the marshal, Stevens replied, "He caused the arrest of my Chinese coachman, for carrying concealed weapons." Stevens did not deny that the coachman was illegally armed; his complaint was that it was *his* coachman who had been arrested.

"Is that all?" Peterson, asked.

"I have other matters against him," Stevens replied, declining to elaborate.[179]

In a dispatch to Secretary of State Blaine the previous April, Stevens had written, about Wilson, 'The queen appears to be largely in his hands. The administration of his office results in very gross abuses, and it is a striking evidence of the forbearance and restraint of the white and native population that they endure it.'[180] Yet, Stevens never offered any proof of his claims that Wilson abused his office or unduly influenced the queen. Wilson's one major fault, to Stevens' bigoted mind, appears to have been the colored blood running through his veins.

Stevens also knew, from Thurston and Smith, but also from personal observation, that the very capable Marshal Wilson would be the one major obstacle to the annexationists seizing power in Hawaii if it came to an armed confrontation. If Stevens could force the queen to remove Wilson from office, he would be doing the Committee of Safety a very great favor. But Peterson and Parker knew that there was absolutely no chance of Liliuokalani agreeing to dismiss Wilson.

Realizing that they were not going to make any headway with the US ambassador, the premier and the attorney general unhappily bade Stevens good night.

13.

CAPTAIN WILTSE'S DECISION

Not long after the sun rose over Honolulu on Monday, January 16, Captain Gilbert Wiltse came ashore from the USS *Boston*, alone, and took a carriage across town to the Nuuanu Avenue residence of US ambassador John Stevens.

All through Sunday, Wiltse's subordinate Lieutenant Lucien Young had been urging him to land armed marines and sailors from the *Boston*, supposedly to protect American lives and property in the city, but in reality to support Lorrin Thurston and the annexationists. All day, Wiltse had resisted. Now he had come ashore to gauge the mood in the city for himself and to consult with the ambassador.

After Stevens counseled Captain Wiltse to wait on developments in the city, the captain returned to the ship through streets that were 'outwardly quiet,' having decided to venture ashore again later in the morning for a second reconnaissance.[181]

Captain Wiltse was back aboard his ship when, at 8.30 a.m., Premier Sam Parker arrived at the Iolani Palace to see the queen. Finding her in the second floor private parlor, eating breakfast, Parker showed Liliuokalani the proclamation drafted by the hastily put together committee of businessmen late the previous day, and already signed by all the cabinet ministers. Liliuokalani was not impressed by their presumptiveness.

But Parker was just as determined as she. "I want you to sign it, Your Majesty," he insisted.[182] Parker had already had the proclamation typeset at the government printing office, and as soon as he had the queen's signature on it he would have copies run off and distributed.

Liliuokalani observed that all was still quiet in the city. 'Even if any great commotion had been going on I would have remained indifferent,' she was to say, for she was stubbornly determined to push through her new constitution sooner or later. She had been prepared for opposition, but from outside, not from her own cabinet, which had up to this time, she believed, supported her intent to change the Bayonet Constitution. 'The reaction was a great strain' to her, she later wrote. And heavy was her heart due to 'the disappointment in my ministry.'[183]

Parker would not be put off. He placed the proclamation, pen and ink in front of his queen. "The cabinet advises you to sign it, Your Majesty," he said firmly.[184]

Liliuokalani had made much of her desire to been seen to follow the Constitution and act on the advice of, and with the consent of, her ministers. Now, she had to practice what she preached. Unhappily, she took the pen and wrote 'Liliuokalani R' at the bottom of the document. Premier Parker hurried away, armed now with a signed piece of paper which, he hoped, would put a stop to a revolution.

The Committee of Safety was due to meet again at 9.00 on Monday morning, this time at Lorrin Thurston's Merchant Street law office. Before that meeting took place, a five-member deputation from the Committee, almost certainly led by Thurston, met with the cabinet at the Government Building, in response to an invitation from the ministers delivered to Thurston the previous afternoon.

'In that interview,' Lieutenant Young was to write, 'the ministers urged the Committee to go no further, stating that the queen had agreed to go no further with the constitution matter.' The cabinet showed the delegation the proclamation signed by the queen. 'The Committee replied they could place no confidence in the queen's pledges, that she had gone too far, and they would proceed with their deliberations without regard to what the queen said or did.'[185] The annexationist delegation returned to Thurston's office. At the same time, the ministers proceeded to police headquarters to meet with Marshal Wilson.

At Thurston's office, the full Committee of Safety met, and proceeded to set the agenda for the afternoon's public meeting at the Armory and make plans for subsequent action, even though the excuse for the Committee's existence–providing support to the cabinet in its quarrel with the queen–no longer existed. While the Committee was in session, there was a firm knock on the door. Thurston rose, went to the door, and opened it, to found Marshal Wilson standing there. Wilson poked his head into the room. Looking past Thurston, the marshal noted the identity of each of the other twelve men sitting in the room.

Withdrawing his head, Wilson said, "Thurston, I would like to speak to you a minute." Thurston accompanied him out into the hall, closing the office door. Wilson then said, "I know what you fellows are up to, and I want you to quit and go home."

Thurston shook his head. "We are not going home, Charlie. Things have advanced too far and we do not intend to have a repetition of the events of Saturday." By this he meant the queen's attempt to promulgate a new constitution.

"The queen will not further attempt to do away with the present constitution, or promulgate another one," said Wilson, "so there is no danger of repetition."

"What assurance have we?" Thurston countered.

"I give you my personal assurance."

"And what value is that? Suppose that the queen goes ahead and attempts to do it anyway? What can you do?"

"If it is necessary, I will undertake personally to lock up the queen to prevent her doing anything further along those lines," said the marshal earnestly.

Thurston was not going to be swayed from his course. "It's no use, Charlie. We will not take any more chances, but are going to wind affairs up now."

Wilson was thoughtful for a moment, then said, "Well, I think you are wrong. But remember–I warned you and told you to quit." The marshal then turned and departed.[186]

Thurston had only just rejoined the others in his office when there was another knock at the door. This time, when Thurston opened the door, he found Archie Cleghorn, Governor of Oahu and the queen's brother-in-law, standing there. The tall, elegant Cleghorn, who had been born at Edinburgh in Scotland, was only fifty-seven years old, but his sun-wrinkled skin, white hair and beard gave him the appearance of a man in his seventies. It is possible that Cleghorn had been waiting on the stairs to find out the outcome of Wilson's conversation with Thurston, and when that outcome had been negative, he came up to take his turn at bat. Cleghorn invited Thurston to talk with him in private, so again Thurston went out into the hall and closed his office door behind him.

"I do not blame you for what you are proposing to do to Liliuokalani, Mr. Thurston," the Scotsman began. "But I wish to submit for the consideration of the Committee of Safety whether it is necessary to overturn the monarchy entirely, and to have you take into consideration the claim of Princess Kaiulani."

Thurston must have raised his eyebrows in surprise at the suggestion that the queen be replaced by Cleghorn's daughter.

"If you remove Liliuokalani from the throne, why not appoint Kaiulani, who is now the heir apparent, to be queen," Cleghorn went on. "You can appoint a board of regents to act during her minority, and I assure you that the community will have a very different state of affairs to deal with from that which Kalakaua and Liliuokalani have presented."

"You know my regard for Kaiulani, Mr. Cleghorn," Thurston responded. Thurston, as a member of the Bayonet Cabinet, had approved sending Kaiulani to school in England at Hawaiian Government expense. The teenaged princess was due to come home from school in England this year. "I think very highly of her," Thurston went on. "If conditions were different, I should be very glad to help promote your suggestion. But matters have proceeded too far for your plan to be an adequate answer to this situation. We are going to abrogate the monarchy entirely, and nothing can be done to stop us, as far as I can see."[187]

According to Thurston, Governor Cleghorn appeared close to tears as he bowed his head, then turned and retreated down the stairs, lamenting the fact that his daughter's once glittering future as queen of her country was now under threat. Thurston watched him go, then returned to his office. Back inside, he informed his twelve co-conspirators of all that had transpired between Wilson, Cleghorn and himself. With smiles all round, the thirteen members of the Committee of Safety got back down to work plotting the details of their revolution.

After the brief conversation outside Thurston's door, Marshal Wilson briskly made his way to the police station, which was just half a block up Merchant Street from Thurston's law office. Unbeknownst to Thurston and the Committee of Safety, the marshal had, by first thing that morning, collected enough evidence to lay charges against Thurston and others for plotting to overthrow the Crown. The most damning of that evidence appears to have come from Fred Wundenberg, the clerk of the supreme court, who had attended the meeting at Thurston's house on Saturday evening. For, within months, Wundenberg would publicly reveal everything that had gone on in the secret Committee of Safety meetings that he attended, and for his trouble would come into the spiteful revolutionaries' sights as a spy in their midst and a traitor to their subversive cause.

When the ministers assembled at the marshal's office after meeting with the deputation from the Committee of Safety, Wilson informed them that he had sufficient evidence to swear out a warrant for the arrest of every member of the Committee. But when he asked Attorney General Peterson for permission to proceed with the warrant and the arrests, as he was required to do under the Bayonet Constitution, Peterson refused point blank to allow it, and the other members of the cabinet backed him.

'The damned cowards would not give me permission!' Wilson was to later complain. 'They said, if we attempted any such action, it might precipitate trouble, which they wished to avoid. They said that, if an attempt were made to arrest the Committee of Safety, Mr. Stevens would take action with the American troops. I did not believe that Mr. Stevens would do anything of the kind, and told the cabinet so, but they would not listen to me. I insisted, however, that we should try to head off the Committee of Safety from doing what they might be intending to do.'[188] So the cabinet had given him permission to attempt to personally persuade the Committee of Safety from proceeding with its plans. And that was what the marshal had just tried to do, without success.

By the time that Wilson arrived back at police headquarters, the members of the cabinet had departed. Despite the reluctance of the government's ministers to act against the simmering revolution, the marshal did not intend to sit around and twiddle his thumbs. He immediately summoned all off-duty policemen to duty, and called in forty-five special constables–respectable citizens who were deputized to serve in emergencies. Of those special constables, around fifteen were white, the remainder Native Hawaiian.

The marshal posted one of those special constables, Charles J. McCarthy, to the Government Building. Thirty-one-year-old

McCarthy had been born in Boston, and was one of a number of Americans in Hawaii who was firmly loyal to Queen Liliuokalani. McCarthy came to Hawaii in 1881 to manage the Hawaiian operations of a San Francisco fruit wholesaling firm. Marrying a local woman, Margaret Morgan, McCarthy was a volunteer fireman and was elected to the House of Nobles in 1890, becoming Secretary of the legislature in 1892. If anyone knew his way around the Government Building, special constable the Honorable Charles McCarthy did.

But McCarthy was the lone defender of the Government Building, and even he was unarmed. Marshal Wilson, being unaware of the secret agreement struck between Thurston, Smith and ambassador Stevens that made rebel occupation of the Government Building key to Stevens giving US recognition to the insurgents as the legitimate government of Hawaii, did not rate the defense of the Government Building highly on his list of priorities. He saw other locations as key to maintaining government control.

Later military manuals would put a national capital's telephone exchange and electric power facility top of the list of targets to be defended in the event of a military coup, but Marshal Wilson had determined that Honolulu's military strong points, if it came down to a battle between insurgents and government forces, would be the Iolani Palace, the Iolani Barracks, and police headquarters. The latter he considered central to the defense of the city. A solid, two-story redbrick building, the police station also had a basement, occupied by cells and the arsenal of weapons collected following the abolition of the Honolulu Rifles.

But Charles McCarthy instinctively knew that the Government Building was a key strongpoint, and that afternoon the special constable sent the marshal a note: 'I believe it would be advisable to send to the Government Building after dark about 20 stand of arms, and about 300 or 400 rounds of ammunition, with the idea of storing them in the office of the attorney general, in case of necessity. I have sufficient employees here to take care of the building in case of attack.'[189]

Wilson took McCarthy's advice seriously. Late in the day, the marshal detailed Senior Captain Robert Parker Waipa, the highest ranking policeman in the kingdom, a crack shot, and a man of proven dependability after the way he had derailed Robert Wilcox's 1889 rebellion, to go to the Government Building with the requested cache of arms, and to station himself there all night with McCarthy until reinforced next morning.

This was the last thing that Thurston and the Committee of Safety wanted.

While the Committee of Safety was meeting, Captain Wiltse again came ashore from the *Boston*, and for a second time that morning went to the home of the US ambassador. Stevens told Wiltse that both he and the longtime British ambassador to Hawaii, John Wodehouse, had been for months advising the queen against tampering with the Bayonet Convention, but she had ignored their advice. The captain and the ambassador discussed the current situation for a time, before they agreed that 'great caution' was required.[190]

By 11.00 a.m., Wiltse was once more back aboard his ship. At that time, the executive officer of the *Boston*, forty-two-year-old Lieutenant Commander William T. Swinburne, who, like Lucien Young, was short, slight, and the wearer of a walrus mustache, put his head in the captain's door to consult him about the cleaning of the ship. He found Wiltse in conversation with a darkly bearded civilian whom he had seen aboard the *Boston* on Saturday. Wiltse introduced the civilian as Henry Cooper, and said that Cooper had brought a message from the Committee of Safety. Swinburne, who had never heard of the Committee of Safety and had no idea of its purpose, withdrew.[191]

After Henry Cooper left the *Boston*, not long after 11.00, Captain Wiltse called Lieutenant Young to his quarters. Young was to say that, 'with closed doors,' the captain informed him of all that he had learned while on shore, and said that on his return to the cruiser he had received a message from parties in the city. That message, he said, reported the need for American forces to be landed at once to prevent a bloodbath when the queen's forces and the armed revolutionaries clashed. According to Young, his captain now sought his advice on what to do in response to that message.[192]

'There were several thousand American citizens and many million dollars worth of American property at the very focus of this cyclonic condition of affairs,' Young melodramatically told his commander.[193] In fact, according to the Annexation Club's figures, a total of 1,350 'Americans' were then resident throughout the Hawaiian Islands; this included American citizens, naturalized Hawaiian citizens of American birth, and people born in Hawaii to American parents. In fact, of the merchants and traders in the country, just eighty-one were American citizens. By contrast, there were 776 Chinese merchants and traders in Hawaii.[194] The vast majority of the retail trade in Honolulu was carried out by its Chinese residents, almost all of whom had been deprived of the vote by the Bayonet Convention.

Young also told Captain Wiltse that in his opinion the Hawaiian Government was 'unable to protect itself, and could not under any circumstances protect life and property.' This claim flew in the face of the fact that the Hawaiian Government possessed a small army and police force made up of several hundred trained, well-equipped men. 'Captain Wiltse,' Young would write, 'after consulting with the American minister and myself, decided that his duty plainly required him to land. He asked me how long it would take to get ready for landing the two revolving cannon, and two Gatling guns, with ammunition. I replied, "Half an hour."'[195]

The captain nodded, and dismissed the lieutenant. Wiltse then summoned executive officer Swinburne, and ordered him to prepare to land four companies of marines and sailors, with artillery, at 4.00 that afternoon. In all the time that Swinburne had been serving as second in command of the *Boston*, not once had Captain Wiltse exchanged a personal conversation with him. And never had Wiltse taken him into his confidence or sought his advice.[196] That role, of the captain's confidant, was reserved for Swinburne's subordinate, Lieutenant Young. Swinburne was aware of that fact, and would have resented it. But he could do nothing about it.

Lucien Young had not long been back in his quarters when Swinburne put his head in through his open doorway. "Young," said Swinburne, "get one revolving cannon, and one Gatling gun, each with their field carriages, and one caisson, ready. Let me know how many men you need to fill up the complement. And get the boats ready for lowering."[197]

Orders were soon issued throughout the ship for nine officers and 153 men to prepare to land that afternoon with packed knapsacks and in heavy marching order. Shortly after, Captain Wiltse again sent for Young. The commander read the lieutenant his confidential written orders from the Navy Department and Admiral George Brown, commander of US naval forces in the Pacific. Those orders appear to have been written by Secretary

Tracy following his meeting with Lorrin Thurston in Washington the previous year.

Wiltse was clearly agitated about this whole affair, and was looking for reassurance from Young, who gave it to him. 'I fully agreed with him as to the necessity of landing a force,' Young later wrote. 'I remarked that the situation was such that great tact and judgment would have to be used to avoid being accused of interfering or taking sides.'

"I intend to maintain a perfectly neutral attitude," Wiltse told the lieutenant. "But I will prevent any injury to Americans or their property, incendiarism or pilfering, even if I have to fight all hands!"[198]

By 10.00 a.m., the proclamation signed by the queen and her entire cabinet had been printed in a special edition of the *Gazette*. Come midday, it had been hand-delivered throughout Honolulu to business houses and all foreign diplomatic representatives. US ambassador Stevens received a copy accompanied by a personal note from Premier Parker in which he expressed the hope that the situation that had developed since Saturday had now been satisfactorily resolved. Stevens did not reply.

The proclamation declared that, 'Her Majesty's Ministers desire to express their appreciation for the quiet and order which has prevailed in the community since the events of Saturday, and are authorized to say that the position is taken by Her Majesty in regard to the promulgation of a new Constitution, was under the stress of her native subjects.' In other words, the cabinet was claiming that the queen had been forced to do what she had done by the Hawaiian people. 'Authority is given,' the proclamation went on, 'for the assurance that any changes desired in the fundamental law of the land will be sought only by methods provided in the Constitution itself.'[199]

This proclamation should have been enough to put the cork back in the proverbial bottle. But, knowing that the relentless Lorrin Thurston and his Annexation Club colleagues were hell bent on smashing that bottle with their 2.00 p.m. meeting at the Armory, the queen also agreed to a competing public meeting, designed to preserve law and order, which would be held at Palace Square, also at 2.00 p.m. This too was promoted in the special edition of the *Gazette*.

* * *

By 1.30 p.m., businesses, saloons and offices throughout Honolulu were closing their doors, and, as 2.00 o'clock approached, a crowd of mostly white males came through the open doors of the Armory on Beretania Street and took seats in the hall, whose walls were draped with Hawaiian flags. The number of people who attended this meeting has long been disputed. The true number would serve to endorse or destroy the claims of the opposing parties. The queen's supporters were adamant that only a very small minority of Hawaiian residents, wealthy white businessmen in the main, supported Thurston and his annexationists. Those calling for the queen's overthrow were to claim that Liliuokalani was widely unpopular and that support for the movement against her was significant.

Pro-annexation Honolulu daily newspaper the *Pacific Commercial Advertiser* reported, the day following the meeting, '1,260 being present, by actual count, while many others came later.' Ambassador Stevens, in a dispatch immediately after the event told Washington that 1,300 were present. Thurston, when talking with the American press in February, 1893, inflated the number to 1,500. By November 21, when he released another statement on the subject, he had upped it to 3,000. Lieutenant Lucien Young, who was not present, wrote in a book five years after the event that this meeting attracted 'about 2,000 men.' Sanford Dole, who was present at this meeting, would write in his memoirs that the gathering was merely 'large and harmonious.'

An indication of the actual number of attendees at the Armory meeting can be found today in the depths of Hawaii State Archives, which holds a receipted invoice to the Committee of Safety from the Pioneer Furniture Warerooms for the hire of a table and forty-two dozen chairs for use at this meeting in the armory bicycle shop.[200] The fact that the Committee of Safety only hired 504 chairs suggests one of three things–either there were already some chairs there; that this was the maximum number of chairs that the Armory could hold; or this was the maximum number of attendees that the Committee was expecting. It was not that the Committee could not afford more chairs. The Committee, representing some of the wealthiest men on the islands, could afford any number of chairs.

It likely that the hall could only accommodate 504 chairs–for

Thurston wrote that 'the hall was crowded to its limits' during this meeting.[201] It might be argued that, in addition to 504 filled seats, there were perhaps a number of people standing at the Armory meeting. Sanford Dole appears to knock that possibility on the head with his report of the meeting, in which he said that, following a number of speeches, 'a resolution was adopted unanimously *by a standing vote* and with much cheering.'[202] That is, those in favor of the resolution were called on the by the meeting's chairman to stand. Had there been a number of men already standing at the back and sides of the hall, such a call would have been totally impracticable. If even a few men were standing, logically, the chairman would have called for a show of hands. Requiring attendees to jump to their feet to endorse the resolution may have looked dramatic, but it betrays the fact that no one was standing prior to this, and that there were little more than 504 men at this meeting, if that many.

The meeting was chaired by Committee of Safety member William Wilder. Born in Canada, to American parents, Wilder had served in the Union cavalry during the Civil War. Since arriving in Hawaii in 1869, he had made a fortune with his Inter-Island Steamship Company, which now had seven vessels on the island trade. He was also developing railroads and importing coal and lumber. Wilder introduced Thurston, who read the meeting a 'report' he had written, narrating the events of the previous Saturday leading to the formation of the Committee of Safety. In this report, Thurston showed his talent for exaggeration and misinformation by claiming that three of the cabinet ministers 'had, or were about to resign' on Saturday in reaction to the queen's intention to promulgate a new constitution. This was not true. He also claimed that the ministers had warned the queen that 'the streets of Honolulu would run red with blood' if she persisted.[203] There is no record of any such thing being said by the cabinet members.

If the cabinet was so opposed to the queen, as Thurston was telling them, some at the Armory meeting might have expected the ministers to be present, to put the case against her. Thurston was not game to tell the crowd that since Saturday the ministers had backed away from taking any action against Liliuokalani, and had that very morning asked the Committee of Safety not to proceed with their planned coup against the queen. Lucien Young would later complain, of this turnaround by the cabinet,

'Without a moment's hesitation, and without replying to the proposition of the Committee of Safety, the cabinet abandoned the citizens whom they had called upon for help, and who had organized in good faith to help them.'[204]

Thurston needed to explain his way around the cabinet's change of heart. Even more importantly, he needed to give legitimacy to the continued existence of the Committee of Safety. So, in his report to the Armory meeting, Thurston stressed that cabinet ministers Colburn and Peterson had attended the meeting at William Smith's offices on Saturday when the Committee was formed, and that Colburn had addressed that meeting. Thurston's report finished with several resolutions, written by Thurston and William Smith. These denounced the queen, ratified the self-appointment of the Committee of Safety, and empowered the Committee to 'devise such ways and means as may be necessary to secure the permanent maintenance of law and order and the protection of life, liberty and property in Hawaii.'[205]

Seven speakers in succession spoke in favor of the resolutions. Thurston was the first. "Hawaii is a wonderful country," he began. "We are divided into parties and nationalities and factions, but there are moments when we are united and move shoulder to shoulder, moved by one common desire for the public good." After railing against the queen, he finished by saying, "The man who has not the spirit to rise after the menace to our liberties has no right to keep them. Has the tropic sun cooled and thinned our blood, or have we flowing in our veins the warm rich blood which makes men love liberty and die for it?"[206]

The other speakers gave similar melodramatic addresses. The last man to speak, R. J. Greene, was a native of Rhode Island. His grandfather had fought the British in the Revolutionary War. His father had fought in the War of 1812. And Greene and three brothers had fought in the Union army during the Civil War. "I have adopted this flag and am loyal to it," he said, pointing to the Hawaiian flag. "But I am not willing to take one step back in the matter of civil liberty, and I will give the last drop of Rhode Island blood in my veins to go forward and not back!"[207]

This latest reference to the spilling of blood, which seemed to characterize annexationist rhetoric–rather than loyalist rhetoric as Lucien Young would later claim–brought cheers from Americans in the Armory audience. Chairman William Wilder called on the audience to show their support for it with a standing vote. Men jumped to their feet, and the resolutions were, according to Thurston, 'adopted without a dissenting vote.'[208] At the end of the meeting, written versions of these resolutions were circulated among attendees, to gain their signatures. But, according to leading Committee of Safety member Henry Waterhouse, only around half the men at the meeting ultimately signed the resolutions.[209]

Those who did sign, put their names to what was only a relatively mild condemnation and denunciation of the queen. Even Thurston had to admit that the phrases 'dethronement of Liliuokalani' and 'abrogation of the monarchy' were not used by any of the speakers at this meeting, just as they were not used in the resolutions. He later tried to pass this off by claiming that everyone present understood that this was the intention, even if it was unspoken.[210] But, apart from the members of the Committee of Safety and an inner circle of some twenty like thinkers, it is highly probable that the vast majority of the men who left the Armory meeting had no idea that they had just voted to authorize the Committee to overthrow the queen, abolish the monarchy, and seek annexation by the United States.

At 2.00 p.m. Monday, the same time that the revolutionaries hosted their meeting at the Armory, the meeting called by the queen was staged at Palace Square, on King Street, outside the Opera House.

As with the Armory meeting, attendance numbers at this Palace Square meeting would be hotly disputed by both sides. William D. Alexander, who was Hawaii's surveyor general and commissioner of public education in 1893, and an ardent supporter of the Committee of Safety, would later write a book in which he stated that the crowd which attended this pro-Government, pro-queen meeting 'has been variously estimated all the way from 500 to 3,000.' Being a civil servant, Alexander himself was apparently present at the official government meeting at Palace Square. He would claim that the government's meeting was 'about half as large as the meeting at the Armory.'[211] Lorrin Thurston would likewise claim that the Armory meeting was the largest in Honolulu that day, far outnumbering the meeting in support of the queen.

This comparison of the size of the two competing meetings

would prove central to the propaganda war that was to unfold following this momentous day. To the annexationists, it was vital for them to show that the majority of public support in Hawaii was against the queen and for her overthrow. To the queen's supporters, it was just as vital to show that the annexationists attracted only meager support and represented a small minority. If Alexander is to be believed, a crowd of perhaps 600, or as few as 250 if the real number at the Armory is used, turned up at Palace Square that afternoon. To this day, Native Hawaiians have been unable to believe that the queen drew such a small crowd. The queen and her ministers had called this meeting. At the very least, all ali'i were obligated to respond to that call and attend.

So, what was the true number? The Committee of Safety's figures of 1,200 at their meeting and around 500 at the government meeting were to become embedded in Hawaiian and American history books as true and accurate. The top end of Alexander's scale, of 3,000 attendees at Palace Square, was probably a figure published in the Hawaiian language press of the day, while the bottom end, 500, was the figure used by the pro-annexation press. File copies of the Hawaiian language papers of the day were subsequently destroyed by the annexationists. An official US inquiry several months after the event put the number at the Palace Square meeting at between 1,500 and 2,000.

There was an unnamed foreign visitor in the crowd at Palace Square that day. He had taken in all the excitement of the past few days, and had read in Honolulu's lurid English language press that morning of fears in the white community that the native Hawaiians would rise up against them for preventing the queen from changing the despised Bayonet Constitution, with the streets running with blood. This visitor was due to board the Oceanic Line's SS *Alameda* that evening for the transpacific steamer's voyage from Honolulu to Sydney, New South Wales, via Samoa and New Zealand. On his arrival in Sydney, the traveler would regale the Australian press with a story of the exciting scenes he had witnessed in Hawaii. With no ax to grind for either camp in the conflict, and having left the kingdom before seeing the local press next day with its estimates of the numbers involved, the traveler would calculate that the crowd at the Palace Square meeting numbered 4,000.[212]

In reality then, as has been demonstrated, there were perhaps

500 men at the Armory meeting, and anywhere between 1,500 (the low end of the US Government's official estimate) and 4,000 at the Palace Square meeting. Whatever the precise numbers, clearly, support for the queen and her government greatly outnumbered that for the cabal of businessmen who were opposed to her. At Palace Square, five speakers used the Opera House steps as their rostrum. Those speakers were headed by Antone Rosa, a successful businessman and former attorney general of Hawaii. Surprisingly, the other speakers were all Liberal Party politicians who for two years past had been vilifying the queen and calling for a Hawaiian republic. Even more surprisingly, they were led by redshirt revolutionary Robert Wilcox and his acid-tongued colleague John Bush. The other speakers, Joseph Nawahi, who had been premier of Hawaii very briefly in 1892, and William White, had both been among Wilcox's redshirts in 1889.

Now, these men all spoke in support of Liliuokalani, being careful to 'express themselves with great caution and moderation.'[213] For, they knew that their country's sovereignty was now at stake, and, to them, loyalty to Hawaii came before everything. They put a resolution to the crowd, that the queen's proclamation of that morning be accepted as a satisfactory guarantee that neither she nor her government would attempt to modify the Constitution by any means other than that provided by law. The crowd, apparently by a show of hands, endorsed the resolution and gave their full support to the queen, in the quiet, gentle, moderate Hawaiian way.

Lieutenant Lucien Young, who was not present at this meeting, was to claim that some of the speakers 'gave vent to expressions of a desire for bloodshed.'[214] Young was contradicted by annexationist author Surveyor General Alexander, who was apparently there at Palace Square. 'The tone of this meeting,' he wrote, 'was constrained and unnatural.' To Alexander's surprise, and perhaps his disappointment, there were no calls for American blood to flow through Honolulu's streets. And when it was over and done the large Palace Square crowd melted peacefully away, paying respect to their queen's call for order.[215]

US ambassador Stevens, in his next official dispatch to the secretary of state in Washington, would describe the Palace Square meeting very differently. 'A counter demonstration was attempted by the queen's party at Palace Square,' he wrote, claiming that 'one of the speakers gave vent to the expression of a wild thirst for bloodshed.'[216] This was at complete variance with Alexander's firsthand report of the meeting. But Stevens had to write in these terms to justify what he was doing behind the scenes. Stevens' account of the meeting would be entered into the official State Department record and be published in the 'Foreign Relations of the United States' congressional record for the year.

In the end, both meetings, held by the annexationists and the loyalists, were superfluous. Events taking their course out on Honolulu Harbor would dictate the future of the Kingdom of Hawaii.

14.

THE US INVASION
OF HAWAII

Aboard the USS *Boston*, once the crew had finished their lunch at 1.30, preparations were made for the armed landing ordered that morning by Captain Wiltse, who had set 4.00 p.m. as the time for the operation to be executed. 'The time set was supposed to be about the hour the two mass meetings would finish their deliberations,' said Lieutenant Young, 'and should they come together in a hostile manner, we would be on the scene in time to prevent riot and bloodshed within the city proper.'[217]

As it was to transpire, the Armory meeting broke up a little after 3.00, and the Palace Square meeting somewhat before that. Both meetings proved to be peaceful, and no reports reached the *Boston* during the afternoon of the two groups coming together 'in a hostile manner.' There was no riot, no bloodshed, no incendiarism. The queen had ordered her native subjects to be peaceful, and they obeyed her. The city was tense, but it was quiet. Not that this would have any influence on Captain Wiltse. The die had already been cast; the necessity of landing US forces in support of Americans ashore had been pressed on Wiltse by ambassador Stevens that morning. Only the time of the landing had been left up to Wiltse.

Approaching 2.30, while the two mass meetings were still taking place in the city, ambassador Stevens set off for the docks from his residence. From Brewer and Company's wharf he was conducted out to the *Boston* in one of the cruiser's boats, and once aboard was taken directly to the captain's quarters. Just after 3.30, all nine officers assigned to the landing were ordered to report to Captain Wiltse. Lieutenant Commander Swinburne would command the 'battalion,' as the shore party was henceforth called. His four companies would be commanded by Lieutenants Young, Draper, Laird, and Coffman. Once they had assembled, Stevens, who remained seated throughout, addressed them.

"Should you land," said the seventy-two-year-old ambassador, "you need not apprehend anyone firing upon you, as they have never done such a thing under other and similar circumstances."[218]

He was referring to 1874 and 1889, when US naval forces had been landed in Honolulu at the request of the Hawaiian Government. Not that Stevens gave any credence to the fighting prowess of the native Hawaiians, even if they did put up a fight. In a dispatch to Washington several weeks after this, he would rate the Household Guard as 'not an effective force equal to 20 American soldiers.'[219] Stevens' estimation seems to have been based on nothing more than the fact that the men of the Guard were Hawaiian natives.

Captain Wiltse was quick to make it clear that he had taken the decision to put troops ashore, telling Stevens, in front of his assembled officers, "I have realized the necessity, and have already given orders to land troops at 4.00 p.m., to protect American interests."[220]

This satisfied Stevens, and Wiltse then addressed the officers, reading aloud a short letter of instructions that he had prepared for them that morning, when he had first taken the decision to land.

Lieutenant Charles Laird, who was to command the color company ashore, then asked, "Now, Captain, how far will these orders and instructions which you have read carry me in case I am detached from the main command and sent off to some other part of the city?"[221]

Turning to Laird, Captain Wiltse replied, "My desire is that you remain neutral. You are to protect the lives and property of American citizens. You have been in Honolulu four months and have been going ashore and meeting the people, and I must depend a great deal upon the discretion of my officers."[222]

Lieutenant Commander Swinburne then asked where the landing force should base itself once ashore, suggesting that the troops be quartered close to the wharf, to be near their base of supply, as Admiral Skerrett had done when he landed US forces in Honolulu in 1874. Both Stevens and Wiltse quickly disagreed with this idea. They declared that they thought it best that the troops occupy the Opera House, downtown.[223]

The fact that the Opera House was well away from all American-owned property in the city bothered Swinburne–he and his troops were being landed to protect US interests, yet here his superiors wanted him based away from those interests. It could not have escaped Swinburne's attention that the Opera House was directly across the street from the queen's Iolani Palace, and right next door to the Government Building. Swinburne was of course unaware that ambassador Stevens had secretly agreed with Thurston and Smith that once the annexationists had taken the Government Building he would recognize them as the legitimate government of Hawaii.

Stevens handed Swinburne a note addressed to William Giffard, Hawaiian representative of Spreckels and Company–Claus Spreckels owned the Opera House. 'Sir,' it read, 'please allow Capt. Wiltse and his men the use of the Opera House hall for a fair compensation for the same. Yours truly, John L. Stevens.'[224] Swinburne did not argue with his superiors, but would have noted that Captain Wiltse did not actually order him to occupy the Opera House.

Once all questions had been answered and arrangements agreed, ambassador Stevens smiled, and said to the officers, "I'm glad you are going to land. It is absolutely necessary."[225]

Captain Wiltse now ordered his officers to proceed to their landing stations.

Once the meeting at the Armory ended, just after 3.00, the members of the Committee of Safety and a small band of supporters walked from Beretania Street to William Smith's law offices on Fort Street, skirting the Iolani Palace. Passing along silent, deserted streets lined with shuttered stores and saloons, they walked as if on air, with the adrenaline pumping hard through their veins after all the uplifting speechifying, cheering, and agreement of the meeting. 'The Committee instinctively felt the necessity for early action,' Lorrin Thurston was to say.[226]

The Committee was aware of ambassador Stevens' commitment to Thurston and Smith that he would recognize the Committee of Safety as a de facto government of Hawaii once they had taken control of the Government Building, and when they reached Smith's premises a number of the members were all for marching on the Government Building at once. 'We were all for going right up, then and there,' Henry Waterhouse later recalled.[227] Waterhouse, a man known for jumping in at the deep end of an enterprise, led the call for instant action.

"But the emergency has come upon us unexpectedly," Thurston argued. "The thing to be done is vital. The details of our course are varied and unknown. Our plans are inchoate." Indeed, they were only rudimentary. "We have no plan of action to meet the queen's government, should it move first. We lack particulars of the military at our command. At the moment, we lack organized troops."[228]

In fact, at the close of Armory meeting, Henry Waterhouse had gone around the attendees asking who had what weapons and whether the men who had just given the Committee of Safety such a strong vote of confidence were prepared to put their lives on the line and shed their blood to remove the queen. Waterhouse now advised his Committee colleagues, at Smith's office, that the response had been poor. Alarmingly so, in Thurston's opinion. There were few weapons in private hands in the city, with few men prepared to use them in the face of Marshal Wilson's determined and very obvious preparations. In the words of Roman historian Tacitus, Hawaii's revolutionaries were 'bold before the dangers came and timid in the moment of peril.'[229]

Thurston railed against this lack of martial support and urged his colleagues to wait until US forces had landed and the Committee had collected a large body of armed men. On present indications, the latter could take days. Thurston decided that 'the first thing to do, before being compelled to act, was to gain time.'[230] He now tried to stall his more enthusiastic colleagues such as Waterhouse and Committee chairman Henry Cooper, who were all for immediate action. Thurston argued that, once the sun set, between 5.00 and 6.00, it would be too dark for successful military operations. If he could waste enough time, Thurston would be able to convince the Committee to at least put off any attempt to take the Government Building until the next day, by which time they may have been able to recruit and arm enough men to mount a credible coup. For, Thurston was sure that the presence on shore of US troops would give faint-hearted locals the courage to join the revolt. But first, time had to be allowed for the US Navy force to land. And, by Thurston's estimation, the rebels would not be ready for that until next morning.

One way to eat up time was by drafting documents to give a veneer of legality to the planned coup. Thurston's stratagem succeeded; his practiced powers of persuasion reined in rash action. Waterhouse, one of those convinced by Thurston to delay, later recalled, 'We hadn't our papers all ready. It was getting dark. We thought it better to have daylight on our side.'[231]

Thurston pointed out that there should be a formal, written request from the Committee of Safety before Stevens could act, and he was now directed by the Committee to draft one, which he proceeded to do, as slowly as possible. 'We are unable to protect ourselves without aid,' said this request from the Committee of Safety to the US ambassador, written by Thurston, 'and, therefore, pray for the protection of United States Forces.'[232]

Then, reminding his colleagues that they should provide the US ambassador with as much legal ammunition as possible before he authorized the landing of US troops, Thurston set to work drafting a note which all the diplomatic representatives in Honolulu could sign and send to ambassador Stevens. In that note, the foreign representatives would request that Stevens land American troops 'for the protection of the lives and property of the countries which we severally represent.' This note, once drafted, was circulated around the foreign diplomatic community that afternoon and evening, but not a single diplomatic representative in Honolulu would sign it or send it to Stevens.[233]

It was 4.00 o'clock by the time that these documents had been drafted and approved by the Committee. Thurston next wanted to stall further by drafting a proclamation announcing the dethroning of the queen, for use once the act had been performed, and he was given some notes on the subject by W. O. Smith. But a majority of those present voted to send the first two documents to ambassador Stevens at once.

Twenty-eight-year-old Charles Carter volunteered to take the documents to the American Legation and to ask Stevens whether he was indeed going to land forces. Carter, the son of H. A. P. Carter, a former Hawaiian ambassador to Washington, was also the nephew of Joseph O. Carter, one of the queen's closest advisers. Enthusiastic young 'Charlie' Carter was all for annexation. And he was always keen to jump right in, as would be the case, with tragic results, in several years' time. The tall, bespectacled, fresh-faced attorney–he was the only clean-shaven man in the room–was sent on his way to the legation on Nuuanu Avenue with the documents.

Some fifteen minutes later, Carter returned from the legation. "The troops are coming ashore," he excitedly reported.[234] He did not say who told him this. It could not have been ambassador Stevens, for he had not returned from the *Boston* by that point. Carter's information must have come from Stevens' daughter Nellie Stevens, who was serving as an assistant to her father. When the Committee asked Carter when the US troops would land, he could not tell them. But it was to be soon.

Thurston threw his hands in the air. The Committee was not ready, he reminded the others. The landing of US forces now, when the annexationists' forces were insufficient to take and hold the Government Building, might spark counter-measures from Marshal Wilson that would turn an assault on the Government Building into a bloodbath. Thurston was able to convince the Committee to delegate Smith and himself to go to Stevens and, in his own words, 'urge him to delay the landing of American troops.'[235] Smith was to recall precisely what was agreed: 'We should request that the troops be not landed until next morning, the hour in the morning being immaterial, whether it was 9.00 or 8.00 or 6.00 o'clock, but we must have further time to prevent bloodshed.'[236] Leaving their disappointed colleagues at the law office, Thurston and Smith hurried out along Nuuanu Avenue.

When they reached the legation, they were informed by the ambassador's daughter that Stevens had been aboard the *Boston* for some time. The pair settled down to wait for the ambassador's return, and before long his carriage drove up. Thurston and Smith met Stevens at the door, and informed him of their mission, and he invited them into his study.

"I don't know what your plans are, gentlemen," Stevens said once they were seated, "and I cannot afford to take chances to find out what the plans of the government may be. The conditions are so serious, and the trouble so great, that it is my duty to protect the lives and property of American citizens with every available means within my power. And I am going to land American troops immediately for that purpose." Thurston tried to convince him to delay, but Stevens stopped him in mid-sentence. "I have already given orders to that effect, and it will not be long before the troops are ashore. That's all I have to say."[237]

Thurston and Smith rushed back to Smith's Fort Street office to alert the other members of the Committee, but when they arrived there it was to find the offices deserted. The other members of the Committee and their hangers-on had all dejectedly gone home. Thurston, now lapsing into despair, believing his revolution to be in tatters, bade goodnight to his friend Smith, and wandered a block down to Fort Street toward the docks. Turning into Queen Street, he saw US Marines and blue-jacketed sailors forming up on Brewer's Wharf. All were heavily armed.

Captain Wiltse's planned 4.00 p.m. landing had been delayed, but only by an hour. At the last minute, reminded by his executive officer that the men should eat before they landed, Wiltse had ordered supper for 4.00 o'clock, with the landing to take place as close to 5.00 as possible. Boats filled with armed marines and sailors had begun to pull away from the Boston not long after 4.30, and the first US troops had stepped ashore at 4.45.

By 5.00, the full contingent was on the dock–one company of marines, three companies of blue jackets including Lieutenant Young's artillery company toting a howitzer and a Gatling gun, plus the ship's band and a medical detachment. Each enlisted man carried two ammunition belts loaded with up to eighty rounds. The artillery company's caisson and ammunition boxes were packed with 174 cannon shells, 14,000 rounds of rifles cartridges and 1,200 bullets for revolvers–enough ammunition to start a small war. And finish it![238]

Knowing that it would soon be dark, the landing force's commander, Lieutenant Commander Swinburne, disregarded ambassador Stevens' advice that he seek to make the Opera House the quarters for his troops, and initially attempted to secure 'an old armory near the boat-landing'–possibly the remnants of the old coral fort at the base of Fort Street. But his request was refused by the landlord. So, with colors flying and band playing, the force set off at the march along Queen Street, then, swinging left, proceeded up Fort Street to Merchant Street.[239] They were followed by a small crowd of the curious and the dazzled, many of them children who marched with broad grins and swinging arms in the column's wake.

At the Merchant Street intersection, the marching force came to halt while Lieutenant Draper and fifteen marines were detached to take up station at the US Consulate on the western corner of Merchant and Fort. To the tap of a pair of kettle drums, another fifteen marines under an orderly sergeant were sent marching out to join ambassador Stevens at the American Legation on Nuuanu Avenue. The main force then swung right into Merchant Street and marched toward King Street, the palace, the Opera House, and the Government Building.

Lorrin Thurston, on foot, had followed the US troops up Fort Street. When the column swung right, he continued on up Fort. Just as he reached the Hotel Street corner, he was assailed by an angry William Rickard. Manager of the Honokaa Plantation, Rickard had been a member of the legislature and was a supporter of the queen.

"Damn you, Thurston!" exclaimed Rickard, a handsome Englishman with a shaggy mustache and sixteen children, shaking a fist in the annexationist's face. "You did this!"

"Did what?" Thurston innocently replied.

"Had these troops landed," said Rickard, as the sound of the Navy band wafted to their ears on the evening air.

"You credit me with considerable influence, to be able to direct the United States troops," Thurston countered. "I had no more to do with their coming ashore than you did, and I have no more idea of what they are going to do than you have." It was a bare-faced lie, one that Thurston had no qualms in recording in his memoirs years later.[240]

Thurston then hailed a taxi, and drove to his Judd Street home, arriving just before sundown. A few weeks earlier, he had suffered what he described as 'grippe,' which was an 1890s diagnosis for stomach or intestinal pains. Thurston would claim that the stresses of the last few days caused him to now collapse when he reached his door. He telephoned his doctor, who, Thurston would assure his revolutionary colleagues, ordered him to bed.[241] And to bed he went. Thurston's friend and co-conspirator William Smith would not be charitable in his description of Thurston's departure from the field of battle; according to him, 'Thurston gave up–sick.'[242]

Thurston seems to have decided that his revolution was now doomed to fail. American troops had landed to add support to a citizen's force and an alternative government that did not exist. The US troops had come too early, and the annexationists too slow to mobilize. Thurston knew his international law. The United

States, in landing her armed forces uninvited by the sovereign government, had just invaded a friendly nation. It was an act of war. An act that might have been justified had there been armed mobs on the streets threatening American lives, and the flames of burning buildings threatening American-owned premises. But in downtown Honolulu, as the sun set on January 16, the buildings were all intact and the streets were deserted but for a marching column of heavily armed US sailors and marines, and silent but for martial tunes being belted out by a US Navy band.

In the twilight, the American column marched through Palace Square, past the Opera House, then along King Street beside the Iolani Palace, where the Hawaiian flag and the royal standard fluttered in the evening breeze. There was a small crowd of Hawaiians outside the palace's front gate, and, just inside it, a white-uniformed sentry of the Household Guard with a rifle on his left shoulder, standing rigidly to attention. Another two sentries of the Household Guard stood on the palace's front steps. As the American troops tramped by the gate, Lieutenant Young saw Her Majesty Queen Liliuokalani come out on a palace balcony to watch them. She was quite alone. Lieutenant Commander Swinburne ordered a royal salute in her honor. A bugle sounded, the colors were drooped, 'port arms' was ordered, and the drums rolled.

A little further along King Street, Swinburne called a halt. The battalion came to a standstill, the band fell silent. As his men stood in the street in their ranks, Swinburne hesitated, as he contemplated his next step. Color company commander Lieutenant Laird now pointed out that the sky overhead was threatening rain and that they should perhaps find shelter for the men. Swinburne agreed, and, temporarily turning command over to Laird, he went along the street to the house of J. A. Hopper. As the troops stood waiting for Swinburne to return, Lieutenant Laird noted Charles Carter and several others known to him, on the sidewalk observing the US troops, and nodded to them.

Lieutenant De Witt Coffman, standing at the head of his company, spotted a white-haired Englishman he knew. Coffman, like all the US officers, had fraternized with the leading members of society in Honolulu, and, recognizing the white-haired gent as

John T. Waterhouse, one of the city's leading businessmen and father of Henry Waterhouse, the lieutenant greeted him cordially.

"I'm glad to see this," said the elder Waterhouse to the lieutenant, resting on his walking stick and looking approvingly up and down the lines of bluejackets.[243] His son Henry had apparently kept him up to date on revolutionary plans, and it seems that Waterhouse senior had been expecting the US forces to land and to focus on this part of town. He had come out onto the street to see the spectacle for himself.

Meanwhile, Lieutenant Commander Swinburne was using Mr. Hopper's telephone. A phone line ran out to the *Boston*'s regular mooring, and Swinburne was able to call Captain Wiltse aboard the cruiser. He now reported that he had not succeeded in securing the Opera House as quarters for the battalion. He had in fact not even attempted to obtain the Opera House. Swinburne was acutely aware of the highly political nature of the choice of the Opera House by Wiltse and Stevens, and did not approve.

Swinburne now suggested to Wiltse that he march the battalion to the property of J. B. Atherton, an American missionary. When ambassador Stevens was on board the *Boston* that afternoon, he had mentioned that Mr. Atherton had called on him at the legation to suggest the landing of US troops. Stevens had told Atherton he was about to do that very thing, and had offered to give the missionary a military guard once US forces were ashore. Stevens and Wiltse had agreed that Atherton's property provided an alternative camp site, and Wiltse now gave Swinburne approval to proceed there.

When Swinburne returned to the head of his troops, Lieutenant Coffman mentioned spotting John T. Waterhouse, and told his superior that he believed Mr. Waterhouse owned a brand new, three-story hotel nearby, on Nuuanu Avenue–ideal accommodation for the battalion. Swinburne quickly dismissed the idea. He may have become aware that Waterhouse's son Henry was a member of the Committee of Safety, and the need for neutrality would not permit Swinburne to consider quartering his US forces in a building associated with one of the sides in the Hawaiian political conflict. Swinburne ordered 'quick march.'

With band playing, the American sailors marched along King Street toward Waikiki, which was then an outlying resort lined with beach-houses of the wealthy but not a single hotel. Five miles from downtown Honolulu, Waikiki was separated from the city by acres of palm groves and watery taro fields. Half a mile out of the downtown area, and in darkness now, Swinburne again halted his column, this time outside J. B. Atherton's property. Atherton, an American, readily agreed to Swinburne's request for a place where his troops could shelter, and, as light rain began to fall, the men from the *Boston* were allowed to stack arms and spread among the trees covering the missionary's sprawling property.

Committee of Safety leader Henry Waterhouse lived directly next door to the American Legation on Nuuanu Avenue. He had made a point of hurrying home to watch for the expected appearance of US troops at the legation, and was standing at his front gate delightedly observing the party of US Marines sent by Lieutenant Commander Swinburne come marching smartly up the avenue and in the legation gate. Now, Henry heard a voice calling his name. Turning, he saw a figure riding toward him–Sam Damon, the wealthy Honolulu banker, a fellow member of the Central Union Church and a family friend.

Damon had been out of town all day, at Monoalua. In the early evening, unaware that US forces had landed in Honolulu, he had ridden back into town and was turning into Nuuanu Avenue when he saw the US marines entering the American Legation. From the back of his horse, Damon saw Waterhouse standing at his front gate watching the marines–and looking 'very much strained and excited' in Damon's opinion.

"Henry, what does all this mean?" Damon called to Waterhouse.

"It's all up," Waterhouse excitedly replied. All up for the queen, he meant.

Damon was later to recall that there was a confident air about Waterhouse, and, in Damon's opinion 'he evinced a feeling of security.'[244] Waterhouse, made to feel secure by the landing of US forces, informed Damon that he intended calling a meeting of the Committee of Safety and its supporters at his house that evening. The Tasmanian revealed that the purpose of the meeting would be the discussion of formation of a Provisional Government to replace the queen and her cabinet. What was more, Waterhouse invited Damon to attend that meeting, and to play a role in that Provisional Government.

Telling Waterhouse that he would think on it, Damon rode on, deeply troubled.

* * *

A little after 5.00, as soon as Premier Sam Parker learned, to his shock and chagrin, that US troops had been landed from the *Boston* and were in the city, he hurried to the Pacific Club and sought out the Governor of Oahu, Archie Cleghorn. While Parker was responsible for paying Hawaii's troops, Cleghorn was officially the nation's military commander in chief.

Parker took Frank P. Hastings along with him. Hastings was Clerk of the Foreign Office, which made him chief of the Foreign Ministry under the minister. American-born, Hastings had nineteen years experience in foreign affairs, having started out at the US State Department in Washington DC. After locating Cleghorn, Parker gave Hastings the job of writing two letters to US ambassador John Stevens. One was from Parker, as Minister for Foreign Relations, the other from Cleghorn, as Governor of Oahu and commander in chief. Both were official letters of protest from the Hawaiian Government.

'The troops from the USS *Boston* were landed in this port at 5 o'clock this evening without the request or knowledge of Her Majesty's Government,' said the letter which the premier signed. 'As the situation is one which does not call for interference on the part of the United States Government, my colleagues and myself would most respectfully request of Your Excellency the authority upon which this action was taken. I would also add that any protection that may have been necessary for the American Legation or for American property and interests in this city would have been cheerfully furnished by Her Majesty's Government.'[245]

The letter from Governor Cleghorn likewise protested the landing without permission, and noted, 'I am compelled to impress upon Your Excellency the international questions involved on this matter and the grave responsibilities hereby assumed.'[246] What Cleghorn was saying between the lines was that, under international law, Stevens had committed the US to an act of military hostility against a foreign nation. In fact, technically, Hawaii and the United States were now at war, although Parker and Cleghorn would never have alluded to that, for they knew that if it came to blows between Hawaiian and American forces the 8-inch guns of the *Boston*, if employed, could level Honolulu. The Hawaiians were totally at the mercy of the American invasion force, and Parker, Cleghorn and Stevens all knew it.

Once the letters of protest were signed, and copies made, Parker had them hand-delivered to Ambassador Stevens.

Telephones jangled around Honolulu as Henry Waterhouse summoned annexationist colleagues to meet at his house that evening at 7.00. In his own words, Waterhouse was determined that they 'get everything in shape' prior to taking action next day, now that they could boast the backing of US troops.[247] For, with the forces of the Queen occupying defensive positions in the city and showing that they were ready to fight any rebel attempt to take over, Waterhouse was aware that some of his colleagues–Thurston in particular–had suddenly lost their revolutionary fervor.

The response to the Tasmanian's summons was, for him, disappointing. Apart from the irrepressible chairman of the Committee of Safety, American Henry Cooper, the only other members of the Committee to turn up were William Smith, Arthur Brown, and Theodore Lansing. Not only did Lorrin Thurston claim to be unwell and unable to leave his bed, a minor epidemic seemed to wash through annexationist circles that evening, with both lawyer William Castle and ship-owner William Wilder professing sudden illness and sending their apologies. Castle and Wilder, it seems, shared Thurston's fear that the US troops had landed too early, without legal justification, and inconveniently prior to the annexationists being ready to move against the queen's government.

Despite this crisis of confidence among many of their colleagues, Waterhouse and Cooper plowed on. The five Committee members were joined at Waterhouse's residence by another enthusiast, young Charles Carter, by John Soper, the former major of the Honolulu Rifles, and by Fred Wundenberg, clerk of the supreme court (and government spy). This group of eight agreed that the Provisional Government should consist of four ministers in the same portfolios that currently existed. But instead of the foreign minister being the premier, he would take the title of President, and would serve as both head of government and head of state.

Who would be that president? Sanford Dole's name was immediately suggested, probably by Waterhouse. If making Dole the figurehead of their new government was not Waterhouse's idea, he certainly quickly endorsed it, for it made great sense. Dole, who had been connected with the annexation movement from the outset, had the reputation and gravitas, as a serving supreme court judge, for the role. Waterhouse would also have known that Dole was a vain man who could be manipulated. A messenger was sent to invite Dole to join the meeting at Waterhouse's residence.

When Dole arrived, he was promptly offered the post of President of the revolutionary Provisional Government of Hawaii by Waterhouse and Cooper. Dole did not rush to reply. 'He debated it in his mind,' Waterhouse later said. 'He wanted to think it over until morning.' Told that the Committee of Safety would meet again next morning at 8.00 at Smith's law office, Dole said that he would give the Committee his final answer then.[248]

Once Dole took his leave, Waterhouse and his companions discussed the military requirements of the overthrow. It was all very well having the moral support of the landed US forces, but when it came down to it the annexationists would need their own little army to affect the overthrow of the queen and her government. They thought that they could round up a hundred men. But who would lead them? 'Major' Soper was promptly offered the military command by Waterhouse and Cooper, with the rank of colonel. Soper had played a leading role in the government's defeat of Wilcox's redshirts in 1889. But the Englishman, tall, thin, with a shiny bald head and extravagant mustache and side-whiskers, was reticent about accepting the role.

"I would rather be with the marshal," Soper frankly responded, meaning he thought the other side would have a distinct advantage in any conflict of arms.[249]

Marshal Wilson had the trained men, and the firepower. Even when Waterhouse revealed something that only the members of the Committee of Safety knew–that there was a contraband shipment of Springfield rifles and ammunition sitting at Hall and Sons, waiting to be collected by the annexationists, Soper was not enthusiastic. The five members of the Committee of Safety present then revealed to Soper that the US ambassador had agreed to support the queen's overthrow, but still the Englishman had his doubts. So, two members of the Committee–almost certainly Waterhouse and Cooper–then took Soper from the meeting next door to the American Legation, to meet with Ambassador Stevens.

According to Fred Wundenberg, when the trio rejoined the meeting at Waterhouse's house a little later, they came back saying that Stevens had given his assurance that any proclamation abrogating the monarchy and establishing a provisional government read 'at the Government Building, or at any other building in Honolulu, for that matter, would receive his immediate recognition.' This finally convinced Soper to throw in his lot with the conspirators. He departed the meeting authorized to form several companies of volunteers and to commission reliable men as officers of the insurgent force.[250]

One of Soper's first recruits would be Charles Ziegler, who headed a society of men of German descent called the Three Hundred. Another was John Good; like Soper, a Honolulu Rifles veteran, Good had the rank of captain bestowed on him, and was appointed by Soper to serve as his ordnance officer. Oscar White, secretary of Hall and Sons, where the crucial secret arms cache lay, was given the rank of lieutenant.

As Henry Waterhouse's seven fellow conspirators departed his home to prepare for the next day's coup attempt, he knew that if he did not continue to drive this revolution forward, now that the courage of Thurston and others had failed them, it would crumble away to nothing.

Bernice Piilani Irwin, a teacher at St Andrews Priory School in Honolulu, that evening learned of the uninvited landing of US troops in her country. Her all-girls school stood behind the Anglican St. Andrews Cathedral on Beretania Street, and was contiguous with the back yard of Washington Place, the family home that Queen Liliuokalani had inherited from her late husband John Dominis.

Bernice and her sister had both attended the Priory School, and only recently, Bernice, who was now in her late teens, had joined the teaching staff. And she was hopping mad. 'We learned that troops from the USS *Boston* had been landed at the order of the American Minister, John L. Stevens,' she was to recall. 'The request was ostensibly "to protect Americans and their interests." Protect them from what, I wanted to know?'[251]

The city was as quiet and peaceful as on any other Monday night. So tranquil was it, that, in the early evening, the men in the temporary US Navy encampment at the Atherton property heard, from the far distance, the sound of band music on the still night air. Back in downtown Honolulu, the Royal Hawaiian Band, an adjunct of the Household Guard, gave a scheduled recital in the grounds of the Hawaiian Hotel. The recital was well attended. None of the concert-goers feared the riot, arson and pillage which Captain Wiltse and Ambassador Stevens were to claim would have broken out at any moment had they not landed their troops.

Not long after 9.00, an aide to Captain Wiltse reported to Lieutenant Commander Swinburne at the Atherton property, bringing new orders. Wiltse had telephoned ambassador Stevens with the report that Swinburne could not secure the Opera House, but Stevens was determined that the US troops be quartered beside the Government Building. Stevens had then personally attempted to gain permission to use the Opera House by contacting Claus Spreckels' deputy in the kingdom, William Giffard, who controlled the building.

But Giffard had flatly refused to hire out the Opera House to the US Government; he had no intention of aiding the United States in an illegal occupation of Honolulu. Giffard's official excuse for refusing to allow Swinburne to use the Opera House was that, 'if any damage occurred while the American troops occupied it, it would affect the insurance, as the building was liable to be damaged.' Giffard added that after government forces had occupied the Opera House in 1889 at the time of Wilcox's redshirt rebellion, it had cost a thousand dollars to repair the damage done by Wilcox's two cannonballs.[252]

Stevens had not given up. He had secured a building that would be just as advantageous to his plans as the Opera House. Lieutenant Commander Swinburne was ordered to march the battalion to Arion Hall, which was situated directly behind the Opera House. So, the *Boston*'s sailors were ordered to pack up their things and fall in, in marching order. Soon, their knapsacks, bedrolls and rifles were on their backs, and the battalion was tramping back down King Street. To make the battalion's return downtown less conspicuous, Swinburne ordered the bandsmen's drums and instruments to remain silent. By 10.00, the column had reached Arion Hall. A single-story wooden building with wide verandas front and back, it had a large yard at the rear, called the Gilson Yard. The entire lot was bounded by a picket fence five to six feet high.

Before the troops could take over Arion Hall and lay out their bedrolls, they had to clear the building of pews. For, Arion Hall, which had been built by the government during the reign of King Kalakaua, was leased to G. J. Waller, on behalf of the Mormon Church in Honolulu, which used it as their house of worship. It was Waller, an American, who had approved the US ambassador's request for use of the hall.

Lieutenant De Witt Coffman, commanding one of Swinburne's companies, would later testify that he felt the choice of Arion Hall as the site of the force's camp very poor indeed if the true intent was to protect American lives and property in Honolulu, for the place was well away from American-owned businesses and residences.[253] But there was an ulterior and very strategic motive behind its acquisition by Captain Wiltse; Arion Hall stood right beside the Government Building, with just a narrow alleyway separating the two structures. Now, the US forces were in a position to influence events in the contest between Government and annexationists, as Stevens and Wiltse had intended when they planned to make the Opera House the shore base for US forces. For, both men knew how critical the Government Building was in the plan for the annexationists' coup and Stevens' intended recognition of the rebel government.

Said Lieutenant Lucien Young, who was now appointed officer of the day by Swinburne. 'I soon saw that this was the best strategical position in the city for the main body of the troops to encamp.' That is, strategic in terms of supporting the rebels and intimidating the queen. Young posted armed pickets around the Arion Hall lot, and set up his cannon and Gatling gun.[254] Later, when questioned, neither Young nor anyone else from the US Navy shore contingent, nor from the annexationist side, would confirm the direction that these guns were pointed; all developed amnesia over this point.

From her palace, Queen Liliuokalani saw the US Navy's guns, and noted that they were pointing her way, toward the palace. She was at a loss as to why the US troops had come ashore in the first place. 'Why had they landed when everything was at peace?' she asked. 'I was told that it was for the safety of the American citizens and the protection of their interests. Then, why had they not gone to the (American) residences, instead of drawing in line in front of the palace gates, with guns pointed at us, when I was living with my people in the palace?'[255]

Once his guns had been pointed and sentries set, Young, with a holstered pistol on his hip, took up a watching position in front of the Opera House, looking directly at the palace across the street. He would have been surprised to learn that, from the darkened Government Building next door, he was in turn being closely watched by Hawaiian police captain Robert Parker Waipa, who was stationed there all night. Parker Waipa, one of Hawaii's finest marksmen, may have even drawn a bead on him with his rifle.

At 10.00 p.m. just as the American sailors were occupying Arion Hall, out on the harbor there was activity, as the Oceanic Line's ten-year-old, 3,000 ton steamer SS *Alemeda* got under way. She was commencing a journey across the Pacific that would end in Sydney in the first week of February. Among her passengers was the visitor who would tell Sydney's *Daily Telegraph* about the two mass meetings in Honolulu that afternoon. The *Alameda* also carried American and Hawaiian mails for Samoa, New Zealand and Australia. And, in the purser's safe, the ship carried a confidential official dispatch from Hawaiian premier and foreign minister Sam Parker, addressed to the Hawaiian vice consul in Auckland, New Zealand.

Sam Parker was to come in for considerable criticism from Hawaiians during his own lifetime, and after it, for what was perceived as his weak performance during this crisis of January 14-17, 1893. Parker was by nature a gentle, genial man. One of the *Boston*'s officers, Charles Laird, who came to know and like him while based in Hawaii, described him as 'more a big boy than a man.'[256] Perhaps an aggressive attitude may have paid dividends in this crisis, perhaps not. Parker chose to employ good sense and diplomacy. The problem was, his opponents did not. But Parker was no fool, as evidenced by the contents of the confidential dispatch to his consul in New Zealand.

Parker had not expected the US to land troops in Honolulu without invitation or permission. It had shaken him up, but he was soon thinking on his feet. Parker knew how the English language press in Honolulu would report the events of the last few days—in favor of the annexationists and against his queen. He also knew that the San Francisco papers would pick up those same reports and run them, and that papers across the United States would follow suit. Between the time that the US troops

landed and the *Alameda* sailed, Parker had written a summary of
the events of the past three days, from the Hawaiian Government's
perspective, making it clear that ambassador Stevens had acted in
contravention of international law in landing US troops.

The Hawaiian consul in Auckland was instructed by Parker
to distribute this summary to the press in New Zealand and
Australia, and to send it on to Great Britain, so that the Hawaiian
Government's position became known throughout the world.
Ultimately, too, he knew, if his version of events were to appear
in the London press, it would as a matter of course be reprinted
in the influential papers in Washington, New York and Chicago.
This was to be the first Hawaiian shot in a protracted propaganda
war that lay ahead.

Lieutenant Lucien Young had not been sitting on the steps to
the Opera House long when several local Americans known to
him approached. Young employed these men 'to scour the town
and obtain all information possible of the situation, disposition
and number of troops on each side.' Reports from Young's spies
would come in several times during the night, and from these he
learned that, apart from patrolling plainclothes special constables,
the government had no forces on the streets. According to the
informants, too, there were sixty Household Guards at the
Palace and the barracks, and eighty police at police headquarters,
making a total of 140 armed men on the government side.[257] Both
these figures would prove to be well below the true numbers.

Young would also claim that he received reports that the
annexationists were massing 175 armed men in three different
places in the city ready for action next day.[258] This was either
Young's invention, or he was misled by an agent of John Soper,
sent to let the US forces believe that the insurgents were mounting
a formidable threat to the queen's forces as a justification for
the continued presence of US troops. No other source, and
particularly no annexationist source, would repeat such a claim.
At this point, the annexationists had neither the arms nor the
men. The only armed forces in Honolulu that night were those of
the Kingdom of Hawaii and of the United States.

Before long, Deputy Marshal John A. Mehrten paid Lieutenant
Young a visit. Mehrten, who had been born in Boston and was
in his thirties, passed on a message from Marshal Wilson, asking

if Young required any assistance. Young replied that he and his troops were in no need of assistance, and gave Mehrten a guided tour of the American camp. As the deputy marshal departed, he promised to send the lieutenant a bottle of liquor, which he later did.

Mehrten reported back to Marshal Wilson at the police station, where every foot of spare floor space was occupied by the beds of the police and reservists who thronged the building. Now that Wilson knew from his deputy that the bulk of the US troops had occupied Arion Hall, he guessed that the Government Building next door would be a prime target for the annexationists once they attempted their coup. Wilson issued orders for one hundred of his men to report to Captain Parker Waipa at the Government Building first thing next morning and prepare to defend it.

There would not be much sleep for any side that night. The US troops at Arion Hall were plagued by mosquitoes. And twice during the night Lieutenant Young led detachments of US sailors to the sites of reported arson, to find outbuildings in flame, with the fires apparently set by boys. But no lives were in danger. On the Hawaiian Government side, Wilson and his men at the police station, and Nowlein and his men at the palace and barracks, were on high alert. On the annexationist side, passionate leaders such as Henry Cooper would have found it difficult to sleep for excitement. Lorrin Thurston, meanwhile, would pass the night worrying that his revolution was about to fail.

Throughout Honolulu, annexationists and government ministers would sleep fitfully. And at the palace, Queen Liliuokalani spent her last night before her life, and the history of Hawaii, changed forever.

PHOTOS

A statue of the ill-fated Princess Kaiulani, where once the young beauty's Waikiki beach house stood. Her property is now home to a hotel.

Iolani Barracks in Honolulu once quartered Hawaiian troops of the royal bodyguard.

This statue of deposed Queen Liliuokalani standing outside the walls of the Iolani Palace in Honolulu is draped with flowers by Hawaiians year-round.

The Iolani Palace, Honolulu. Queen Liliuokalani's home during her reign, it became her prison after her 1893 overthrow.

Best known to viewers worldwide as the headquarters of the fictional Hawaii Five-O Taskforce in the remake of the 'Hawaii Five-O' television series, the Aliiolani Hale in Honolulu, known today as the Judiciary Building, was the Government Building at the centre of the armed overthrow of Hawaii's Queen in January, 1893. The statue out front is of King Kamehameha the Great, revered founder of the Hawaiian Kingdom.

Entrance to the vault at Mauna ‘Ala where lie the remains of twenty-one Hawaiian royals including the kingdom's last ruler, Queen Liliuokalani.

William Kaihe'ekai Maioho, Curator of the Royal Mausoleum, Mauna 'Ala, puts the key in the lock of the mausoleum's vault.

Taking Hawaii author Stephen Dando-Collins outside Washington Place, Queen Liliuokalani's private residence in Honolulu, where the queen spent the years following her overthrow.

Famed Diamond Head, seen from Kapiolani Park. From this park, forces of the rebel government shelled royalists holed up on top of Diamond Head during the failed counter-coup of 1895.

15.

PREPARING TO STRIKE

THE COMMITTEE OF SAFETY CONVENED AT 8.00 a.m. on Tuesday, January 17, at their headquarters, William Smith's law office on Fort Street. Lorrin Thurston and William Castle were again conspicuous by their absence, but the other 'sick' committeeman William Wilder turned up, as did several other leading white businessmen who were not members of the Committee.

As promised, Sanford Dole came to the meeting to give his answer to the offer of the presidency of the Provisional Government once it was established. When he arrived, he noticed several large, uniformed, but unarmed Hawaiian policemen stationed across the street, watching the Smith office and all who came and went. Once he joined the meeting, Dole told the crowded office that he had thought hard on the situation overnight, and was inclined to feel that if Liliuokalani was removed she should be replaced by her heir apparent, the young Princess Kaiulani. Adopting the same line as the princess's father, Governor Cleghorn, Dole suggested that a board of regents be established to rule in Kaiulani's name until she came of age.

Judge Hartwell endorsed this idea, but he and Dole were in a meager minority; Henry Waterhouse and the others present all vetoed it. Now that US troops were ashore, the annexationists would accept nothing less than a total overthrow of Hawaii's current political system and annexation by the United States. The Committee put it to Dole that he either accept the presidency on those terms, or decline it. 'I returned home to breakfast, with my mind fairly well made up to accept the position,' Dole was to write.[259]

John Soper reported to the Committee that he expected that Ziegler's German militia could be relied on to back the Committee of Safety once it moved against the government, and it was agreed that all parties should converge on the Government Building at 3.00 p.m. that afternoon, where Cooper, as chairman of the Committee, would read a proclamation declaring Liliuokalani deposed and announcing the formation of a provisional government.

This timing was influenced by the fact that Henry Waterhouse and fellow members of the Committee had learned, from an unidentified informant in government ranks, that Marshal Wilson was planning to transfer one hundred armed men to the Government Building that morning. The Committee also knew, again from their undisclosed source, that by the middle of the day Marshal Wilson would be forced by higher authority to remove those men from the Government Building, leaving it undefended and open to seizure by the Committee.

A timetable was set down by the Committee. At 2.00 p.m. they would all gather here at Smith's offices, ready for action. At 2.30, John Good and several reliable men would retrieve the arms cache from Hall and Sons and take the weapons and ammunition to the old Armory, where Charles Ziegler and his men were to assemble. Just before 3.00, the Committee would set off for the Government Building from Smith's office, and Ziegler's company, now armed with the weapons from Hall and Sons, would march there from the Armory. All parties would converge at the Government Building at the same time, and at 3.00, Cooper would read the Committee's proclamation from the Government Building's steps. Shortly after, Ambassador Stevens would recognize the Provisional Government as the de facto government of Hawaii. And that would be that.

Thurston had promised to write the proclamation that Cooper was to read, and had taken away Smith's notes on the subject. The Committee therefore dispatched a messenger around the corner to Thurston's Merchant Street office to see if his law clerk Fred Peterson could obtain the draft for them. The Committee, which continued to sit through the morning, now decided the shape of the Provisional Government. It would consist of a four-man Executive Council, or cabinet, headed, they felt certain, by

Sanford Dole. The other executive councilors would be Committee of Safety members William Smith and Peter Jones, plus Scotsman James A. King, a former sea captain in the employ of William Wilder. In addition to the Executive Council, there would be a fourteen-member Advisory Council, chosen by the Committee of Safety and made up of Committee of Safety members and their friends, which would take the place of an elected legislature.

It was expected that this governmental structure would only be short-lived–just several months–until the US Congress had ratified annexation. To ensure that annexation was brought forward without delay, it was agreed by the Committee of Safety that, as soon as government was in their hands, they would send a delegation to Washington seeking annexation by the US. William Wilder offered to take one of his steamers, the relatively new 785-ton *Claudine*, off the inter-island run and charter her to the Committee of Safety, for three hundred dollars a day, to whisk a delegation from the Committee to San Francisco on the first leg of that mission to Washington. It was agreed that Wilder's offer should be taken up, and Wilder sent instructions to the Inter-Island Shipping Company to have the *Claudine*, which was then docked in Honolulu, readied to sail with just a few hours notice.

It was also agreed that Lorrin Thurston should head this delegation to Washington. Thurston was not particularly well-liked by a number of his fellow conspirators, and his sudden bout of ill health, just when he was needed most, did not endear him to his colleagues. In Washington, Thurston, first among Hawaii's annexationists, could use his silver tongue to push the case before Congress. And, while Thurston was in Washington, others could run Hawaii without fear of interference from him. Two other delegates were also chosen for the mission to Washington–the other absentee Committee member, William Castle, and the owner of the *Claudine*, William Wilder.

A little after 8.30, Thurston's law clerk Fred Peterson appeared on his employer's Judd Street doorstep. Shown into his boss's bedroom, the clerk found Thurston in bed. Peterson told Thurston that he had been sent by the Committee of Safety to procure the proclamation to be used in the overthrow of the queen, as the Committee expected to use it that afternoon.

'I had not done a stroke of work on it,' Thurston later

confessed, 'and I did not know what had become of the notes on the subject.' He sent Peterson back to his office downtown to collect his typewriter, and when the clerk returned, not long after 9.00, he set the machine up on a table in his master's bedroom. Thurston, from his bed, began dictating the document. 'Although I was still exhausted,' Thurston said, 'the exigencies were such that I had to supply the proclamation.'[260]

At 9.00 a.m., Sam Damon arrived at the Iolani Palace and asked to see Her Majesty the Queen. Liliuokalani considered Damon one of her most trusted advisers. Damon's missionary father, Reverend Samuel C. Damon, had presided over her wedding to John Dominis, and Liliuokalani was personally in considerable financial debt to banker Damon. She immediately had him shown up to see her in the parlor.

'He told me that he had been asked to join a revolutionary council, but had declined,' the queen later wrote. As this revolutionary council only came under discussion by the Committee of Safety that same morning, Damon must have attended, and come directly from, the 8.00 a.m. meeting at the Smith law office. 'He asked me what he should do,' the queen recalled, 'and whether he should join the advisory or executive council, suggesting that perhaps he could be of service to me.' The idea of having a friend among the enemy hierarchy appealed to Liliuokalani. 'So I told him to join the advisory council.' But, she was to say, 'I had no idea that they intended to establish a new government.'[261]

Damon seems to have deliberately misled the queen into believing that he was still on her side. She would continue to believe it for months to come. Yet, having seen the American troops in Honolulu the previous evening, Damon had apparently come to the conclusion by Tuesday morning that the monarchy was doomed, and had decided to join the winning side, while attempting to prevent any blood being split. Damon returned to the Committee of Safety meeting at Smith's office to advise that he was prepared to serve in the Provisional Government. From this point forward, he would always refer to the revolutionaries in terms of 'we' and 'us.'

The Committee of Safety was so delighted to have the influential banker and defecting royalist in its ranks that it appointed him president of their Advisory Council. Before long, too, they would create a new position for him in the Executive Council, that of vice president, making him second only in the official revolutionary hierarchy to Dole.

While the Committee of Safety was meeting at Fort Street, just around the corner in Merchant Street the Parker cabinet met at the fortified police headquarters, which, while US troops remained on shore, Premier Parker had decided to make the headquarters of the government. The office of Deputy Marshal Mehrten became the temporary Cabinet Room.

Now, Attorney General Arthur Peterson instructed Marshal Wilson to cancel his intended transfer of one hundred men to the Government Building. Wilson was outraged, but Peterson was backed up by Parker and the remainder of the cabinet. Putting one hundred armed men in the Government Building, just seventy-five yards from the US Navy force at Arion Hall, was much too provocative in the opinion of the attorney general. He dreaded the possibility that the US might take this as an act of war, and open fire. Just one man with an itchy trigger finger could ignite a war, the same way that a lone rifleman at the Opera House had sparked hostilities in 1889. The nervous attorney general even instructed Wilson to remove Captain Parker Waipa from the Government building, to ensure the Americans were not incited by the sight of an armed man in uniform.

So it was that no Government forces were sent to the Government Building, and Captain Parker Waipa was recalled to police headquarters. Just a single policeman, special constable Charles McCarthy, was now left at the Government Building. The rifles and ammunition sent to the Government Building in the night at McCarthy's request were left there, stored, not in the attorney general's office as he had suggested, but in the office of the Interior Department, at the front of building, with the intention that McCarthy could arm the civilian clerks working in the Government Building to defend it.

The way was now open for the Committee of Safety to occupy the building unopposed by regular forces, declare the queen overthrown, and be recognized by the US ambassador. Either Attorney General Peterson was a party to the conspiracy to overthrow his queen, and deliberately had the Government

Building demilitarized, or, in his dread of the United States Government, he was intimidated by the presence of US troops at Arion Hall into playing right into the hands of the annexationists. The fact that Henry Waterhouse and the rump of the Committee of Safety knew in advance that Peterson would instruct Wilson not to send troops to the Government Building strongly suggests that Peterson was, at this point, in league with them.

During the late morning, Sanford Dole, having decided to accept the post of President of the Provisional Government, went to the courthouse, tidied up several legal matters, then wrote his resignation from the bench of the supreme court. After giving the resignation to a messenger with instructions to deliver it to the attorney general and cabinet at police headquarters, Dole proceeded to William Smith's office, where the Committee of Safety was still in session.

To the delight of the Committee, Dole confirmed that he would head up the new government, and told them that he had sent in his resignation as an associate justice. Law clerk Fred Peterson had just delivered Thurston's draft for the all-important document which was to be proclaimed that afternoon at the Government Building, and by this time the Committee had received information that the marshal's order to send one hundred men to the Government Building had been rescinded. The road seemed clear. With a copy of the proclamation in his pocket, and, agreeing to join the Committee back here at 2.00 prior to launching their coup at 3.00, Dole went home for lunch.

By 11.00 a.m., Marshal Wilson had received word from his spy close to the Committee of Safety that the Committee intended seizing one or more Government buildings at 3.00 that afternoon, after which it would proclaim a new government. Wilson immediately sent word to Major Nowlein at the Iolani Palace to be ready to repel an assault at 3.00, in case the rebel move was directed at the palace or the barracks, and he himself put his own force at police headquarters on full alert.

Despite the spy's report, and perhaps because of it, Premier Parker was determined not to give up hope of suppressing the annexationist revolt. During the middle of the morning, searching around for support for the queen's government, the premier sent messages to the leading members of the foreign diplomatic corps in Honolulu, inviting them to meet with the full cabinet at police headquarters.

Four ambassadors and consuls accepted the invitation. The most senior and most influential of these was James Wodehouse, British minister to the Kingdom of Hawaii for many years past. Wodehouse's son Hay was the man who had lobbed dynamite bombs onto the roof of the Bungalow during the 1889 Redshirt Rebellion. Hay Wodehouse had since married Annie Cleghorn, a daughter of Governor Cleghorn and half sister of Princess Kaiulani. Minister Wodehouse mixed in the royal circle and had been a close and respected adviser to both Queen Liliuokalani and her predecessor King Kalakaua.

Parker reasoned that if Wodehouse threw his support, and therefore the British Government's support, behind the queen's government, there was yet hope that the US troops now in Honolulu would refrain from becoming involved in the rebellion on the side of the annexationists–for fear of sparking a conflict with Britain. This would allow the government to move in and arrest the rebels without worrying about American military interference.

The other diplomatic representatives who attended the meeting with Parker and his cabinet colleagues were Ambassador Carnavara, representing Portugal, Ambassador Vizavona, representing France, and Mr. Fujii, the Japanese consul general. As a matter of course, and form, John Stevens of the United States was also invited, but he declined the invitation–'which did not surprise us,' Finance Minister Cornwell was to say, 'knowing his sympathy for the revolutionists.'[262] Stevens was suddenly feeling sickly, and 'he sent word that he was not well enough' to attend the meeting, Sam Parker would recall.[263]

The cabinet informed the diplomats that 'we had heard that there was going to be trouble,' and Premier Parker went on to ask for the support of the foreign governments. But, led by Britain's Wodehouse, the ambassadors all shook their heads. 'The advice from them was to offer no resistance,' said Parker. 'Not to have any bloodshed, because they all knew we had a big force.'[264] This, to Parker, was the most frustrating thing of all–from the intelligence that Marshal Wilson had gathered, the number of men whom the Committee of Safety could rely on when push came to shove and the bullets were flying would be pitifully small compared to the forces now assembled under the marshal. The cabinet also knew that the ali'i in the royal ranks would be prepared to fight to their last drop of blood. Without the support of US forces, the Committee of Safety's coup was doomed to fail.

As the ambassadors departed police headquarters, Premier Parker was aware that the future of Hawaii's monarchy, and the little nation's independence, lay with the US troops now in Hawaii. Twice in the past, the Hawaiian Government had sought and received the aid of the US military when riot and rebellion had erupted in Honolulu. The US ambassador on those occasions had not even contemplated throwing US military support behind the rioters or rebels. So, Parker now held out the hope that the current US ambassador might be convinced to again support the Hawaiian Government in its time of need, rather than throw his support behind the rebels–as Marshal Wilson's spies were telling him could be expected.

Parker's cabinet colleagues Colburn and Cornwell had mentally surrendered by this point; they saw no point in opposing the Committee of Safety while Stevens supported them. Yet, with Marshal Wilson and his men making it very clear that they intended fighting the annexationists should they make a move to grab power, the two ministers could only see bloodshed as the outcome. Fearful for their own lives, the pair declared they would not leave the safety of police headquarters. So, when the premier urged the cabinet to go as a body to see ambassador Stevens and win his agreement to support the government in any conflict with the insurgents, only Attorney General Peterson found the courage to accompany him out to Nuuanu Avenue.

It was close to 1.00 p.m. when Lieutenant Commander Swinburne saw attorney Charlie Carter enter the yard at Arion Hall. Swinburne had kept his men busy all morning, some with military drills, others digging latrines and drains. The lieutenant commander had absolutely no idea what the situation was in the city as regards the Government and the annexationists, but he was about to find out from the young attorney, whom had come to know reasonably well since the *Boston*'s stationing at Honolulu.

"It is the intention of the Committee of Safety to take possession of the Government Building," Carter blithely informed the US

Navy officer. "You will recognize them by Mr. Dole. You know Mr. Dole–he is the tallest man in the party. If you see him in the party you will know what he is doing. They are going to take possession of the Government Building."[265]

Determined to play a middle course, Swinburne thanked Carter for the information, but made no comment or commitment.

Carter now spotted Swinburne's written orders from Captain Wiltse, which lay open on a table. "Have you any objection to my seeing your orders?" he asked.[266]

Swinburne said that he had no objection, and handed the piece of paper to Carter.

The attorney read the orders, which, in just a few short paragraphs, were concise and to the point. As Carter was handing the orders back to him, Swinburne said, "You see my orders are to protect the legation, the consulate, and the lives and property of American citizens, and to assist in preserving order. I do not know how to interpret that. I can do it in but one way. If the queen calls upon me to preserve order, I am going to do it."[267]

This came as a rude shock to Charlie Carter, who had been led to expect that the US troops would support the Committee of Safety, not the queen. He nodded, then turned and hurriedly left the Arion Hall grounds.

At 1.30, Sanford Dole left home and set off for the Smith law office and his appointment with destiny. But first, he diverted to the American Legation on Nuuanu Avenue.

Ambassador Stevens saw Dole at once, and Dole informed him of the Committee of Safety's plans for the afternoon, and handed him a duplicate copy of a letter that Dole hoped to send him shortly after 3.00 that afternoon, 'announcing the abrogation of the monarchy and the organization of a new government in its place,' and seeking the US ambassador's official recognition of that government.

As Dole was leaving, Stevens said to him, "I think you have a great opportunity."[268]

Dole had not long departed the legation when, at 2.00, a hack pulled up and Premier Parker and Attorney General Peterson stepped out. A garbled response had been received to the previous evening's two Hawaiian Government letters of protest at the unauthorized landing of US forces. Late that morning,

Stevens had written to Parker and Cleghorn: 'My responsibility as the United States minister plenipotentiary at this critical time in Hawaiian affairs it is impossible for me to ignore. I assure you that in whatever responsibility the American diplomatic and naval representatives have assumed or may assume, we shall do our utmost to regard the welfare of all present and interests concerned.'[269]

Now, in the words of Attorney General Peterson, the two ministers had come 'to learn if possible the truth of the statements made publicly by the leading members of the so-called Committee of Safety to the effect that Mr. Stevens had promised that if a proclamation declaring a provisional government was issued he, (Mr. Stevens), on behalf of his government, would immediately recognize such government and support it with the United States forces at his command.'[270]

The two Hawaiian Government ministers walked past the US marines guarding the legation and were formally received by ambassador Stevens' new young military aide, Cadet Pringle, a naval cadet detached from the *Boston*'s crew by Captain Wiltse. After a short wait, Parker and Stevens were shown into the ambassador's office. They found Stevens lying on a sofa, affecting illness, 'as if in a weak and exhausted state,' said Peterson.[271] The epidemic affecting the backbone of key players in this coup had evidently reached Nuuanu Avenue.

Premier Parker began bluntly, by asking, in reference to the landing of US troops, "What's this all about?"[272]

"I gave orders," Stevens replied vaguely, speaking with apparent difficulty.[273]

"Mr. Stevens," said Peterson, "what action would be taken by you in case the insurgents attacked Her Majesty's Government, and the government called on you for assistance?"

"In that case, I could not come to the assistance of the government," Stevens answered croakily.

"What then, would be your action in case Her Majesty's Government should treat the insurgents as rebels and attack them and arrest them?" Peterson asked.

Stevens replied, "In that case, I should feel it my duty to interfere with the force at my command."[274]

Parker looked at Peterson with dismay. Both now knew, if they hadn't known it before, that the queen's goose was well and truly cooked–if Stevens followed through with this intention.

"I have made up my mind," Stevens went on, "that if any number of what I consider responsible citizens should ask my assistance in establishing a provisional government, I should grant that assistance and should recognize them as such and support them."[275]

On his way from visiting Stevens, Sanford Dole stopped in at Judd Street to briefly see Lorrin Thurston and collect drafts of two public decrees that Dole planned to publish once the Committee of Safety had seized power. Thurston's illness had seemingly rapidly improved, but still he was not associating with the Committee of Safety.

By 2.00, Dole rejoined the Committee of Safety at Smith's Fort Street office. Including himself, just eighteen men had arrived to participate in the afternoon's coup. But at least this was better than the turnout the previous evening at Henry Waterhouse's house. Sam Damon was here, having accepted Waterhouse's invitation of the previous evening to play a part in proceedings, along with Waterhouse himself and William Smith. During the morning, Waterhouse and Smith had done the rounds of their revolutionary colleagues, urging and cajoling them, trying to give them the courage to proceed, with the result that Charlie Carter and most of the remaining members of the Committee of Safety were now present.

John Soper, their military commander, was here, now looking resolute. William Wilder had again dragged himself from his sick bed. But neither Thurston or Castle came; the two lawyers, once so eloquent in the call for the Queen's removal, were convinced that the coup must fail and that prison and perhaps the hangman's noose awaited all who participated in it. Henry Waterhouse, who had never been particularly friendly with either Thurston or Castle, had not paid either a visit during the morning to try to talk them into turning up for the revolution. He was perfectly happy to proceed without either of them.

All present at Smith's office were tense; some, excited. At the request of Waterhouse, Smith and Cooper, Sanford Dole signed several rebel commissions, including one for John Soper as colonel of the Provisional Government's armed forces. Once Dole had done that, unable to sit still, he went out onto the sidewalk. Vehicles and pedestrians were passing, as on any other tropic Tuesday in Honolulu. Dole knew from Soper that, just down the street, John Good and his companions were at Hall and Sons, loading the Springfield rifles and ammunition into a wagon for delivery to Ziegler's men at the Armory. Across the street, the policemen that Dole had spotted that morning were still in place, continuing to watch the law office. 'What were the plans of the government regarding us?' Dole pondered to himself. 'The queen's opportunities for checking the movement against her royal status were fast slipping by, while the venture of the revolutionists, then still in suspense, was nearing solid ground.'[276]

Dole checked his fob watch–it was approaching 2.30. And then, from the direction of Hall and Sons, a police whistle began to blow. Summoned by the whistle, the police officers across the street suddenly came to life and set off at the run toward Hall and Sons.

At police headquarters, a plainclothes officer had reported to Marshal Wilson that he had seen a wagon driven by suspected annexationists go into the yard behind Hall and Sons on the corner of Fort and King.

One of the marshal's agents had informed him that the annexationists were planning to make a move of some kind at 3.00 that afternoon, and Hall and Sons was one of three Honolulu firms suspected of receiving contraband arms shipments in the past. The two pieces of information convinced Wilson that the wagon had been sent by the Committee of Safety to collect arms in preparation for their 3.00 o'clock move.

In response to the report about Hall and Sons, Wilson had sent a policemen to watch the store and be ready to prevent the wagon from leaving the store's yard. But as he thought on it, the marshal began to worry that, if they were collecting arms, the annexationists might be prepared to use them to force their way out of the yard. To be on the safe side, at around 2.25 p.m., Wilson handed two loaded pistols to special constable James W. Pratt, manager of the Mutual Telephone Company in Honolulu, and sent him on his way to join the officer watching the store with orders to prevent any weapons leaving Hall's.

With the pistols jammed in his belt, Special Constable Pratt left the sandbagged police building and walked quickly along busy Merchant Street. As he went, he passed the US Consulate, where an armed US marine stood sentry duty at the door. Pratt had reached the corner of Merchant and Fort, and was turning into Fort, with the Hall and Sons store just a block away. It was just on 2.30. It was then that Pratt heard a shot ring out from the direction of Hall and Sons.

16.

LAUNCHING THE COUP

JOHN GOOD'S ACT OF SHOOTING DOWN A policeman to enable his wagon, laden with arms and ammunition, to escape from Hall and Sons, set the Hawaiian coup in motion thirty minutes ahead of schedule. But it also served to draw a vast crowd to the site of the shooting, and to draw off the police officers who had been watching the rebel Committee of Safety's assembly point at William Smith's Fort Street law office. The Committee of Safety knew that this was the time to move.

'Colonel' John Soper left at once, planning to hurry to the Armory, from where he would send Ziegler's men to the Government Building once they had been armed with the weapons that John Good was to deliver to them. Soper would also round up all the other volunteers he could find. Fred McChesney dashed out the door and hailed a hack, planning to go home, grab his pistol, and then meet the other members of the Committee of Safety at the Government Building. 'Members of our party were restive and eager to start,' Sanford Dole would recall. But it was not a good idea for the unarmed Committee of Safety to arrive at the Government Building before they received the armed support of Ziegler's and Soper's men. 'We had to give time for their movement,' said Dole.[277]

There was also the question of whether the intelligence the Committee had received about the Government Building being free of Government forces was accurate. Sanford Dole, calm and cautious by nature, assigned former legislator Albert S. Wilcox the task of going to the Government Building and checking that everything was as hoped there. Wilcox apparently took a hack all the way there and back, for, said Dole, 'he returned in a few minutes and reported that everything was quiet, and the steps of the Opera House were occupied by a lot of Hawaiians.'[278]

Now, Dole announced, the Committee should set off for the Government Building. The group surged out the door of Smith's office, bent on making history. But once outside, there was disagreement about which route should be used. Henry Waterhouse wanted to go via Queen Street, which would take them to the rear of the Government Building. William Wilder backed him up, thinking this a route less likely to draw attention to them all. But Dole and Cooper wanted to take the more direct route, via Merchant Street, which would bring them out at Palace Square.

So, Waterhouse and Wilder set off on the Queen Street route, and the others followed the prominent, long-striding Dole and black-bearded Cooper as they took the Merchant Street route. As they made their way, several of them 'expected at every corner to be fired on.'[279]

There was now considerable activity in the streets. Hundreds of people were running to Fort Street, attracted by the shooting as ghouls everywhere are attracted to the site of accidents and bloodshed. Others, dreading more shooting, panicked, filling Merchant Street and clamoring to be allowed into the heavily defended police station.

The doors of police headquarters had been closed on Marshal Wilson's orders as soon as the shot rang out around the corner. The government forces bunkered down, expecting an assault at any moment. Inside, to Marshal Wilson's disgust, cabinet ministers Colburn and Cornwell 'rushed to the rear of the room and stood there trembling.'[280]

The crowd that had gathered on the Opera House steps had departed and hurried toward Fort Street and the scene of the shooting when, at 2.40, a panting man came rushing into the Arion Hall camp of the US Navy's landing force. He wore a business suit and hat, carried a Winchester rifle, and had an ammunition bandoleer draped over one shoulder. Lieutenant

Commander Swinburne did not know the man, but recognized him as an American as soon as he spoke.

"The police have attempted to stop our ammunition wagon," the man with the rifle gushed excitedly. "It was necessary for it to go on, and the policeman was shot and killed. There is a large crowd collected on Merchant Street. I was ordered to come and tell you."

"Who are you, and what is 'our ammunition wagon'?" Swinburne demanded, eyeing the man's Winchester.

"I belong to one of the companies raised by the Committee of Safety," said the man. He turned out to be Oscar White, secretary of E. O. Hall and Sons. As 'Captain' John Good had fled the scene of the shooting with the ammunition wagon, Good had yelled to 'Lieutenant' White to inform the US commander at Arion Hall of what had taken place. White had run all the way from Hall and Sons to the temporary US Navy camp. He now told Swinburne that the Committee of Safety's ammunition wagon had been loading at Hall and Sons since morning, and he repeated that it had been necessary to shoot the policemen when he tried to stop it leaving. Now Swinburne had the picture.

"Can I stay here at your camp until my company arrives?" the highly agitated White asked the lieutenant commander.

'He was an American citizen and could stay anywhere,' Swinburne was later to say.[281] He agreed to White remaining with the US force. Alerted now that the Committee of Safety had launched its bid for power, and that they meant to occupy the Government Building right next door, Swinburne ordered his men to assemble in the yard behind Arion Hall, there to stack their arms and remain in their companies and out of sight, with no one permitted to leave the premises. The astute Swinburne, who would in years to come be made a rear admiral and commander of the US Pacific Fleet, was determined that his men were not seen to play, nor play, any part in the drama that he now knew was about to play out at the Government Building.

As his men were being assembled by their petty officers, Swinburne and several of his officers, including Lieutenant Young, took station at the gate to the Arion Hall yard, looking across the alley-way to the Government Building seventy-five yards away. Rebel Oscar White joined him.

* * *

At police headquarters, news of the shooting of the police officer galvanized former attorney general Antone Rosa into taking the bull by the horns. The fact that the rebels were prepared to shoot down an unarmed policeman in cold blood sent a chill message, and, with Premier Parker and Attorney General Peterson not yet returned from their meeting with Ambassador Stevens at the American Legation, there was a possibility the two ministers had either been detained by the US marines at the legation, taken prisoner by the rebels, or, worse, had themselves been shot.

With cabinet ministers Colburn and Cornwell quaking in fear and apparently incapable of making any decisions, Rosa hurriedly wrote a note addressed to Ambassador Stevens. That note stated that 'certain treasonable persons' had claimed to have declared a provisional government in opposition to the lawful government, and asking, 'Has Your Excellency recognized said Provisional Government? And if not, Her Majesty's Government, under the above existing circumstances, respectfully requests the assistance of your government on preserving the peace of the country.'[282] Placing the letter in front of Colburn and Cornwell, Rosa had them both sign on behalf of the cabinet. Rosa then gave the letter to former legislator Charles L. Hopkins, who was serving as a special constable.

"Wait for an answer," Rosa instructed urgently.[283]

Hopkins pocketed the letter then made his way out into the crowded street and pushed his way through the throng. Hailing a hack at an intersection, Hopkins set off on his mission to the US Legation.

Four parties converged on the Government Building simultaneously. From Queen Street, Waterhouse and Wilder came up Mililani Street, the alley separating Arion Hall and the Government Building. Dole, Cooper and the larger group arrived via Palace Square, and came down Mililani Street to enter the Government Building's grounds via a side gate. Simultaneously, a hack pulled up; Fred McChesney jumped out, revolver in hand, and ran to join them. Seeing them all coming, Oscar White trotted across the alley from the Arion Hall gate and was waiting for all parties to join him at the Government Building's side gate.

Dole, his white beard flowing, and with a straw boater on his head, strode purposefully toward the gate, with Cooper and Damon close on his heels, and the others straggling along behind like schoolboys late for a bus. When banker Damon saw Oscar White alone at the gate, he was very surprised indeed. "Oscar, this is not very prudent for you to be here with only one rifle in this street," he said.[284]

Damon could hardly miss the fact that an armed sentry of the Household Guard stood at the palace gate across the street and another two on the palace steps, or that a light cannon mounted on the upper balcony of the palace by Guard commander Major Nowlein on Saturday was still in place and pointing in their direction. Most worrying of all, the annexationists seemed only able to muster Oscar White and a single rifle to enforce the queen's overthrow.

Charlie Carter, walking just behind Damon, sensed the banker's alarm. He quickly pointed out the US Navy sentries posted around Arion Hall and told Damon that he had personally spoken with the Navy's commander at Arion Hall little more than an hour earlier, on the very subject of US military support. He added, "After you are in possession of the Government Building the troops will support you."[285]

Carter was referring to US troops, and Damon seemed reassured by this. Damon was unaware that Carter was quite deliberately lying, having learned just the opposite from Lieutenant Commander Swinburne at Arion Hall–that, if called on to provide military support to anyone in this conflict, Swinburne intended providing that support to the queen and her government.

After collecting at the side gate, the group walked briskly past the statue of Kamehameha the Great and up the front steps of the Government Building. Fleetingly, Sanford Dole saw Special Constable Charles McCarthy standing in the Government Building doorway ahead. McCarthy, who was armed with nothing more than a police whistle, had never been told why the hundred government men that he had been expecting to join him never turned up. Now, seeing the weapons carried by Oscar White and Fred McChesney, he decided that he had no time to arm the clerks of the building and that discretion was the better part of valor. McCarthy withdrew inside and escaped out the back way to join the marshal and the cabinet at police headquarters. The pro-annexation press would later poke fun at McCarthy, calling him a one-man army for his solo stint as guardian of the Government Building on January 16-17.

The men who had come to declare themselves the new government of Hawaii gathered on the front veranda of the Government Building, by the front door, and summoned John A. Hassinger, American-born Clerk of the Interior Department, and demanded that he hand over the building to them. 'The demand was immediately complied with,' said Dole later; Hassinger would prove a compliant servant of the rebels.[286]

The revolutionists began a nervous wait for their military support to join them, urgently checking their watches as the time dragged by. As they waited, a dozen 'loafers' gathered at the foot of the steps and looked up at them as if they were curiosities in a sideshow. Members of the revolutionary party became extremely tense. Where were Ziegler's militia from the Armory? Where were the other armed men Soper was supposed to collect? 'We counted on a hundred men,' Fred McChesney was to say.[287] So, where were they? How could Sanford Dole declare the queen and her government overthrown if the Committee of Safety did not have the armed force to back their claim to power?

As 3.00 p.m. approached and there was still no sign of any armed support, banker Sam Damon began to fret. He had been led to believe that the US Navy force had been landed to support the overthrow of the queen. That was why he had changed sides, after all. So Damon was expecting US troops to now march on over from Arion Hall. But they didn't. And the annexationists' army was nonexistent. Damon was not the only one looking worried. 'With others, I was convinced that we were in a position of danger,' Damon later said. 'I could not imagine why we were there without being supported by American troops, prior to the troops coming from the Armory. We were not supported in any way.'

So, Damon took Charlie Carter aside. Where were the US troops, he demanded. 'He gave me to believe that we would be protected,' he said, 'and when we were not protected by them I wanted to know the reason why.'[288] Carter seems to have answered vaguely, perhaps suggesting that the US troops would appear at any moment.

The anxiety of the group got the better of them, and several leaders decided that they had better proceed without further delay to proclaim Liliuokalani overthrown and the Provisional Government in existence. The longer they waited, the more likely that government troops or police would arrive to arrest them all. If Carter was to be believed, once the revolutionists had claimed power they could expect US recognition and protection from arrest. But not before. Henry Cooper took the proclamation from his pocket.

There on the steps to the Government Building, Cooper, an American citizen who had been living in Hawaii for less than two years, proclaimed the nation's head of state dethroned and its constitutional government replaced. The proclamation, written by Lorrin Thurston, was relatively long, and took some fifteen minutes to read. As Cooper read, the clerks of the various departments in the Government Building, many of them of full or part Hawaiian blood, came out of their offices and clustered in the doorway behind the Committee of Safety to find out what was going on.

Fred Wundenberg, the clerk of the supreme court, was among these civil servants watching the rebel proceedings. Having attended most of the meetings of the Committee of Safety, Wundenberg knew exactly what was going on. But even he was bemused by what he perceived as 'the utter absence of organization at all adequate to the undertaking.'[289] The other clerks stood, astonished and disbelieving, as they listened to their kingdom being taken from them by this gaggle of capitalists supported by one man with a rifle and another with a pistol.

Sam Damon was now so 'perfectly astonished that we were in that position without any support' that, as Cooper was reading the proclamation aloud, he asked one of the others to run across the alley to Arion Hall and ask Lieutenant Commander Swinburne 'if he was not going to send someone over to support us.' The messenger returned, and whispered Swinburne's response to Damon, "Captain Wiltse' orders are, 'I remain passive.'"[290] Damon's large round eyes must have widened on hearing this.

Finally, support appeared. Cooper had almost finished reading the proclamation when Charles Ziegler arrived from the Armory at last with his company of German volunteers, which John Soper had styled Company A of the Provisional Government's army. Many annexation supporters would claim that Ziegler brought sixty men to the Government Building that day, but Committee of Safety member Fred McChesney, the man with the revolver, put the number at twenty-five to thirty. This estimate was supported by supreme court clerk Fred Wundenberg, who, in an affidavit, numbered Ziegler's men at 'about thirty.' According to Wundenberg, Ziegler's party, 'variously armed, came running into the side and back entrances to the yard and gathered about the Committee.'[291] They may have been few in number, but, said Sam Damon, 'there were enough came in to make us feel more decidedly at ease than before they arrived.'[292]

With great relief now that troops were on the scene, and while Cooper continued to read the last paragraphs, Sanford Dole instructed Charlie Carter to set off at once for the American Legation to formally deliver Dole's letter announcing the abrogation of the Hawaiian monarchy and the establishment of the Provisional Government. With the letter in his pocket, Carter hurried out to the street, hailed a hack, and set off on his mission.

Cooper finished reading. His colleagues applauded, and then Sanford Dole led the way into the Government Building to commence his government. Ziegler posted sentries at the gates, cleared the yard, then lined most of the remainder of his men down both sides of the Government Building. A crowd was beginning to swell beyond the iron railings that separated the Government Building's grounds from King Street. From the Government Building steps, Committee of Safety member John Emmeluth, a thirty-eight-year-old native of Cincinnati, Ohio, spotted men in that crowd who had formerly served in the Honolulu Rifles during the crises of 1887 and 1889. Furious that these men were making no attempt to come forward and serve in the ranks of the Provisional Government's fledgling army, Emmeluth stormed out to the street.

'As soon as Company A entered the building I went out and found the old standbys of 1887 and 1889,' Emmeluth later said, 'and had a conversation with them .They were all ready for doing any duty that was required of them.'[293] This was Emmeluth's way of saying that he badgered and bullied several of these men, and probably dragged one or two by the ear, so that they went into the grounds of the Government Building and joined two more companies of volunteers that gradually formed up, one out front of the building, the other in its rear.

The base of these companies materialized when John Soper before long arrived with several men including Joseph H. Fisher, George C. Potter and Hugh Gunn. John Good also came in with

his men Paris and Rowald, armed with Springfields from the
Hall and Sons cache. But the Provisional Government's armed
force was still pitifully small. The Committee of Safety had been
expecting a hundred men to converge at 3.00 o'clock, but it
didn't work out that way. Annexation apologist Lucien Young
would claim that the Provisional Government soon had 175 men
under arms at the Government Building. A later US Government
investigation put the total now at sixty-five men.

Pushing by the gathered clerks, Dole led his colleagues across
the Government Building's entrance hall and through a door to
the left, into the office of the Interior Department. There they
found young stenographer Anne Vida sitting at her typewriter,
in tears. Dole assured her she had nothing to fear. But Miss Vida
was not afraid. One of her closest friends was Princess Kaiulani,
the queen's niece and heir apparent to the throne. Anne Vida
was in tears because, in depriving Liliuokalani of her throne, the
rebels were depriving her dear friend Vicki of her future as the
next monarch of Hawaii.

Miss Vida was told to wipe her tears and go home, and, for
the moment, the Provisional Government made the Interior
Department office its headquarters. To make room, the
government rifles they found in here were stood up against the
wall, and the crates of ammunition were carried out and stacked
in the hall. Dole quickly signed the declaration of martial law and
another two documents that had also been provided by Lorrin
Thurston that morning.

Thurston's 'Order Number One' required all residents to
deliver any weapons and ammunition in their possession to the
Government Building. Order Number Two declared martial
law throughout the island of Oahu; from this moment forward,
it was to be under a military dictatorship. Habeas corpus was
suspended, and anyone could now be arrested by the Provisional
Government's troops without a warrant. Anyone disobeying an
order from the Provisional Government's military could be shot.
Dole gave instructions for this declaration of martial law to be
published in English, Hawaiian, and Portuguese. The nation's
large Chinese and Japanese populations were ignored. Dole also
authorized the closure of all saloons.

The declaration of martial law by a new government was all very
well, but there remained several obstacles to that new government
enforcing its authority. The country's constitutional government

was still in existence; the queen had not acknowledged the authority of the new government; and the existing government's troops and police had superior numbers and superior weapons and held major bastions north and south of the Government Building, which, with several smaller government buildings on the Government Building's two-acre lot, was all that the rebels held.

Dole and the Provisional Government ignored these obstacles, acting as if they did not exist. With the enthusiastic help of the American-born Clerk of the Foreign Office, Frank Hastings, who, the previous evening, had written the letters of protest to Ambassador Stevens from Premier Parker and Governor Cleghorn, the rebel president quickly penned notes to all the members of the diplomatic corps in Honolulu, announcing the overthrow of the monarchy and formation of the new government, and inviting their official recognition of that government. These were soon being carried away by messengers.

At the Iolani Palace, the atmosphere had been tense ever since the 11.00 a.m. warning from Marshal Wilson to expect an assault at 3.00. Apart from the regular white-uniformed sentries outside, who were changed at the usual times, Major Sam Nowlein kept all his men indoors and out of sight. Four cannon were in place on the second floor balconies, with ammunition stacked ready for use, but Nowlein made sure the gunners remained inside the palace so that the sight of them at their guns did not provoke the rebels and draw fire.

The queen was being stoic, keeping up a brave face for all those around her, which included her ladies in waiting, among them the wife of Marshal Wilson. Shortly after 2.30, a telephone message would have come through to tell of the shooting of the policeman on Fort Street. The unimaginable seemed a reality–a coup was being staged against Liliuokalani. Not for the first time that day, the queen's pessimistic brother-in-law Archie Cleghorn warned her that the rebels would succeed in setting up a rival government. But the queen had total confidence in her marshal and the Guard.

The tension grew as the expected assault at 3.00 p.m. grew nearer. Then, from the windows of the upper floor, it was possible to see a crowd gathering out the front of the Government Building on the far side of King Street. Liliuokalani and those with her

could only speculate about what was going on over there, but
before long they found out. A visitor was admitted to the palace
and brought to the queen by Chamberlain Robertson. That
visitor was J. S. Walker, finance minister in several past cabinets.
Walker had been in the crowd that had heard Henry Cooper read
the Provisional Government's proclamation. As soon as he had
known the contents of the proclamation, which culminated in the
call for the removal of queen, cabinet and marshal from power,
the loyal legislator had rushed to the palace to inform the queen.

When Walker was ushered in, he found Liliuokalani clustered
with her anxious ladies in waiting and the two princes, Kawanakoa
and Kuhio. The princes lived at the palace; their bedrooms were
on the second floor, along with that of the queen. Governor
Cleghorn and Major Nowlein were also present.

"Your Majesty, I have come on a painful duty," said an
ashen-faced Walker to Liliuokalani. "The opposition party has
requested that you abdicate."[294]

The queen looked at Walker in astonishment. When she had
overcome her shock, she replied, "I have no idea of doing any
such thing!"

Walker looked awkwardly at the queen, not knowing what to
do or say next.

Liliuokalani thought for a long moment, then said, quite
calmly, "I would like to see Mr. Neumann."[295]

So, the man considered by many the best lawyer in the
kingdom was sent for.

Charles L Hopkins had arrived at the American Legation. Seeing
no sign of Premier Parker or Attorney General Peterson, Hopkins
alighted from his taxi and walked up onto the veranda, where he
was met by Ambassador Stevens' daughter Nellie.

Miss Stevens took Antone Rosa's letter from Hopkins. "Any
answer required?" she asked.

"Yes," Hopkins responded.

For ten minutes, Hopkins waited on the legation veranda,
under the gaze of a US Marine on sentry duty, until Nellie Stevens
returned.

"My father is too unwell to write an answer now," she said,
"but if you will go and return in about an hour's time he will have
the answer ready."

Hopkins shook his head. "My instructions are to wait for an answer."[296]

Again Miss Stevens adjourned indoors. After another lengthy pause, she returned to say that her father would write a reply while Hopkins waited.

A little after 3.30, annexationist Charlie Carter returned to the Government Building from the American Legation, accompanied by Cadet Pringle, Ambassador Stevens' military aide. Pringle had come 'to see if we actually had possession' of the building, according to Fred McChesney.[297]

"You see we have possession, and have troops here to protect us," said Sanford Dole to the naval cadet.[298]

Pringle did not reply. Fred McChesney watched Pringle as 'he took a look around, and politely bowed and left.'[299] The members of the new government looked at each other with concern. The promised official recognition from Stevens was vital to their future, and to their very lives. If this coup failed, under the Hawaiian Constitution they would all be guilty of treason, a hanging offense.

Shortly after Pringle's departure, British ambassador James Wodehouse arrived with his deputy, the British consul general, and found Dole and members of his Provisional Government sitting around a table in the Interior Department. Wodehouse spoke privately with Dole, and then the ambassador and the consul general left, after which Dole told his colleagues that Wodehouse had said he would recognize their government once Stevens had done so. Not many more minutes passed before Japanese consul general Saburo Fujii also arrived at the Government Building. Without speaking with anyone, he took a look around, and then departed.

Everything, as far as the rebel Provisional Government was concerned, still depended on US Ambassador Stevens.

17.

THE GREAT BLUFF

Premier Parker and Attorney General Peterson had returned safely to the government headquarters at the police station. At 2.30, when the annexationists' coup prematurely exploded into action on Fort Street, Parker and Peterson had been in the process of climbing into their carriage on Nuuanu Avenue after their disheartening meeting with Ambassador Stevens. Unwittingly, on their way back, they had passed Charles Hopkins going the other way with Antone Rosa's letter for the ambassador.

At approximately 3.45, Charles Hopkins returned from his trip to the legation. He came with a letter penned by Ambassador Stevens and addressed to Sam Parker, as Minister for Foreign Relations. Hopkins handed the letter to Parker, who disappeared into the deputy marshal's office with it. Several minutes later, Parker gave the letter to Marshal Wilson to peruse. Wilson read that, on behalf of the United States Government, Ambassador Stevens had extended official recognition to the Provisional Government as the *de jure*, or legal, government of Hawaii.

Later, Wilson, Peterson, Colburn, and Charles Hopkins would all give affidavits that they had read this letter at this time, and that in it Stevens had stated that he had that day, January 17–some time prior to 3.30 p.m., when the letter was written–officially recognized the Provisional Government. Later, Paul Neumann would take this letter to Washington and tender it to the State Department as evidence of Stevens' action. There in Washington, the letter would disappear. For, Stevens had lied to the Hawaiian Government. By 3.30 on January 17, he had still not officially recognized, in writing, the Provisional Government; he was awaiting confirmation that the rebels had gained control of the situation before he did so.

As a consequence of receiving this letter, the cabinet decided that it was time for a conference with the members of the Provisional Government, and Marshal Wilson called in Deputy Marshal Mehrten to act as the cabinet's emissary.

Not long after, at the Government Building, the members of the Provisional Government were informed that Deputy Marshal John Mehrten was at the gate, demanding entry. Ziegler's men refused to let him pass, so Mehrten sent in an invitation from Premier Parker for Dole and the other members of the rebels' Executive Council to come to the police station for consultations with the queen's cabinet. Dole, fearing a trap, rejected the invitation. Instead, he had a copy of the Provisional Government's proclamation given to Deputy Mehrten, along with an invitation for the Parker cabinet to come to the Government Building for a meeting with the Provisional Government there, on their territory.

At this point, unlike the queen's cabinet, the Provisional Government had not received any indication from Ambassador Stevens that he had recognized their legitimacy, and Sanford Dole, like Sam Damon, was feeling far from secure. Dole now wrote a note to Lieutenant Commander Swinburne, next door at Arion Hall, asking him to come over to see for himself that the Provisional Government had control of the situation. The note was conveyed across the alley to the commander of US forces on the ground.

Swinburne had just finished reading this note from Damon when Captain Wiltse himself unexpectedly arrived at Arion Hall, having come ashore from the *Boston* to find out what was going on. Swinburne, who continued to command the *Boston*'s landing party, showed Damon's note to Wiltse, after which he went across the alley to find Dole and pass on the news that the captain was there and wished to see him.

When Swinburne walked into the Government Building, the Provisional Government's companies were making a military show, drilling in the yard. Swinburne was conducted into the office of the Interior Department. 'A large number of arms was piled up in the room' Swinburne would recall, and 'a large quantity of ammunition was stacked in the hall.'[300] Swinburne saw Dole and obtained a note from him which invited Wiltse to visit the Government Building, which he took back to his captain.

Wiltse and Swinburne subsequently ventured to the Government Building together, and were ushered into the Interior Department office, where all the Provisional Government members came to their feet, and Dole greeted Wiltse warmly. Swinburne would remember that Henry Cooper and William Smith did most of the talking for the rebels, telling Wiltse that they had formed a *de facto* government and overthrown the queen by proclamation, and that they had taken possession of the archives, treasury and legislature–all of which were contained in the Government Building. They then asked Wiltse if he was prepared to recognize their government.

Fred McChesney, who was present, was to testify that Captain Wiltse looked at Dole, and asked, "Have you got possession of the palace, barracks, and station house?"

"No, not yet," Dole replied. "We are arranging that."

"Well, you must have them before we can recognize you as a power," said Wiltse. "We cannot recognize you when there is another government across the street."[301]

Lieutenant Commander Swinburne also remembered what appears to have been a comparatively stressed Sanford Dole saying, "We have not charge of the police station at present, but it is a mere matter of time. It is bound to be given up in a few minutes. I expect to hear that it is given up at any moment."[302]

The meeting was interrupted by a tap on the door, and it was announced that members of the queen's cabinet had arrived outside for a conference. Wiltse and Swinburne then withdrew. After the two US Navy commanders had departed, Sam Parker and Billy Cornwell were ushered in to the room. Colburn and Peterson had been too afraid to leave the police station, being certain that the rebels would murder them all. Parker, as usual, had no fear, and was able to share some of his courage with Cornwell.

No one on the government side was aware that the Provisional Government had not received written recognition from Ambassador Stevens, or that, on the contrary, the US Navy had just given the Provisional Government a tough 'to do' list before they won US recognition. Obviously, none of the rebels was going to let the queen's men know it, either. What was more, Parker and Cornwell would have seen the two Navy officers depart the Government Building as they were led in, and this added to the impression that the US forces were in league with the rebels.

Just the same, Premier Parker did not reveal that he had received the letter from Stevens, especially when Sanford Dole was unable to show him any letter of recognition from the US ambassador. Dole, acting as if US recognition had been formally received, asked that the cabinet give up the police station and the other government property under their control, 'in the interests of law and order.'[303] Parker, suspicious, and sensing a lack of certainty on the part of Dole and his colleagues, did not commit to any action. He did agree to allow Sam Damon and another Advisory Council member, forty-year-old Charles Bolte, German-born manager of the Hawaiian interests of San Francisco sugar concern Grinbaum and Company, to accompany Cornwell and himself back to police headquarters. There, said Parker, Damon and Bolte could discuss the situation with the full cabinet.

The four of them took hacks back to Merchant Street and the police headquarters. There, after passing through a lobby crowded with stern-faced police, fidgety reservists, and worried politicians loyal to the queen, this quartet went into the deputy marshal's office, where they were joined by Peterson and Colburn. Behind a closed door, the six men conferred. Damon now said declared it was pointless for the queen's forces to resist, and he urged the cabinet to, in his own words, 'yield up their power.'[304] According to ministers Colburn and Peterson: 'Mr. Damon stated that Mr. Stevens had recognized the Provisional Government and that the United States forces would assist them and that it was useless for us to resist, but asked us in the interest of peace, and to save bloodshed, not to do so.'[305]

Damon was bluffing; Stevens had not yet advised the Provisional Government of his official recognition, and, since receiving the message from Lieutenant Commander Swinburne that he was under orders to remain passive, Damon had good reason to doubt that US forces would intervene on behalf of the rebels. But the fact that Damon had been one of the queen's chief advisors until just the previous day meant that the cabinet was likely to believe him before they believed anyone else from the other side.

Peterson then read aloud the Provisional Government's proclamation. After some lively discussion, the torn cabinet invited attorney Paul Neumann to join them and contribute his thoughts on the legal issues involved. Neumann had just returned from the palace, having been summoned by J. S. Walker. There, Liliuokalani had, in her own words, explained her position to Neumann, and sought his advice. In response, Neumann had counseled the queen to consult all her friends on the best course of action. Now, after talking with Neumann, the cabinet asked for time to confer alone for a few moments, and Damon and Bolte withdrew to the corridor outside.

Spotting Marshal Wilson in the corridor, Damon took him aside, into an empty cell at the rear of the building, and 'urged him very strongly to give up any hope or any thought of making any attack, or resistance.' Wilson had by this time read the Provisional Government's proclamation, which, in addition to declaring the queen overthrown and her cabinet dissolved, also dismissed Wilson from the office of Marshal of the Kingdom. When Wilson scoffed at the idea of surrender, Damon said, "Now, if you will cooperate with us, if in future I can be of service to you, I will do so."[306]

This offer made no impression on Marshal Wilson. He was ready to fight. And he was not alone–Damon soon gauged that the mood of the queen's forces in the police building was solidly for resisting the rebels. He came to feel that 'if they (the government's forces) had only to contend with the Provisional Government and the forces of the Provisional Government, that they would not give up. That was the impression that I gathered from them; that they felt themselves equal to the occasion as far as the Provisional Government went.'[307]

The queen's forces had every reason to feel confident. They were distributed between three strong points. The Iolani Palace was protected by Major Nowlein with fifty men of the Household Guard and four cannon. The thirty remaining men of the Household Guard occupied Iolani Barracks, just across Palace Walk from the palace, commanded by the adjutant of the Guard, and equipped, in addition to their rifles, with a Gatling machinegun. At the crowded police headquarters with Marshal Wilson were eighty regular police, forty-five special constables, and volunteer Household Guard reservists–the number of which would be the cause of much dispute in the future–with rifles, pistols and two Gatling guns; although there were not enough arms for every man.

Interior Minister John Colburn would later make a foolish claim in a letter to a friend in the US that the queen's government had 700 men under arms on January 17. This exaggeration was designed to support his assertion that the government was perfectly able to maintain law and order and therefore the US troops need not have come ashore. After the letter was published in the *New York Times* on February 9, Lorrin Thurston would seize on the number of 700 and bandy it about the US press to show what enormous odds the annexationists had overcome. Thurston would himself contradict this number in a written submission to the US Government, in which he said, 'The queen then having about four hundred men under arms.'[308]

Even the figure of 400 was high. There were at this time three reserve companies of the Household Guard, down from four in the time of King Kalakaua. These companies were based on the then US military model, which provided for companies of thirty to forty men. The four companies of sailors and marines landed from the *Boston*, had, for example, a maximum of thirty-four men each. On this basis, the complements of the three reserve companies of the Household Guard would, at most, have totaled 102 men.

A figure of 272 government soldiers in Honolulu would be bandied about by some later authors. Some would add this to the eighty full-time soldiers of the Household Guard, eighty regular police, and forty-five 'specials,' which suggests a total of 477 men under arms for the queen's government. But it is much more likely that 272 was the grand total, and of these, only sixty-seven were Guard reservists, in two companies. It is also possible that thirty or so more reservists, making up the third reserve company, may have been stationed out of town at the old Punchbowl battery, which was maintained throughout this era, and that they never figured in events in the city on January 17. Detailed records of the Guard and its reserve units during this period no longer exist, so there is no way of knowing for sure.

Of the number of men on the rebel side, the Provisional Government's Fred McChesney was to claim: 'Had fighting actually been necessary, we would have had six hundred men armed and ready with plenty of ammunition.'[309] This was pure hot air. The sixty-five armed men holding the Government Building for the Provisionals in the late afternoon on January 17 were joined in the early evening by a band of Portuguese led by J.

M. Camara, and these men were formed into a fourth Provisional Government company. With the addition of the Portuguese, the US Navy's Lieutenant Commander Swinburne was to estimate the total number of Provisional Government men under arms at 6.00 that evening to be one hundred.[310] And they had no artillery or heavy weapons. The rebel Provisional Government was outnumbered and outgunned. And both sides knew it.

While Sam Damon was waiting on the cabinet's decision, he asked a special constable at police headquarters whether he was prepared to fight. The man in question was John T. Bowler, an American-born plastering and stone contractor who had made himself comfortably wealthy during his years in Hawaii. Like a number of Americans in the kingdom, 'Johnny' Bowler admired and was loyal to the queen. Answering Damon's question, he said, "We are all prepared, but I will never fight against the American flag."[311]

This, Damon knew, was the ace up the rebel sleeve. While the queen's men *believed* that the US sailors and marines would intervene in any fighting on the side of the Provisional Government, the rebels had an insurmountable advantage. Ambassador Stevens had come right out and told Parker and Peterson that the US troops would support the insurgents, but in reality the US force had strict orders from Captain Wiltse not to become involved. Lieutenant Commander Swinburne later testified that, had fighting broken out between Government and rebel forces, he would have withdrawn his men from Arion Hall and relocated them to a place out of the firing line, to ensure that they *did not* become involved.[312]

But perceptions can sometimes be more powerful than facts. And the perception that the US troops would intervene on behalf of the primarily American rebel government was what turned the tide in favor of Hawaii's rag-tag revolutionaries. 'We realized then that any steps from our side to dislodge and arrest the rebels would unavoidably lead us into conflict with the United States forces,' said the kingdom's finance minister Billy Cornwell later, in error, 'and we decided to surrender.'[313]

Damon and Bolte were called back into the deputy marshal's office. Peterson, Colburn and Cornwell had been able to convince the doubting Sam Parker that capitulation was the only safe and sane option, and the premier informed Damon and Bolte that the cabinet had agreed that it should surrender to the Provisional

Government. The rebel bluff had worked. Almost. There were still one or two more obstacles for the rebels to overcome–a defiant queen and an even more defiant marshal of the kingdom and his hundreds of loyal Hawaiian fighting men who might choose to fight rather than surrender. And the cabinet knew it. When asked by Damon to surrender all Hawaiian Government forces and assets, the cabinet hesitated. Said Cornwell: 'We answered that it would be necessary for us to consult first with Queen Liliuokalani.'[314]

Around 5.00 p.m., Joseph Carter, one of the queen's most trusted advisers, was sitting down to dinner at his Honolulu home when a hack rolled up his drive and Deputy Marshal John Mehrten jumped out and came running to his door. Informed that his presence was urgently required at the Government Building by the cabinet, Carter joined the deputy for the ride to King Street.

Inside the Government Building, the Provisional Government had transferred from the Interior Department at the front of the building to the Finance Department, at the back. The Provisional Government was still very nervous about coming under attack from the queen's forces, and someone must have pointed out that the Interior Department was in direct line of fire of the Household Guard cannon mounted on the palace balcony several hundred yards away.

Passing through the ranks of rebel troops after his arrival, Joseph Carter was ushered into the Finance Department, which he found filled with thirty or so men. He immediately recognized his nephew Charlie, and Sanford Dole, Sam Damon, and other members of the Provisional Government, as well as all four members of the queen's cabinet and several other advisers to Liliuokalani. Everyone seemed to be talking at once. 'There was a deal of excitement,' Carter would recall, 'and earnest discussion going on among groups of persons, and while standing among them I overheard among other things that Minister Stevens had recognized the new government.'[315]

In the conversations going on all around Joe Carter in the crowded Finance Department room, he would have heard the members of the Provisional Government and the queen's cabinet all express sentiments that the receipt of formal US recognition was the final nail in Liliuokalani's proverbial coffin as monarch of Hawaii. Carter also heard talk 'that a steamer was to be made ready at once to carry to San Francisco, en route to Washington, commissioners of the new government.'

Glumly accepting the overthrow of his queen as inevitable, Carter asked, "What is required of me?"

He was informed that he would be a member of a delegation headed by Sam Damon that would now go across the road to the palace, 'to inform Her Majesty the Queen that she was deposed.'[316]

With her nephews the two princes, Kawanakoa and Kuhio, standing behind her chair, a grave-faced Liliuokalani was seated in the Iolani Palace's Blue Room when the members of this deputation filed in. Not a word was spoken; the air was thick with tension. The queen ran her eyes over the men who formed up in front of her and bowed. Sam Parker and his three fellow cabinet members were all here, along with Joe Carter, Paul Neumann, Judge Henry Widemann, and Ed Macfarlane. Leading the group was Sam Damon, a man the queen still considered her trusted and firm friend.

Damon was the first to speak. Joe Carter later recalled: 'Mr. Damon informed Her Majesty of the establishment of a provisional government, and of her being deposed, and that she might prepare a protest if she wished to. An awkward pause followed, which I broke.' Carter began by expressing his sympathy to the queen for what had come to pass. Then he told her, "Your Majesty, any demonstration on the part of your forces would precipitate a conflict with the forces of the United States. It is desirable that such a conflict be avoided."[317]

Henry Widemann then spoke up, disagreeing. The crusty old German was all for fighting the rebels, and cited the fact that 'the queen's government had possession of the station house, barracks and palace, nine-tenths of the arms and ammunition on the island except that in the hands of foreign governments, and a large body of men under arms.' But Widemann was a lone voice. His fellow German Paul Neumann told him this was foolish, as it would implicate the US forces. The queen, said Neumann, had no option but yield. Each of the others had their say, and all, including downcast Sam Parker, 'came to the conclusion that it was not advisable to oppose the United States' forces.'[318]

"It is useless to carry on, Your Majesty," said one of the cabinet ministers. "It will be provocative of violence and trouble if you persist in this matter longer."[319]

The queen was thoughtful for a moment, then, to the surprise of many in the room, asked, "Might I surrender pending a settlement in Washington?"[320]

Sam Damon saw where her thoughts were leading. "Surrender under protest? To the United State Government?"

Joe Carter grasped the idea as a drowning man grasps for a life preserver. "Yes, Your Majesty, your case would be considered at Washington. A peaceful submission to force on your part would greatly help your case."[321]

"You have a perfect right to be heard at a later period," said Damon.[322]

Widemann now reentered the debate to enthusiastically endorse the idea, adding, "I believe that the result would be a repetition of the scenes of 1843, when the sovereign and flag were restored to Hawaii by Great Britain."[323]

The old German was referring to Lord Paulet's arrogant seizure of control fifty years before, and of the full restoration of the Hawaiian monarchy five months later by Admiral Thomas. Archie Cleghorn, once he became Governor of Oahu, had even given the name of Thomas Square to a square in downtown Honolulu in honor of the admirable admiral.

This concept now gave Liliuokalani growing hope–she could surrender to the United States Government, not to the Sanford Dole's Provisional Government, on condition that her case was heard by the US President. She felt that John Stevens was clearly behind the coup, and that the US President would very quickly perceive the injustice of her illegal removal by the US ambassador, and restore her to her throne. Liliuokalani asked Paul Neumann and Joe Carter to immediately prepare a protest for her signature. They agreed, went to a table, and were provided with pen and ink.

As the two men commenced work on the document, Sam Damon stressed the need to ensure that hostilities did not break out at this late stage, and suggested that Arthur Peterson be sent to police headquarters to instruct Marshal Wilson to disband the force he commanded there, and to surrender the building and the arms and ammunition it contained. Liliuokalani agreed, and Peterson was sent on his way.

The document was completed, and read to the queen. In

it, she protested against 'all acts done against myself and the constitutional government of the Hawaiian Kingdom by certain persons claiming to have established a Provisional Government of and for this kingdom.' Now came the key words: 'I yield to the superior forces of the United States of America.' And she agreed to 'yield my authority' until the United States Government undid the action of Ambassador Stevens and reinstated her.[324] Annexationists would crow that this was an abdication by the queen, but it was not. Liliuokalani made sure that Sam Damon fully appreciated this distinction between a temporary yielding of authority and abdication, and had him agree that until her protest was decided in Washington she would be entitled to continue to live at the palace and fly the royal standard.

It was around 6.00 that the queen placed her signature on this document. Not long after, a flustered Arthur Peterson arrived back from police headquarters, to report that Marshal Wilson had refused to surrender–unless and until he received the order in writing from the queen herself. This must have brought a smile to the faces of Sam Parker and Henry Widemann, but the queen had already chosen her course, and Wilson's display of loyalty was now only an annoyance to her. An order was written, which the queen signed, and Peterson set off to deliver it.

The sun was just beginning to set when yet another official arrived at the American Legation on Nuuanu Avenue. A troubled Chief Justice Judd stepped down from a hack and hurried to the legation's door.

When Judd was shown into the ambassador's study, he said to Stevens, "We have a rumor all through the streets that the American minister has refused to recognize the Provisional Government." And Judd demanded to know why Stevens had failed to give the promised recognition.

"I have just recognized," Stevens replied.

Later, Stevens would claim that he wrote the letter of recognition 'about 5 o'clock.' But he would not be able to recall to whom he gave that letter of recognition, nor at what time he handed it over, although he did remember that Judd arrived as dusk was beginning to fall.[325]

It is likely that Stevens only now parted with the letter, handing it to Judd, doing so at dusk–the sun set at 6.15 that evening–

and only then after Judd had informed him that Damon was at the palace, that the queen had agreed to surrender, and that the instrument of surrender was being prepared for her signature as they spoke.

Judd would have hurried the letter back to Dole at the Government Building, so that the Provisional Government finally received the US ambassador's official recognition shortly after 6.15. That was after Liliuokalani signed the surrender document, believing–as Damon and her own ministers had assured her–that the Provisional Government had received US recognition hours before this.

Dole immediately sent back a written acknowledgment to Stevens, and a request that, as the sun was setting and the police headquarters had not yet been surrendered by the queen's forces, the US military commander on shore take command of Provisional Government troops so that both US forces and rebel troops could act together. Stevens declined this request, telling Dole in a short note that he believed Captain Wiltse would not agree to taking charge of the Provisional Government's forces.

Word having reached Arion Hall that the queen had surrendered and that Ambassador Stevens had finally recognized the Provisional Government, by 6.30 Captain Wiltse felt able to return to the *Boston*, leaving Lieutenant Commander Swinburne in change of the battalion on shore.

During the day, Swinburne had arranged to have a telephone hooked up at Arion Hall, and, at 7.30, it jangled. When Swinburne answered, it was to find the US Marines' Lieutenant Draper on the line from the American Consulate on Merchant Street, which was only several doors up from the police station. Draper reported that he had just been out on the sidewalk, and had witnessed Marshal Wilson assemble all his men in the street, give them a short speech, and then dismiss them. John Soper had arrived, accompanied by pistol-packing Fred McChesney, Clerk of the Supreme Court Fred Wundenberg–who now became the Provisional Government's Acting Marshal in place of Wilson– and a number of men from Ziegler's German company. They had taken over the police station in the name of the Provisional Government. All was now quiet, Lieutenant Draper reported.

Special Constable Charles Hopkins was one of those men

dismissed by the marshal. He hung around for a time, in case he was needed by the queen's side. By 8.00 o'clock, with Soper's men patrolling the streets and declaring a 9.00 p.m. curfew, which sent the crowds melting away, and with all ships banned from leaving Honolulu Harbor to ensure that the queen could not send for help, Hopkins caught a trolley car, and went home.

Committee of Safety member John Emmeluth was sitting in the Finance Department office at the Government Building, reflecting on the amazing change that he and his Committee colleagues had just wrought on the Hawaiian Islands, and the comparative ease with which it had been achieved. He would recall that it was sometime between 8.00 and 9.00 p.m. when, to his surprise, the uniformed Major Sam Nowlein, commander of the Household Guard, walked in. Spotting Sanford Dole at the end of the room, Nowlein presented himself to him, and came to attention, giving him a salute.

On the queen's instructions, Nowlein had come to arrange the surrender of the Household Guard to the Provisional Government. But Dole knew he did not have the manpower to handle the night-time surrender of the royal troops. John Emmeluth would record: 'The President told him (Nowlein) to keep his men together and all arms inside the barracks for the night. Nothing should be disturbed and he should simply carry on their routine duties within the enclosure for the night. Nowlein asked whether he would mount a guard as usual in the enclosure, and he was told "No."'[326]

Nowlein saluted, then marched out the way he had come.

Later that evening, with Hawaii's revolution brought to a civilized and almost bloodless conclusion–contrary to Oscar White's claim, the policeman shot by John Good was not dead and would recover–the US Navy's Lieutenant Lucien Young came off duty. With all the saloons in Honolulu closed by order of the Provisional Government, Young made for the bar of the Hawaiian Hotel. Here he would quench his thirst and celebrate a political outcome that he welcomed. He was to gleefully describe the coup as 'the complete and final overthrow of the rank hypocrisy and unconcealed paganism of the house that Kalakaua founded and his sister Liliuokalani brought to grief.'[327]

When Young walked into the hotel, he spotted Charles Wilson, the now out of work former marshal. The pair knew each other, and they sat down for a long chat. 'He was intense in his loyalty to the queen and bitterly denounced the ex-ministers as cowards and traitors,' Young would write. 'He had intended to resist, and said that it was fully understood that if a fight took place the Government Building and palace grounds were to be the scene of battle.' In Young's opinion, 'had the marshal been permitted to carry out those plans, there would have been loss of life and the Provisional Government would have had difficulty in establishing itself that day.' But Young thought that the whites would have prevailed in the end, partly because of their 'superior intellect.'[328]

Word was soon carried that evening to Lorrin Thurston at his Judd Street home that his Committee of Safety colleagues had carried the day and successfully staged the military coup that he had thought doomed. He was astonished. Delighted, but astonished nonetheless. Years later, he would write: 'Knowing every detail of what happened, I still do not comprehend exactly how it all came about, yet happen it did.'[329]

The tale of the almost farcical turns of events, with the fortunes of both sides swaying back and forth through the second half of January 17 like a loose sail blowing in a gale, was stranger than fiction. 'The whole situation would be ridiculous were it not so tragical," said Thurston. He laid the success of the queen's overthrow at Liliuokalani's own feet. 'Her assumption that any provision of the constitution was binding upon her was purely assumption.'[330] Putting on his lawyer's hat, he was of the opinion that the monarch did not need the approval of her cabinet to promulgate a new constitution. In striving to obtain her ministers' approval, which they had declined to give, she had given the annexationists the leverage they needed to claim that the queen was in revolt against her own cabinet.

'Her views prevented her from taking the bull by the horns, abrogating the constitution, promulgating a new one, and putting her terms into effect by force,' said Thurston.[331] That was what he would have done, in her place. But Liliuokalani was not Lorrin Thurston.

* * *

Liliuokalani had been so stressed by the events of the past three days that she had been unable to bring herself to write in her diary each night before bed.

During this momentous Tuesday in particular, the fear that she might be killed by the rebels had been a very real one, even if concealed behind her royal mask. Now, with the coup over, but still with protecting ali'i of the Household Guard at her door, and with the hope of regaining her throne within a few months with the help of President Benjamin Harrison of the United States, Liliuokalani wrote in her dairy for Tuesday, January 17, 1893: 'Things turned out better than I expected.'

18.

IN THE LIGHT
OF THE NEW DAY

THE PEOPLE OF HONOLULU AWOKE ON WEDNESDAY, January 18 to the realization that the Queen of Hawaii had been overthrown and their country was now under a military dictatorship. A small minority of residents, American and German in the main, rejoiced. The great majority were stunned. Native Hawaiians would soon be grieving as if a loved one had died. Most residents with British blood or connections were unhappy. Apart from John Soper and one or two others, Britons had played no part in the coup, and resented the idea of annexation by the United States–there had long been tension between the British residents and the American and German communities, with the British preferring annexation by Britain if by anyone at all.

At St. Andrews Priory School first thing that morning, Bernice Irwin, her fellow teachers, and their students could not believe the news that their monarchy had been taken from them. Said Irwin, 'We were all stunned. The teachers, of whom I was now one, and the older pupils, were indignant, and the Sisters Beatrice and Albertina walked about the school with sad and anxious faces. No one could give proper attention to studies.' As for Bernice herself, 'I went around in a daze. I felt it must all be a tragic mistake, a nightmare from which we would all soon awaken.'[332] She was not alone in that regard.

* * *

At 8.00 a.m., Hawaiian soldiers of the Household Guard stood at ease in a line in the courtyard at the center of the Iolani Barracks, wearing their undress uniforms. On the orders of their commander, Major Nowlein, they had removed their ammunition belts and wrapped them around their stacked rifles. Authorized by the Provisional Government to record the event, a photographer from one of Honolulu's pro-annexation newspapers set his camera on a wooden tripod and pointed it their way, to the discomfort of the humiliated Hawaiians, who would have fought to the death had the queen ordered it.

Rangy John Soper, commander of the Provisional Government's small army, his bowler hat making him look even taller than usual, stood facing the men of the Guard, a written order in his hand. Beside him stood a dejected Sam Nowlein, wearing a white 'duck' suit and straw boater hat, his smart Household Guard uniform consigned to history.

Soper read out a discharge notice for sixty-four fulltime men of the Guard. Friends of the queen had managed to convince the Provisional Government to allow Liliuokalani to retain a personal bodyguard of sixteen men of the Guard, under the command of Sam Nowlein. There was a genuine fear that some fanatical anti-monarchist would make an attempt on Liliuokalani's life, so that she no longer presented a problem to the Provisional Government. Liliuokalani herself would hear that John Good, the annexationist who had shot down the policeman to precipitate her overthrow, had been overheard to say that he would personally shoot the queen if the US Government came out in her favor.

The sixteen chosen bodyguards, who were at this moment with Liliuokalani at the palace, were permitted to retain their rifles and a limited amount of ammunition, and would continue to wear their old Guard undress uniforms, although their unit would have no name. The Provisional Government would pay their salaries, for now. As for the remaining men of the Guard, they were informed by Soper, as he read the order to disband, they would be paid to the end of the month, and then they would be on their own.

Some of the tall, muscular guardsmen looked lost. Others looked angry. To serve in the Guard had been a great honor, with ali'i son following ali'i father into the ranks over the decades.

Now, that honor was being taken away from the proud guardians of the *wahine moi*, as the queen was called in Hawaiian. As soon as the dismissed men of the Guard departed the barracks, John Good marched a contingent of Provisional Government's irregulars in to take possession of the building and the arms and ammunition it contained.

At 10.00 a.m., Sam Nowlein and his sixteen men of the bodyguard escorted Liliuokalani from the palace. Liliuokalani had decided to move across the street to her family home. 'I moved to Washington Place of my own accord,' she was to write.[333] The Provisional Government made it clear it considered the Iolani Palace to be government property, which would have made Liliuokalani feel like a prisoner. Washington Place was her own personal property, and there she could do what she liked and receive whomever she liked, without having to seek permission. As it was, the queen's chamberlain, James Robertson, was to have a long, drawn-out battle with the Provisional Government over what items at the palace were the queen's personal property and what was state property.

The Provisional Government was glad to see Liliuokalani go. They immediately took possession of the palace. The two thrones, crowns and anything else connected with the monarchy would be removed from the Throne Room, and auctioned off. Even the carpet on the floor of the Throne Room would be taken up, cut into portions, and auctioned. Looting also began. According to one apocryphal story, the troops of the Provisional Government's Portuguese company made souvenirs of the crystal baubles hanging from the chandeliers in the palace's Blue Room, and gave them as gifts to their wives and girlfriends.

That first full day of the new rule, contrary to the assurance given by Sam Damon, the Provisional Government ordered the royal standard lowered from the palace flagstaff. A campaign to remove all connections with royalty was launched that same day. Police and military badges which had previously been topped by a crown would be replaced with badges with an American-style five-pointed star on top. The royal crown on the Hawaiian coat of arms was removed and a star likewise put in its place. All Government employees were required to take an oath of allegiance to the new Provisional Government. Any man who refused to do so was fired on the spot, and banned from taking any future government employment, in any capacity. One of the first to go was Deputy Marshal John Mehrten, who proved too loyal to his former boss Marshal Wilson for the rebels' liking.

The new regime's first priority was the building of an army with which to guarantee its control of the country. That first day, recruiting began for an army which would soon boast 170 full-time soldiers, paid forty dollars a month, backed by several hundred reservists. John Soper, the man who had orchestrated the military side of the coup, would be appointed Adjutant General of the nation's military, and, before long, Marshal of the Kingdom after Fred Wundenberg went back to his supreme court post.

Thirty-five-year-old, San Francisco-born Joseph Fisher, a junior partner of Sam Damon's at Bishop's Bank, was made a lieutenant colonel and commander of the Provisional Government's military. Fisher had been a co-founder of the Honolulu Rifles after service with the California National Guard. To quarter their new army, the Provisional Government not only took over the Iolani Barracks but before long also turned the Armory into a barracks.

Lorrin Thurston made a remarkable overnight recovery, as did William Castle. Both assured their colleagues that they would be quite well enough to travel aboard William Wilder's *Claudine* when the chartered steamer sailed next day to convey the Provisional Government's new Annexation Commission to San Francisco. That trio now joined the eleven other members of the Advisory Council and the four-member Executive Council for a joint sitting that lasted throughout Wednesday. Letters were hand-delivered to these two councils during the day, as the Provisional Government received conditional recognition from eight members of the local diplomatic corps, all dated January 18. Even Ed Macfarlane, one of the queen's closest advisers, provided recognition in his capacity as Danish consular representative.

Contrary to what Sanford Dole had led his colleagues to believe, it would be another day before British ambassador Wodehouse also granted recognition, conditional on instructions from London. Unofficially, Wodehouse would make it clear that he was not happy with the turn of events, and, unbeknownst to the Provisional Government, he sent a letter requesting his government dispatch a British warship to Hawaii.

Buoyed by this flood of official recognition, the eighteen

leaders of the Provisional Government decided on a number of initiatives on this first full day of their rule. The main focus of the revolutionary councils was the framing of the submission that their Annexation Commission would present to US secretary of state John W. Foster, the man who had replaced James Blaine at the State Department. The previous evening, the Provisional Government had added two more members to the Annexation Commission that it was sending to the United States–another lawyer, the indefatigable young Charlie Carter, and forty-five-year-old English-born Joseph Marsden, an owner of the Honokaa Sugar Company. Marsden was included on the Commission to lobby the so-called Sugar Trust, the US sugar producers, to ensure they did not come out against Hawaiian annexation; for annexation would put Hawaii's sugar producers back on the same footing as US producers. Lorrin Thurston's clerk Fred Peterson would also be going along, as the Commission's secretary, complete with his trusty typewriter.

Sitting at the head of the council table, Sanford Dole, the unelected president of an unelected government, must soon have begun to realize that the true power of the new regime lay in the hands of just several men–Thurston and his close friend William Smith, the two motivating figures behind the formation of the Committee of Safety. Thurston would the following day be departing for the States, but Smith would be remaining behind, with significant power as both one of the four members of the Executive Council and Hawaii's new attorney general and head of the police. At Advisory Council level, Smith would be strongly supported by Henry Waterhouse and Henry Cooper–that determined troika of Waterhouse, Cooper and Smith had driven the agenda on Sunday evening, when even Thurston had balked at the challenge of pulling off the coup.

Dole seems to have joined the coup believing that he would keep a restraining hand on Committee of Safety firebrands, but in the light of the new day he was finding the agenda now being driven by those firebrands, whose approach was hard-headed and iron-fisted. He was also finding himself powerless to stop them. That night, as Dole was driven home through streets deserted because of the martial law curfew and patrolled by heavily armed Provisional Government men on horseback, he was composing a revealing letter to his brother George on Kauai, a letter he would write next day.

'How I have regretted this whole affair,' Dole would confess to his brother, just two days after the queen's overthrow. 'Had I my way about the matter I would have used far more tactful ways than the treatment that we have this far rendered.' At least, in talking in terms of 'we,' Dole had the decency to accept responsibility for the acts of the government he headed. 'I have reiterated time and again my desire that we hold the power of the throne in trust and we hold the regency in the name of the young Princess Kaiulani.'[334]

Each time that he raised the regency option, Dole had been outvoted by the others, who were all for US annexation. He had either to go along with them and keep quiet, against his better judgment, or resign as President of the Provisional Government of Hawaii. Stay, as a powerless puppet, or leave, as a man of principle? Dole's choice was to indicate what sort of man he really was. He stayed on, and stayed quiet.

19.

A SUGAR COATING

THE *CLAUDINE* DROPPED ANCHOR OFF SAN FRANCISCO
at 1.00 a.m. on Saturday, January 28, after covering the 2,000
miles from Honolulu in just under nine days. Apart from mail
and a few paying passengers approved by owner and annexation
commissioner William Wilder, the ship had only carried the
Provisional Government's five commissioners.

At the last moment, Liliuokalani had announced that she
too wished to send a delegation to Washington, to put her case
for restoration by the US Government, and she had asked the
Provisional Government for permission to send her envoys on the
Claudine with their commissioners. The Provisional Government
had denied her request. The deposed queen's delegates–Paul
Neumann, Prince Kawanakoa, and Edward Macfarlane–were
forced to wait for the next regular steamer sailing to San
Francisco, that of the SS *Australia*, on February 1. This gave the
annexationists a valuable head start in the race to reach America
and put their case to the US press and politicians. Annexation
commissioner William Castle had chortled in his diary as the
Claudine sailed from Honolulu without the queen's delegates:
'No doubt kahunas are praying us to death.'[335]

Lorrin Thurston was so anxious to launch the annexation
campaign in the US that he had a boat take him ashore almost as
soon as the *Claudine* anchored in San Francisco Bay, in the early
morning darkness. This allowed him to distribute an account of
the Hawaiian coup from the Provisional Government's perspective
to all the San Francisco newspapers before the sun came up. In
his account, Thurston deflated and inflated the numbers for and

against the queen, claimed that Liliuokalani threatened the lives of her cabinet ministers, asserted that 'practically the entire business community' was against her, and stated, incorrectly, that she had abdicated. Uniquely, he also accused the Hawaiian-language press of 'race prejudice' against the white minority in Hawaii, because the 'native press' had been critical of the American and European businessmen who opposed the queen.

Thurston and his fellow commissioners checked into San Francisco's Occidental Hotel, and over lunch at the Palace Grill pressed the case for annexation with the San Francisco Chamber of Commerce. That evening, while Thurston did the rounds of the city's newspaper editors, his attorney colleagues William Castle and Charlie Carter went to the Palace Hotel for a meeting in a private parlor with representatives of the sugar trust. It would not have escaped the attention of Castle and Carter that it was at the Palace Hotel that King Kalakaua had passed away; and here were they, bent on killing the Hawaiian monarchy, in the very same place. Some of the richest men in San Francisco attended this meeting. The majority, like W. H. Dimond, who was related by marriage to Henry Waterhouse, and M. S. Grinbaum and Charles Reed Bishop, had sugar interests in Hawaii as well as in the US. By far the most important man in the room—and he knew it—was Claus Spreckels, banker, sugar baron, and by this time, too, a US railroad owner.

Lorrin Thurston had done legal work for Spreckels in Hawaii in the past. 'Claus Spreckels was most vigorous and forceful,' Thurston would say of him, 'reputed a most generous friend and an unrelenting and dangerous enemy.'[336] Thurston knew how clever Spreckels could be when confronted with competitors who opposed his will. When Spreckels built a sugar refinery in San Francisco, eastern competitors built one there too, to put him out of business. So Spreckels went east and built America's most modern sugar refinery in Philadelphia, on the doorstep of his eastern competitors. In the end, those competitors bought Spreckels' Philadelphia mill from him and closed down their San Francisco refinery, leaving Spreckels as sugar king of the Pacific coast.

Portly, gray-bearded Spreckels, who was accompanied by his sons Rudolph and Gus to this sugar summit, sat back, and, with imperial aloofness, listened as Castle put the case for American annexation of Hawaii. It turned out that Spreckels was only interested in one thing–a guarantee of the continued importation of cheap Asian contract labor to work Hawaiian sugar plantations. Under US law, this was illegal in American states and territories. But when Castle and Carter assured Spreckels that they intended negotiating an annexation treaty with the United States which recognized existing Hawaiian law and permitted the continued importation of Asian labor, Spreckels was all smiles.

'Claus takes the floor,' Castle wrote in his diary, 'talking in a general sort of way of the vital importance of the assistance of himself and the (sugar) trust, of how annexation will fail without it, and of his great power and influence.' As the discussion continued, and Castle guaranteed that any annexation treaty he signed would permit the continued importation of Asian labor to the Hawaiian islands, he could see that his annexation argument had triumphed. 'It wins!' he exalted in his diary. 'The mighty Claus is won. He says he will cause annexation to become an accomplished fact.' Spreckels went on to say that he would even take his private railroad car to Washington to push the case, and offered use of the car to the annexation commissioners.[337]

As the meeting wound up, with the sugar men agreeing to form an annexation bureau in San Francisco to promote Hawaiian annexation by the US, Castle told the businessmen that he had to go on and meet Thurston at several newspapers before midnight, to have their photographs taken for the next day's editions. "It is well to get the papers on our side," Castle remarked.

"Damn the newspapers!" Spreckels declared. "Let them alone, they have no influence. Snub the reporters. They will do more harm than good."[338]

Spreckels may have been a shrewd businessman, but he was a poor publicist. And he obviously appreciated nothing of the power of the press. The following day, the story of Hawaii's revolution was splashed across all the city's front pages. To American newsmen, the overthrow of Hawaii's monarchy by men who wanted Hawaii to become part of the United States made for exciting copy–especially the way Lorrin Thurston told it. 'The papers are full of annexation,' Castle delightedly noted in his diary on January 29. And the press wanted more, hounding the annexation commissioners wherever they went. 'Reporters without end!' Castle recorded with undisguised glee.[339]

Premier Sam Parker had been wise to try to put the queen's version of events before the world's press via the diplomatic packet that he sent to the Hawaiian consul general in Auckland. But that packet was still on the high sea when the story broke in San Francisco. Via the telegraph wires, the San Francisco stories were flashed the length and breadth of the United States, to appear next day in virtually every city and town in the nation. These news stories then crossed the Atlantic, to be picked up in London, Paris, Berlin, and all the other European capitals, and beyond. As Lorrin Thurston had intended, those first stories that the world's press ran telling of a revolution in Hawaii were based on his version of events.

20.

AN AMERICAN
PROTECTORATE

I_T WAS THE MORNING OF FEBRUARY 1, AND, IN their companies and with band playing and colors flying, the US marines and sailors from the *Boston* marched through the streets of Honolulu from Camp Boston, their new shore base. Two days after the January 17 coup, Lieutenant Commander Swinburne had transferred his men from Arion Hall to a large former hotel some three hundred yards back down King Street. The stone, two-story building, which was empty, was surrounded by airy verandas and sat on a large lot separated from the street by a high stone wall. The property, which was given the temporary name Camp Boston, was rented by Ambassador Stevens on behalf of the US Government from the representative of its owner, San Francisco sugar baron and annexation supporter Charles Reed Bishop.

Every day since the move to Camp Boston, the *Boston*'s battalion had staged a dress parade in Palace Square in the early evening. To American residents, this was a reassuring presence. To Hawaiians, it was a very public demonstration by an army of occupation. But this morning, things were different. The American column marched to the Government Building, where the members of the Provisional Government stood on the steps and veranda with their little rebel army arrayed in front of them. The US force marched in, formed up in neat ranks, and came to attention in front of the Provisional Government force.

At the stroke of 11.00 a.m., the adjutant of the American battalion read out a proclamation signed by John L. Stevens 'establishing a protectorate over the Hawaiian Islands in the name of the United States, pending negotiations and action in Washington.'[340] The US flag replaced the Hawaiian flag flying over the Government Building. In the harbor, the guns of the *Boston* boomed out a twenty-one-gun salute. And US marines took charge of the Government Building. It was all over in minutes. Hawaii was now a US possession.

John Stevens took this action, of declaring the sovereign nation of Hawaii a protectorate of the United States, entirely on his own authority and without consulting Washington. The previous day, he had suggested to the Provisional Government that it send him a written request to declare Hawaii a US protectorate, and it had obliged. Stevens would later say that he had taken this step to prevent Hawaii falling into British or Japanese hands. Yet, there was no indication that annexation of Hawaii was being contemplated by the government of either country.

Perhaps Stevens' success in engineering the overthrow of the queen had gone to his head. On reading his dispatches, a case could be put that Stevens had been mentally unstable throughout his years in Hawaii. Just days before he initiated the Provisional Government request for him to give Hawaii protectorate status, an event had occurred that may have been enough to seriously unhinge him, even only temporarily, and provoke his taking possession of the Hawaiian Islands. When Stevens had sailed aboard the *Boston* on its cruise to Hilo earlier in the month, one of his daughters, Grace Stevens, who worked as his secretary at the legation, had accompanied him. Grace had remained on the Big Island when the *Boston* sailed on back to Honolulu, vacationing with friends at remote Hamakua. It was also rumored that, while on the Big Island, Grace collected Americans' signatures on a petition in favor of annexation, for her father.

On January 20, Grace Stevens had set off to return to Oahu by the inter-island steamer *Kinau*. Her departure point was a rocky promontory at Kukaiau where there was no jetty or landing place for the steamer's boat. It was arranged that Miss Stevens would be lowered down the cliff on a rope, into the ship's boat waiting below—an exciting but perilous exercise. Miss Stevens successfully reached the boat, and was just taking her seat when an unexpected wave flipped the boat over and threw everyone in it into the sea. Grace Stevens had drowned. Word of this tragedy reached Stevens before the proclamation of protectorate status was initiated. Months later, Stevens would say that he was still 'suffering a terrible affliction at the recent sad drowning of a gifted and beloved daughter.'[341]

Grace Stevens' body arrived in Honolulu aboard the *Kinau* on January 31. Coincidentally, the day before, January 30, the body of James G. Blaine, Stevens' close friend and the former secretary of state who had appointed Stevens and furtively supported Lorrin Thurston's plan to overthrow the Hawaiian Government and seek annexation, had been interred in Washington DC.

21.

SELLING ANNEXATION
IN WASHINGTON

AFTER PROTECTORATE STATUS WAS PROCLAIMED, there was a great outcry in Honolulu's pro-monarchy press. The Provisional Government, feeling buttressed by the fact that the stars and stripes flew over the Government Building, moved to clamp down on criticism. Lieutenant Lucien Young would write: 'A paper edited by a Canadian, and one by two adherents of the ex-queen, filled their columns with abuse of the United States officials, and with weird utterances in the native dialect urged the people to rise against the government, whereupon the editors were arrested and brought before the courts, and their papers suppressed.'[342]

The Provisional Government's crackdown against freedom of speech and freedom of the press extended to John C. White, manager of the Honolulu Water Works Company, who was dismissed from his post after he wrote a letter to the *New York Times* condemning John L. Stevens for his role in the overthrow of Queen Liliuokalani's Hawaiian Government. White's job as water works manager was given to Andrew Brown, a member of the Provisional Government's Advisory Council. These were lessons to critics of the dictatorship that speaking out would not be tolerated.

The Provisional Government's annexation commissioners arrived in Washington DC from the west coast by train on Friday, February 3, two days after the US flag was raised in Honolulu. The commissioners' hotel, the gracefully decaying Wormleys, flew the Hawaiian flag and gave the rebel Hawaiian delegation a parlor and seven rooms. 'A good deal of style about this!' William Castle noted approvingly in his diary, but added, 'A bill ahead!'[343] A bill which the Provisional Government would pay from the Hawaiian Treasury that it had just illegally seized.

The commissioners had been besieged by reporters at every stop on the way east. 'All along we find the papers full of Hawaii and our mission,' Castle wrote. 'Most in favor of annexation.'[344] With some glaring exceptions, such as the Chicago *Herald*, the press had indeed been generally supportive, and four state legislatures–in Pennsylvania, Oregon, Washington, and California–quickly passed resolutions in support of American annexation of Hawaii, based purely on press reports of the rebellion. Similarly, former secretary of state Thomas Bayard had been quick to come out and say, 'The annexation of Hawaii to America is the logical result of the policy of the Republic, which enjoys virtual supremacy in Hawaii, by reason of the treaties of 1875 and 1887.'[345]

But many Democratic politicians in Washington DC were not so supportive. Democrat Joseph H. Outwaite, who had replaced the now retired James Blount as chairman of the House of Representatives Foreign Relations Committee, was not fooled by Lorrin Thurston's spin. He declared to the press, 'America committed a great outrage upon the Government of Hawaii in landing marines, which virtually amounted to an act of war.' Outwaite went even further, calling for the immediate recall of US ambassador Stevens.[346] If Lorrin Thurston and his colleagues had previously thought their mission would be an easy one, they now knew different.

The day following their arrival in the federal capital they were taken to the State Department by Hawaii's ambassador to the US, Dr. John Mott-Smith, who, despite Thurston's suspicions of him, proved more than helpful. On February 1, Mott-Smith, who was of English descent, had told representatives of the British press in Washington that he believed a joint Anglo-American protectorate over Hawaii was possible. Under protectorate status, the Hawaiian monarchy might be preserved, and, at this early stage at least, preservation of the monarchy seems to have been Mott-Smith's underlying objective. 'He says that the native government (the queen's government) will not be wiped out without a struggle,' one London paper reported.[347] Yet, once Thurston and his cronies arrived in Washington, Mott-Smith had changed his tune, telling the *New York Times*, 'The restoration of the native dynasty to control the affairs in Hawaii was an impossibility in any circumstances.'[348]

At 10.00 that Saturday morning, Mott-Smith conducted the five annexation commissioners into the State Department's reception room, where Secretary of State Foster briefly greeted them. Accepting their letter of introduction from the Provisional Government's President Sanford Dole, Foster accorded them full diplomatic status. 'Mr. Foster is a white-haired gentleman of pleasant aspect,' wrote William Castle after this brief preliminary meeting. 'He impressed me with his friendly manner.'[349]

But the commissioners were made to wait until 3.00 o'clock for a sit-down meeting with the secretary of state. Thurston, as chairman of the Annexation Commission, then took the lead. 'The commission expressed a desire to have Hawaii annexed as a (US) state,' he was to say. 'Mr. Foster replied that he had no personal objection, but he added that our main problem was to secure annexation, and that whether Hawaii should be annexed as a state or territory was secondary.' Foster said that he anticipated opposition to Hawaiian annexation in any form, so it was better to leave the status–state, territory, or even protectorate–out of any treaty, to speed ratification by Congress.[350]

All parties knew that rapid treaty ratification was imperative. The previous November, Republican President Benjamin Harrison had lost the 1892 presidential election to Democratic candidate Grover Cleveland, who had won with the largest vote margin in US presidential history to that time. Cleveland was due to take office as America's twenty-fourth president on March 4, when John Foster would be replaced at the State Department by Cleveland's appointee, Walter Q. Gresham. The annexation commissioners had told the press on their way to Washington, that 'an intimation had been received that Mr. Cleveland, the President Elect, was in favor of annexation.'[351] Whether Thurston and his colleagues genuinely believed that, is unclear, but there was a widespread belief in Washington at the time that Cleveland would not oppose annexation. Just the same, knowing that the Harrison Administration was entirely in their corner, it made sense for the annexationists to push their treaty through before Cleveland came into office on March 4.

As their meeting progressed, Thurston presented Foster with a draft for the annexation treaty document that had been approved by the Provisional Government's councils prior to the commission's departure from Honolulu. After reading it, Foster worried the commissioners with a shake of his head. One clause in particular, he said, would have to go. This was the clause covering the use of foreign contract labor in Hawaii, the one clause that Claus Spreckels and other members of the sugar trust wanted included. Foster declared that the treaty had no hope of ratification while it contained that provision. Without it, he said, the treaty stood a good chance of being accepted.

The commissioners looked at each other. Realizing that they would be making powerful enemies, not the least being Claus Spreckels, they all nonetheless agreed that the foreign labor provision would have to be sacrificed. The 'Claus clause' as they called it, was struck out, and the meeting was adjourned until the following Tuesday. As it was to turn out, the initial vocal support for annexation shown by Spreckels and his colleagues soon led the press to declare that annexation was all about 'big sugar' and the greedy self-interest of the rich Hawaiian sugar producers. Thurston would expend a great deal of energy convincing editors that annexation was not about sugar, which, once the deletion of the Claus clause became known, it certainly was not. Spreckels, once he learned of the commissioners' action, was absolutely furious at what he considered a betrayal. Determined to take his revenge on Thurston and his crew, Spreckels not only subsequently declared himself annexation's greatest enemy, he actively set out to wreck it.

On the Monday, February 6, the New York *Herald* reported that it had canvassed both houses of Congress on the Hawaiian annexation issue. Eighty members of the House had told the paper they were in favor of annexation, forty-six said they were opposed, and seventy-seven would not commit either way. In the Senate, twenty senators were said to be in favor of annexation, while thirty-five favored making Hawaii a protectorate, and twenty-five would not commit to any policy. It all added up to a lot of work on behalf of the administration if it was to have the treaty speedily endorsed by both houses.

With this in mind, when Foster met with Thurston and his colleagues at 10.00 a.m. on February 7, he again took the editing pencil to the treaty. William Castle noted: 'He says it is important to make a treaty which the Senate can ratify without going to the House, or the business cannot be done now. This will necessitate the deferring of much of our requirements.'[352] The bare-bones treaty that remained did little more than hand the islands over to the US, but even that was acceptable to Lorrin Thurston. Anything to achieve annexation and do away with the monarchy.

The commissioners' lack of bargaining power became all the more apparent when Foster pointed out that unless the cuts were made, 'the House might take a hand, and this means much delay, possibly defeat.' Then the cagey secretary of state played his trump card. Castle wrote: 'Mr. Foster intimates that the President might desire a plebiscite at the Islands.'[353] Thurston and his cohorts knew that a referendum in Hawaii on the subject of annexation would be overwhelmingly defeated by the Hawaiian people. A plebiscite was the last thing they wanted. The commissioners went away to compose a new document, one that avoided the need for a plebiscite.

By Friday the 10th, Mott-Smith, the commissioners, and several friends who had joined them in Washington finalized their deliberations: 'We all agree to the short and concise treaty necessary to get action by the Senate,' Castle wrote in his diary. At 10.00 that morning, they presented the treaty to Foster. 'After some further discussion and suggestions of ours we came to terms.' The commissioners had won one tiny concession: 'The Hawaiian flag is to be kept as a district banner.' The following morning, the commissioners again met with Secretary Foster and signed the final treaty document. 'I retained the pen,' Castle noted proudly.[354]

Foster then escorted the commissioners to the White House to meet the President at a public reception. 'Mr. Harrison shook hands very mechanically,' said Castle, 'and seemed surprised, perhaps annoyed, if any exhibited pleasure or would speak.' Harrison was totally disinterested in the subjects of Hawaii or annexation. That agenda had, apparently, been driven by Blaine, Tracy, and, more recently, Foster. Benjamin Harrison seemed incapable of driving anything. 'It is rather surprising how such a man becomes President,' Castle observed.[355]

The following Tuesday, February 14, the commissioners asked Secretary Foster to withhold the treaty from the Senate until the following day, when the SS *Australia* set sail from San Francisco on its latest run to Honolulu. Said Castle, this was 'so that the text will not go to Honolulu till we can go—or someone—and explain.'[356] The necessary explaining would be to their colleagues of the Provisional Government, for the annexation treaty that was submitted to the US Senate on February 15 bore little resemblance to the treaty which the commissioners had been sent to Washington with.

22.

A PRINCESS IN THE WHITE HOUSE

In Britain, Queen Liliuokalani's heir apparent, the seventeen-year-old Princess Victoria Kaiulani, was staying with the family of her British guardian, Theo Davies, at 'Sundown,' the Davies' Welsh estate on the Irish Sea. On January 30, three telegrams arrived at 'Sundown' in quick succession. Addressed to Theo Davies by Hawaiian ambassador Mott-Smith in Washington, they read: 'Queen deposed,' 'Monarchy abrogated,' then, 'Break news to Princess.'[357]

Kaiulani was staggered by the tidings. She would confide to her dairy, 'I feel my life is over before it has really begun.'[358] Groomed as a queen in waiting, and, considered by many of her people to be 'the Hope of Hawaii,' she could not imagine any other life. Yet, here the annexationists had taken her future from her in one fell swoop.

From the British press, Kaiulani soon learned more details of her Aunt Lydia's overthrow. 'Revolution in Hawaii!' declared the *Times* of London that same day that the telegrams reached the Davies estate. 'The long-threatened revolution has broken out,' the *Times* went on. 'The Queen and Government overthrown, and a provisional Government and President have been appointed.' London's *Daily Telegraph* and the *Evening Standard* both expressed opinions in favor of the restoration of the Hawaiian monarchy, although not necessarily of Queen Liliuokalani herself.[359]

The British Government's first reaction to the overthrow of the Hawaiian monarchy by American annexationists was one of concern. British Foreign Minister Lord Roseberry was reported as saying, on behalf of his government, 'While the present attitude was a passive one, Great Britain and France could not allow the annexation of the islands by America,' and he immediately dispatched the Royal Navy cruiser HMS *Garnett* to Honolulu.[360] But, with bigger problems on its plate–the country was divided over the Irish Home Rule Bill, and the British Army was about to become embroiled in a bruising war in Egypt–Great Britain would before long wash its hands of Hawaii.

Canadian Premier Sir John Thompson huffed that 'Canadian interests were involved in the integrity of Hawaii, especially in view of the construction of the Pacific Cable,' which Canada wanted laid from its shores, rather than from California.[361] But, ultimately, Canada also turned its official gaze elsewhere. The New Zealand Government protested to London, deploring the Hawaiian coup and likely US annexation, but, as its foreign policy was then dictated by Britain, the New Zealand protest went no farther. The colonial governments of Australia were similarly restricted. Germany, meanwhile, said that Britain and the US should sort out the Hawaii situation between them, and France laughed at Britain's discomfort over the situation in the islands and went back to enjoying the Naughty Nineties.

The best that Britain could do, it seemed, was to focus on the part-British Hawaiian princess on their shores, with one London paper speculating 'that the British Government will be prepared to press her claim' to the Hawaiian throne.[362] Soon, the talk in British editorial columns was increasingly of young Kaiulani assuming the throne in her aunt's place. Within a day of the first news of the Hawaiian revolution, a London daily was reporting, 'The Princess Kaiulani is likely to return to Honolulu shortly.'[363]

The princess would not be going home to Honolulu just yet. With international interest in the Hawaiian revolution quickly fading, it became clear that Hawaii's fate lay in the hands of the United States, and Theo Davies convinced Kaiulani that she should go to Washington to support her aunt's case for restoration. Davies sent a telegram to Mott-Smith to say that they were coming. Mott-Smith cabled back: 'Cannot use help yet.' 364 Davies ignored the message. He, his family members, and the princess began to make preparations to sail from Southampton to New York on February 25 aboard the transatlantic passenger liner SS *Teutonic*.

In the interim, Davies and the princess composed a statement which was released to the press in Kaiulani's name: 'Four years ago, at the request of Mr. Thurston, then a Hawaiian cabinet minister, I was sent away to England to be educated privately and fitted to the position which by the Constitution of Hawaii I was to inherit. For all these years I have patiently and in exile striven to fit myself for my return this year to my native country. I am now told that Mr. Thurston is in Washington asking you to take away my flag and my throne. No one tells me even this officially. Have I done anything wrong, that this wrong should be done to me and my people? I am coming to Washington to plead for my throne, my nation, and my flag. Will not the American people hear me?'[365]

When the *Teutonic* sailed into New York Harbor on March 1, a massive contingent of newspaper reporters and photographers was waiting on the pier to greet Princess Kaiulani. A boat made its way out to meet the liner before it docked, and ambassador Mott-Smith and Ed Macfarlane–one of Queen Liliuokalani's envoys from Honolulu, who had by this time reached New York– transferred to the *Teutonic* to welcome the young princess, and to brief her.

Macfarlane, Prince Kawanakoa and delegation leader Paul Neumann had all arrived in Washington DC in the middle of February, but had experienced difficulty making any headway with the Harrison Administration as they strove to put Liliuokalani's case for restoration. The annexation commissioners were scornful of Neumann. 'He is not received officially,' wrote William Castle in his dairy with glee. 'I do not think he will accomplish much.'[366] The only good news that Ed Macfarlane was able to pass onto Princess Kaiulani as she prepared to land in Manhattan was that Lorrin Thurston's Hawaiian annexation treaty had become stalled in the Senate, where Democrats had been made suspicious by the unseemly rush of the secretary state for ratification of the treaty. The document now lay on the table, awaiting the March inauguration of new president Grover Cleveland.

On the negative side of the ledger, Paul Neumann had attempted to arrange an interview with the president elect, but had not been granted one, and the US press was speculating that Cleveland would support the annexation treaty once he was in office. Neumann, Prince Kawanaoa, and Mott-Smith were all against Princess Kaiulani coming to America and entering the debate. Neumann knew that many in the United States had the same historical abhorrence of monarchy that John L. Stevens had come to exhibit, and the lawyer was reluctant to expose the young heir to the throne to the jackals of the press.

Prince Kawanakoa was against the princess's coming for another, more personal reason. There was a time when Kaiulani and the dashing Koa, as he was known in the family, and who was a decade older than the princess, had been romantically linked. But lately they had fallen out. Kawanakoa believed that Vicki was coming to promote her own elevation to the Hawaiian throne, rather than to support her aunt's cause. As for Dr. Mott-Smith, it appears that he had thrown his lot in with the annexationists, having given Hawaii's monarchy up for lost.

Against the advice of Liliuokalani's envoys, the princess had come to America, and now that she was here Macfarlane and Mott-Smith were bent on making the most of it. They were also prepared to launch into damage control mode should the teenager make a fool of herself, of Liliuokalani, and of them. As the *Teutonic* docked, it was agreed that Kaiulani would read a statement which she and Theo Davies had prepared, and then Davies, Macfarlane and Mott-Smith would field questions from the press on her behalf.

The press corps had been told that a Hawaiian princess was coming to town, and many were expecting to see a dark-skinned 'savage.' Some had inquired whether they would need an interpreter, and they were astonished to learn that, in addition to Hawaiian, the young woman was fluent in English, French and German. But it was the image of her as she came down the gangway that took the breath away. Just prior to Liliuokalani's overthrow, Theo Davies had purchased a new wardrobe for Kaiulani, in Paris, in preparation for a vacation tour of Europe before her return home to Hawaii. In France, this was *La Belle Époque*, and the latest French high fashion was all about long, elegant, tight-fitting dresses, corseted waistlines, and glamorous broad-brimmed hats with plenty of feathers. Kaiulani was well proportioned–tall, slim, with a naturally slender waist–and as she stepped onto the dock in her best French high-necked gown and feathered hat, followed by her entourage of worried minders, she looked like a fashion model.

Cameras popped and flashed, and dazzled reporters jostled each other to get close and throw questions at her. Kaiulani had been nervous prior to landing, but now she relaxed. Smiling, she lay her large round brown eyes on each of the male reporters in turn; and they swooned at her feet. Journalists would rave about those dreamy, almost mesmerizing eyes, not knowing that Kaiulani was severely near-sighted. She wore spectacles out of the public eye, but would never allow herself to be photographed in them. So, when she gazed at reporters with what became her trademark far-away look, it was because she could barely see them. Her secret remained undisclosed, and the New York press corps was conquered before she even opened her mouth. 'Beautiful.' 'Enchanting.' 'Fascinating.' 'Captivating.' The adjectives would flow when the press room keyboards clacked.

Stout, bearded Theo Davies announced that Her Highness wished to make a statement, and a hushed descended on the throng. Reading the statement, which was no doubt writ large so she could manage it without her eyeglasses, Kaiulani said, in a sweet, sing-song voice: "Seventy years ago, Christian America sent over Christian men and women to give religion and civilization to Hawaii. Today three of the sons of those missionaries (Thurston, Castle and Carter) are at your Capitol, asking you to undo their fathers' work. Today, I, a poor, weak girl, with not one of my people near me and all of these statesmen against me, have the strength to stand up for the rights of my people. Even now I can hear their wail in my heart, and it gives me strength and I am strong. Strong in the faith of God. Strong in the knowledge that I am right."[367]

And then came a torrent of reporters' questions, about what the princess would do, where she would go, who she would see. As planned, they were dealt with by Davies, Macfarlane and Mott-Smith, after which they, the princess and the Davies party moved on. In their wake, reporters dashed for telephones and typewriters. With just her presence and a few words, Kaiulani had won over the press. One reporter with a way with words would write, 'Her accent says London, her figure says New York, but her heart says Hawaii.'[368]

Castle, Carter and Thurston were in Washington on Saturday March 4 for what Castle jokingly described as 'America's coronation'– Grover Cleveland's presidential inauguration.[369] The other two annexation commissioners had gone home to

Hawaii. When Castle got out of bed that morning and threw
back the curtain of his Wormleys Hotel bedroom, he was met
with a very un-Hawaiian sight: 'It was snowing fast and with
big flakes. Damp and raw, with wind in gusts. It grew worse all
day.'[370]

While the trio attended Cleveland's bitterly cold inauguration
day festivities as official guests, Princess Kaiulani was in Boston,
taking a sleigh ride and keeping a low profile. The annexation
commissioners were not much worried by Kaiulani's arrival in
the US. They could not see a teenage girl having any impact
on the situation. Besides, Secretary of State Foster had publicly
disparaged Kaiulani as 'a potential English sovereign for Hawaii.'

Foster was referring to Kaiulani's British father, British
guardian, and British education, and playing on the widespread
American dislike of British influence—in Hawaii, and anywhere
else. Foster and the annexationists received unexpected support
from Prince Kawanakoa, who pointed out to reporters that in
her statements Kaiulani had said nothing about the restoration of
her aunt. Kawanakoa accused the princess of being controlled by
Theo Davies, and accused Davies of working against the interests
of Liliuokalani.[371]

On March 8, Princess Kaiulani and the Davies family arrived
in Washington from Boston and checked into the Arlington
Hotel, where the princess was again a press sensation. By this
time, Davies had worked out that Mott-Smith was in the enemy
camp, and he told the crowd of reporters at the Arlington that,
although the good doctor was his friend, he would no longer
grant him access to the princess, as Mott-Smith represented
the Provisional Government. Davies also announced that the
annexation commissioners were banned from any contact with
Kaiulani.

The annexation commissioners were not bothered by this
news, nor by the news that a petition against US annexation
signed by thousands of Hawaiians throughout the islands has
arrived in Washington. Ambassador Stevens had written to the
State Department disparaging this petition, declaring that the
signatures had been obtained by unscrupulous means and false
representations. 'This dirty work,' he assured the secretary of
state, 'is managed exclusively by the same white men, American
renegades, Australians, and Canadians, who have thrived on the

palace corruptions under the recent King Kalakaua and his sister, the deposed queen.'[372]

The annexation commissioners were so full of confidence that Thurston wrote to Sanford Dole during this week, 'I believe that Gresham is heartily in sympathy with the annexation proposition, and will do all he can to forward it. All our information has also been that Mr. Cleveland is in favor of the general proposition, although he has been so closed-mouthed that it is impossible to say exactly what his intentions are.'[373]

On the morning of March 10, the annexation commissioners were staggered to learn, from reporters flooding to Wormleys with their notebooks at the ready, that Walter Gresham, Grover Cleveland's newly installed Secretary of State, had that day withdrawn the Hawaiian annexation treaty from the Senate. Annexationists and the Republican press would now turn on Gresham, accusing him of being a poor loser after twice being rejected by the Republican party as a presidential candidate. 'He could not be nominated by Republicans,' William Castle wrote bitterly in his diary, 'so satisfies his revengeful soul by trying to undo what the Republican President has done.'[374]

Castle, Thurston and Carter were thrown into a tailspin. 'Our friends the reporters,' wrote Carter, 'are anxious to learn our next move. We don't know ourselves. At home we shall have to "hold it down" some way. Liliuokalani and her friends will be filled with courage.' The three commissioners had invitations to go to a formal State Department reception that evening. Dazed, they went along. They felt even worse when they found that the reception was held in the very room where they had signed the now withdrawn treaty. 'How different the surroundings,' Castle wrote. 'No longer friendly officials. Frowns where there were smiles.' The trio met the new secretary of state, Walter Gresham, 'a large man with much gray in both hair and beard,' noted Castle. 'Rather of a pleasant voice. However, not pleasant for *us!*' Gresham informed that commissioners of his 'stern disapproval of the policy of the Republican President Harrison.' Castle left the encounter deeply shaken by their encounter with Gresham. 'There is trouble in store,' he wrote. 'He may ruin us all.'[375]

Thurston, as he had once before, immediately lost hope, and lapsed into depression. His spiraling spirits infected Carter. The pair began packing their bags, and made arrangements to leave Washington next day. Castle was made of more resolute stuff, and the following day he sought and received a solo interview with Secretary Gresham, who 'was chilly, and evidently wishes me to regard my call as an intrusion. In answer to my direct question about intentions of the administration regarding Hawaii, (he) intimated that nothing is to be done at present.'[376] Gresham had no intention of telling the annexationists that something was indeed being done by the Cleveland Administration, and at that very moment.

That afternoon, on the heels of Castle's disheartening meeting with Secretary Gresham, he, Thurston and Carter met with several friends at Wormleys Hotel for a farewell. 'None of us are hopeful of present action,' Castle wrote. 'Certainly nothing favorable to annexation.' Now came wisdom in hindsight. 'We ought to have got the ear of the new administration, but risked and staked *all* on Foster's success. It was the correct thing to have gone at once to Cleveland, as Neumann and Ed Macfarlane did for the queen.'[377]

Their overconfidence, based on Thurston's assurances that the Harrison Administration would endorse their annexation treaty, showed their lack of Capitol Hill lobbying experience. Washington politics are never that simple. Without congressmen on side, an administration's gleaming policy desires frequently end up on the scrap-heap of rusty spurned initiatives. That evening, Thurston, Carter and Castle all boarded the night train for New York City, and in Thurston's words, 'melted away.'[378]

James Blount, the fifty-six-year-old former chairman of the House Foreign Relations Committee, had only been back home in Macon, Georgia a matter of weeks after retiring from the House, when, on March 10, his son brought him a telegram from Secretary of the Interior Hoke Smith in Washington. The cable read: 'I ask can you come here immediately prepared for a confidential trip of great importance into Pacific Ocean?'[379]

After all the recent press coverage about Hawaii and annexation, Blount immediately had a very good idea where this Pacific mission would take him. 'When I first got the telegram,' he was to say, 'I made up my mind very promptly that I would not go.' Showing the telegram to his wife, Eugenia, he told her that he was going to turn down the request.[380]

Blount's son was thoughtful for a while, then said, "Father, mother's health is very bad." Eugenia Blount was apparently suffering from consumption. "And I think it would add five years to her life to go."

"I will do anything for your mother's benefit," Blount responded. "I will go."[381]

And so, as the retreating annexation commissioners rattled and rolled their way to New York, James Blount prepared to take his wife and himself to Washington, for a briefing at the White House, and thence to Honolulu via San Francisco. His confidential brief was to launch an investigation on behalf of Grover Cleveland, as the President's 'special commissioner,' into the circumstances surrounding the overthrow of Queen Liliuokalani.

The *New York Times* would say on March 15, as the Blounts headed west, 'Mr. Blount will make a very safe representative of the conservative interest in his country.' He was, opined the *Times*, 'a man of great adaptability to men, one who managed to be a good Democrat and yet to get along with Mr. Blaine without quarrelling with that exacting statesman.' As to Blount and his mission, details of which the Cleveland Administration had not made public, the *Times* said, 'If he makes a report of conditions in the islands, it will be a faithful report of things as he sees them. His integrity is beyond question.'

The same day that James Blount received the request to go to Washington and the three annexation commissioners departed the capital, Princess Kaiulani and Mr. and Mrs. Davies received an invitation to join the President and First Lady at the Executive Mansion–that very afternoon, at 5.30.

In a flurry of excitement the young princess prepared, and at 5.30 she and her party were shown into the oval Blue Room, the White House's state reception room, and were greeted by First Lady Frances Cleveland and President Cleveland. The President's wife had a boyish face and bubbly charm that endeared her to the press. Kaiulani was enchanted by her, just as the First Lady was enchanted by the Hawaiian teenager. Kaiulani would tell reporters, back at the Arlington Hotel later, "I was simply infatuated with Mrs. Cleveland. She is very beautiful. But all beautiful women are not sweet, you know. But Mrs. Cleveland is both, and I have fallen in love with her."[382]

At the time of the Cleveland's invitation, it had been made clear that this was to be a social visit, not a state visit. So there were not the usual formalities, and no politics were discussed. President Cleveland even surprised the princess by displaying a talent as a mimic. And then, after a delightful hour, it was over, and Kaiulani and her escorts were in a carriage on their way back to their hotel. Kaiulani would have plenty to tell her father, Archie Cleghorn, who would soon arrive from Honolulu to join her.

Supporters of annexation, inside Congress and out, would criticize the President for hosting the princess at the White House. They claimed that it signaled Cleveland's personal support for Kaiulani's cause, and that it, as one newspaper suggested, 'technically committed this government to a consideration of her position.' The administration quickly countered this argument. 'It is asserted at the Department of State,' said Boston's *Evening Transcript*, 'that the character of the audience granted to the princess was a subject of purely informal arrangement, that the princess was so specifically informed, and accepted the accorded interview on those conditions. Therefore, this incident has no bearing whatever on the main matter.'[383]

Yet, despite the administration's take on the princess' visit to the White House, that visit sent an encouraging signal to the many supporters of the monarchy in Hawaii, and an equally discouraging signal to the annexationists. And perhaps it was intended that way—by Frances Cleveland, if not by her husband.

By March 22, Princess Kaiulani was on the Atlantic aboard the SS *Majestic*, on her way back to England, having successfully courted the US media for three weeks. She had done no harm for her cause or her aunt's cause, and probably did a great deal of good. At the same time, James Blount, his wife Eugenia, and the US State Department's Ellis Mills, Blount's Hawaiian mission secretary, were on the Pacific aboard the United States Revenue Service's cutter *Richard Rush*, which had been put at Blount's disposal by his government, bound for Honolulu.

The story of Hawaii's monarchy was about to enter a new phase.

23.

LOWERING THE US FLAG

'COMPARED WITH COMMISSIONER BLOUNT, THE Sphinx is a chatterbox,' said one frustrated reporter who attempted to interview James Blount while he was in San Francisco.[384] 'The most simple thing I might say would be likely to be construed as significant,' Blount himself later explained. 'It was important for me not to take any position one way or the other.'[385] Despite this, news of his mission reached Hawaii before he did, by mail steamer. The Provisional Government had Honolulu decked out in American flags when the USRS *Richard Rush* arrived in crowded Honolulu Harbor on the morning of March 29.

The USS *Boston* had by this time been joined at Honolulu by a second US Navy cruiser, the *Mohican*, and both were at anchor in the harbor when the USRS *Rush* arrived. Beside the American cruisers, within hailing distance, lay the elderly British sloop of war HMS *Hyacinth*, which had recently replaced the cruiser *Garnet* in port. Also at anchor was the trim Japanese cruiser HIJMNS *Naniwa*, the most advanced ship of its kind in the world when launched in Scotland seven years before. Unbeknownst to the Provisional Government, Japanese consul-general Fujii had sent a dispatch to his government aboard the *Claudine* when it carried the annexation commissioners to San Francisco in January. Mr. Fujii had expressed concern to the Japanese Government that the thousands of Japanese residents of Hawaii would be discriminated against by the all-white Provisional Government, and asked for a warship to be sent to Honolulu to help safeguard Japanese interests.

The powerful *Naniwa*, pride of the Japanese fleet, larger than the *Boston* and *Mohican* and with a larger crew, had arrived on February 23. Since then, her commander, Captain Heihachiro Togo, later an admiral of note, had been at odds with the Provisional Government–after a Japanese prisoner had escaped from Oahu Prison and swam out to the *Naniwa*, Captain Togo had refused to hand him back.

When the *Richard Rush* docked, an immense crowd of curious Honolulu people was gathered on the pier to see President Cleveland's man in the flesh. A little after 10.00 a.m., ambassador John Stevens led a delegation of Annexation Club members up the gangway and aboard the little steamer. This was a very different Annexation Club from the secret seventeen-member society originally established by Lorrin Thurston. A very public organization, this latest version of the Club had been set up by annexationists since January 17 to counter the native Hawaiian patriotic societies, whose membership was in the tens of thousands. This Annexation Club boasted that it had five thousand members who were in favor of US annexation–James Blount came to hear that many were plantation employees ordered to sign up by their bosses.

Blount received Stevens and his party in the forward cabin of the *Rush*. Stevens had an offer to make. 'He informed me that this Club had rented an elegant house, well furnished, and provided with servants and a carriage and horses for my use,' Blount would report. Ambassador Stevens told Blount 'that I could pay for this accommodation just what I chose, from nothing up! He urged me very earnestly to accept the offer. I declined it, and informed him that I should go to a hotel.'[386]

At 11.00, after Stevens and his disappointed friends trooped off the ship, Liliuokalani's chamberlain, James Robertson, came aboard and offered Blount the use of the queen's carriage. Blount courteously declined that offer, too. As their residence in Honolulu, Blount, his wife, and his secretary occupied one of the several cottages that sat in the park-like grounds of the Hawaiian Hotel. But from the start, the commissioner could see that the boorish, blinkered US ambassador had unashamedly allied himself to the annexationist movement.

The next day, Blount, looking dapper in a white, three-piece suit and white hat, went to the Government Building to pay an official call on Sanford Dole, President of the Provisional Government. Cordially received by Dole, Blount passed over his letter of accreditation from President Cleveland, in which Cleveland said that Blount's mission was to 'make report to me concerning the present status of affairs in the country.' And, Cleveland stressed in the letter, 'in all matters affecting relations with the Government of the Hawaiian Islands his authority is paramount.'[387]

From this reference would grow the derisory nickname given to Blount by the annexationists–Paramount Blount. The authority bestowed on Blount by the President made him superior in rank to Ambassador Stevens, a fact which Stevens resented and resisted. He would later rant about what he perceived as Blount's 'inferiority of official rank,' and would tell the US press that it was all he could do to be polite to the President's man, only 'with the utmost effort of will controlling my outraged sensibilities.'[388]

Blount's also carried credentials from the Secretary of the Navy which empowered him to issue orders to the US Navy commander in the islands, who was now Rear Admiral Joseph S. Skerrett. Captain Wiltse's two-year tour of duty had not been extended by the Navy when it expired in February. Nor had the Navy Department given him another appointment. Wiltse, who had come in for criticism in some US newspapers for landing troops on January 16 and then participating in the February 1 declaration of protectorate status, had gone home to New York City, to be replaced as commander of the *Boston* by Captain B. F. Day. In the meantime, the *Mohican*, flagship of the US Navy's Pacific station, had steamed into Honolulu Harbor carrying Admiral Skerrett.

Blount meant to exercise his authority immediately. Prior to leaving Washington, he had met with Secretary of State Gresham, who had expressed the opinion that there was no principle in international law that he thought justified the hoisting of the American flag in Honolulu and the declaration of Hawaii as a US protectorate by Stevens. Gresham's Republican predecessor, Secretary of State Foster, had actually sent Stevens a dispatch on February 14 in which he disavowed the ambassador's action in raising the flag in the first place–Stevens would later refuse to acknowledge the validity of that disavowal. But despite his condemnation of the act, Foster had not instructed Stevens to haul the flag down again, so he hadn't.

At 11.00 on the morning of March 31, Blount again called on Dole, and asked him whether the Provisional Government's police and military were capable of preserving order in the country. Dole assured him they were. That being the case, said Blount, he intended taking down the US flag at 4.00 that afternoon, running up the Hawaiian flag once more in its place, and withdrawing all US marines and sailors from Camp Boston to their ships. Dole, stunned, asked for a delay of twenty-four hours, so Blount set 11.00 a.m. next day for the flag-changing ceremony.

At the same time that Blount was meeting with Dole, Provisional Government Advisory Council member John McCandless was at the American Legation on Nuuanu Avenue, chatting with Ambassador Stevens. When McCandless asked the ambassador what his feelings were about the present situation in Hawaii, Stevens responded, "I am very well satisfied with everything as it is."

McCandless then mentioned that some people believed that Commissioner Blount would haul down the US flag currently flying over the Government Building. Stevens had no idea that Blount's authority also extended to the US Navy in Hawaii– Blount had not shown Stevens his letters of authority from the secretaries of State or the Navy. In fact, Stevens was still convinced of Blount's 'inferiority of rank' to him. In answer to the question from McCandless, Stevens pompously declared, "The flag will never come down!"[389]

That evening, Blount received an unexpected visit from Ambassador Stevens at his Hawaiian Hotel cottage. President Dole had obviously used the requested delay as an opportunity to contact Stevens, who now not only knew about the intended flag lowering, he had brought along a reinforcement in a bid to halt it– Walter G. Smith, editor of the *Hawaiian Star*, a pro-annexation newspaper set up in Honolulu by the Annexation Club since the queen's overthrow.

Speaking 'with intense gravity,' the newspaper editor told Blount, "I know beyond doubt that it has been arranged between the queen and the Japanese commissioner that if the American flag and troops were removed, the troops from the Japanese man of war *Naniwa* would land and reinstate the queen."[390]

Supporting Smith's dramatic declaration, Stevens said that it was important that American troops remained on shore until Blount could communicate with Secretary of State Gresham, and then after Gresham had communicated with the Japanese Government and obtained assurances that no Japanese troops would be landed in Hawaii to force any policy on the government of Hawaii. This could all take months. But Blount could see right through Stevens and Smith. 'I was not impressed with these statements,' he later said.[391] Shortly after this, Blount would tell Consul General Fujii about Smith's claim. Fujii, horrified that his government could be accused of interfering in Hawaiian affairs, wrote to Japan, with the upshot being that within a matter of weeks Captain Togo received new orders, and the *Naniwa* sailed away.

In the meantime, Commissioner Blount was determined to run up the Hawaiian flag and withdraw US troops to their ship. He had two strong reasons for doing this. Firstly, Secretary of State Gresham had told Blount that, for reasons of international law, 'protectorate status ought not be continued' in Hawaii.[392] But Blount was more concerned that, while American forces were seen to be in occupation of Honolulu, potential witnesses to his inquiry might be intimidated into keeping their mouths shut. To mollify Stevens, Blount agreed to leave a marine guard at the American Legation. But the flag-changing ceremony at the Government Building and the withdrawal of all remaining troops would proceed.

Several hundred yards from the Government Building, at Washington Place, Queen Liliuokalani was living under increasingly difficult circumstances. In February, the Provisional Government had stopped paying the salaries of the members of her bodyguard and disbanded them. Sam Nowlein had stayed on as the queen's sole, unpaid protector, and Liliuokalani allowed Nowlein and his wife, and Charles Wilson and his wife, to move into cottages in the Washington Place grounds, rent-free. Then, on James Blount's third day in Hawaii, as if to punish Liliuokalani for the commissioner's announced intention of lowering of the US flag and the removal of US troops, the Provisional Government informed Liliuokalani that it was stopping her salary, too, and the salary of her chamberlain. Officially, she was told that this was because she had supposedly encouraged the writing of articles in a Hawaiian-language newspaper that were critical of the Provisional Government and Ambassador Stevens.

This was going to make things difficult for Liliuokalani. To pay for Neumann, Kawanakoa and Macfarlane to make the trip to Washington on her behalf, she had borrowed ten thousand dollars from Sam Damon, mortgaging her Palama and Waikiki houses. Already owing the banker seven thousand dollars prior to her overthrow, she was now in debt to the second highest-ranking member of the Provisional Government for a total of seventeen thousand dollars.

The annexationists' *Hawaiian Star* had in February called for Liliuokalani to be deported, a call that Lorrin Thurston, who had remained in the US, supported from afar. But Liliuokalani was permitted to stay in the islands, probably because the Provisional Government feared a mass uprising by Hawaiians if they attempted to remove her. Now, while she remained on Hawaiian soil, and remained a thorn in the Provisional Government's side, they would increasingly put pressure on her. To raise money and keep her household running, Liliuokalani was forced to give her Hawaiian Agricultural Company shares to Sam Parker, asking him to sell them at the best possible price.

The arrival of Commissioner Blount was, to the queen, a signal that the US Government would restore her to her throne. To her mind, it was just a matter of holding on until that occurred. Early on the morning of April 1, after Liliuokalani had heard that the US flag was to come down at 11.00 and the Hawaiian flag returned to its place over the Government Building, and, realizing that this was no April Fool's joke, she sent for Joseph Carter, who continued to be her faithful adviser.

"What should we do when the flag is raised?" she asked Carter when he arrived at 9.00 a.m.

"Keep perfectly quiet, and not cheer, Your Majesty," he replied.

"No cheering?"

"It would be aggravating to the Americans."[393]

Liliuokalani immediately sent for ali'i Joseph Nawahi, and, when he came to her, she instructed him to tell the people to be quiet when the flag ceremony took place.

With their band playing, the men of the USS *Boston* marched along King Street, having left Camp Boston for the last time, and made their way to the Government Building. Two hundred soldiers of the Provisional Government had formed up outside the building, resplendent in new blue uniforms of US Army pattern. The US marines and blue jackets also formed up in neat ranks.

Beyond the iron railings which separated the Government Building's grounds from King Street, a large crowd of mostly Hawaiian men, women and children swelled, with much smiling and laughter. The crowd watched in silence as, with due ceremony, the US flag came down. Out on the harbor, the guns of the US flagship *Mohican* sounded a salute. Then, up went the Hawaiian flag in its place–without a single cheer from the crowd. A company of Provisional Government troops then formally took over the Government Building from the squad of US marines that had been in occupation since February 1. It all went off peacefully; no protest by Americans, no exaltation by Hawaiians. 'There was not the remotest evidence shown, by the crowd of natives present and others about the Government Building, of any feeling,' a surprised Admiral Skerrett reported to the navy secretary in Washington. 'No demonstration of any description.'[394]

Commissioner Blount chose not to attend the ceremony–so that he did not antagonize one side or the other. Captain Calvin L. Hooper, commander of the USRS *Richard Rush*, went in Blount's stead. Hooper, who had some renown for a book he'd written about his explorations in Alaskan waters, took along his teenage son Calvin Jr., who was serving under him. Hooper reported back to Blount: 'I was surprised not only at the absence of the indication of the violent and partisan feeling that I had been led to expect, but by the apparent apathy and indifference of the native portion of the assembled crowd.'[395] The English-language press would also report this apparent apathy and indifference, declaring it evidence that the queen had no popular support, and that the locals did not care for their own flag and were not bothered about Hawaii being annexed.

Liliuokalani knew different. She had given her orders, and her people had obeyed their *wahine moi*. 'The people listened to my voice,' the queen would write, 'and obeyed my will with a submission that kept the community free from disorder far more than any law or restraint of that which has called itself a government.'[396] In her diary for that day, Liliuokalani recorded what was reported back to her. She had told the people to be quiet–'which they did, and behaved very well. Their feelings of joy were suppressed, while the men all took their hats off, while tears of joy streamed down the cheeks of men as well as women.'[397]

Lieutenant Lucien Young, who was on duty aboard the *Boston* at the time of the flag-changing ceremony, felt anything but joy. He claimed that his feeling was shared by his crewmates. It was, he said, 'a humiliation which was keenly felt by men and officers.' He would also claim that Admiral Skerrett lodged a complaint with the navy secretary against Commissioner Blount over the whole affair; but Skerrett did no such thing. Following the ceremony, the American sailors and marines marched down to the docks, and were ferried back to their ship. Once the color party came aboard the *Boston*, the bitter Lieutenant Young claimed the now furled US flag that had been flying over Honolulu's Government Building, and hid it.[398]

Young was not the only American who was outraged by the lowering of the US flag in Hawaii. The outcry across the United States, once the news of Blount's action arrived, took Blount, Secretary of State Gresham, and the White House by surprise. One Republican member declared in the House, "Mr. Speaker, I had grown into the idea that the American ensign could not be hauled down. In times past, an order had been given under other circumstances, to shoot any man who attempts to haul down the flag." A Democrat asked, if the flag had to be hauled down, could it not have been done at night, so that no one witnessed its coming down?[399]

And not a few Republicans were up in arms about 'the deplorable fact that an ex-Confederate should have hauled down the American flag.'[400] James Blount had served in the Confederate Army during the Civil War. Initially a Georgia rifleman, he had ended the war as a lieutenant colonel of his own cavalry regiment. Despite the fact that the Civil War was close to thirty years in the past, some northerners had long memories, and many of Cleveland's political opponents would from now on describe his Hawaiian commissioner James Blount as 'the Confederate colonel.'

Despite the furor in the US, Blount was able to report that, in Hawaii, all was quiet. Now he could settle down to the many months of interviewing that would characterize his inquiry into the overthrow of Liliuokalani, and of the part that John L. Stevens, Captain Gilbert Wiltse and US forces had played in it.

* * *

On April 19, Liliuokalani wrote in her diary, 'I think he will, I mean Mr. Blount, reinstate.' That is, reinstate her to the throne. It was wishful thinking.

Blount strove to be as impartial as possible. He only met with Liliuokalani twice, and then only briefly. He refused many social invitations from annexationists and royalists alike, while treating the members of the Provisional Government with the utmost courtesy. Just as the queen thought that Blount would favor her, Sanford Dole believed that he had made Blount his friend, and that Blount would take the side of the Provisional Government. Dole wrote, in a confidential memorandum to the members of the Executive and Advisory Councils, that, although he had come to believe that President Cleveland had no intention of annexing Hawaii, he was confident that the Provisional Government would be able to secure a treaty with Cleveland which guaranteed US Government assistance for them–'especially with Blount's friendly services.'[401]

On April 20, a day after Liliuokalani made her optimistic diary entry, thousands of miles away in New York City, fifty-five-year-old Captain Gilbert Wiltse, former commander of the USS *Boston*, and the man who had ordered US troops to invade Hawaii, collapsed at his home on East 53rd Street. His doctors diagnosed 'congestion of the brain.'[402] Six days later, Wiltse was dead.

Some of the more superstitious people in Hawaii may have felt that perhaps William Castle was right, that the kahunas were praying the leading players in the overthrow of Queen Liliuokalani to death.

24.

RESTORE THE QUEEN

JAMES BLOUNT FORWARDED HIS COMPLETED Hawaiian report to Secretary of State Gresham in July, and departed the islands a few weeks later. His four months of investigation had been hampered by the fact that, as he was in a foreign country, he was unable to subpoena witnesses or compel testimony. Some of the Provisional Government figures he approached for interviews declined to talk to him; they provided written affidavits instead, as was the case with most of the members of the queen's last cabinet.

One man Blount would liked to have questioned but could not was Lorrin Thurston, who, in April had been appointed the Provisional Government's ambassador to Washington, replacing John Mott-Smith. Nonetheless, Blount very astutely came to the conclusion that the two key figures in the coup had been Henry Waterhouse and Sam Damon. Waterhouse for driving the faltering revolution forward on the night before the coup when Thurston, Castle and Wilder lost their courage, and again on the morning of the coup. And Damon for changing sides and bluffing the Queen into believing that the US marines and sailors from the *Boston* were siding with the rebels when they were not. Blount secured interviews with both men.

Waterhouse was guarded when he spoke to Blount, but what he did say made it clear that he had carried the coup forward when, in his own words, Thurston 'gave up, sick.' As Blount came to realize, had the Tasmanian not picked up the baton and run with it on the evening of January 16, Liliuokalani's overthrow was likely not to have occurred.

Sam Damon, on the other hand, was remarkably candid in his interview with Blount. The commissioner came to appreciate that, had Damon balked on January 17 once he realized that the Committee of Safety's armed force was paltry and that Swinburne had no intention of allowing US forces to become involved in the coup on the rebel side, the queen's surrender would not have been obtained. And it was Damon who had convinced Liliuokalani that the US troops sided with the rebels, that it was madness to take them on, and that she could surrender under protest and seek redress from the US president.

Several months after Blount departed Honolulu, a new ambassador took up residence at Nuuanu Avenue. Early in Commissioner Blount's four month stint in the islands, controversial ambassador John L. Stevens had been recalled to the United States. Stevens never again received a US Government appointment. In May, after Stevens' removal, Blount had himself temporarily taken on the role of US ambassador to Hawaii. The post was vacant after his departure until, in September, Democrat congressman Albert S. Willis was given the job. Willis retained the services of Ellis Mills, Blount's efficient English-born secretary. Mills, a former private secretary to Secretary of State Thomas Bayard, had stayed behind in Honolulu when Blount returned to the US, becoming consul general.

The Blount Report, which ran to well over a thousand printed pages, was handed to President Cleveland by Secretary Gresham on October 18, together with a letter containing Gresham's recommendations. The last sentence of the secretary of state's recommendations read: 'Our government was the first to recognize the independence of the islands, and it should be the last to acquire sovereignty over them by force and fraud.'[403] James Blount had found that Queen Liliuokalani had been overthrown as the result of a conspiracy between US ambassador John L. Stevens and the members of the Committee of Safety, and that Captain Wiltse had landed US forces in Hawaii with the intention of influencing the outcome of the coup staged by the annexationists against the legitimate and lawful Hawaiian Government.

Back in May, during his investigation, Commissioner Blount had taken Admiral Skerrett on a walk around Honolulu, retracing the steps of US forces landed by Wiltse on January 16. It turned out that Skerrett was unaware that Wiltse had based his blue jackets at Arion Hall–Wiltse had led the admiral to believe that his troops had only been quartered at the Reverend Atherton's property, omitting to tell his superior that they had relocated to Arion Hall after just a few hours. Once in possession of the facts, gained from Lieutenant Commander Swinburne, Lieutenant Young, and the other officers who had led the landing, Admiral Skerrett gave a written report to Blount about the placement of US forces at Arion Hall. The commissioner included this in his report to the President.

Admiral Skerrett wrote: 'In my opinion it was unadvisable to locate the troops there (at Arion Hall) if they were landed for the protection of the United States citizens, being distantly removed from the business portion of the town and generally far away from the United States Legation and Consulate General, as well as being distant from the houses and residences of United States citizens. It will be seen from the accompanying sketch that had the Provisional Government troops been attacked from the east, such attack would have placed them (US troops) in the line of fire.'[404]

The admiral also felt that, had the queen's forces seized the Opera House, the American troops 'would have been under their fire.' He went on, 'It is for these reasons that I consider the position occupied as illy selected. Naturally, if they were landed with a view to support the Provisional Government troops then occupying the Government Building, it was a wise choice, as they (the US forces) could enfilade any troops attacking them (the Provisional Government forces) from the Palace grounds in front.'[405]

Blount's report, and Gresham's subsequent recommendations to the President, were for the moment confidential, but word soon leaked out that Blount had damned Stevens and Wiltse and that Gresham was recommending the restoration of Queen Liliuokalani. President Cleveland endorsed both the Report and Gresham's recommendations, and on December 18 would send the Blount Report to Congress together with a lengthy, eloquent, and passionate message from the President. In that message, he said, among other things, 'Thus it appears that Hawaii was taken possession of by the United States forces without the consent or wish of the government of the islands, or of anybody else so far as shown, except the United States Minister.' That landing was, 'wholly without justification,' he said.[406]

'But for the notorious predilections of the United States Minister for annexation, the Committee of Safety, which should be called the Committee of Annexation, would never have existed,' President Cleveland went on. 'But for the landing of the United States forces upon false pretexts respecting the danger to life and property, the Committee would never have exposed themselves to the pains and penalties of treason by undertaking the subversion of the Queen's Government. But for the presence of the United States forces in the immediate vicinity and in position to afford all needed protection and support, the Committee would not have proclaimed the Provisional Government from the steps of the Government Building.'[407]

As Cleveland informed Congress, he had sent instructions with new ambassador Albert Willis, who did not arrive in Honolulu until November 4, to meet with Queen Liliuokalani and inform her 'of my desire to aid in the restoration of the status existing before the lawless landing of the United States forces at Honolulu on the 16th of January last.'[408] President Cleveland intended to restore Liliuokalani to her throne.

On the morning of Monday, November 13, the queen's carriage drew up outside the American Legation on Nuuanu Avenue, and Chamberlain Robertson and Queen Liliuokalani stepped out. The queen's thick, curly hair was noticeably grayer compared to ten months earlier, but as usual she was immaculately if conservatively dressed. With a regal stride, she proceeded to the door, with Robertson coming a respectful distance behind, and was met, with a slight bow, by Ellis Mills. While Robertson was led into a separate room to wait, the queen was ushered into the legation's parlor, where she was greeted formally by a stiffly correct Ambassador Willis.

A disheveled, bald man with a bushy beard and the perpetual look of a polar explorer just returned from some failed icy adventure, Willis did not appear the ideal choice for one of the most delicate US diplomatic postings of the time. The fifty-year-old Kentucky Democrat had served in the House of Representatives for many years, and this was his first diplomatic posting. He had risen to become chairman of the House Committee on Rivers and Harbors. This was considered a position of some importance, but whether this equipped him to settle a revolution remained to be seen.

Liliuokalani was a little miffed that Willis had sent for her, rather than calling on her at Washington Place, but, she answered the summons, because, she was to write, 'I simply felt that I would undertake anything for the benefit of my people.'[409] She, like everyone else in Hawaii, had heard the rumors that President Cleveland intended restoring her to the throne. But her hopes had been raised and then dashed more than once since her overthrow.

In May, it had been Claus Spreckels who had given her false hope. As the annexation commissioners had dreaded, Spreckels had turned from their friend to their foe after they dropped the Claus clause, and by late May he was in Honolulu, meeting with Liliuokalani and promising to personally hit annexation on the head. Leading members of the Provisional Government were in debt to Spreckels to the tune of ninety-five thousand dollars, and overnight he called in their debts–unless they walked away from annexation.

Liliuokalani had been convinced that the all-powerful Spreckels was her savior, but to the astonishment of both the queen and the financier the rebels raised what they owed, principally via Sam Damon, and cleared the ledger with Spreckels. The German had slunk back to San Francisco–with his money but without ejecting the annexationists from power. Spreckels, it turned out, was not as powerful as either he or the queen had believed.

Ambassador Willis now informed the queen that he had an important communication for her from the President of the United States, and asked whether she was prepared to receive it alone and in confidence. 'She answered in the affirmative,' Willis afterward reported to Secretary Gresham.[410] Wary of what Willis might have to say, Liliuokalani took a seat on a sofa. Willis sat on a chair opposite, with a large, folding Japanese screen, which divided the room, behind him. Liliuokalani was to later say she heard rustling behind the screen at one point, but Willis assured her they were entirely alone, with Mrs. Willis in another part of the house and Ellis Mills at the front door to ensure the meeting was not interrupted.

Willis passed on Grover Cleveland's regrets about the manner of Liliuokalani's overthrow, then said, "He hopes that, with your consent and cooperation, the wrong done to you and your people might be redressed."

Liliuokalani bowed her head in acknowledgment.

"The President expects and believes that when reinstated you will show forgiveness and magnanimity," Willis continued, "that you will wish to be queen of all the people, native and foreign born." When the queen did not reply, Willis asked her if she was prepared to answer certain questions which he was required to ask.

"I am willing," she replied.

"Should you be restored to the throne, would you grant full amnesty as to life and property to all those persons who have been or who are now in the Provisional Government, or who have been instrumental in the overthrow of your government?"

The queen had had ten long months to think about this, and now, Willis was to report, after hesitating a moment, she slowly and calmly answered. "There are certain laws of my government by which I shall abide. My decision would be, as the law directs, that such persons should be beheaded and their property confiscated to the government."[411]

Later, Liliuokalani would maintain that she did not use the word 'beheaded.' She claimed that she said 'executed.'[412] But Willis was adamant that she said 'beheaded.' The use of that word, in fact, was to dictate Willis' future actions. And, within weeks of this meeting, Willis would present the queen with a transcript of their conversation, which he claimed to have recorded from memory–Liliuokalani became convinced that someone on the other side of the Japanese screen took notes during this half-hour conversation. Willis asked Liliuokalani to read the transcript, and, if she agreed that it was a true and accurate record of their initial discussion, to sign it. Liliuokalani read and signed the transcript, which contained the word 'beheaded.' Why would she say such a thing? Possibly, like Lorrin Thurston, Liliuokalani was a student of the French Revolution, which gave the guillotine so much employment.

The ambassador looked at the queen in disbelief. Then, to be certain he had not misheard her, he asked, "Is it your feeling that these people should be beheaded and have their property confiscated?"

"It is," she affirmed.[413] Liliuokalani was bitter, and understandably so. Even the ministers of the churches she had generously endowed with funds over the years had vilified her in their sermons since the January coup. Her diary entries after January 17 show her often in deep depression, and determined to punish those who had trespassed against her and her people.

Willis gave the queen a second opportunity to back away from such a provocative position. "Do you understand the meaning of every word which I have said to you, and of every word which you have said to me, and, if so, do you still have the same opinion?"

"I have understood and mean all I have said, but I might leave the decision of this to my ministers," she said.

Willis then asked if the queen would be prepared to issue a royal proclamation of clemency, but she replied that she had no legal right to do that. Thinking for a moment, she added that there would never be peace while the annexationists were in the country. "They must be sent out of the country, or punished, and their property confiscated."[414]

With a sigh, Willis said that he could have nothing more to communicate to her until he heard from his government, in three to four weeks time. As Liliuokalani was leaving, the ambassador gave her the option of moving from Washington Place to the legation or to one of the US warships in port, for her protection, and pressed her to do so. Two days after his arrival in Honolulu, Willis had learned that the Provisional Government had that day shipped in 276 new rifles, plus ammunition, and all the signs about the city were of the Provisional Government going on a war footing, distributing arms to men whom Willis privately thought nothing more than irresponsible children.

"I believe it is best for me at present to remain at my own residence," said the queen resolutely, thanking Willis for his offer.[415]

After the queen departed, Willis was so troubled by her use of the word 'beheaded,' which, to many whites would have barbaric overtones that stretched back into pre-Christian times in the islands, he wondered if she was not as fluent in English as he had been led to believe. Over the coming days he asked around about Liliuokalani's language skills. As a result, Willis wrote in a December 5 report to Secretary Gresham, 'I have made further inquiries into the queen's understanding of the English tongue, and find that she is perfectly familiar with it, having been a classmate of Chief Justice Judd and other prominent citizens.'[416]

By the end of November, Honolulu was looking increasingly like an armed camp. In June, the Provisional Government had moved into the Iolani Palace, changing the structure's name to the Executive Building, while the Government Building was renamed the Judiciary Building. The palace's Throne Room, stripped of all its royal trappings, became the Executive Chamber, where the Executive and Advisory Councils met. President Dole's chair now adorned the dais where the two royal thrones had previously sat. Briefly, one night in September, the palace had again resounded to the sound of music and gaiety as in royal times past, as two thousand Provisional Government guests bade farewell to the officers of the *Boston*, before the cruiser that had been at the heart of January's coup sailed for California, where it was to be laid up.

By November, the palace's vandalized rooms were crammed with the desks of Provisional Government employees, particularly its fast-growing military, which now accounted for much of the government's expenditure. A letter from dismissed government employee John C. White published in the *New York Times* on November 15 claimed, 'The Provisional Government has not spent one cent on public improvement since it came into power. It has been spending all the people's money on soldiers, rifles, ammunition, and clothes for the soldiers, so as to keep them in power.' The palace basement had been turned into an additional barracks. Outside, the building's balconies and steps were sandbagged and equipped with cannon. Sandbag emplacements dotted the palace grounds, and new recruits stood about, some bored, some nervous and uncertain. Outside the barracks, Armory, and Arion Hall, men were drilling.

On November 24, Secretary Gresham's October 18 letter to President Cleveland, in which he severely censured Stevens and recommended the restoration of Liliuokalani, appeared in Honolulu newspapers. This came about because the *Chicago Evening Post* published what it claimed were extracts from the Blount Report on November 7, followed by the New York *Herald* next morning, as a result of which Secretary Gresham two days later released his letter to the President to all the press. Resultant joy at Washington Place and in thousands of Hawaiian homes was matched by utter dismay and dejection in annexation quarters. Crowds gathered on the streets to discuss the news, and the Annexation Club called a meeting for the following evening.

The annexationist press claimed that 1,600 attended this protest meeting, while the royalist papers put the number at 700 to 800. One of the seven speakers, New Englander Francis M. Hatch, had been living in California at the time of the queen's overthrow. Now president of the Annexation Club and Vice President of the Executive Council in Sam Damon's place, Hatch declared that it was wrong to "decide this great issue upon the petty technicality as to whether or not Stevens recognized the power of this community five minutes too soon or not!" There was much similar rhetoric from other speakers, but the most sobering comment of the evening came from Chief Justice Judd, who now unashamedly stood with the annexationists: "I will say only one thing more, that we will all have to hang together, or hang separately."[417]

The audience laughed at this, but they were well aware that the queen wanted her revenge. Early in December, it would become known that former marshal Charles Wilson had given Ambassador Willis a restoration plan which called for the Provisional Government to parade its troops in Palace Square and then surrender them to the US forces, who would in turn hand them over to the queen's forces, after which the rebels 'be dealt with by a special court.'[418] The only alternative, as the Provisional Government's men saw it, was to fight.

And as November came to an end, a fight seemed imminent to all parties, with the word circulating through annexationist ranks that Rear Admiral John Irwin, commander of the two US ships in port, the *Philadelphia* and the *Adams*, was making preparations to land a large force of US sailors and marines from the two cruisers, to forcibly restore the queen. Irwin later confirmed that he was indeed making ready to land, but 'solely for the purpose of suppressing riot, and to protect the lives and property of the defenseless,' a statement which must have had a familiar ring to the former members of the Committee of Safety.[419]

The British warship HMS *Champion*, a 2,380-ton corvette, had dropped anchor in the harbor beside the *Pennsylvania* and *Adams* on November 24, the same day that Secretary Gresham's letter was published. The Japanese cruiser *Naniwa Kan*, a sister ship of the *Naniwa*, arrived nine days later. The captains of the British and Japanese ships both had orders from their governments to remain at Honolulu until the situation in Hawaii was resolved, to safeguard their nationals should hostilities break out. In an ironic twist of fate, those hostilities would be between the Provisional Government and the United States, even though the Provisional Government had been formed with the express purpose of making Hawaii part of the United States!

On November 29, Sanford Dole wrote to Ambassador Willis rescinding previous permission for US marines and sailors to drill onshore. Two days later, On December 1, an open letter would appear in the Honolulu *Star*, addressed to US ambassador Willis. It was headlined: 'He is reminded that interference by his government will be an act of war!'

On November 29, the same day that Sanford Dole wrote to Ambassador Willis to ratchet up the tension in Honolulu, in Augusta, Maine, Willis' bitter predecessor John L. Stevens was posting off a letter to the US press to answer the now widely published findings of the Blount Report and Secretary Gresham's recommendations to President Cleveland.

Said the *New York Times*, when it ran his letter, 'Ex-Minister Stevens' Reply: Devotes Much Space to Vilifying Commissioner Blount.' He certainly did that. First in this November letter, and in a second broadside fired seventeen days later, the seething Stevens vilified and belittled Blount and everyone else who had dared to speak against him in Blount's report, in particular the members of what he called Hawaii's 'palace gang.' And he took no pains to hide his racial prejudice. The queen's 'half-caste paramour,' as Stevens described Marshal Wilson, again came in for malicious treatment. Premier Sam Parker was, Stevens said, 'mostly of native Hawaiian stock; he has a small fraction of Anglo-Saxon blood,' and was 'ignorant, fond of luxurious living, and a spendthrift.' Paul Neumann and Judge Widemann he dismissed as 'German Jews.'[420]

When Stevens did use ink to answer Blount's findings, he twisted and turned the truth, and lied outright. To the charge that he recognized the Provisional Government when it only held the Government Building, while the queen's forces held the palace, barracks and police station, he responded in fanciful tone: 'When I did recognize it, the Provisional Government was the complete master of the situation, had full control of the city and the Government archives, the police station being surrounded and at the mercy of the Provisional Government. It was a small building in which the disorganized and powerless followers of the fallen queen's paramour marshal took refuge, and they must have surrendered in a few hours by mere force of hunger.'[421]

Many people would believe Stevens, taking the word of a

white northerner against that of a Confederate colonel and a colored queen. In a bid to clear his name, Stevens embarked on a national speaking tour, delivering his bigoted views and concocted version of events to large, supportive audiences. At the same time, Lorrin Thurston, as the Provisional Government's ambassador in Washington, also went on the war path, touting his and Stevens' take on the queen's overthrow in a long, sly answer to the Blount Report which, via the Associated Press and the United Press agencies, was widely published, and widely accepted.

'Blount Pulverized, His Report Torn to Tatters,' yelled the headline in the pro-annexation New York *Tribune* on November 22. Thurston had another ally–American patriotism. There were many editors, and readers, who could not accept that an ambassador of the United States could do the things that Blount had accused Stevens of doing. Said the New York *Journal* on November 23, in a typical editorial: 'We do not need to rely on Mr. Thurston's unsupported testimony to be convinced that Uncle Sam was guiltless of undue pressure in Hawaiian politics.'

Grover Cleveland had declared that he wanted to impose a solution to the Hawaiian problem which was 'consistent with American honor, integrity, and morality.' His solution, born of a desire to do the right thing in the face of a clear and unmitigated injustice, blew up in his face like an erupting Hawaiian volcano. Five years later, Harvard lawyer James A. Gillis would be moved to publish a book in defense of President Cleveland and his Hawaiian policy. 'No act of Mr. Cleveland's administration had met with such severe criticism,' Gillis would write. 'No epithets have seemed sufficient to characterize his "base and ignoble policy".' That policy, said Gillis, had uncharitably been called 'unscrupulous' and 'opposed to all republican and democratic ideas.'

The criticism of the president had been so unrelenting, Gillis would observe, that even some of Grover Cleveland's supporters came to believe there must be something in the accusations against him.[422] Unfortunately for the well intentioned President Cleveland, the Hawaiian mud stuck.

As Lorrin Thurston wrote from Washington to Sanford Dole on November 19, 'With the ignorant, unthinking masses, the word "monarchy" is enough, and that fact is in our favor.'[423] With populist papers such as Charles Dana's New York *Sun* daily savaging Cleveland for even thinking about supporting a monarchy, and questioning why he would do such an 'un-American' thing, the tone was set for the roasting of a president and the toasting of the annexationist cause.

December in Honolulu was tense. Admiral Irwin, observing 'the great parade of preparation for war' by the Provisional Government onshore, saw that some of his own men were inclined toward the annexationist cause of their brother Americans, and he was forced to issue a general order informing his sailors and marines of 'the manifest impropriety of taking sides with either political party in Hawaii,' and prohibiting them from 'the expression of political opinion or the wearing of badges.'[424]

If push came to shove and the US forces were ordered to fire on Provisional Government forces, there was, at the very least, the likelihood of a lack of enthusiasm on the part of Irwin's men. At worst, mutiny might flare. Not that such a situation was contemplated by Washington; the very presence of the US Navy was thought to be enough to pressure the Provisional Government into bending to US will, the same way that Liliuokalani's government had been intimidated into surrendering in the face of US force of arms eleven months earlier.

On Friday, December 15, Ambassador Willis had received new instructions from Washington with the unheralded arrival of the USRS *Corwin* from San Francisco. 'The excitement consequent upon the unexpected arrival of the *Corwin* is intense throughout the city,' Willis reported to the secretary of state.[425] Armed with his new orders, Willis again invited the queen to visit him, and next day, Saturday, Liliuokalani came to the legation once more. This time, her trusted adviser Joseph Carter also came along, at Willis' suggestion.

Willis began by running the transcript of the November 13 meeting by the queen and Carter, to receive Liliuokalani's acknowledgment that it was an accurate account of what had been said at that time, which she did. This was all news to Carter, who was totally unaware of what the queen had told Willis at their previous meeting. Carter was shocked, and disturbed, just as Willis had been, by the 'beheading' reference. Willis then asked the queen if she had modified her views about what should happen to the members of the Provisional Government in the event that she was restored.

"I feel that, if any change should be made," Liliuokalani replied, "that they must not be permitted to remain in the country, and that their property should be confiscated. That is my view." She had clearly had second thoughts after her first interview with Willis had not produced any positive result.

Carter now asked her, "You do rescind so much of that interview as pronounced upon them the death penalty?"

"I do in that respect," she agreed.

The queen went on to say that her government, if restored, would assume responsibility for Provisional Government expenditure, even their heavy military outlays, on the basis that the confiscated property of exiled men would cover those expenses. She also said that she would want to change the constitution to return the vote to those of her subjects who had been disenfranchised by the Bayonet Constitution, to limit the term of supreme court justices to six years, and to increase her cabinet from four to six members.[426] Liliuokalani and Carter then departed. But Carter returned shortly after, asking on the queen's behalf for another interview in two day's time.

The Provisional Government's attorney general, William Smith, the real driving force behind the annexationist government and the key influencer to its decisions, had been pestering Willis for days for an indication of the US Government's intentions. So, Willis now sent Smith a note to say that he expected to relay his government's attitude to the Provisional Government within forty-eight hours.

On the Monday, December 18, in the middle of the day, Ambassador Willis and Consul General Mills went to Washington Place to confer with the queen and Joseph Carter. Carter informed Willis that he had been shocked to learn what Liliuokalani had told Willis at their November 13 meeting. He said that since the most recent meeting, he had advised the queen to be magnanimous, as President Cleveland had asked. 'I told her that I took it as the wish of the President that she should grant amnesty as to life and property.'[427]

In Willis' presence, Carter now asked the queen if she was prepared to do that. But Liliuokalani still believed the rebels should be exiled and their property confiscated, and she said so. This had been in her mind for months; as far back as May, she had written in her diary, 'They must suffer for those Missionaries overthrowing my government, and their property *must* pay for all.'[428] Now for the first time, the exasperated Willis revealed his detailed confidential instructions from President Cleveland, who had set, as his requirement for US support of the queen's reinstatement, an undertaking by her of a full amnesty for all who had participated in her overthrow.

Liliuokalani protested, "I want to say in regard to the request of Mr. Cleveland asking for complete amnesty–how shall I know that in future our country will not be troubled again, as it has been in the past?"[429]

The meeting concluded on that note.

That evening, back at the legation, Willis waited for Ellis Mills to finish typing up the report of the morning's meeting. He intended sending the report to Washington the next day aboard the *Corwin*. The revenue cutter had been anchored in the harbor since its arrival on the 15th, with orders to carry away the ambassador's latest dispatch to the secretary of state with news of Liliuokalani's responses to the President's terms for reinstatement. At 5.30 p.m., a terse letter was delivered to Willis from Sanford Dole, who advised that his government was aware that the ambassador had met with Liliuokalani and was discussing restoration with her, and demanded to know whether Willis was 'acting in any way hostile to this government.' Dole requested an immediate answer.[430] He did not get one.

At 6.00 p.m., Joseph Carter called at the legation and read Willis a note from the queen in which she now agreed to grant full amnesty. This changed everything. Or so it seemed.

The next morning, Tuesday, at 9.30, Joe Carter brought the US ambassador a letter signed by the queen, in which she said, 'I must forgive and forget the past, permitting no proscription or punishment of anyone.'[431] Carter also handed over an agreement signed by Liliuokalani in which she set out the details of the full amnesty she was prepared to grant, agreed to abide by the Bayonet Constitution, and agreed to assume the financial obligations of the Provisional Government. Liliuokalani had finally bowed to the terms of restoration set out by President Cleveland. Willis immediately sent to Dole and asked for a meeting with the Provisional Government. Shortly after, a hand-delivered reply came back, inviting the ambassador to the Executive Building at 1.30 p.m. that same day.

Willis kept the appointment, and, promptly at 1.30., was shown into the former Throne Room of the former Iolani Palace, where sat the stony-faced members of the Executive Council. Five men awaited the US President's verdict–Sanford Dole, William Smith, James King, Peter Jones, and Sam Damon. The Provisional Government's finance minister, Damon had a very personal interest in the government's finances–Liliuokalani had heard that he'd declared 'he has loaned so much to the Provisional Government that if the queen were restored he would have to leave Hawaii, a ruined man.'[432]

Willis proceeded to read the Executive Council a lengthy communiqué which began by stating that, based on James Blount's report, 'the President has arrived at certain conclusions and determined upon a certain course of action.' President Cleveland believed, said Willis, that 'the Provisional Government was not established by the Hawaiian people or with their consent or acquiescence, nor has it since existed with their consent.' After a brief review of Blount's findings, the document informed the executive councilors that, as the US Government, via John L. Stevens and the crew of the USS *Boston*, had a hand in the removal of Queen Liliuokalani, the US Government felt duty bound to have a hand in restoring her to her throne, and to that end had obtained an agreement of full amnesty from her for all participants in her overthrow.[433]

Willis read out the queen's agreement, then said that the President of the United States expected the Provisional Government to promptly hand over constitutional power to the queen. The ambassador ended by saying, "I submit to you the question, are you willing to abide by the decision of the President?"[434]

After what a long, chill pause, Sanford Dole responded, "The government will take the matter under consideration and answer as soon as they are ready."[435]

As the Provisional Government set about preparing a response to the US Government's demand, they were informed that, out on the harbor, stands of rifles were seen to be stacked on the decks of the two American cruisers, and that their boats were lowered and loaded with Gatling guns and crates of ammunition.

On the morning of December 23, the combined Executive and Advisory Councils met at the Executive Building, and considered a lengthy document that had been drawn up in response to the declared US Government position. That meeting went on all day, and did not end until well after 11.00 p.m. Just on midnight, the Provisional Government's reply, signed by Sanford Dole, was delivered to Ambassador Willis. That reply rejected the Blount Report, and rejected the US Government's right to dictate to the sovereign government of the Hawaiian Islands. It concluded: 'The Provisional Government of the Hawaiian Islands, respectfully and unhesitatingly declines to entertain the proposition of the President of the United States that it should surrender its authority to the ex-queen.'[436]

The Provisional Government had decided to call Grover Cleveland's bluff. There were enough lawyers in their ranks for them to know that Cleveland could not authorize the use of force to reinstate Liliuokalani. Under international law, that would be an act of war, and under the US Constitution war could only be declared by approval of Congress. And the Provisional Government knew that there were simply not the votes in Congress for America to go to war against tiny Hawaii's American-led government.

Cleveland knew it, too. Prior to giving Albert Willis his instructions, the President had taken advice from his attorney general, Richard Olney, and as a result knew that, if the Provisional Government refused to surrender power, without the support of Congress he was powerless to enforce his decision to reinstate Queen Liliuokalani. Secretary Gresham had stressed this in Willis' initial instructions, reiterating, in a December 3 dispatch to the ambassador, 'You will say (to the queen) that the President cannot use force without the authority of Congress.'[437]

On December 24, Willis sent the *Corwin* on its way with the Provisional Government's defiant answer–their dare to Grover Cleveland that the United States to go to war with them.

The Provisional Government now tightened its grip. When twenty Hawaiian policemen refused to bear arms for them, they were dismissed. And after word had reached Honolulu that the Clerk of the Supreme Court, Fred Wundenberg, had given detailed testimony to Commissioner Blount about what had gone on at the meetings of the Committee of Safety in January, he was hauled before the three judges of the Hawaiian supreme court. The Provisional Government had trusted Wundenberg enough following the queen's overthrow to appoint him acting marshal, and then to offer him the post of Collector of Customs, which he had declined. Wundenberg told Blount that after the US flag had been raised over the Government Building he had applied himself to his job and had nothing more to do with the annexationists. Now, he was charged with 'misconduct.' Details of the charge were never released. Despite Wundenberg's request for a public hearing, on December 6 he was tried behind closed doors by the three supreme court justices, convicted, and dismissed from government service.

By this stage, all those connected with the Provisional Government had acquired the scornful nickname of 'PGs' from their many opponents in Hawaii. Priory School teacher Bernice Irwin later recalled, 'One of the Priory girls suggested it would be *apropos* to insert the letter 'i' between the letters P G'–to create PiG. 'These were dark days at the Priory,' Bernice said, 'and we prayed for the queen and for the heir apparent, the beautiful Princess Kaiulani.'[438]

The queen's lone permanent bodyguard, Sam Nowlein, had by this time been augmented by former Household Guard soldiers, twenty to twenty-five men who took turns as unpaid volunteer sentinels, armed only with clubs, around the clock. One night, those guards had discovered several white men loitering in the grounds of the Priory School, behind Washington Place, and scared them off. One story that reached Liliuokalani's ears had it that two of her faithful Hawaiian guards, Joe Aea and Willie Ahia, had been offered five thousand dollars to assassinate her, but they'd scoffed at the proposition. As anxiety grew in the city in December, Liliuokalani asked the Provisional Government to provide Washington Place with a guard of armed PG soldiers, which they did.

Tensions ran high into January. A fuming Admiral Irwin, in a January 2 dispatch from Honolulu to the navy secretary, reported, 'The military preparations for defense continue to be made by the Provisional Government and the excitement is unabated. The newspapers assume that I, as the military representative of the US Government, intend to use force to restore the queen. At the same time they quote me as saying that I would not obey any order which I considered unlawful, also, that the officers and men under my command had assumed the same attitude. These sensational reports are intended to influence public opinion in the United States and are entirely without foundation.'[439]

A flurry of diplomatic correspondence flew back and forth between Dole and Ambassador Willis well into January. But by the 17th, the first anniversary of the queen's overthrow, which was celebrated by the Provisional Government with a street parade, a reception at the Executive Building, and fireworks, Dole was telling the US ambassador that it no longer considered they had anything to discuss. For they had learned that President Cleveland had washed his hands of the entire affair and handed it over to Congress to settle. And so he had.

Cleveland had enough problems to worry about. He had come into office in March, 1893 with a large reform agenda which had to take a back seat to the financial crisis which hit the United States in April. When it was learned that the US gold reserve had slipped under 100 million dollars, panic hit the financial markets. Share prices crashed. Short selling was banned. Banks failed. Unemployment skyrocketed. The Panic of 1893, as it became known, would, like the Great Depression of the 1930s and the Global Financial Crisis of modern times, paralyze the US economy, and spread around the globe.

The US economy had already been in recession for some time, partly because of the ill-conceived McKinley Tariff and also through a downturn in the Midwest, but now it slumped into a nationwide depression that would last for three years. One of the causes of the fall in the gold reserve was an obligation placed on the US Government to buy silver under the Sherman Silver Purchase Act. This was great for silver-producing states, but bad for the federal government. Determined to reverse this, Grover Cleveland took on the 'silverites' in Congress, and in October, 1893, after a bitter battle, won. The silver purchase act was repealed. But the battle had bitterly divided Congress, and lost Cleveland many supporters. So much so that, when he attempted to reduce the damaging McKinley tariffs, the House supported him but the Senate amended the bill severely, and actually increased some tariffs in a recourse to protectionism which many saw, wrongly, as the solution to the financial crisis.

In this fractious atmosphere, the Hawaiian problem, a storm

in a distant teacup to most Americans, landed in the lap of the Senate Foreign Relations Committee, as the frustrated President Cleveland turned his attention to more pressing matters. Into the void stepped Senator John Morgan.

25.

THE MORGAN REPORT

JOHN TAYLOR MORGAN WAS A DEMOCRAT SENATOR
from Alabama with very fixed ideas on monarchy and the
American annexation of Hawaii. By demonstrated act he was
against the former and very much in favor of the latter. Morgan
was chairman of the Senate Foreign Relations Committee which,
between December 27, 1893 and February 26, 1894, took
evidence from witnesses in what became an investigation into
James Blount's report to President Cleveland about the Hawaiian
coup, and into Cleveland's subsequent attempt to restore Queen
Liliuokalani to her throne.

Unlike James Blount, Morgan's Senate committee had the
power to subpoena American citizens to appear before it,
although that power did not extend to foreign nationals. Unlike
Blount, too, the Senate committee did not leave Washington
DC and never once set foot in Hawaii, the very place it was
inquiring into. The witnesses called by the committee included
former US ambassador to Hawaii John L. Stevens, officers
from the USS *Boston*, Provisional Government members
and annexation supporters who came to Washington from
Hawaii, and Commissioner Blount. No representative of Queen
Liliuokalani or her cabinet was called to give evidence, nor were
any Hawaiian Government officials serving at the time of the
queen's overthrow, or members of the Hawaiian community
who supported the queen. To give a perception of balance, the
committee's subsequent report would include selected excerpts
from Blount's report. But Morgan cynically made no attempt to

secure evidence from anyone who supported the queen or was opposed to her overthrow.

This blatantly one-sided Senate inquiry could have only one outcome. On February 26, Senator Morgan tabled a report in the Senate. Written solely by him, and signed by him alone, it approached the Blount Report in length. Morgan declared that James Blount, a fellow Democrat, had made an earnest attempt to uncover the truth of the matter and 'executed his instructions with impartial care.' But the very fact that Blount had been in Hawaii, with its 'agitated state of opinion and feeling,' had only made it all the more difficult for him to find the truth, according to Morgan. Whereas, said Morgan, the Senate committee, sitting at a distance in Washington, was able to consider evidence 'taken under circumstances more favorable to the development of the whole truth,' because it was not embroiled in the turmoil that existed in Hawaii.[440] A novel argument.

Morgan found that Blount had been right to lower the US flag on February 1, and that Stevens had been wrong to raise it without authority from Washington. But in all other respects, Morgan exonerated Stevens and the late Captain Wiltse from any wrongdoing in relation to the queen's overthrow: 'The purposes of Captain Wiltse and of Minister Stevens were only those which were legitimate.' Morgan said that 'in what occurred in landing the troops there may have been an invasion,' and that if the queen or her supporters had opposed the landing of US troops on January 16, that 'invasion would have been an act of war.' However, he said, 'when their landing was not opposed by any objection, protest, or resistance, the state of war did not supervene, and there was no irregularity or want of authority to place the troops on shore.'[441]

In making this blatantly incorrect statement, Morgan overlooked or totally disregarded the official, written protests from the Hawaiian Premier and Minister of Foreign Affairs and by the Governor of Oahu, which were lodged with the US ambassador on January 16 following the unauthorized landing of US forces, and which were acknowledged, in writing, by Ambassador Stevens. By Morgan's own definition, the US had indeed committed an act of war against the sovereign Kingdom of Hawaii.

Morgan erred in fact throughout his report. For example, he wrote that, 'Except the queen and cabinet, no officer of the

Government was removed.' This ignored the fact that, in their proclamation dethroning the queen, the Committee of Safety very specifically included the Marshal of the Kingdom among those it removed from office. Morgan went on, 'The legislative body, including the House of Nobles and House of Representatives and their presiding officers, remained in commission.'[442] This was also incorrect. On January 14, the queen had prorogued the legislature at the end of its session, as provided for under the Constitution. The members of the legislature were no longer in office; new elections were due.

Morgan supported the need for US troops to be landed, and backed the claims by the Provisional Government, and by ambassador Stevens, that law and order had entirely broken down in Honolulu by January 17, and that the queen's government was incapable of governing. As an example of this, he cited the fact that a policeman was shot down in the street, yet 'no action was taken for the purpose of arresting or putting on trial the man who did the shooting.'[443] The fact that a military coup was going on at the time or that within five hours of the shooting the government fell, preventing the arrest and trial of John Good, the man who shot the policeman, did not seem to enter Morgan's thinking.

As for the PGs, they didn't consider Good a lawbreaker; to them, he was a hero for gunning down the unarmed officer. Sanford Dole would write, some years later, 'To the quick decision and courage of Captain Good is undoubtedly due, in large measure, the success of the bold and unhampered movement that resulted in the promulgation of the order which accomplished the overthrow of the monarchy.'[444]

Morgan accepted, without any proof, the Provisional Government's assertion that it, and the Committee of Safety before it, represented the majority of the citizens of Hawaii in their wish to overthrow the monarchy and seek annexation with the United States. The senate committee did not question the fact that five of the members of the Committee of Safety were American citizens and several others were citizens of other countries, yet purported to represent the majority of the citizens of Hawaii.

The most glaring lapse of all, to modern eyes, is perhaps the fact that the Senate Committee on Foreign Relations did not think it strange that not one person of native Hawaiian blood or part native Hawaiian blood, or representatives of Hawaii's large Chinese or Japanese communities, joined the Committee of Safety or sat on the Provisional Government's Executive or Advisory Councils. The Portuguese had also come to make up a sizable component of the Hawaiian population, but, because they had neither money nor influence, while they were permitted to serve in the PG army, like Hawaii's other majorities they were excluded from the corridors of power.

The annexationists, representing a handful of wealthy whites, had not been able to find a single native Hawaiian, Chinese or Japanese who wanted to overthrow Hawaii's queen, call for annexation, or participate in the white dictatorship of their nation. Not even Wilcox of redshirt rebellion fame, or his influential partner the publisher Bush, or their Liberal Party friends, men who had called for a Hawaiian republic after Liliuokalani shunned them, none of these men had supported the queen's forced overthrow, annexation by America, or the PG autocracy.

How could this be overlooked? Sadly, in 1893, even some of the most learned and good-hearted men in America believed that colored people and Asians were inferior to whites. In 1893 America, the question of the lack of inclusion in the Hawaiian annexation movement of the majority of Hawaii's population, her native and Asian people, did not arise. Not that other Western countries were any more moral, or any less discriminatory. For example, in 1893, the parliament of New South Wales in Australia passed a law banning the immigration of Asians.

Senator Morgan entirely accepted John L. Stevens' account of his actions and the events of January 17. Morgan's report stated unequivocally that, in opposing the queen that day, 'the people' had 'captured her small force of policemen and soldiers before the American minister had recognized the Provisional Government.'[445] Which was, of course, demonstrably untrue–the kingdom's police and military were never captured, and the Household Guard was only dissolved the day following the queen's overthrow. Morgan had swallowed the demented US ambassador's fabrications, hook, line, and sinker. Perhaps, because he wanted to.

As for Liliuokalani, and her claim for restoration, Morgan declared that, 'The attitude of Liliuokalani at the conclusion of this proceeding is that of waiting for a pleasant retirement from the cares of public life.'[446] Without talking with the deposed queen or her representatives, Morgan felt qualified to state that Liliuokalani had no interest in regaining her throne. And Morgan had no interest in seeing her restored to it, strongly condemning his own President for his support of foreign royalty: 'American opinion cannot sustain any American ruler in the attempt to restore them, no matter how virtuous or sincere the reasons may be that seem to justify him.'[447]

Besides, said Morgan, the Queen of Hawaii's overthrow was all her own fault. He declared: 'The revolutionary movement in Hawaii originated with Liliuokalani.'[448] He claimed that the unrest in Hawaii originated from the queen signing into law on January 14 two bills that had just been passed by the legislature prior to its being prorogued. One bill provided for a government license for the import and sale of opium, the previous opium license having been discontinued by the Bayonet Cabinet. The other bill provided for a license to a syndicate which would operate a lottery in Hawaii, in return for an annual fee of half a million dollars.

In fact, both bills had been put up by the Reform Party cabinet voted out of office on January 12, both had been passed by the legislature, and both were subsequently endorsed by the new cabinet of Sam Parker, which intended to apply the funds raised by the licenses to the building of a leper hospital and an undersea telegraphic cable to the US. Both bills were unpopular with the church in Hawaii, but opium and the lottery had rarely rated a mention in the revolutionary rally cries of January, 1893.

Morgan's report, clearing the US and its officers of any complicity in the overthrow of the Hawaiian monarchy, and laying the blame squarely at the feet of Queen Liliuokalani, was accompanied by several minority reports from other committee members. Morgan's four fellow Democrats wished to absolve Captain Wiltse of any blame over the affair but were critical of John Stevens' role in it. The four Republicans on the committee submitted a report which attacked James Blount, and attacked Cleveland's appointment of him, which they claimed was unconstitutional. Blount's actions, including the hauling down of the US flag, had been, in their opinion, unlawful. The actions of their fellow Republican John Stevens and of Captain Wiltse, on the other hand, received their fullest endorsement.

The release of the Morgan Report was a slap in the face for Cleveland, Blount, and Liliuokalani. Despite Morgan's errors, omissions and misrepresentations, his conclusions were accepted by many in the US, with the stamp of the Senate Foreign Relations Committee giving his document credibility. The Morgan Report heartened Cleveland's political enemies and annexationists alike, and dampened any enthusiasm which the President may have retained for righting the wrong in Hawaii. In May, Senator David Battle Turpie, an Indiana Democrat, proposed a resolution which called on the United States Government to cease all further attempts to meddle in the affairs of Hawaii. The 'hands off' Turpie Resolution was passed by the Senate on May 31.

Liliuokalani and her people were now on their own.

26.

THE HAWAIIAN REPUBLIC, AND THE COUNTERREVOLUTION

THE MEMBERS OF THE PROVISIONAL GOVERNMENT knew that their adversary Grover Cleveland could not again run for US President once his current term ended, for he had previously served a term as twenty-second president. The Provisional Government, in the letter in which it had refused to surrender power to Liliuokalani, had stated, 'We shall therefore continue the project of political union with the United States as a conspicuous feature of our foreign policy, confidently hoping that sooner or later it will be crowned with success.'[449]

The PGs had decided to sit it out, until a new administration took office in Washington in 1897, with the intent of pursuing annexation with that new administration. As an interim measure, and to banish all hopes of a return of the monarchy, they moved to turn Hawaii into a republic. The first step would be a new constitution, to be approved by a constitutional convention. Through the early spring of 1894, residents of Hawaii were encouraged to register to elect fifteen men who would sit with the Executive and Advisory Councils to approve the new constitution for a Hawaiian republic. The vast majority of supporters of the queen, and that covered most of the population, refused to register. A letter of protest against the convention was sent by native Hawaiian representatives to Ambassador Willis, but he declined to forward it to Washington.

The convention's delegates were elected in May, and on May 30 they sat down to consider the new constitution. The document had been drafted by Sanford Dole and Lorrin Thurston–the PGs ambassador to Washington had temporarily returned home early in 1894 so that he could play a leading role in deciding Hawaii's future direction. The new constitution of the republic provided for an elected legislature comprised of two houses, Representatives and Senate. Via property and English language qualifications, its provisions continued to exclude the majority of native Hawaiians and Asians from standing for elected office or voting in elections. It included an additional requirement that voters must also take an oath in which they swore not to aid in any attempt to restore the monarchy.

Not coincidentally, the constitution was approved by July 3. Next day, July 4, America's Independence Day, the Republic of Hawaii was proclaimed. From the steps of the Executive Building, and in front of a large crowd of whites, the proclamation was read by Sanford Dole, the republic's unelected President, who had been appointed to a six year term by the constitutional convention. The members of the Republic's unelected government were the same as those of the unelected Provisional Government, and despite the name change, the people of Hawaii would continue to call them the PGs.

The new Republic of Hawaii was officially recognized by numerous foreign governments, including that of Great Britain. As soon as the proclamation of the Hawaiian republic was in the wind, Liliuokalani had sent a delegation headed by Paul Neumann to Washington, to beg the US Government not to recognize the Republic of Hawaii. But now America, too, gave the official nod to the regime. Grover Cleveland had burned his fingers over Hawaii, and wanted nothing more to do with the islands. Despite this, Liliuokalani would remain grateful to Cleveland. 'He has always had from me the utmost respect and esteem,' she would write in 1898. Her people felt the same way, she said. 'The Hawaiian people almost worship the name of President Cleveland; for he has tried to do what was right, and it was only because he was not supported by Congress that his efforts were not successful.'[450]

The proclamation of the Republic, and the fact that the US Government had turned its back on them, caused many Hawaiians to begin thinking about an alternative way of restoring their queen to power. Several different secret Hawaiian groups sprang up in the summer of 1894 and began plotting a counterrevolution. Over the next five months, money was secretly collected to buy arms and munitions in California, sympathizers were sounded out, and reliable men were recruited to lead various elements of a military coup of the kind that had deposed the queen, this time to depose the PGs. So that government suspicions were not aroused, the plotters only met in small groups, using the excuse of business or socializing, and communication between groups was kept to a minimum, so that members of each group, or cell, were ignorant of the identities and roles of others.

The counterrevolution, it was decided, should take place early in the new year of 1895. The general in command of the operation was the former commander of the Household Guard, now Liliuokalani's chief bodyguard, Major Sam Nowlein.

On the evening of November 23, the schooner *H. C. Wahlberg* cleared the port of San Francisco. It was bound, its master Captain Matthew Martin told the US authorities, on a sea otter hunting expedition to the North and South Pacific Oceans. The *Wahlberg* did not go far before making a stop, crossing San Francisco Bay to the village of Sausalito. Between 10.00 and 11.00 p.m., a cargo of wooden crates was loaded aboard the schooner at Sausalito, watched over by Major William T. Seward, an ex US Army officer who had lived in Hawaii for many years. The vessel was then towed to sea by a steam tug, with neither tug nor schooner showing lights. Once out of sight of land, Captain Martin parted company from the tug and set the *Wahlberg* on a course for Hawaii.

Major Seward did not sail with the *Wahlberg*. Instead, he crossed the bay, back to San Francisco, from where, two days later, he set off for Honolulu aboard the regular mail steamer, arriving back in Hawaii on December 8. In Honolulu, Seward lived at the house of John A. Cummins, an elderly, well to do planter of part Hawaiian blood who had served as minister for foreign affairs in 1890-91. For a number of years, Major Seward had worked as Cummins' secretary, and he now informed his employer that an important shipment was on its way from California.

The PGs had a new Marshal of the Republic, Edward G. Hitchcock. Previously an assiduous sheriff of Maui, and looking a great deal like Sanford Dole, Hitchcock had married the eldest daughter of Castle and Cooke co-founder Samuel Castle. By

December, Marshal Hitchcock began receiving reports from his spies in the community that something was brewing, but no one knew exactly what. Information was then received that John Bush, former cabinet minister Joseph Nawahi and several others were plotting something, and on December 9 they were arrested, charged with conspiracy, and thrown in jail.

While, under questioning, none of these three revealed anything incriminating, the edgy Dole Government now began to question the loyalty of some of its Hawaiian and part-Hawaiian employees, and several men were dismissed when they refused to take an oath to support the Republic. Christmas Day arrived, and only now did the PGs relax a little, to celebrate the Yuletide.

On Wednesday, December 26, Sam Parker paid a visit to Liliuokalani at Washington Place. Liliuokalani noted in her diary that Parker urged her to call Judge Widemann, Joe Carter, Ed Macfarlane and several other trusted advisers 'to consult on the situation.' The following day, Parker returned, and asked whether she had sent for Widemann and the others. 'I said "No,"' the queen recorded. 'He was disappointed,' she added. '(I) told him it was treason.'[451]

Exactly what Parker and the queen were talking about was never revealed, but it seems to have involved a new Hawaiian constitution. Based around a return to constitutional monarchy, this had been drawn up over a week and completed by Christmas Day, at Sam Nowlein's behest, and transcribed by Liliuokalani's secretary, William Kaae. The inference from Liliuokalani's diary is that she was aware of, and wary of being implicated in, a plot to overthrow the PGs. That same day, Liliuokalani heard that Sam Parker's cousin, Robert Parker Waipa, would be dismissed by the government on the last day of the month from his position as senior captain of police. Clearly, the PGs were worried about an Hawaiian ali'i serving in such a senior law and order post. But, as it turned out, Captain Parker retained his post.

The following Saturday, December 29, Sam Nowlein and Charles Gulick met with Liliuokalani at Washington Place. Fifty-three-year-old Gulick, nephew of a Congregational Church missionary, was a wealthy planter and attorney of part native Hawaiian blood. He had served as interior and finance minister under King Kalakaua, and briefly as finance minister under Liliuokalani. In September 1893, Gulick had reestablished the previously PG-suppressed Hawaiian-language newspaper *Holomua*. One of the counterrevolution's organizing committees met three times a week at Gulick's Honolulu house. It was Gulick who had drawn up the new constitution, at Nowlein's request. The other members of Gulick's group were Nowlein, William Rickard, the English plantation manager who had confronted Lorrin Thurston in the street after the January 16, 1893 landing of US troops, and Major Seward–considered 'a good old soul' by Liliuokalani.[452]

Liliuokalani would note in her diary for December 29, 'Signed eleven commissions.' Those commissions, it would later be said, were for four cabinet ministers, four island governors, and supreme court justices. At the top of the list of ministers, as premier, was the name of Robert Wilcox, of redshirt rebellion fame. Liliuokalani also noted in her dairy that Nowlein and Gulick witnessed her 'political will' during this meeting.[453] The two men then departed. Hawaii's counterrevolution was a week away.

In the darkness, the schooner *Wahlberg* stood off Rabbit Island, near Kailua. It was the night of Tuesday, January 1, 1895. Close by, the small, rusty, interisland tramp steamer *Waimanalo* also lay at anchor. Cloaked by the night, a boat from the *Wahlberg* ferried packets containing one hundred revolvers ashore to four waiting native partisans led by George Townsend.

The shore party had brought a lantern, and with this they had answered a blue light from the *Wahlberg* with a red light, as they had been instructed by Major Seward. George Townsend had then been rowed out to the schooner and passed over a letter from Seward which confirmed that he was authorized to receive the pistols. After the pistols had been landed, a boat from the *Waimanalo* transferred crates and bulging sacks from the schooner to the steamer in two trips. The crates contained 288 Winchester carbines; the sacks were filled with hundreds of ammunition belts filled with 30,000 bullets.

From the bridge of the *Waimanalo*, her master, Captain William Davies, watched his Swedish first mate supervise the loading of the crates into the steamer's hold. Davies had once captained the *Claudine*, the ship that had carried the annexation commissioners to San Francisco in 1893 and considered the cream of the inter-island steamers. Davies had come down in the world a little since then, but his fortunes were set to rise; the royalists had promised him ten thousand dollars in exchange for landing weapons for their coup, plus the post of pilot or harbormaster at Honolulu once they had regained power. The royalists intended bringing in the new year with a bang. But first, there was still organizing to be done, and intelligence to be gathered.

A day or two later, plastering and stone contractor John F. Bowler made a call on the premises of the Mutual Telephone Company in downtown Honolulu. This was the same Johnny Bowler who had told Sam Damon on the day of the queen's overthrow that he would not fire on the American flag. As recently as November 28, the Honolulu *Advertiser* had branded Bowler 'a prominent royalist.' Bowler's good friend and fellow American, James T. Pratt, was manager of the telephone company; both Bowler and Pratt had been special constables in the service of the queen's government. At Bowler's request, his friend Pratt happily arranged for the telephone company's superintendent to give him a guided tour of the telephone exchange, or 'Central' as it was known.

Sam Nowlein had given Bowler the task of seizing the telephone exchange when the royalists staged their coup a few days later. Nowlein, unlike the Committee of Safety in 1893, perceived the strategic importance of the telephone building in a military coup. It was one of three buildings that he intended be seized by royalist forces. The others were the electric company, and the police headquarters. Partisan groups had been formed to rise up within Honolulu and occupy each of these targets once two large forces, led by Nowlein and Robert Wilcox, had moved into the city from the north and east. Nowlein's and Wilcox's forces would then link up in the city, surround the Executive Building, and demand the surrender of the Republic's government.

Bowler, tasked by Nowlein with raising a company of thirty-seven men to take and hold the telephone exchange, had quickly enlisted eager recruits. Now, courtesy of his guided tour, he knew the exact interior layout of the building. All he needed now were weapons and a date and time for action.

On the evening of Thursday, January 3, Sam Nowlein left Washington Place at 5.00 o'clock. In his absence, Charles H. Clark, whose wife now served as a lady in waiting to Liliuokalani, took charge of the queen's bodyguard. Clark had for several years been an officer in the royal guard, serving under Nowlein, having been made a lieutenant in the King's Guard back in 1884. After dark, Clark distributed rifles to forty former soldiers of the Household Guard who slipped, in ones and twos, into the Washington Place grounds. Their assignment was to defend the property and protect their queen from any counter attack by the Republic's military. Their stealthy arrival went totally unnoticed by the Republic's authorities.

During the evening, at various places around Honolulu and nearby, hundreds of other men set off for rendezvous points, knowing that the uprising was set to launch at 2.00 in the morning. Junius Kaae was assigned to lead one of the royalist companies. The Government's chief recorder during the reign of King Kalakaua, Kaae had been intimately involved in the scandal involving the 'gift' of $71,000 for the opium license, and had been forced by the Bayonet Cabinet to retire. After dark that evening of January 3, ten native partisans gathered at Kaae's house. Before setting off to take part in the coup, Kaae and his friends filled glasses and raised them in a toast proposed by Kaae's wife: "The health of our queen, and success to the expedition!"[454]

It was intended that, in the early evening, the carbines and ammunition would be landed from the *Waimanalo* at two separate locations–at Kakaako, which lay to the east of the city between Ala Moana and Waikiki, and at the Honolulu fish markets. The tramp steamer's Captain Davies had sent a note ashore to Major Seward asking for boats to be sent out to the steamer to speed the landing. Davies had no desire to loiter close offshore for too long; that risked attracting Government attention. So Seward purchased a skiff, and Sam Nowlein sent several men to the royal boathouse, which was still in the possession of Liliuokalani, who acquired another rowboat there.

But now the coup struck several obstacles. To begin with, the *Waimanalo* could not get in past a dredge that lay at anchor in its path. Next, a large band of royalist fighting men gathering at the old immigration depot at Kakaako to receive their weapons and orders attracted the attention of the Honolulu Police's Detective Larsen. The detective led a police detachment to the site, arrested several men for illegal assembly, and scattered the remainder. Sam Nowlein, on his way to take charge of the royalist group at the fish markets, arrived in time to see the arrests being made, and slipped away unnoticed.

Marshal Hitchcock, meanwhile, feeling there was something in the wind, stationed several special constables on the beach at Kakaako to keep an eye on the stretch of sand. Seeing the policemen there, Carl Widemann, twenty-seven-year-old son of Judge Widemann, together with two royalist friends, Will Greig and Louis Marshall, detained the special constables in friendly conversation to allow the weapons to be landed without being detected. But the landing never took place there.

With the help of several royalist foot soldiers, William Rickard launched a boat into the rolling surf from the beachside Waikiki house of Henry Bertelmann, former aide de camp of the queen, and rowed out to sea. Locating the *Waimanalo*, Rickard climbed aboard and passed on a message from Charles Gulick to Captain Davies. The message asked him to put to sea for twenty-four hours then return and land the weapons at Kaalawai Beach the next night. With Rickard remaining on board, the little *Waimanalo* turned her bow away from Oahu and steamed away. Before long, she had disappeared over the horizon with her precious cargo.

The Hawaiians arrested at the old immigration depot kept their mouths shut about their reason for being there, so that neither Marshal Hitchcock nor anyone else in authority had any idea that the Republic of Hawaii had just averted a coup. In the shadows across the street from the telephone exchange, after 2.00 a.m. came and went and no royalist army made an appearance in the city, John Bowler realized with a sigh that the uprising was not going forward. He traipsed home, to hide the revolver that had been under his coat, and to await word of a renewed coup attempt.

From his location near Merchant Street, another royalist commander, Englishman Thomas B. Walker, also made his way home, in his case with two revolvers under his coat. Nowlein had given him the task of leading the capture of police headquarters. A well-to-do stonemason, Walker had manufactured some of the royalist 'bombs' that were to be used in the counterrevolution. As Bowler and Walker went home and went to bed, other disappointed royalist partisans elsewhere followed suit, putting their weapons in hiding places and their hopes on hold.

First thing next morning, Friday, Liliuokalani rose early, as she always did, and went for a stroll in her garden. Most of the forty men who had assembled to defend Washington Place had gone home by this time. Only the usual sentinels were now in place. 'I remember that I had occasion to scold my gardener for the disturbed condition in which I often found my plants,' she would later say.[455] It is likely that Liliuokalani had a sneaking suspicion that the rifles handed out to Nowlein's men the previous night now lay buried in her garden beds, but she said nothing about that to the gardener, the elderly Joseph Kaaewai, when he greeted her this morning.

"Any news of last night, Joseph?" Liliuokalani asked.

Kaaewai, who had served the royal family for many years, said, "Our work did not get along favorably, Your Majesty."

The queen nodded unhappily. "Yes," she absently responded, as she kept walking.[456]

A little later, Sam Nowlein reported to her, in the house.

"That affair of last night was a failure, Your Majesty," Nowlein advised.

"I had heard so," Liliuokalani replied.

"But Warren and Townsend have landed arms and ammunition beyond Diamond Head," Nowlein went on, referring to the shipment of revolvers, and trying to sound upbeat.[457]

Liliuokalani looked at Nowlein with a scowl. She had made it perfectly clear that she wished to be in possession of absolutely no details of the coup until it was over and done. But Liliuokalani knew perfectly well that it was afoot. Three years later, she would say, of the royalist plotters: 'I could no longer hold them in check with reason; if they were now, by one accord, determined to break away, and endeavor, by a bold stroke, to win back their nationality, why should I prohibit the outburst of patriotism? I told them that if the mass of the native people choose to rise, and try to throw off the yoke, I would say nothing against it, but I could not approve of mere rioting.'[458] Nowlein had just told her more than she wished to know. Without another word she terminated their brief exchange.

That evening, A. M. Hewitt, a cargo supervisor at the Honolulu docks, called on his acquaintance Charles Peterson, keeper of the Diamond Head signal station. Hewitt suggested that, should Peterson happen to see a tramp steamer without lights off Diamond Head during the night, it would be a favor to him if Peterson failed to report it, and Peterson agreed.

Sure enough, the *Waimanalo* returned that night, and, without displaying navigation lights, or lights of any kind, she lay just to the east of Diamond Head. The signal station keeper kept his word, and no official report of the steamer's presence was made. In the darkness, Rickard came ashore from the steamer, after which boats were launched from Kaalawai Beach by George Townsend and his men. By 1.00 a.m., the carbines and ammunition had been brought ashore from the steamer.

The *Waimanalo* then departed, to dock at Honolulu. The carbines she had landed were by now loose, having been removed from their packing crates, and the consignment was buried in the sand of Kaalawai Beach, not far from a beachside estate owned by former attorney general Antone Rosa. The Reverend S. K. Kaili, who had been retired from the ministry for the past three years, had fishing rights on this stretch of beach and lived nearby; a party to the counterrevolution, the reverend took on the task of watching over the buried cache of arms.

At noon on Saturday, Sam Nowlein arrived at the Waikiki Beach house of Henry Bertelmann and lunched with Bertelmann and Robert Wilcox. Wilcox had stumbled on the plot a week or so earlier, and had been brought in at the last moment as premier designate and one of the royalist field commanders. Over lunch, the three ali'i agreed to make the second bid to launch the royalist countercoup that night. Again, the starting time was to be 2.00 in the morning. Nowlein and Wilcox then set off to alert their subordinates to prepare.

Royalist company commanders were soon setting off for Antone Rosa's property at Kaalawai Beach, collecting their foot soldiers as they went. By late afternoon, hundreds of royalists, the vast majority of them native Hawaiian or with native Hawaiian blood, including a number with mixed Portuguese/Hawaiian ancestry, were sitting cross-legged around the grounds of the Rosa house under the palm trees, with Diamond Head looming up beside them to the west.

The youngest partisan was just fifteen. Some, like former Captain of the Guard John Kahalewai, had military experience, but most had never fired a gun in their lives. Cleaning sand out of carbines, strapping ammunition belts around their waists, drinking gin, whiskey, and *okotehao* distilled from the ti plant, and chattering and laughing, the partisans were in high spirits. During the afternoon, and later during the early evening, a smiling Prince Kuhio was seen moving among the partisans, talking with them and offering encouragement for the business ahead.

During the afternoon, too, J. J. McDonald and Carl Lukinger, *haole* residents of the area, happened to be conducting members of their families and visitors on a Sunday afternoon stroll along the beautiful Kaalawai Beach. At the sight of all the armed natives gathered in the grounds of the beachside Rosa property, the ten whites all froze with terror. The Hawaiians, too, froze for a moment. Then royalist commanders barked orders in Hawaiian, and several of their men rushed onto the sand and took the *haoles* captive. At gunpoint, the prisoners were herded into the Rosa house. The intent was to keep them there until the countercoup was over.

During that afternoon, Liliuokalani went for an outing in her carriage, accompanied by Charles Clark and another of her bodyguards. After spending several hours with the students at the Kamehameha School, she returned to Washington Place around five, by which time Nowlein had also returned.

After dinner, just before 8.00, Nowlein came to Liliuokalani and said, "The time has come." The queen nodded. Nowlein added, "Every provision has been made for your safety, Your Majesty."[459] And then he set off, just as hundreds of churchgoers were arriving for an evening service at the Central Union Church, a large bluestone Congregational church immediately across Beretania Street from Washington Place which had only been completed several months before.

The forty men assigned to defend Washington Place had again slipped into the grounds by this time, and as Nowlein rode away, his deputy Charles Clark was handing out the rifles that had just been dug from the queen's flower beds. He also handed out 'bombs.' More correctly, these were grenades, improvised explosive devices consisting of round shell casings, some iron, some concrete, made expressly for the uprising, packed with gunpowder and small pieces of metal, with a fuse attached.

"The time has come," said Clark to his men, emulating Nowlein. Clark's orders were simple; he was to hold Washington Place 'at all hazards.'[460]

27.

FIGHTING FOR THE QUEEN

Hawaii's 1895 counterrevolution began in the Sunday evening darkness of January 6, with a squad of royalist troops creeping up to the signal station on Diamond Head. Without a shot being fired they captured it. After making the attendant their prisoner, then cut the telephone line to the city.

By 9.00, Sam Nowlein had arrived at the assembly point at the Rosa property. He found Robert Wilcox there, ready and waiting. Wilcox was resplendent in the smart Italian military uniform that he had worn during his redshirt rebellion of 1889, complete with cloak, cap and sword. The two men shook hands and wished each other luck, and then Nowlein led away his part of the force. Nowlein's plan was to skirt around Diamond Head to Punchbowl Hill, secure that, then enter the city from the northeast while Wilcox led his part of the force in from Diamond Head. At 2.00 a.m., they would link up in the city, just as the partisan groups assigned to seize the police headquarters, telephone exchange and electric company rose up and went into action. The plan may have worked, too, had it not been for Robert Wilcox.

Prior to coming out to the Rosa property to meet up with Nowlein, Wilcox had dined early with Henry Bertelmann, at Bertelmann's house beside Waikiki Beach. Wilcox had been accompanied by one of his captains, George Markham, a Wilcox subordinate during the Redshirt Rebellion. Before being recalled by Lorrin Thurston's Bayonet Cabinet in 1887, Markham had, like Wilcox, been in Italy undergoing military training. Markham had been severely wounded in the 1889 rebellion, but had recovered to go on to become Honolulu's port surveyor. Since the proclamation of the Hawaiian Republic, Markham had formed the Hawaiian Republican Club, which had as its declared aim the support of the new Republic's government. The PGs had been so impressed with this, and the fact that here was an ali'i who had turned his back on the monarchy, that Marshal Hitchcock had hired Markham as a police detective. Among Markham's recent duties had been guarding the home of President Sanford Dole, and the home of Attorney General William Smith, the true chief executive of the republic. Bodyguards for the pair had been made necessary by the fact that both Smith and Dole had recently received death threats.

But Markham had fooled Hitchcock. Markham was, and always had been, a royalist, and he was about to take part in the royalist coup. Or, at least, that was his intention. For, something very odd occurred over dinner at Bertelmann's. An argument broke out. The nature of that argument has never been revealed, but it had two dramatic outcomes. First, Henry Bertelmann refused to have anything more to do with the coup, and told Wilcox to leave. And, Wilcox escorted George Markham to the Rosa property at gunpoint, lodging him with the other prisoners there. It seems that Wilcox had declared, over dinner, perhaps primed by wine or gin, that, once Sanford Dole's government of the Republic of Hawaii had been overthrown in this coup, *he intended to make himself the new President of Hawaii*, and damn the queen! And both Bertelmann and Markham had reacted to this.

From the outset, some of the coup's leaders had doubts about Wilcox, and he knew it. 'The people who got up the rebellion I think had no confidence in me,' he himself was to say, 'and I did not like it at first.'[461] For years, Wilcox had led the Liberal Party's demands for a Hawaiian republic. Now, Hawaii was a republic, and yet when Wilcox discovered the counterrevolution plot just before Christmas he had overnight proclaimed himself, at least to Nowlein and the other coup leaders, once more a royalist, and the enemy of the republic. On that basis Liliuokalani had chosen him to be her premier and Nowlein had made him his fellow military commander. Liliuokalani, Nowlein, Gulick, Rickard and Seward may have been naïve. Or perhaps the loquacious Wilcox was very convincing. Then again, maybe the coup leaders felt they had no option but include him now that he knew their plans.

This affair at Bertelmann's had taken place in the early evening of January 6, while Nowlein was still at Washington

Place. Wilcox, to preserve his secret once he arrived at the Rosa property, promptly sent twelve men under Lot Lane, a handsome, charismatic, powerfully built Hawaiian rancher, around Diamond Head to Bertelmann's house. Wilcox later made up a complicated tale about sending these men to prevent the police interfering with royalist recruits heading for Kaalawai Beach. But in reality Wilcox had sent them to seal off Bertelmann and prevent him from making contact with the authorities and warning them of the upcoming coup. Bertelmann, a queen's man, had no intention of doing any such thing. Just the same, Lot Lane's men took up positions around the house, and settled down for a long night on watch.

Unfortunately for the royalist cause, some members of Lot Lane's squad, who Wilcox had instructed to only carry concealed pistols, had come bearing carbines, and they were spotted arriving at the Bertelmann house by a neighbor who rushed to a telephone and alerted the authorities. In response, Marshal Hitchcock ordered Arthur Brown, who had been brought over from Hilo by the PGs to replace John Mehrten as deputy marshal, to immediately obtain an arrest warrant and bring in Bertelmann and any armed men with him.

Brown in turn phoned Senior Captain Robert Parker Waipa, instructing him to assemble an armed squad of his most reliable policemen. The captain joined Brown with Lieutenant Holi and five Hawaiian policemen armed with rifles. At this point, neither Brown nor Parker Waipa had any idea what the armed men reported to be out at Bertelmann's were up to, or who they represented. Soon, Brown, Parker Waipa and their men were in hacks heading for the Waikiki Road.

On reaching Waikiki, Deputy Marshal Brown stopped off at the house of Charlie Carter, to invite him to come along. Carter, the young attorney who had been such a solid supporter of the Committee of Safety two years before and who went on to become a member of the PGs' Annexation Commission, now worked on the staff of President Dole. Carter, always the enthusiast, rubbed his hands together with relish on receiving Brown's invitation. After jamming two loaded revolvers in his belt, Carter summoned his cousin Alfred, an attorney, and neighbor James Castle, Honolulu's collector general of customs, to join the party. After telling his wife and two young children he would be back soon, Carter set off with his companions to follow Brown, who had taken his police party on ahead.

To reach Bertelmann's house, Deputy Marshal Brown's party walked warily down a lane opposite Kapiolani Park. The house was quiet. Lights were burning inside. Brown, Captain Parker Waipa and a constable entered the house via the unlocked front door, and found Henry Bertelmann sitting calmly reading a newspaper. When Brown, a man in his late thirties with dark hair and a neat goatee beard, began to read out his warrant, Bertelmann denied knowing anything about armed men. Brown was only part way through reading the warrant when a shot was heard outside, followed by two answering shots.

Charlie Carter, arriving at Bertelmann's in the wake of the police party, had decided that he and his two friends should skirt along Waikiki Beach to cover the house from the ocean side. There was a fine moon that night. In the bright moonlight, and with pistols and rifles in hand, the three young men crunched their way along the soft sand. Spotting movement at Bertelmann's canoe shed, just eight yards from the house, on the edge of the beach, Charlie Carter immediately raised a pistol, and, without warning, fired. His shot was answered by two rounds from a royalist carbine fired by part-Hawaiian Tom Poole, a carpenter by trade. A carpenter with a good eye, for both bullets found their mark—one hit Charlie Carter in the chest, the other in the abdomen. Carter fell to the sand. At first, Carter assured his companions that he was fine; only later was it realized he was badly hurt.[462]

These shots ignited a fusillade at the front of the Bertelmann house, with Lot Lane's men opening fire, shooting at the trio on the beach and at the policemen standing outside the front door. Lieutenant Holi took a round in the chest and collapsed; a bullet had passed through one of his lungs. Logan, one of the officers with Holi, had his elbow shattered by a royalist bullet. The other officers pulled the two wounded men into cover, and kept their heads down, as Lane's men kept up a rapid rate of fire. The uprising had begun, and it was an inauspicious beginning for both sides.

Poole and his royalist companions on the beach ran off, but the rest of Lot Lane's men poured bullets into the Bertelmann house from a clump of palm trees. Still not knowing who these armed men were, or what their intentions were, Captain Robert Parker Waipa dived out the back door of the house and sneaked around to the front. Encountering the brother and cousin of Lot

Lane, William and James Lane, skulking in the undergrowth, the
captain bailed them up, disarmed them, then forced them ahead
of him and into the darkened house. There, Brown, Bertelmann
and a constable were all lying flat on the floor, as bullets continued
to scythe in through the shattered windows. The Lane boys were
made to join Bertelmann in a corner.

Again the plucky police captain ducked out into the night.
Parker Waipa was once more making his way toward the firing
when he bumped into more royalists coming from the east. Tom
Poole had gone to Robert Wilcox for reinforcements, and Parker
Waipa walked into two more royalist rifle squads coming up at
the double, the second led by Wilcox himself. The police captain
was recognized–Wilcox had put a price on Parker Waipa's head
for continuing to serve the PGs–and, with bullets flying all
around him, the captain had to make a speedy retreat. He ended
up hurling himself into a thicket and lying low for the rest of the
night as royalist rifleman searched for him close by.

Meanwhile, the quick-thinking police officer covering the
prisoners in the house yelled to the royalists outside, in Hawaiian,
that he would shoot Bertelmann and the Lane boys if they did
not stop shooting into the house. Lot Lane ordered his men to
cease fire. But the royalists held their position around the house.
While this was all going on, Alfred Carter, cousin of wounded
Charlie Carter, was able to slither back the way he had come,
along Waikiki Beach, and go for help. A phone call was soon
received at police headquarters from Alfred Carter, saying that
there was a firefight going on at the Bertelmann house and that
Charlie Carter badly needed a doctor.

Liliuokalani would write that about this time, from
Washington Place, she heard a considerable disturbance at the
Central Union Church across the street, where leading lights
of government, the military, and the white business community
were attending the church service. A policeman had arrived with
news of the Bertelmann battle, and PGs came rushing out to their
horses and carriages and set off to their assigned stations. A large
part of Company E of the republic's National Guard, as the PGs'
standing army was now called, immediately set off for Waikiki in
horse-drawn omnibuses. Members of all other PG units went to
their assigned locations.

The Dole Government had been expecting some sort of
military demonstration by royalists ever since the previous July

4, and had a plan in place to meet the emergency when it came. Republican troops immediately encircled Washington Place, making the Central Union Church their headquarters. They kept far enough back so as not to spark a gun battle with Liliuokalani's bodyguards, but sealed off the queen's residence to prevent anyone coming or going. Charles Clark and his men spotted the troops in the moonlight, and, as his soldiers hunkered down and prepared to shed their last drop of blood should the PGs attempt to storm Washington Place, Clark informed Liliuokalani that her home was surrounded by government troops.

Out at Bertelmann's, Alfred Carter returned with a doctor to tend his cousin, but the royalists saw them coming along the beach and opened fire, forcing them back. The arrival of the PG soldiers in the omnibuses a little later made the royalists abandon their position, and only then was the doctor able to reach the unconscious Carter on Waikiki Beach. As Bertelmann and the Lane pair were handcuffed and taken away, the unconscious Charlie Carter was removed to his own home, while the two badly wounded policemen were conveyed to hospital. Rash Charlie Carter did not regain consciousness; he died a little after 5.00 next morning.

By late Sunday evening, Sam Nowlein and his royalist force of close to one hundred men had occupied Punchbowl Hill. The cannon up here had been rendered inoperable by the PGs by keeping essential parts in a safe. Shortly after midnight, as Nowlein prepared to march down into Honolulu, his men saw a force of twenty-five special constables and ten mounted Hawaiian policemen commanded by American-born businessman T. B. Murray, moving up toward their position. From behind stone walls and almost impenetrable lantana bushes, Nowlein's men opened fire. And, to the terror of the thirty-five ambushed government men, several of the royalists' homemade 'bombs' were thrown at them.

The explosions caused no injuries, but were frightening enough for Murray to believe that the other side was using a cannon. He ordered a retreat. Plump, middle-aged, mustachioed Murray, who ran a carriage-making business in Honolulu's King Street, was president of the American League, an association of US citizens founded in Honolulu in November, 1893 to support the PGs and to rival the Annexation Club for influence with the Government. Murray was also a captain in the Citizen's Guard.

The Citizen's Guard was a highly secretive organization of police auxiliaries. Set up by the PGs in June, 1893 for emergencies like this one, it answered directly to Attorney General Smith. The Citizen's Guard was confined to white men, and membership was by invitation only. There were no uniforms, but the Citizen's Guard was organized in companies and with military ranks, with its men expected to supply their own arms. Supreme court justices served in the Citizen's Guard alongside some of Honolulu's wealthiest businessmen and ministers of the cloth.

Cabinet minister Sam Damon was one such Citizen's Guard member, as was Henry Cooper, the manic former chairman of the Committee of Safety. Henry Waterhouse, the determined driver of the original Hawaiian revolution and now a member of the Republic's senate, was a lieutenant in the Citizen's Guard's Sharpshooters Company. Waterhouse was in mourning. Just two days earlier, his father, the redoubtable John T. Waterhouse, had passed away, aged seventy-eight, at his Waikiki beach house–later the site of Fort de Russy.

Henry Waterhouse, despite his personal loss, and despite having distanced himself from Smith and Thurston since the queen's overthrow and taking a back seat in the Provisional Government, had no desire to see the monarchy restored. He knew, as the other PGs knew, that the queen and her followers would treat them as traitors if she regained power. Fearing that he stood to lose his property, and quite possibly his very life, to vengeful Hawaiians, Henry Waterhouse immediately dropped everything as soon as he heard of the battle at Bertelmann's. Arming himself with rifle and ammunition, he reported for duty with his sharpshooting company. He would be prominent in the counterrevolutionary events of the coming days.

Combined, the Citizen's Guard and National Guard had five hundred men under arms–the PGs claimed to have a thousand, but the records show their ranks numbered half that. The assigned task of the Citizen's Guard was to patrol the streets of Honolulu and guard major assets in the city. In the current emergency, this freed up uniformed National Guard regulars to surround Washington Place and do battle with the two royalist forces out of town. Citizen's Guard patrols were also tasked with arresting men in the city who looked suspicious. Men such as royalist cell leaders Johnny Bowler and Tom Walker, who would be in position near their downtown targets in the early hours of Monday morning ready to link up with Nowlein and Wilcox when fought their way into the city.

In response to news that sizable royalist forces were at Punchbowl, with a cannon, Lieutenant Colonel J. Fisher, the republic's military commander, dispatched Company F regulars under Captain Charles Ziegler to the spot. These men were mostly the Germans who had been the first to support the PGs at the queen's overthrow. In support of Ziegler's riflemen, Fisher sent a field gun plus six marksmen of the Citizen's Guard's Sharpshooters Company.

Once they arrived below Punchbowl Hill, the forces under Captain Ziegler dug in along the Moiliili Road, facing Sam Nowlein and his men, who had withdrawn to occupy a volcanic crater which made an excellent natural defensive position. Nowlein's men, who had the advantage of the higher ground, opened up a furious though inaccurate fire with their carbines. 'Bullets dropped all around the soldiers for an hour,' wrote Edward Towse, a sergeant major with the PGs' National Guard.[463] Nowlein's men had been given no training with their weapons, and their lack of marksmanship showed in the lack of government casualties. By 3.00 p.m., the government's howitzer had been pushed into position, and it now opened fire, lobbing shells up into the crater.[464]

Following each detonation, the royalist fighters would pop up, fire, then sink back down into cover again to await the next shell. Under cover of the shelling, Ziegler ordered his deputy, Lieutenant H. Ludewig, to conduct a flanking attack. Ludewig rose from cover and was leading his men off to one side when he was hit in the thigh by a royalist bullet. Ludewig dropped like a stone. His men quickly dived for cover, and the outflanking move stalled in its tracks. But the PG shells were soon having a devastating effect in the confines of the crater. After fifteen explosions, three royalists had been killed. Someone yelled down from the crater that they wanted to surrender. The PG troops ceased fire.

Seven Hawaiians came down from the crater under a white flag and with hands raised. Several other groups of royalist fighters eventually came down, in dribs and drabs, until there was a total of thirty-three prisoners. When the republican troops plucked up the courage to rush the crater, all they found was seventeen discarded carbines. 'The attempt to hold it evidenced a desperate madness,' commented Sergeant Major Towse.[465] But Sam Nowlein and the bulk of his force had escaped from the crater, taking their dead with them.

As the sun rose over Diamond Head on Monday morning, a hail of fire was directed down onto the bullet-riddled Bertelmann house from the ridges of Diamond Head by Robert Wilcox and his royalist force. Under this withering fire, government troops were forced to abandon the house, but Lieutenant Arthur Coyne, who was leading Company E in the absence of its ailing commander, the notorious John Good, regrouped his troops and led them on a counterattack into the western foothills of Diamond Head. But this failed, with the terrain too difficult and royalist fire too sustained. The rifle of Company E man Urband Conklin, a Union army veteran of the US Civil War, jammed at the height of the firefight, and he was trying to free it up using a ramrod when a royalist bullet struck the ramrod. "Well, they are shooting close," he calmly remarked while studying the damaged ramrod.[466]

Coyne ordered his men to withdraw to the San Souci Hotel, below Diamond Head. Wilcox, rather than press home the attack on the retreating government troops and push toward the city to link up with Nowlein as planned, led his men to the top of the extinct volcano, deciding to hold out up there. As a result, in the face of persistent but generally inaccurate fire from the eighty royalists high on Diamond Head, government forces established a firing line at Kapiolani Park, and sent for artillery. By midday, one field gun was set up in the park, normally the site of race meetings and church picnics, and began shelling Diamond Head. Its gunners were not particularly accurate, and they did little more than deface the beauty of the craggy heights. But the gun was good for the morale of the government troops, and annoying to the royalists, as it kept up a relentless fire.

Down at the docks, another cannon was laboriously installed aboard the harbor tug *Eleu*, under the command of James Pratt. Formerly a supporter of the queen, Pratt, Robert Bowler's friend, was now a reserve captain in the republic's National Guard, and, unlike George Markham, his new loyalty did not waver. Eventually, the tug got under way and steamed out of Honolulu harbor. By 4.00 p.m. the *Eleu* was off Diamond Head and its gun was also shelling the royalists on the heights, with much more accuracy than the Kapiolani Park gun.[467]

All through the day, government riflemen also kept up a steady fire at the summit. Seeking shelter, Wilcox's men retreated into the Diamond Head crater. The royalist fighters were not only outgunned by the artillery. Only Wilcox and Lot Lane were armed with rifles. Their men carried the Winchester carbines shipped in aboard the *Wahlberg* and *Waimanalo*. Major Seward had purchased carbines in California because they were lighter and easier to conceal than rifles, and cheaper. But carbines had a shorter range, which meant that government troops could stay out of carbine range and pepper the royalists with rifle fire with little fear of being hit themselves.

Despite this, the royalists on Diamond Head held their position all day. From his lofty vantage point, Wilcox could see Nowlein's men fighting at the Moiliili Road, but was unable to coordinate with them–a courier sent to Nowlein with a message from Wilcox was captured by government troops.[468]

"It's no use," declared a cursing Wilcox late in the day, as the *Eleu*'s shells fell too close for comfort and scattered his men. With darkness, he ordered a withdrawal into mountainous country to the north.[469]

Some of the royalist fighters on Diamond Head, sick of the government shelling, and fed up with Wilcox's leadership, or lack of it, deserted the cause and set off for home. But even though the revolutionaries were in retreat, the government could not rest, for more than one hundred armed royalist fighters under Nowlein and Wilcox were still on the loose.

Martial law had been declared early on Monday morning, and, with the streets of Honolulu in the hands of the Citizen's Guard, parties of troops and armed police moved through the hills and valleys north and northeast of the city through Tuesday and Wednesday. Then, in the late afternoon of Wednesday, the government's Company A stumbled on Robert Wilcox and fifty men at Manoa, just as the royalists came out of hiding and attempted to march to the Koolau Mountains to the north.

Wilcox, whose men outnumbered the Company A troops, went on the attack, striving to capture the other side's rifles. But the government troops fended them off until reinforcements including more infantry, a field gun and sharpshooters arrived. Wilcox held his ground for some time, even after shells began lobbing into his position, but the shelling demoralized many of his men. So, leaving a ten-man rearguard to delay the government forces, he withdrew the remainder of his men and headed into the Pauoa Valley. An hour after sunset, two men of the rearguard came down to the government commander under a white flag.

When the government troops moved up into what had been the royalist position, they found Robert Wilcox's discarded Italian military cloak and the body of another member of the royalist rearguard with a bullet in the brain. The Hawaiian was the only fatality of the encounter, on either side.

Through Thursday, government forces were out looking for the royalist partisans in the hills and valleys of Oahu. That night, two sentries on duty at the camp of Company F saw an Hawaiian walking toward them with his hands raised.

"Hands up," said the man, to emphasize that he was unarmed. The two edgy sentries both pulled their triggers, and both hit the Hawaiian, who fell down dead with one bullet in the head and another in the heart.[470]

As the search for the royalist leaders continued through Friday and the weekend, a 9.30 p.m. to 5.00 a.m. curfew was strictly enforced by government forces.

At 7.30 on Sunday morning, January 13, the female boarders at the Priory School on Beretania Street looked up from their breakfast to see a haggard Hawaiian royalist soldier standing at the refectory door. Sisters Albertina and Beatrice rushed to see what the man wanted, then left the room with him. When the sisters returned, thirty minutes later, they were both visibly excited.

There was a small school infirmary building at the end of the playground, and all the students were now warned by the sisters not to enter it. Sister Albertina herself remained in the yard for much of that day, patrolling up and down outside the infirmary door. At noon she went to the infirmary with a well provisioned tray, although no student patient was inside at the time.

When Priory School teacher Bernice Irwin returned to work next day, her students told her all about these strange goings on. 'We knew someone was in that room and suspected it was the queen,' Bernice later wrote.[471] Whoever it was that the pro-royalty sisters had secreted in the school infirmary, this person had moved on by Monday. It was not the queen; she was right next door at Washington Place, and had no reason to hide at the Priory.

It is more likely that the person who spent a day and a night in the school infirmary was Robert Wilcox, who, it is known, was by this time back in Honolulu. For the first few days after the fight at Manoa, Wilcox and ten men who remained with him kept to the hills, but by the weekend they had slipped into the city via the Kalihi Valley. Wilcox's companions went home, but Wilcox himself had gone into hiding. It was probably one of his ten men who had appeared in the doorway of the school refectory on Sunday morning, to help find shelter for Wilcox before he himself had gone home.

Deputy Marshal Brown and Captain Parker Waipa had been in the hills all day Saturday and Sunday, leading a party of thirty well armed and well provisioned Hawaiian police in search of Sam Nowlein. On Monday morning, Parker Waipa, using his local contacts, tracked down a Hawaiian who confessed to him that he knew roughly where Sam Nowlein was in hiding with three comrades.

Henry Waterhouse and Marshal Hitchcock now joined Brown's party, and, following Parker Waipa's directions, located and arrested his informant, handing him over to Chief Justice Judd and William Kinney, a National Guard captain. This pair interrogated the prisoner until he 'yielded the desired information.'[472] They learned that four royalist fugitives were being provided with food and information by an Hawaiian woman, and that they were planning to try to get a ship to one of the other islands once the hullabaloo had died down.

A large Government force moved into the area indicated by the informant. That area, to the surprise of the authorities, was near Kanewai Springs. Close to Honolulu, it had escaped PG attention, as Nowlein had hoped. The woman was arrested, along with her son, after which the authorities threatened to shoot the son if the woman did not help them capture Nowlein and his associates. She agreed, and sent her boy into the brush with a message for Nowlein, urging him to surrender to prevent bloodshed.

Out came Nowlein and his three young comrades–Carl Widemann, son of Judge Widemann, Will Greig, a young Hawaiian educated in the US, and nineteen-year-old English lad Louis Marshall. Nowlein shook hands with his senior captors, knowing them all well. Young Marshall grinned as he was handcuffed, and whistled all the way into the city. Come noon, the Nowlein quartet was being led into police headquarters on Market Street, passing through a vast crowd that had swiftly materialized on news of their arrest.

Late that afternoon, acting on a tip-off from Charles Hopkins, previously a pro-monarchy legislator, seven special constables armed with revolvers and rifles closed in on a small house at Iwilei, not far from Oahu Prison. The house was owned by Hopkins, and it seems that Robert Wilcox thought him an ally and had approached him for shelter there that morning, after leaving the Priory. As the government's men were surrounding the Hopkins house, a hack drew up outside. Wilcox emerged from the house, and walked quickly toward the taxi. Determined not to let him get away, the constables rushed forward and threw Wilcox to the ground. As he was being handcuffed, Wilcox protested that he was just on his way to give himself up to Attorney General Smith. By 5.00 p.m., Wilcox was behind bars at police headquarters.

Three days later, Thursday, January 17, the last royalist leader at large, Lot Lane, gave himself up. That morning he had taken refuge at a relative's house at Manoa. At noon, he heard cannon firing a salute in the distance. Lane thought this signaled that martial law, under which he could be shot on sight, had ended. In fact, the salute was to celebrate the second anniversary of the January 17 overthrow of Queen Liliuokalani; martial law would continue until March 1. Lane only learned of his mistake when he walked into the city and surrendered to the Citizen's Guard. But he wasn't shot. Lane ended up behind bars.

"I went into this thing with my eyes open and on principle," Lane told the arresting officer. "We are whipped and I only hope that none of my friends on either side are hurt."[473]

In the eleven days since the uprising had begun, five royalists and one government man, Charles Carter, had been killed. The government of the Hawaiian Republic subsequently lionized Carter; they did not even record the names of the royalist dead. Since noon on January 7, after marital law came into force, three hundred royalists had been arrested. With Oahu Prison soon overflowing, the Iolani Barracks was pressed into use as a jail. Some prisoners had surrendered, others had been captured. But a number of those arrested in the martial law crackdown, including the editors of the Hawaiian-language newspapers *Holomua* and *Ka Leo*, and citizens who had written press articles or published letters critical of the Dole Government, were incarcerated purely on suspicion of involvement in the uprising. A new file was opened at the Government Archives; it was entitled 'Political Prisoners.'

Now that they had the royalists in their net, the Dole Government intended stamping out any possibility of future resistance. They would begin by putting the royalist rebels on trial, for treason, a hanging offense. But they would not be stopping at the three hundred. The person the PGs chiefly suspected of treason, and most dearly wanted to put on trial, was Queen Liliuokalani.

28.

THE QUEEN ON TRIAL

At 9.30 on the morning of Wednesday, January 16, 1895, under the provisions of martial law, the Hawaiian Republic's adjutant general, John Soper, issued an order to Marshal Hitchcock for the arrest of Mrs. Liliuokalani Dominis, as the PGs had persisted in calling Liliuokalani since the day of her overthrow. At 10.00, two hacks drew up outside Washington Place. Deputy Marshal Arthur Brown and the police department's Senior Captain Robert Parker Waipa stepped out, then quickly walked up the long path to the door and rapped the knocker. All but a handful of the queen's forty guardians had gone home; their weapons were once more buried four feet down in the queen's garden. The Hawaiian guards at the queen's door looked at the two officials uncertainly.

One of Liliuokalani's ladies in waiting, Charles Wilson's wife Evelyn, (called Kitty by those close to her, including the queen), hurried to the queen's bedroom, where Liliuokalani was resting after breakfast. The queen had been under her doctor's care for mental exhaustion for months; the events of the past ten days had only sapped her strength all the more. Mrs. Wilson told the queen that she had seen the two uniformed men coming up the path, and Liliuokalani instructed her to show the pair into the parlor, which she did. After a short while, Liliuokalani came into the room, dressed entirely in black, followed by her ladies in waiting–Mrs. Wilson and Mrs. Charles Clark. Ignoring Brown, Liliuokalani glowered at the Hawaiian police captain, whom she had considered a traitor ever since he had so faithfully served her late brother the king.

This was the most difficult thing that Robert Parker Waipa had ever done, or would ever do in his life. For, he was still an Hawaiian ali'i, and still considered Liliuokalani his queen. Robert would explain to his children that he had taken an oath to uphold the law and obey his orders, as he had when he held the palace for King Kalakaua. And Robert Parker Waipa always kept his oath. He would be given gifts totaling $875 and a diamond encrusted badge by supporters of the republican government for his role in putting down the counterrevolution of 1895. He could use the money—he had eighteen children. And the badge was handsome. But as far as he was concerned, he was only doing his duty, and keeping his oath.

"Oh, my queen," the captain now said in Hawaiian to Liliuokalani, "I must arrest you."[474]

Her ladies gasped, but Liliuokalani calmly turned to Arthur Brown for an explanation. Opening a warrant for her arrest, Brown read it to her. When she asked to see the document, he refused, and curtly asked her to accompany him. PG soldier Edward Towse, who penned a very pro-government firsthand account of this counterrevolution, nonetheless wrote admiringly of Liliuokalani at this moment, saying that she 'was always rated a strong woman.' Now, faced with arrest, Towse said, 'she did not faint, or cry, or start back, or give any evidence of weakness.'[475]

"All right," Liliuokalani responded. "I will go."[476]

Brown informed her that Mrs. Clark could accompany her. Sending Mrs. Clark to fetch her handbag, Liliuokalani put on her hat and coat, then walked with Brown and the captain out the door. Lost as to what they should do, her Hawaiian guards stood by and watched as their queen was escorted down the path to the waiting taxis. Brown sat beside the queen in the lead hack, and Parker Waipa climbed up beside the driver. Mrs. Clark bustled to take her seat in the second taxi. Then with a mounted policeman riding in front and another behind, the little convoy crossed Beretania Street into Richards Street.

A block and a half down Richards, the taxis swung in the palace's Kinau Gate. This was the former tradesman's entrance, but its use on this occasion was probably not intended as an insult to the queen; the government was concerned about Hawaiians rioting once they learned of their queen's arrest, so Liliuokalani's transfer from Washington Place had to be carried out via the fastest route possible, and with the least fuss—hence the small escort.

The last time that Liliuokalani had been here, this had been the Iolani Palace, and she had been leaving for self-imposed exile at Washington Place. Now that she was returning, it was the Executive Building, and the grounds were filled with army tents, horses, and PG soldiers standing around talking, or lounging on the grass. 'The men looked as though they had been on the watch all night,' Liliuokalani would recall. Lot Lane's surrender was a day away at this point, so the army was still on alert. The queen was surprised that she had been brought here. She had been expecting to be taken to police headquarters, 'to undergo some sort of trial,' she thought.[477]

Her hack pulled up at the foot of the palace steps. Lieutenant Colonel Joseph Fisher, chief of the republic's army, trotted down the cast iron steps to meet her. Of medium build, with a neat beard, he had a pleasant face. Wearing full dress uniform and sword, he offered the queen his arm and helped her step down to the ground. Liliuokalani looked up, and saw the muzzles of two brass cannon projecting from the lower veranda. She did not see the newspaper photographer on the same veranda who snapped her mounting the steps under escort. Alerted by the government, that photographer now had a priceless image for his editor. All in a row, Captain Parker Waipa, Deputy Marshal Brown, Liliuokalani and Lieutenant Colonel Fisher went slowly up the steps.

Inside, government employees at desks stopped what they were doing and looked around as Fisher escorted the queen up the central, carpeted, koa staircase to the second floor. The Dole cabinet was meeting in the queen's former library to the right. The members all now came to the room's door, to watch Liliuokalani's arrival with considerable satisfaction, and she paused, just for a moment, to gather her composure, with a white linen handkerchief in her hand. She did not realize that she was standing beneath a life-size portrait of herself in full regal attire, that still hung on the wall.

Colonel Fisher now escorted her to a room at the front corner of the former palace. Two years before, this had been the bedroom of one of the two princes. For the past eighteen months, it had been the office of Hawaii's auditor general. The shutters were drawn. The carpet had been pulled up, and sold off, exposing the naked floorboards. A single, hard bed had been installed in one corner. The room also contained a small sofa, a chair, a table, and a few other sticks of furniture. A bathroom and an empty dressing room led off the bedroom. Mrs. Clark had caught up with the queen by this time, and she followed her into the room. The two women looked around uncertainly.

"I suppose this is to be your future abode, madam," said Fisher apologetically. "If there was anything that you wanted...?"[478]

Liliuokalani, realizing that this was now her prison suite, asked that her steward be permitted to bring meals to her and Mrs. Clark three times a day. Fisher agreed, then withdrew, leaving the two women looking at each other. The door closed. Outside, a guard locked the door.

After dark, all the noise of government industry beyond that locked door ceased. A distraught Mrs. Clark attempted to sleep on the sofa, sobbing and sighing without relent. Liliuokalani lay awake on her little bed all through that first night, staring at the ceiling. It was, Liliuokalani would write, 'the longest night I have ever passed in my life; it seemed as though the dawn of day would never come.'[479]

When the new day did come, Liliuokalani asked for Mrs. Wilson to come and take the place of Mrs. Clark, who, with her husband Charles arrested on January 7 and now also imprisoned, was not dealing with the situation at all well. Mrs. Wilson agreed, and the two ladies exchanged places.

Instead of trial by jury, the Dole Government created a military commission to try the hundreds they had arrested after the failed royalist countercoup. Attorney Paul Neumann, who defended a number of the accused, began by protesting the commission's legality, but his protest was dismissed by the commission. Secretly, the Dole Government knew that the legality of its military commission was doubtful. 'We recognize the force of objections to (the) jurisdiction of (the) military commission,' Attorney General Smith wrote to his colleague Lorrin Thurston in Washington. 'But in a great measure the existing conditions must govern. Such means are justifiable as will protect the state.'[480] The same questionable argument, that of the ends justifying the means, had been, and would continue to be, used by despots down through history.

At Oahu Prison, royalist prisoners whom the prosecution particularly wanted to crack were isolated and kept in 'dark cells' into which no light could reach. After a week or two of light depravation and no human contact, a handful of prisoners offered to testify against their colleagues in exchange for reduced sentences. Others broke down when told they would hang for their part in the uprising, and they likewise agreed to testify. Sam Nowlein, on the other hand, took full responsibility for the coup attempt. He also freely named his senior colleagues, who, he must have assumed, would, like him, acknowledge their guilt and loyally shelter the queen from any blame. To his later astonishment, Gulick, Rickard and Seward would all plead not guilty and deny everything, despite damning evidence.

Wasting no time, the military commission convened on January 17, just the day after Liliuokalani's arrest. The hearings were held in the former Throne Room of the palace, with a small public gallery permitted to watch. To save time, the commission tried the accused in batches. First to be tried were Nowlein, Wilcox, Bertelmann, Widemann, Greig, Marshall, and Lot Lane's brother and cousin. All were charged with treason and open rebellion. Nowlein, Wilcox and Bertelmann pleaded guilty. Not that it mattered. After three days of hearings, all eight were found guilty. Next, on January 21, came Gulick, Rickard, Seward, and Tom Walker. And they too would be found guilty. In fact, very few of the 191 accused who were brought to trial over the thirty-five days during which the commission sat were exonerated.

While the trials took place, Liliuokalani was under lock and key with her lady in waiting, in her improvised cell directly above the improvised courtroom. During this time, the Dole Government agreed to former marshal Charles Wilson acting as Liliuokalani's 'agent,' to serve as intermediary between the queen and themselves. Curiously, although Wilson was still living on the grounds at Washington Place, he was not implicated in the uprising in any way and was not arrested. On January 21, Wilson brought attorney Paul Neumann up to meet with Liliuokalani in her cell. Neumann gravely informed the queen that Sam Nowlein and several other men had been sentenced to hang.

"In the event that it should decided that all the principal parties to the revolt pay with your lives, Your Majesty," said Neumann, "are you prepared to die?"

"Yes," Liliuokalani firmly replied. "I have no anxiety for myself, and feel no dread of death."[481]

The following day, Wilson brought Liliuokalani a document

which had been drawn up by 'Judge' Alfred Hartwell. It was a formal declaration, to be signed by Liliuokalani, in which she abdicated her throne and called on all her subjects to recognize the Government of the Republic of Hawaii as the nation's legitimate government. This document, Liliuokalani declared, was 'an insulting proposition written in abject terms.' She refused to even contemplate it.[482]

Over the next two days, Hartwell and a number of men whom the queen considered her friends, including Wilson, Neumann, Sam Parker, and Henry Widemann, came to her and urged her to sign the abdication. The military commission had just handed down more death sentences, to Gulick, Rickard, and Seward. 'I would have chosen death rather than to have signed it,' she would say, 'but it was represented to me that by signing this paper all the persons who had been arrested, all my people now in trouble by reason of their love and loyalty toward me, would be immediately released.'[483]

In the presence of her advisers, Liliuokalani signed the abdication. Hartwell was the last to leave the cell once the act was completed. Before he withdrew, he shook the now ex-queen by the hand. As he did, tears streamed down his cheeks. Once the door had closed behind him, Mrs. Wilson, who had been standing behind Liliuokalani's chair throughout the signing process, said bitterly, of Hartwell, "Crocodile tears!"[484]

The next day, Liliuokalani received a document signed by William Smith, in his capacity as attorney general of the Republic. While acknowledging receipt of the instrument of abdication, Smith said that the rights surrendered by Liliuokalani had, to the mind of his government, ceased to exist on January 14, 1893 anyway. The fact that she had signed the document, he said, in no way exempted her from investigation and trial in relation to the recent revolt.

Smith had been jolted by the royalist revolt. As soon as first word of the uprising had reached his ears, he had rushed to police headquarters, which, as it had during his own coup two years earlier, became the bunker of the government of the day. For several weeks, Smith slept there most nights. On January 30, he wrote to Lorrin Thurston, 'I have slept at (my) house 2 nights in three weeks. As also have several others. We have got what sleep we could at the Station House, lying down in our clothes.' Now, Smith wanted to punish the royalists, and ensure there were no more uprisings, ever again. 'Very many of our best men feel it imperative for our future safety that some examples should be made,' Smith told Thurston. Smith agreed with those 'best men.'[485]

Contrary to what Liliuokalani had been led to believe, the trials would continue and death sentences handed out. And the process would be capped by the ex-queen's own arraignment before the military commission. 'Whatever hope may have existed in her mind was ill-founded,' PG official 'Professor' W. D. Alexander was to gloat.[486]

At 10.00 a.m. on February 8, Liliuokalani was escorted into the former Throne Room by two Hawaiian policemen, for her own trial. Paul Neumann had suggested she not attend the hearing, as it would be undignified and humiliating for her. 'Humiliating!' she later railed. 'What had I left?' Besides, she was determined to attend. 'I was a martyr to the cause of my people, and proud of it.'[487]

The Throne Room's gallery was crowded with diplomatic representatives, clergymen, reporters, leading businessmen, several women, and a long-haired character later identified to Liliuokalani as the California poet Joaquin Miller, who would write verse in praise of her. As the queen took a seat on a high-backed chair and adjusted her black dress, her police escorts, a sergeant and a constable, took station directly behind her. In the middle of the room, the members of the military commission sat around a long table, some with their backs to the accused; Liliuokalani knew almost all of them.

The judge advocate was William A. Kinney, who had been hastily given a captain's commission in the PG army by the Dole Government so that he could fulfill this role. A Canadian-born attorney, Kinney had been, along with his lawyer friend Lorrin Thurston, a founding member of the Hawaiian League. He had served a brief term in the legislature before leaving Hawaii, and had been working as an attorney in Salt Lake City, Utah, at the time of the queen's overthrow. After going to Washington in 1893 to try to help Thurston and the failed Annexation Commission, he had resettled in Honolulu.

The senior member of the military commission was William A. Whiting, a Harvard law school graduate. He had resigned as one of Hawaii's circuit court judges to accept this position, having been made a colonel overnight to enable him to sit on the military commission. Most other commission members had been deeply implicated in Liliuokalani's 1893 overthrow–Joseph Fisher, Charles Ziegler, William Wilder, J. M. Camara, and the turncoat James Pratt. John Good and Oscar White sat as alternate commission members during some of the countercoup trials. The only commission member Liliuokalani would not have known was the most junior, J. W. Jones, a deputy company commander in the Dole Government's army.

The prosecuting attorneys were the late Charlie Carter's cousin, Alfred Carter, and Alexander Robertson, assisted by Advisory Council members William Castle and Cecil Brown. Under overnight pressure from the ambassadors of the US and Britain, who strongly counseled against capital punishment for the former queen, the Dole Government reduced the original charge against Liliuokalani, that of treason, to one of misprision of treason–concealing knowledge of a treasonous act, which was not a capital crime.

The prosecution set out to prove that Liliuokalani had known about the uprising prior to the event, and had encouraged it. Later, after this trial, Liliuokalani would admit to having been aware of the planned coup. 'Preparations were undoubtedly made amongst some in sympathy with the monarchy to overthrow the oligarchy. How and where these were carried on, I will not say. I have no right to disclose any secrets given in trust to me.'[488] But at the time of the trial, infuriated after the promise that the trials would be discontinued once she abdicated her throne had not been kept, she denied everything.

With none of the coup leaders implicating her in their evidence, it was up to the prosecutors to prove that Liliuokalani was an accomplice to the crime. But not a single witness would say where the money for the weapons purchased by Seward had come from–all testified they had no idea of its source–so it could not be proven that Liliuokalani had anything to do with financing the attempted coup. Nor could the prosecution place her in any meeting where the revolt was discussed or planned.

The testimony of Sam Nowlein and his deputy Charles Clark was the most damaging to Liliuokalani, for both told of brief but incriminating conversations they'd had with her on January 3, 4 and 6, which made it clear that she had known that some act against the government was in motion. Liliuokalani denied these conversations. And her lawyer Paul Neumann called eleven witnesses who testified that Charles Clark was not a man who could be believed. After which, Clark, realizing that he had damaged his queen's defense, recanted, and, falling on his proverbial sword, claimed he had made up his conversations with Liliuokalani. But it was to no avail; the military commission did not believe him, and Liliuokalani would never forgive him. Clark was doubly damned.

It was Liliuokalani who provided the most damning evidence against herself. Following her arrest, Washington Place had been ransacked in a search for incriminating evidence, and the garden turned upside down. Rifles and 'bombs' were found beneath her flower beds. And, in the house, her diary was located. Liliuokalani had burned various documents prior to her arrest, but the diary she had left untouched. The prosecutors were able to present the entry for December 29th last, in which the queen had written, 'Signed eleven commissions.' Liliuokalani could not explain this away. And when it was shown that she had sighted Charles Gulick's constitutional draft, she agreed that she had seen it, but argued that she had a right to consider a new constitution in case she should one day be returned to power.

In her overall defense, Liliuokalani presented a lengthy written statement. 'I owed no allegiance to the Provisional Government,' she declared, describing how her legitimate government had been overthrown. 'I must deny your right to try me in the manner and by the court which you have called together for this purpose.' She reminded the members of the commission, 'I would ask you to consider that your government is on trial before the whole civilized world, and that in accordance with your actions and decisions will you yourselves be judged.' She concluded, 'I shall never harbor any resentment towards you, whatever may be your decision.'[489]

After consulting briefly, the commission ordered the bulk of Liliuokalani's statement–those paragraphs in which she had denied the right of the military commission to try her and criticized the Provisional Government and the Government of the Republic–be struck from the record, so that neither the press nor the public could read them. Paul Neumann protested, to no avail, then delivered a detailed summing up for the defense which lasted many hours. After a summing up from the advocate general, the court adjourned, and the prisoner was returned to her quarters above the improvised courtroom.

* * *

Through February and March, concurrent with the trials of the
royalists, the Dole Government conducted a purge of government
ranks, sifting out all employees whose loyalty was suspect
and who may have been involved in the January uprising but
were never caught or implicated. To achieve this, the Executive
and Advisory Councils set up a largely secret Committee of
Investigation, comprising cabinet ministers William Smith,
Francis Hatch and J. A. King. This committee had one basic
stated tenet: 'Loyalty to the government is the first, essential and
indispensable qualification which every holder of office under the
government must possess.'[490]

The principals of the mysterious Committee of Investigation
sent out demands to the heads of all government departments
and agencies, requiring them to furnish Loyalty Reports on
listed employees. Many of the men on the committee's lists had
questions hanging over them that went back to the second half
of 1894, when government employees had been required to take
a special oath of allegiance to the Republic of Hawaii. Some,
it seems, had not taken the oath as quickly as they might have
done. 'The question of loyalty must be settled in each individual
case by evidence,' said the Committee of Investigation's demand.
The department heads were instructed to require the named
employees to provide evidence of where they were and what they
were doing during the week of January 6.[491]

From the Honolulu Fire Department to the Custom House,
Finance Department to the Honolulu Water Works, managers
passed on these demands to their workers. Sometimes, jittery
supervisors did not wait for the employee to hand in their written
responses, instead summarily dismissing men whose loyalty
was suspect. The Committee of Investigation's final Reports on
Loyalty of Government Employees would be presented to the
Executive and Advisory Councils on April 13. Typical of the
many reports to the Committee of Investigation was one which
said that Lionel Hart, a clerk with the Foreign Office, had been
'removed for political reasons.' Jonathan Shaw, an assessor with
the Finance Department, reported on March 9, of D. L. Kalawaia,
'He gave no support to the government and has not taken the
oath of allegiance up to the evening of the 6th instant. He has

since been discharged.' Sixteen-year-old messenger D. K. Maalo was dismissed by Shaw on similar grounds.[492]

None of the men dismissed in this purge were permitted future government employment in any capacity. And the activities of all would come in for intense police scrutiny in future. Hawaii was now truly a police state.

At 2.00 p.m. on February 27, Liliuokalani's police guards led her back into the Throne Room, accompanied by Charles Wilson and his wife. Liliuokalani would have only recently learned that, nineteen days earlier, former US ambassador to Hawaii John L. Stevens, the man who had made her overthrow possible, had suffered a heart attack at his home in Maine, and died. In Liliuokalani's present predicament, that news would have been slight consolation to her.

The room was empty when the deposed queen was brought in. Liliuokalani took a seat. Mr. and Mrs. Wilson stood behind her chair, and the trio waited in tense silence. Before long, two PG military officers hurried into the room. Liliuokalani went to rise, but one of the officers, George Potter, another stalwart of her overthrow and now a major in the Republic's army, told her that she could remain seated.

Potter read out the verdict of the court. Liliuokalani had been found guilty as charged. The sentence of the court was that she be imprisoned for five years, with hard labor, and pay a fine of $5,000.

'I think we will take our own course in regard to the sentences,' William Smith had written to Lorrin Thurston on January 30. Smith had never forgiven President Grover Cleveland for quashing the annexation treaty. Complaining about the pressure being brought to bear by the US Government for clemency, he told Thurston, 'Cleveland and Liliuokalani are the most guilty. Sometimes it seems horribly wrong to think of executing Kanakas and not Liliuokalani and Grover. Damn him!'[493] But by February 17, Smith was confessing to Thurston that he was in a quandary: 'Three times my judgment has swung–for executions–and against them.'[494]

In the end, pressure from the Cleveland Administration and the friends of annexation in Congress influenced the final sentencing.

As Dole Government soldier Edward Towse wrote, 'Word came from the United States that the execution of captive rebels would militate against annexation. That about settled it.'[495] Many of the Republic's fulltime soldiers had signed petitions calling for the death sentences to be proceeded with, but, as William Smith had written to Thurston, there was an overriding priority: 'We must have annexation.'[496]

On February 28, just one day after Liliuokalani's sentence was announced, a lengthy decree from President Sanford Dole, as Commander in Chief, commuted most of the military commission's sentences. A dozen more commutations would be released on March 12 and 15. No death sentences would be carried out. Gulick, Rickard and Seward were now each to serve thirty years imprisonment and pay fines of $10,000. Thomas Walker's sentence was thirty years and $5,000. For Widemann, Greig, and Marshall, it was twenty years and $10,000. Tom Poole, the man who shot Charlie Carter, received ten years, and Lot Lane and John Bowler five years and $5,000. John Kahalewai, former commander of the King's Guard, who was captured under arms, received five years. Many others received sentences ranging from six months to ten years. Prince Kuhio was sentenced to one year in prison, and even the Reverend Kaili, who had watched over the buried carbines, was to be imprisoned for a year.

Sam Nowlein and Henry Bertelmann were pardoned, in recognition of their confessions and cooperation with the prosecutors. Charles Clark and George Townsend were released on parole. Captain Davies of the *Waimanalo*, who had been sentenced to five years and a $10,000 fine, was deported. George Markham, the wayward detective, was discharged, after Robert Wilcox had testified that he had forced him to go to the assembly point at Antone Rosa's property. Wilcox himself, 'Hawaii's Garibaldi,' had his death sentence commuted to thirty-five years imprisonment, with hard labor, and a $10,000 fine.

A number of 'foreign nationals' were released from custody without being charged, but were immediately deported. These men sent into exile included Fred Wundenberg, the dismissed clerk of the supreme court, and Alfred Peterson, the attorney general whose lack of backbone had contributed to Liliuokalani's overthrow. Peterson had never sided with the PGs, and remained supportive of the queen to the end. Even John Colburn had supported the queen up to the point of the counterrevolution, so disgusted was he by the PG dictatorship. But Colburn received such a fright by the military commission trials that he became an annexationist, with embarrassingly contrived enthusiasm.

As for Liliuokalani, the hard labor element of her sentence was eliminated by Dole. And she was informed that her five year incarceration would be in the Executive Building room that had been her home for the past few weeks. She was to continue to be a prisoner in her own palace. And the man who would be in charge of her incarceration was Captain John Good, the same John Good who had shot the policeman and launched Liliuokalani's overthrow, the same John Good who had threatened to kill the queen.

29.

ANNEXATION

By April, 1895, US Secretary of State Gresham and President Cleveland had put up with enough of what they considered Lorrin Thurston's objectionable and undiplomatic conduct as the Dole Government's ambassador to Washington. In particular, they objected to Thurston releasing confidential diplomatic correspondence to the press. Cleveland informed Congress, 'Mr. Thurston having given abundant reason for asking for his recall, that course was pursued.'[497] Declared *persona non grata* by the United States, Thurston was recalled by the Dole Government. On his return to Hawaii, he purchased Honolulu newspaper the *Pacific Commercial Advertiser*. Not only would this give him a money-making machine, the newspaper was to provide him with a powerful tool that would give full rein to his skills as a political propagandist and manipulator of events.

Thurston arrived back in a Hawaiian police state that was in lockdown. The exiled Volney Ashford told the New York *Evening Post*, 'There is a perfect reign of terror in the islands; informers are everywhere.'[498] In San Francisco, where most of the Hawaiian deportees gathered, the Dole Government's consul Charles Wilder expended large sums employing private detectives to keep watch on these potential troublemakers.

In Honolulu, where political gatherings were banned, wives of political prisoners in Oahu Prison made themselves outfits from the same striped material as their husband's prison uniforms, and wore them every time they visited the prison. It was a very effective visual protest, one which ensured the plight of the prisoners was always in the public eye. And there was not a thing the government could do about it. One wife was overheard saying to her imprisoned husband, pointing to his prison garb, "I am prouder to see you in this uniform than in any you ever wore."[499]

There had been much international concern at Liliuokalani's conviction and imprisonment, and the fear had not left the Dole Government of another popular uprising to free her. They saw just one answer. As William Smith told Thurston, 'After annexation, no more revolutions.'[500] It was agreed that all efforts must be focused on winning annexation by the US once their enemy Grover Cleveland left office. To make annexation more palatable to the US Congress, it was also agreed that Hawaii's political prisoners would have to be freed before the next US presidential election.

In September, 1895, after being locked in the room at the Executive Building for eight months, Liliuokalani was released into the 'custody' of her agent Charles Wilson, and went home to Washington Place. She was on parole, and not permitted to leave Oahu. Before long, because Wilson insisted on following the terms of her parole, to ensure she was not locked up again, Liliuokalani came to see her faithful friend as her jailer, and enemy. By March, 1896, the last of the prisoners convicted over the 1895 coup attempt had been released from 'the Reef.' Among them was Prince Kuhio, who had spent a year behind bars.

In November, 1896, Republican candidate William McKinley won the US presidential election, becoming 25th president of the United States. This was the same McKinley who, as a senator, had sponsored the disastrous McKinley Tariff in 1890. McKinley was inaugurated in March, 1897, and two months later Hawaii's Dole Government sent its latest Annexation Commission to Washington, comprised of Lorrin Thurston, Francis Hatch, and William Kinney. Because Thurston had previously left the US capital in disgrace, Hatch was chairman of this commission. But Thurston still called the shots.

Thurston found a fresh and very helpful ally in Washington, in the person of the new assistant secretary of the Navy, Theodore Roosevelt–'an enthusiastic annexationist,' Thurston was to describe him.[501] On May 3, at the very time that the Dole Government was forming its Annexation Commission, Roosevelt was writing to the US Navy's Captain Alfred Thayer Mahan: 'As regards Hawaii, I take your views absolutely.' A noted military historian, Mahan had written an article in the journal *Forum* which many annexationists latched onto. Mahan argued that Hawaii was strategically essential to the military interests of the United States, and was needed as a US base. 'If I had my way,' said Roosevelt to Mahan, 'we would annex those islands tomorrow.'[502]

Roosevelt also confided to Mahan, 'As regards Hawaii, I am delighted to tell you that (Navy) Secretary Long shares our views. He believes we should take the islands, and I have just been preparing some memoranda for him to use at the Cabinet meeting tomorrow. If only we had some good man in the place of John Sherman as Secretary of State there would not be a hitch, and even as it is I hope for favorable action.' Sherman, younger brother of General William Tecumseh Sherman, was famously against US territorial expansion. 'I have been pressing upon the Secretary,' wrote Roosevelt, 'and through him the President, that we ought to act now without delay.'[503]

Roosevelt welcomed Thurston and his fellow annexation commissioners when they arrived in Washington. He even had maps prepared by the Navy Department depicting Hawaii at the strategic center of the Pacific, and gave them to Thurston to distribute to members of Congress. For, this time, Thurston was playing the Capitol Hill game, and was lobbying congressmen to support an annexation treaty. He included Roosevelt's maps in a persuasive little booklet, *A Hand-Book on the Annexation of Hawaii*, which he wrote, printed, and handed out to congressmen and the press.

In that booklet, Thurston wrote, 'The issue in Hawaii is not between the monarchy and the Republic. That issue has been settled.' The American acquisition of Hawaii, said Thurston, writing in an era when the 'yellow peril,' the dread of Asians flooding into the US, affected even the most liberal of the country's leaders, would be 'the preliminary skirmish in the great coming struggle between the civilization and the awakening forces of the East and the civilization of the West.'[504]

Despite Secretary of State Sherman's reservations, President McKinley negotiated an Hawaiian annexation treaty with Thurston and his colleagues. In the end, Secretary Sherman not only signed the treaty on behalf of the United States, he consented to having his photograph taken doing so. McKinley then sent the treaty to the Senate for ratification. But Liliuokalani was also in Washington. Apparently to placate critics in the US, the Dole Government had lifted her house arrest, and she was now free to travel. Gray-headed now, and looking tired after her imprisonment, she brought with her a petition raised by the Hawaiian Patriotic League which contained thousands of signatures from Hawaiians opposed to annexation. She also lodged an official protest of her own with the McKinley Administration, opposing annexation.

With considerable opposition to annexation voiced in the press and in Congress, the treaty languished on Capitol Hill, failing to find the majority in both Houses required for it to be approved. It was looking as if the annexation of Hawaii would again fail to be endorsed by the US Government. But on February 15, 1898, the US battleship *Maine* blew up in Havana Harbor, in Cuba, then a Spanish possession. Patriotic anger, and jingoistic fervor, surged throughout the United States. On March 16, the Senate Foreign Relations Committee reported in favor of a joint resolution of both Senate and House to annex Hawaii, which would make a handy base in operations again Spanish possessions in the Pacific. On April 20, Congress authorized McKinley to take the US to war against Spain in Cuba. When McKinley declared war on Spain on April 25, Secretary of State Sherman resigned in protest.

In the middle of May, with the US gripped with war fever, the House of Representatives Foreign Relations Committee endorsed the joint resolution proposal for the annexation of Hawaii, which was now touted as an essential base for US operations against the Spanish in the Philippines and on Guam. In June, US troopships began calling at Honolulu on their way to the Philippines. The joint resolution for the annexation of Hawaii passed the Senate on June 15, and the House on July 6. On July 7, 1898, President McKinley signed into law the Newlands Joint Resolution for the annexation of Hawaii.

It was done. In the blink of an eye, the sovereign nation of Hawaii was now a possession of the United States of America. Without endorsement by a vote of the Hawaiian people. And, unlike the Gadsden Purchase and Alaska Purchase, apart from the US agreeing to take over the Hawaiian national debt from Dole's government, Hawaii changed hands without a cent in compensation being paid.

Under an oppressively gray sky, on Friday, August 12, hundreds of sailors and marines from the cruisers USS *Mohican* and USS *Philadelphia* came to attention in their ranks in front of Honolulu's Executive Building. A crowd of whites lined the building's verandas–'the elite of Honolulu,' according to Lucien Young. Dole Government officials filled a wooden platform built in front of the former palace's front doors.[505]

Not far away, at Washington Place, Liliuokalani had been joined by her family and friends. As she sat in her crowded parlor, Prince Kawanakoa and Princess Kaiulani stood beside her. Kaiulani had remained in England for more than four years, in self imposed exile, but she had come home in 1897 and was with her aunt at this traumatic moment for them both, and for their people. Liliuokalani and Kaiulani wore black; they were in mourning, for their lost country. The Washington Place shutters remained closed all day, as did the shutters in every native Hawaiian home. No Hawaiian ventured out of doors in Honolulu, said Liliuokalani.[506] 'It was a very sad and tragic day for the Hawaiians,' recalled schoolteacher Bernice Irwin, who was at Hilo the day that the annexation ceremony took place. There, she said, 'Many wept unabashed.'[507]

Outside Honolulu's Executive Building, on the temporary platform, US ambassador Harold Sewall, who had succeeded Albert Willis, read the annexation resolution passed by the US Congress. Sanford Dole, who had never been popularly elected to any post of responsibility in Hawaii, made a short speech in which he yielded the sovereignty and public property of Hawaii to the United States. He was not stepping down from power–he would remain caretaker governor of Hawaii, and William McKinley would appoint Dole to be the first Governor of the US Territory of Hawaii, for a term of three years, on the recommendation of a congressional delegation sent to Hawaii by McKinley and which included none other than Senator John Morgan–of Morgan Report fame.

As the former Royal Hawaiian Band played the Hawaiian national anthem, Hawaii Ponoi, the little nation's flag was lowered from the Executive Building's flagpole. According to one account, some of the Hawaiian musicians could not bring themselves to finish this final rendition of their proud national anthem, and, dropping their instruments, ran off in tears.[508] Once the anthem had ended, National Guard cannon on shore fired a twenty-one-gun salute, which was answered from the harbor by the guns of the USS *Philadelphia*.

Then, the United States flag was run up, the US Navy band played the Star Spangled Banner, the crowd cheered, and again the cannon boomed out in salute. This flag that now flew over Honolulu was the very same US flag that had been lowered from the Government Building on February 1, 1893 on the orders of Commissioner Blount, and subsequently retained by Lieutenant Lucien Young. 'I gave this flag to L. A. Thurston,' Young later revealed, 'with the request that it be re-hoisted on the same flagstaff from which it had been lowered. Mr. Thurston communicated with President McKinley, and he approved of the proposition.'509

Several miles away, on Punchbowl Hill, Senior Captain Robert Parker Waipa, posted well away from the main ceremony, watched as the Hawaiian flag was also lowered for the last time at the old Punchbowl Battery, to be replaced by a US flag. As the cannon nearby boomed out their own twenty-one-gun salute, Robert Parker Waipa took possession of the lowered Hawaiian flag, reverently folding it. He took it home, and retained it for the rest of his days. Despite having been dismissed by Queen Liliuokalani from command of the Guard, he had been under arms for her at the time of her 1893 overthrow and would have given his life for her had she ordered it. Yet, for years after her abdication, he worried that he was despised by some Hawaiians for being the officer who had arrested the queen in 1895. Many years later, he would feel forgiven when invited by his fellow ali'i to ride at the head of the annual King Kamehameha Day parade as its grand marshal, which he continued to do every year from 1922 until he retired from the police force.

For the rest of her days, Liliuokalani was treated as, and addressed as, a queen by her native people and by many foreigners. Over time, the bitterness Liliuokalani felt at her overthrow faded, and she became resigned to the American occupation of her country. When King Kamehameha Day was celebrated at Washington Place in the years following annexation, having been reintroduced by the Hawaiian ali'i in 1904, it was noted that, when Hawaii Ponoi was played by the band, Liliuokalani remained seated, but when the Star Spangled Banner was played, she respectfully came to her feet, and stood, like everyone else. Liliuokalani died, peacefully, at Washington Place, on November 11, 1917, at the age of seventy-nine.

Princess Kaiulani met a more tragic end. After riding in a

rainstorm in late January, 1899, she fell ill. She lingered between life and death for many weeks, until, in the early hours of March 6, she passed away. The beautiful Kaiulani was just twenty-three years of age. The story goes that when she died, peacocks she kept in the grounds of her home at Waikiki–where the Sheraton Princess Kaiulani Hotel now stands–began an unearthly screeching. Her funeral was attended by thousands, and she was mourned for decades. She was, said the Honolulu *Advertiser*, 'the most beloved of the Hawaiian race.'[510] Kaiulani had not married, so that neither she nor Liliuokalani left any descendants.

In 1901, William McKinley, the President of the United States who annexed Hawaii, was assassinated, at Buffalo, New York. It was early in his second term, on September 6–the same date that Liliuokalani had been released from imprisonment in Honolulu's Executive Building. McKinley was shot by an anarchist, Leon Czolgosz. But it is not unlikely that a kahuna or two claimed credit for 'praying him to death.' Hawaiians certainly continued to believe in the power of the kahuna. Robert Parker Waipa's children would tell the story of the day that two kahunas knelt in the drive of the family home and began the *anaana* ceremony, praying their beloved father to death. Parker Waipa put an end to the kahunas' work with a blast of shotgun pellets; fired into the drive in front of the pair, it sent the kahunas running.

Lorrin Thurston and Sanford Dole both appear to have escaped kahuna attention, with both living to ripe old age. Dole died in 1926. Thurston died in 1931, after having built Honolulu's *Advertiser* into Hawaii's most successful newspaper. Although, he did not escape disaster entirely–Thurston's house was burned to the ground in 1920; among the valuables lost in the fire were all Thurston's records and mementos of the annexation years.

Henry Waterhouse, the 'Tasmanian' who propelled the 1893 coup forward when Thurston lost his courage, suffered considerable personal loss after the overthrow of the monarchy. First, his father died on the eve of the counter-revolution in 1895. His elder brother John passed away a year later, aged just 52. Henry's wife Julia died in 1897. Henry himself died in 1904, at the relatively young age of 59. Although he served in the Hawaiian Republic's senate, and was active in putting down the 1895 counter-revolution, Henry refrained from taking another prominent role in Hawaiian politics after his Committee of Safety experience, preferring to serve as president of Hawaii's

Evangelical Society and the YMCA. In 1992, the handsome
Waterhouse family mansion on Honolulu's Nuuanu Avenue was
acquired and restored by the Girl Scouts, who used it as their
Hawaiian headquarters. Ironically, when the Girls Scouts were
founded in Hawaii in 1917, Queen Liliuokalani was their official
sponsor. And to this day the Hawaiian Girl Scouts proudly
display the queen's silk personal standard.

Henry Waterhouse never spoke or wrote about the overthrow
of the monarchy subsequent to his testimony to the Blount
Commission. So, we will never know if he had any doubts or
regrets about his leading part in the coup of 1893, or whether
he deliberately distanced himself from the more anti-Native
Hawaiian attitudes and activities of some of his more rabid
revolutionary colleagues. Colleagues within the church and the
YMCA would cite a long list of his activities and achievements
as evidence of his piety and determination to do good by the
community. But which community? Or, in his enthusiasm to
dethrone a stubborn queen, did it naively fail to occur to Henry
Waterhouse that his colleagues would disenfranchise the native
people of Hawaii to ensure that the annexationists' will, and their
power, permanently prevailed?

Why was my fellow Australian so determined to overthrow
Hawaii's monarchy? Having been born under the British flag, to
British parents whose native land had a crowned head of state,
it is unlikely he grew up with a principled dislike of monarchal
rule, unlike many Americans. Was Henry's distaste for monarchy
purely directed toward Hawaii's native form of this style of
government? Had his objection been to Liliuokalani alone, he
would surely have sided with Sandford Dole and Archie Cleghorn
in 1893 in supporting Princess' Kaiulani's claim to the throne in
her aunt's place. Was Waterhouse's principal objection to rule by
a woman? Was he driven by racism, as some of his colleagues
appear to have been? Or, did Henry simply enjoy using the power
that his money, position, and influence gave him? Perhaps it was
a mixture of all these things.

Banker Sam Damon, the other key figure in Liliuokalani's
overthrow, the man who perpetuated the bluff that convinced his
trusting queen to surrender her throne rather than see bloodshed
as a result of a battle between US sailors and marines and her
loyal forces, lived well into old age, almost reaching his eightieth
year. Damon served as the PGs' first and last finance minister. He

died immensely rich. But long life did not spare him tragedy; in 1904, his eldest son and the light of his life, Ned Damon, was stabbed to death. A victory for the kahunas, the superstitious might have said.

As for the Native Hawaiian peoples, they had revenge for the loss of their country in subtle ways. From 1900, Hawaii, as a US territory, was entitled to send a single delegate to the US Congress. Despite the expressed intent that the domination by Americans and persons of American descent in the government of the islands be continued, the more relaxed US election laws that now applied in Hawaii meant that many of those who had been disenfranchised since 1887 could at last exercise their right to vote. And as their first delegate to the U.S. Congress, the Hawaiian people in 1898 elected none other than 'Redshirt Robert' Wilcox. In 1903, they made an even more emphatic statement, electing Prince Kuhio as Hawaii's delegate to Congress. They continued to send Prince Kuhio to Washington until 1922, when he retired. Widely known as Prince Cupid, he was a popular figure on Capitol Hill.

In 1918, President Woodrow Wilson appointed the Territory of Hawaii's fifth governor since annexation. That governor was Charles J. McCarthy, the very same Charles McCarthy, who, in Queen Liliuokalani's service as a special constable, had been the 'one man army' at the Government Building when the PGs seized power on January 17, 1893. Governor McCarthy convinced the territory's legislature to acquire Washington Place, the home of the late Queen Liliuokalani, as the official residence of the governors of Hawaii, and McCarthy was the first governor to move in there. Liliuokalani's house continued to be the home of Hawaii's governors until 2001, when a new governor's mansion was built in the grounds of Washington Place. Liliuokalani's home is now a museum, dedicated to her, and restored to much the way it was in the 1890s.

Iolani Palace has also been restored to its former glory. It continued as Hawaii's Executive Building until 1968. After an ultramodern new Capitol Building was opened next door, the Friends of Iolani Palace acquired the former palace, saving it from planned demolition. The Friends have since painstakingly restored Iolani Palace, and continue to search for items pillaged from it in the 1890s. Iolani Palace, and the similarly restored

Queen Emma's Summer Palace in Oahu's Nuuanu Valley, now also a museum, are the only royal palaces in the United States.

There is one more chapter to tell in the history of the overthrow of Hawaii's monarchy, and that was written by the US Congress and President Bill Clinton in more recent times.

30.

AN OFFICIAL APOLOGY

H AWAII WAS ADMITTED TO THE UNION AS THE fiftieth state of the United States of America on August 21, 1959, seven months after Alaska became the forty-ninth state of the union. On June 27 of that year, a referendum was put to the people of the Territory of Hawaii, with just two options–did they want Hawaii to gain statehood, or to remain a US territory? The vote was seventeen to one in favor of statehood.

Thirty-four years later, in 1993, the 103rd Congress of the United States passed a joint resolution: 'To acknowledge the 100th anniversary of the January 17, 1893 overthrow of the Kingdom of Hawaii, and to offer an apology to Native Hawaiians on behalf of the United States for the overthrow of the Kingdom of Hawaii.' The resolution was signed into law by President Bill Clinton, as Public Law 103-150, on November 23, 1993.[511]

It was a resolution which recognized the illegal complicity of US Minister John L. Stevens, and of US forces landed from the USS *Boston*, in the armed overthrow of the legitimate, sovereign government of Hawaii. Echoing President Grover Cleveland, this had been, the congressional resolution said, an act of war. At the same time, the Eighteenth General Synod of the United Church of Christ, 'in recognition of the denomination's historical complicity in the illegal overthrow of the Kingdom of Hawaii in 1893,' also offered a public apology to the Native Hawaiian people.[512]

After the earnest but inadequate Blount Report, the personally and politically biased Morgan Report, and the dashing of Native Hawaiian hopes that came with annexation in 1898, finally, the crimes and the prejudicial treatment of the past had been recognized. Has it changed anything? No. A sovereignty movement quickly sprang up in Hawaii on the back of the congressional apology, with some Native Hawaiians demanding that Hawaii be given back its sovereignty as a separate nation. That is unlikely to happen. There are more than 120 US military bases in Hawaii today. Pacific Command, located in Hawaii, is the largest of all US military commands. The US military presence contributes massively to the Hawaiian economy. Incidentally, it also makes the paradise of Hawaii a leading nuclear target.

Hawaiians received no compensation for the Crown Lands surrendered to the United States by Sanford Dole–surrendered as if Hawaii were a conquered country. Financial compensation, rather than sovereignty, is spoken of by most Native Hawaiians today. Many descendants of the ali'i of 1893 have served, and do serve, in the US military, and proudly salute the US flag. They want to be able to send their children to college and would appreciate a little help with college fees. Some would like a little government help with their mortgages; a special, low or no interest rate for Native Hawaiians in Hawaii, perhaps, by way of compensation for their lost heritage.

But the Kingdom of Hawaii is long gone, and the wise ali'i know that it is impossible to turn back the clock and regain it. Grover Cleveland, for all his good intentions, was foolish, or naïve, to attempt to turn the clock back to prior to the queen's overthrow, and expect all in the garden to be rosy again. It was an impossibility, particularly if the Provisional Government refused to step aside, as they did. Sam Parker, deposed premier and firm friend of Liliuokalani, had accepted the inevitability of change by the time that he was interviewed by Commissioner James Blount in the middle of 1893. He told Blount, 'The restoration of the Queen under an American protectorate would be a more stable government than the old regime. There is a feeling that unless we are under some country like the United States it would be the same old trouble coming up all the time.'[513]

It may just have worked–Hawaii as a US protectorate, with the monarchy restored but with the US in charge. Especially if Liliuokalani could have been convinced to step aside in favor of the adored Kaiulani, for the sake of Hawaii. Cleveland was not in favor of this; protectorate status was felt to give the US responsibility for all Hawaii's problems without any compensatory benefits. And then there was the almost rabid hatred of monarchies that existed in many quarters in the United States at that time. To anti-monarchists, the idea of the US flag flying over a monarchy was anathema. To make a more modern analogy, it would have been about as acceptable as the US Government making Castro's Cuba a US protectorate and leaving the existing regime in power.

Could the overthrow of Liliuokalani have been prevented? It is unlikely. In one respect, the Morgan Report was correct—the queen had brought about her own downfall by attempting to promulgate a new constitution. It was not that this act was necessarily illegal; Lorrin Thurston subsequently expressed the view that Liliuokalani did not need her ministers' approval and could have gone ahead and brought in the new constitution. But her action gave the men of the Annexation Club the excuse they needed to brand Liliuokalani a revolutionary, and to demand her replacement.

Ever since Thurston's 1892 trip to Washington, when he'd been assured of the Harrison Administration's firm support for annexation, Thurston and his colleagues had been waiting for Liliuokalani to give them a premise to move against her. Had it not been a new constitution, they would have found another excuse. It was just a matter of time. In the end, Thurston thought that luck played a part in their successful overthrow of the queen. As an old saying goes, luck comes when preparation meets opportunity. The Annexation Club was prepared, and in January 1893 Liliuokalani gave them the opportunity.

Dole, Damon and many others who climbed aboard the annexation train were a mixture of fools and tools. Thurston, Smith, Cooper, Castle, Wilder, and the ill-starred young Carter—this was the diabolically determined, wickedly clever, and blindly prejudiced cabal that would have unseated the 'native dynasty' sooner or later and subsequently consummated the annexation with the United States. It was a union after which they had lusted for years.

During the research for this book, a present day relative of Henry Waterhouse expressed the hope, to me, that Henry, my fellow Tasmanian, would not come out of this study of the overthrow of the Hawaiian monarchy too badly painted. It is true that Henry was a deeply religious man. It is also true that, apart from serving in the Republic's Senate, he had little to do with the illegal government that followed the monarchy. Yet, when the 1895 counter-revolution erupted, Henry was among the first to take up arms in defense of the rebel administration.

That rebel administration, illegal in formation and in action, never gave a thought to the rights of the Native Hawaiian and Asian peoples of Hawaii. As far as they were concerned, those people were without rights. The unelected Provisional Government and the subsequent Republic of Hawaii police state regimes were racist–if not in intent, certainly in deed. And those who enabled or participated in both can only be tarnished with the same sorry brush. This is not to say that the government of my own country, Australia, and many of my fellow Australians, were not racist in word and deed at that time, and well into the second half of the 20th century. But good men, and women, did exist in those times. Men such as Lieutenant Commander William Swinburne, who was determined to keep US forces out of the struggle of January, 1893. And Grover Cleveland and James Blount, who recognized the injustice done to the Hawaiian people, and damaged their own reputations in attempting to right the wrong.

There can be no escaping the fact that, had Henry Waterhouse not pursued the coup on January 16 and 17, when other revolutionaries faltered, there is a strong likelihood that the 1893 overthrow of the Hawaiian monarchy would not have occurred. And it is true that, to some extent, Queen Liliuokalani brought about her own downfall, through her stubborn determination to claw back some of the power lost to the Hawaiian monarchy in the Bayonet Constitution.

Yet, if it was not that, the Queen's enemies would have found some other reason to bring down the monarchy and form an attachment with the United States. Lorrin Thurston wrote, when promoting annexation in Washington in 1897, 'The recognition of the strategic value of Hawaii's geographical position, and the determination that under no circumstances should it pass under the control of any foreign people, constitute one of the most conspicuous examples of consistent and persistent foreign policy in the international history of the United States.'[514]

Had Henry Waterhouse and Sam Damon not played their pivotal roles in events, could we still have a monarchy in Hawaii today? That is unlikely. The taking of Hawaii from its traditional owners was a matter of 'when,' not 'if.' As Thurston pointed out in his *Hand-Book on the Annexation*, America had long had an eye to taking Hawaii. This Pacific paradise was simply too good a plum not to pluck. As far back as 1853, US Secretary of State William Learned Marcy had said of the Hawaiian Islands, 'It seems to be inevitable that they must come under the control of this government.'[515]

In the end, like any successful robbery, all the taking of Hawaii needed was a mildly competent gang, a few helpers on the inside, and a host of intimidated victims. The great Hawaiian nation robbery of January 17, 1893 had all three.

NOTES

1. THE FIRST SHOT

1. Executive Documents of 53rd Congress, 'Affairs in Hawaii.'
2. Ibid.
3. McChesney, in *Blount Report*.
4. Today's Maole language spoken and written by Native Hawaiians is a adaptation of the original tongue by early Christian missionaries to the islands, in particular William Ellis, an Englishman who came to Hawaii for two years from Sydney, New South Wales in 1822 and who reduced the local language to a written form so that an Hawaiian language Bible and Christian hymns could be used by the native population. Ellis, and other missionaries, changed the language spoken by Hawaiians by discarding some sounds which they considered too close to others–for example keeping the 'k' sound but discarding the 't', and keeping the 'i' but discarding the rolling 'r'.
5. The alii classes were the pio, niaupio, naha, wohi, lo, papa, lokea, laau, kaukau, alii noanoa, and makaainana.
6. The lani sub-groups comprised the alii nuii, kalaimoku, pukaua, kuhina, mookuauhau, aii kaulana, alii okana, ilikupono, alii aiahupuaa, konohiki, and luna.
7. The four classes of the noa caste were the ino, hu, noanoa, and the laolao.

2. THE HAWAIIAN MONARCHY

8. Liliuokalani, *Hawaii's Story*.
9. Gregg to Marcy, Executive Documents of 53rd Congress, 'Affairs in Hawaii.'
10. Marcy to Gregg, ibid.

3. THE ROYAL ELECTION RIOT

11. She had been betrothed to Kamehameha V at birth, but when, much later, she told Kamehameha that she wished to marry Charles Reed Bishop, the king acceded to her wishes and gave her up.
12. The Punahou School is today the largest independent school in the United States.

4. AT THE BAYONET'S POINT

13. Dole, *Memoirs.*
14. Ibid.
15. Ibid.
16. Ibid.
17. Liliuokalani, *Diary*, June 12, 1893.

5. CASTRATING THE KING

18. Liliuokalani, *Hawaii's Story.*
19. Dole, *Memoirs.*
20. Ibid.
21. Ibid.
22. Ibid.
23. Ibid.
24. Ibid.
25. Ibid.
26. Thurston, *Memoirs.*
27. Dole, *Memoirs.*
28. History has treated Gibson better than it has most of his opponents; in the 20th century, the Honolulu Police Station on Merchant Street, a 1931 building which replaced the original 1885 redbrick station house, was named the Walter Murray Gibson Building.
29. Wisniewski, *The Rise & Fall of the Hawaiian Kingdom.*
30. Judd testimony, *Blount Report.*
31. Ibid.
32. Dole, *Memoirs.*
33. Liliuokalani, *Diary*, Sept. 26, 1887.

6. WILCOX THE ASSASSIN

34. Sobrero, *An Italian Baroness in Hawaii.*
35. Ibid.
36. Liliuokalani, *Diary*, Nov. 20, 1887.
37. Liliuokalani, *Hawaii's Story.*
38. Kimberly to Secretary of the Navy, Oct. 18, 1889. *Blount Report.*
39. Sobrero, *An Italian Baroness in Hawaii.*
40. Ibid.
41. Liliuokalani, *Hawaii's Story.*
42. Liliuokalani, *Diary*, Dec. 11, 1887.
43. Liliuokalani, *Diary*, Dec. 23, 1887.
44. Ibid., Jan. 9, 1888.
45. Ibid., Jan. 14, 1888.
46. Ibid., Jan 16, 1888.
47. Ibid., Jan. 24, 1888.
48. Sobrero, *An Italian Baroness in Hawaii.*
49. Ibid.

50. Ibid.
51. Ibid.
52. Ibid.
53. Thurston, *Memoirs*.

7. THE REDSHIRT REBELLION

54. David Waipa Parker to the author, Nov., 2008. Most Hawaiian histories incorrectly refer to Robert as 'Captain Parker.' As official records at the Hawaiian State Archives prove, and his family knows, his name was Robert Parker Waipa. The white community tended to refer to him by his English middle name, but Hawaiians knew him as Waipa. Captain Waipa's superior, Captain John Paul Kahalewai was arrested in connection with the Redshirt Rebellion. Charges were subsequently dismissed for lack of evidence, but Kalakaua believed that Kahalewai had deliberately absented himself from duty so that he did not have to fight Wilcox and his men, and the king had the cabinet discharge Kahalewai from the Guard and appoint Robert Parker Waipa in his place as commander.
55. Liliuokalani, *Hawaii's Story*
56. Ibid.
57. *Ko Hawaii Pae Aina* (Hawaiian-language newspaper), August 3, 1889.
58. Ibid.
59. Liliuokalani, *Hawaii's Story*.
60. Dole, *Memoirs*.
61. Ibid.
62. Liliuokalani, *Hawaii's Story*.
63. Ibid.

8. LONG LIVE THE QUEEN

64. Foreign Office & Executive (FO&E) 41
65. Liliuokalani, *Hawaii's Story*.
66. Thurston, *Memoirs*.
67. Ibid.
68. Ibid.
69. Ibid.
70. Ibid.
71. Ibid.

9. CEMENTING WASHINGTON'S SUPPORT

72. Thurston, *Memoirs*.
73. Ibid.
74. Blount testimony, *Morgan Report*.
75. Thurston, *Memoirs*.
76. *Morgan Report*.
77. Thurston, *Memoirs*.
78. Blaine to Harrison, Aug. 3, 1891, Executive Documents, 53rd Congress.

79. Ibid.
80. Thurston, *Memoirs.*
81. Ibid.
82. Ibid.
83. Ibid.
84. Ibid.

10. THE CRUISE OF THE BOSTON

85. Young, *The Real Hawaii.*
86. Ibid.
87. Ibid.
88. Ibid.
89. Ibid.
90. Ibid.
91. Ibid.

11. THE TIME HAS ARRIVED

92. Samuel Parker testimony, *Blount Report.*
93. Liliuokalani, *Hawaii's Story.*
94. Parker testimony, *Blount Report.*
95. Ibid.
96. Thurston, *Memoirs.*
97. Ibid.
98. Ibid.
99. Ibid.
100. Young, *The Real Hawaii.*
101. Ibid.
102. Ibid.
103. Ibid.
104. The princes were related to Liliuokalani through both their father, who was Liliuokalani's cousin, and their mother.
105. Young, *The Real Hawaii.*
106. Ibid.
107. Dole, *Memoirs.*
108. Young, *The Real Hawaii.*
109. Ibid.
110. Ibid.
111. Ibid.
112. Ibid.
113. Liliuokalani, *Hawaii's Story.*
114. Ibid.
115. Ibid.
116. Ibid.
117. Parker, *Blount Report.*
118. Dole, *Memoirs.*
119. Parker, *Blount Report.*

120. Liliuokalani, *Hawaii's Story*.
121. Ibid.
122. Parker, *Blount Report*.
123. Young, *The Real Hawaii*.
124. Parker, *The Blount Report*.
125. Ibid.
126. Young, *The Real Hawaii*.
127. Liliuokalani, *Hawaii's Story*.
128. Parker, *Blount Report*.
129. Ibid.
130. Thurston, *Memoirs*.
131. Ibid.
132. Ibid.
133. Ibid.
134. Ibid.
135. Ibid.
136. Parker testimony, *Blount Report*.
137. Thurston, *Memoirs*.
138. Ibid.
139. Ibid.
140. Bolte testimony, *Blount Report*.
141. Ibid.
142. Waterhouse testimony, *Blount Report*.
143. Thurston, *Memoirs*.
144. Young, *The Real Hawaii*.
145. Ibid.
146. Ibid.
147. Ibid.
148. Parker testimony, *Blount Report*.
149. Liliuokalani, *Hawaii's Story*.
150. Ibid.
151. Ibid.
152. Ibid.
153. Young, *The Real Hawaii*.
154. Ibid.
155. Ibid.
156. Dole, *Memoirs*.
157. Young, *The Real Hawaii*.
158. Dole, *Memoirs*.
159. Young, *The Real Hawaii*.
160. Dole, *Memoirs*.
161. Ibid.
162. Thurston, *Memoirs*.
163. Ibid.
164. Ibid.
165. Ibid.
166. Dole, *Memoirs*.
167. Ibid.

334 *Stephen Dando-Collins*

168. Young, *The Real Hawaii.*

12. SUNDAY: THE MAKING OF A COUP

169. Peterson statement, *Blount Report.*
170. Thurston, *Memoirs.*
171. Peterson, *Blount Report.* His fresh recollection, only months old, should be more reliable than that of Thurston, who wrote of the event many years after.
172. Smith statement, *Blount Report.*
173. Thurston, *Memoirs.*
174. Ibid.
175. Smith, *Blount Report.*
176. Parker, *Blount Report*
177. Ibid.
178. Peterson, *Blount Report.*
179. Stevens to Foster, Sept. 14, 1892, Exec. Docs, 53rd Congress.
180. Peterson, *Blount Report.*
181. Stevens to Blaine, Apr. 2, 1892, Exec. Docs, 53rd Congress.

13. CAPTAIN WILTSE'S DECISION

182. Young, *The Real Hawaii.*
183. Parker testimony, *Blount Report.*
184. Liliuokalani, *Hawaii's Story.*
185. Parker testimony, *Blount Report.*
186. Young, *The Real Hawaii.*
187. Thurston, *Memoirs,* for the entire exchange.
188. Ibid.
189. Young, *The Real Hawaii.*
190. Dole, *Memoirs.*
191. Young, *The Real Hawaii.*
192. *Morgan Report.*
193. Young, *The Real Hawaii.*
194. Ibid.
195. *Blount Report.*
196. Young, *The Real Hawaii.*
197. Swinburne testimony, *Morgan Report.*
198. Young, *The Real Hawaii.*
199. Ibid.
200. Liliuokalani, *Hawaii's Story.*
201. FO&E 41
202. Thurston, *Memoirs.*
203. Dole, *Memoirs.*
204. *Morgan Report.*
205. Young, *The Real Hawaii.*
206. Exec Docs, 53rd Congress.
207. Ibid.

208. Ibid.
209. Thurston, *Memoirs*.
210. Waterhouse testimony, *Blount Report*.
211. Thurston, *Memoirs*.
212. Alexander, *History of Later Years of the Hawaiian Monarchy*.
213. Sydney *Daily Telegraph*, Feb. 6, 1893.
214. Alexander, *History of Later Years*.
215. Young, *The Real Hawaii*.
216. Alexander, *History of Later Years*.
217. Stevens to Foster, Feb 1, 1893, *Morgan Report*.

14. THE US INVASION OF HAWAII

218. Young, *The Real Hawaii*.
219. Ibid.
220. Stevens to Foster, Feb. 1, 1893, *Morgan Report*.
221. Young, *The Real Hawaii*.
222. Laird testimony, *Morgan Report*.
223. Ibid.
224. Swinburne testimony, *Morgan Report*.
225. *Morgan Report*.
226. Young, *The Real Hawaii*.
227. Thurston, *Memoirs*.
228. Waterhouse testimony, *Blount Report*.
229. Thurston, *Memoirs*.
230. Tacitus, *Histories*, II, 68.
231. Thurston, *Memoirs*.
232. Waterhouse testimony, *Blount Report*.
233. Thurston, *Memoirs*.
234. FO&E 41.
235. Waterhouse testimony, *Blount Report*.
236. Thurston, *Memoirs*.
237. Smith statement, *Blount Report*.
238. Thurston, *Memoirs*.
239. Young, *The Real Hawaii*.
240. Swinburne testimony, *Morgan Report*.
241. Thurston, *Memoirs*.
242. Ibid.
243. Smith statement, *Blount Report*.
244. Coffman testimony, *Morgan Report*.
245. Damon testimony, *Blount Report*.
246. *Blount Report*.
247. *Blount Report*.
248. Waterhouse testimony, *Blount Report*.
249. Ibid.
250. Ibid.
251. Wundenberg statement, *Blount Report*.
252. Bernice Irwin, *I Knew Queen Liliuokalani*.

253. *Blount Report.*
254. Coffman testimony, *Morgan Report.*
255. Young, *The Real Hawaii.*
256. Liliuokalani, *Hawaii's Story.*
257. Laird testimony, *Morgan Report.*
258. Young, *The Real Hawaii.*
259. Ibid.

15. PREPARING TO STRIKE

260. Dole, *Memoirs.*
261. Thurston, *Memoirs.*
262. Liliuokalani, *Hawaii's Story.*
263. Cornwell statement, *Blount Report.*
264. Parker testimony, *Blount Report.*
265. Ibid.
266. Swinburne testimony, *Morgan Report.*
267. Ibid.
268. Ibid.
269. Dole, *Memoirs.*
270. Gillis, *The Hawaiian Incident.*
271. Peterson statement, *Blount Report.*
272. Ibid.
273. Parker testimony, *Blount Report.*
274. Ibid.
275. Peterson statement, *Blount Report.*
276. Ibid.

16. LAUNCHING THE COUP

277. Dole, *Memoirs.*
278. Ibid.
279. Ibid.
280. Young, *The Real Hawaii.*
281. Ibid.
282. Swinburne testimony, *Morgan Report*, entire exchange.
283. Hopkins statement, *Blount Report.*
284. Ibid.
285. Damon testimony, *Blount Report.*
286. Ibid.
287. Dole, Memoirs.
288. McChesney statement, *Blount Report.*
289. Damon testimony, *Blount Report.*
290. Wundenberg statement, *Blount Report.*
291. Damon testimony, *Blount Report.*
292. Wundenberg statement, *Blount Report.*
293. Damon testimony, *Blount Report.*
294. Emmeluth statement, *Blount Report.*

295. Liliuokalani, *Hawaii's story*.
296. Ibid.
297. Hopkins statement, *Blount Report*.
298. McChesney statement, *Blount Report*.
299. Ibid.
300. Ibid.

17. THE GREAT BLUFF

301. Swinburne testimony, *Morgan Report*.
302. McChesney statement, *Blount Report*.
303. Swinburne testimony, *Morgan Report*.
304. Dole, *Memoirs*.
305. Damon testimony, *Blount Report*.
306. Colburn & Peterson statement, *Blount Report*.
307. Damon testimony, *Blount Report*.
308. Ibid.
309. FO&E 41.
310. McChesney statement, *Blount Report*.
311. Swinburne testimony, *Morgan Report*.
312. Damon testimony, *Blount Report*.
313. Swinburne testimony, *Morgan Report*
314. Cornwell statement, *Blount Report*.
315. Ibid.
316. J. Carter statement, *Blount Report*.
317. Ibid.
318. Ibid.
319. Ibid.
320. Damon testimony, *Blount Report*.
321. Ibid.
322. J. Carter statement, *Blount Report*.
323. Damon testimony, *Blount Report*.
324. Ibid.
325. Liliuokalani, *Hawaii's Story*.
326. Stevens testimony, *Morgan Report*.
327. Emmeluth statement, *Blount Report*.
328. Young, *The Real Hawaii*.
329. Ibid.
330. Thurston, *Memoirs*.
331. Ibid.
332. Ibid.

18. IN THE LIGHT OF THE NEW DAY

333. Bernice Irwin, *I Knew Queen Liliuokalani*.
334. Liliuokalani, *Hawaii's Story*.
335. Sanford Dole to George Dole, Jan. 19, 1893. Irwin, *I Knew Queen Liliuokalani*.

19. A SUGAR COATING

336. Castle, *Diary*.
337. Thurston, *Memoirs*.
338. Castle, *Diary*.
339. Ibid.
340. Ibid.

20. AN AMERICAN PROTECTORATE

341. Young, *The Real Hawaii*.
342. *New York Times*, November 30, 1893.

21. SELLING ANNEXATION IN WASHINGTON

343. Young, *The Real Hawaii*.
344. Castle, *Diary*.
345. Ibid.
346. *Sydney Morning Herald*, Feb. 3, 1893.
347. *Sydney Morning Herald*, Feb. 1, 1893.
348. *Sydney Morning Herald*, Feb. 2, 1893.
349. *New York Times*, Feb. 4, 1893.
350. Castle, *Diary*.
351. Thurston, *Memoirs*.
352. *London Times*, January 31, 1893.
353. Castle, *Diary*.
354. Ibid.
355. Ibid.
356. Ibid.
357. Ibid.

22. A PRINCESS IN THE WHITE HOUSE

358. Linnea, *Princess Ka'ialani*.
359. Ibid.
360. *Sydney Morning Herald*, Jan. 31, 1893.
361. *Sydney Morning Herald*, Feb. 1, 1893.
362. *Sydney Morning Herald*, Feb. 4, 1893.
363. *Sydney Morning Herald*, Feb. 1, 1893.
364. Ibid.
365. Linnea, *Princess Kaiulani*.
366. Ibid.
367. Castle, *Diary*.
368. Linnea, *Princess Kaiulani*.
369. Ibid.
370. Castle, *Diary*.
371. Ibid.
372. Thurston, *Memoirs*.

373. Stevens to Foster, Feb. 1, 1893. *Morgan Report*.
374. Thurston, *Memoirs*.
375. Castle, *Diary*.
376. Ibid.
377. Ibid.
378. Ibid.
379. Thurston, *Memoirs*.
380. Blount testimony, *Morgan Report*.
381. Ibid.
382. Ibid.
383. Linnea, *Princess Kaiulani*.
384. Boston *Evening Transcript*, Apr. 15, 1893.

23. LOWERING THE FLAG.

385. Unattributed. Reported on the website of Jones, Cork and Miller, the Georgia law firm co-founded by James Blount, www.jonescork.com.
386. Blount testimony, *Morgan Report*.
387. Ibid.
388. *Blount Report*.
389. *New York Times*, Nov. 30, 1893.
390. McCandless statement, *Blount Report*.
391. Blount testimony, *Morgan Report*.
392. Ibid.
393. *Morgan Report*.
394. Liliuokalani, *Hawaii's Story*.
395. Skerrett letter, *Blount Report*
396. Hooper letter, *Blount Report*.
397. Liliuokalani, *Hawaii's Story*.
398. Liliuokalani, *Diary*, Feb. 1, 1893.
399. Young, *The Real Hawaii*.
400. Gillis, *The Hawaiian Incident*.
401. Ibid.
402. FO&E 41.
403. *New York Times*, 27 Apr., 1893.

24. RESTORE THE QUEEN

404. *Morgan Report*.
405. Skerrett letter, *Blount Report*.
406. Ibid. In the fall of 1893, Skerrett was relieved of duty by the Navy Department. The fact that he had supported the protectorate status established by Stevens, even though he did not land men from his own ship to add to those of the Boston in Honolulu, counted against him. Skerrett voluntarily retired in 1894.
407. *Morgan Report*.
408. Ibid.
409. Ibid.

410. Liliuokalani, *Hawaii's Story*.
411. *Morgan Report*.
412. Ibid.
413. Liliuokalani, *Hawaii's Story*.
414. *Morgan Report*.
415. Ibid.
416. Ibid.
417. Ibid.
418. Dole, *Memoirs*.
419. *Morgan Report*.
420. Admiral Irwin dispatch, *Morgan Report*.
421. *New York Times*, Nov. 30, 1893.
422. Ibid.
423. Gillis, *The Hawaiian Incident*.
424. Dole, *Memoirs*.
425. Admiral Irwin dispatch, *Morgan Report*.
426. Willis dispatch, *Morgan Report*.
427. Ibid.
428. Ibid.
429. Liliuokalani, *Diary*, May 29, 1893.
430. Willis dispatch, *Morgan Report*.
431. Ibid.
432. Ibid.
433. Liliuokalani, *Diary*, Feb. 9, 1893.
434. Cleveland's Message, *Morgan Report*.
435. Willis dispatch, *Morgan Report*.
436. Ibid.
437. Dole, *Memoirs*.
438. *Morgan Report*.
439. Bernice Irwin, *I Knew Queen Liliuokalani*.
440. Admiral Irwin dispatch, *Morgan Report*.

25. THE MORGAN REPORT

441. *Morgan Report*.
442. Ibid.
443. Ibid.
444. Ibid.
445. Dole, *Memoirs*.
446. *Morgan Report*.
447. Ibid.
448. Ibid.
449. Ibid.

26. THE HAWAIIAN REPUBLIC, & THE COUNTER COUP

450. Dole, *Memoirs*.
451. Liliuokalani, *Hawaii's Story*.

452. Liliuokalani, *Diary*, Dec. 26 & 27, 1894.

453. Liliuokalani, *Diary*, Dec. 1, 1894.

454. Liliuokalani, *Diary*, Dec. 29, 1894.

455. Towse, *The Rebellion of 1895*.

456. Liliuokalani, *Hawaii's Story*.

457. Towse, *The Rebellion of 1895*.

458. Ibid.

459. Liliuokalani, *Hawaii's Story*.

460. Towse, *The Rebellion of 1895*.

461. Ibid.

27. FIGHTING FOR THE QUEEN

462. Towse, *The rebellion of 1895*.

463. *New York Times*, Jan. 19, 1895 describes the shooting of Carter. Poole is identified as the man who shot Carter by Towse in *The Rebellion of 1895*. Alexander, in *History of the Later Years of the Hawaiian Monarchy*, gives details of Carter's wounds.

464. Towse, *The Rebellion of 1895*.

465. *New York Times*, Jan. 19, 1895.

466. Towse, *The Rebellion of 1895*.

467. Ibid.

468. *New York Times*, Jan. 19, 1895.

469. Ibid.

470. Towse, *The Rebellion of 1895*.

471. Ibid.

472. Bernice Irwin, *I Knew Queen Liliuokalani*.

473. Towse, *The Rebellion of 1895*.

474. Ibid.

28. THE QUEEN ON TRIAL

475. David Waipa Parker to the author, Nov., 2008.

476. Towse, *The Rebellion of 1895*.

477. Ibid.

478. Liliuokalani, *Hawaii's Story*.

479. Ibid.

480. Ibid.

481. Jan. 30, 1895. In Thurston, *Memoirs*.

482. Liliuokalani, *Hawaii's Story*.

483. Ibid.

484. Ibid.

485. Ibid.

486. Thurston, *Memoirs*.

487. Alexander, *History of the Later Years of the Hawaiian Monarchy*.

488. Liliuokalani, *Hawaii's Story*.

489. Ibid.

490. Towse, *The Rebellion of 1895*.

491. FO&E 44.
492. Ibid.
493. Ibid.
494. Jan. 30, 1895. In Thurston, *Memoirs*.
495. Feb. 17, 1895. In Thurston, *Memoirs*.
496. Towse, *The Rebellion of 1895*.
497. Jan. 30, 1895. In Thurston, *Memoirs*.

29. ANNEXATION

498. Thurston, *Memoirs*.
499. *New York Evening Post*, May 16, 1895.
500. Towse, *The Rebellion of 1895*.
501. Jan. 30, 1895. In Thurston, *Memoirs*.
502. Thurston, Memoirs.
503. Roosevelt, *The Letters of Theodore Roosevelt*.
504. Ibid.
505. Thurston, *Hand-Book on the Annexation of Hawaii*.
506. Young, *The Real Hawaii*.
507. Liliuokalani, *Hawaii's Story*.
508. Bernice Irwin, *I Knew Queen Liliuokalani*.
509. Linnea, *Princess Kaiulani*.
510. Young, *The Real Hawaii*.
511. Linnea, *Princess Kaiulani*.
512. Congressional Record, Vol. 139, 1993.
513. Ibid.
514. Parker testimony, *Blount Report*.
515. Thurston, *Hand-Book on the Annexation of Hawaii*.
516. Ibid.

BIBLIOGRAPHY

Numerous books and papers were consulted in the writing of this book, many of them providing the author with insights into the history of Hawaii and her people. In terms of the overthrow of the monarchy, the following sources proved the most useful.

Alexander, W. D., *History of Later Years of the Hawaiian Monarchy and the Revolution of 1893*. Honolulu, Hawaiian Gazette, 1896.

Allen, H. G., *The Betrayal of Liliuokalani, Last Queen of Hawaii 1838-1917*. Honolulu, Mutual, 1982.

Budnick, R., *Stolen Kingdom: An American Conspiracy*. Honolulu, Aloha, 1992.

Castle, W. R., *American Annexation of Hawaii* (diary). Honolulu, 1951.

Chaplin, G., *Presstime in Paradise: The life and times of the Honolulu Advertiser, 1856-1995*. Honolulu, Advertiser, 1995.

Coffman, T., *Nation Within: The Story of America's Annexation of the Nation of Hawaii*. Kaneohe, (Hawaii), EPICenter, 1998.

Cohen, S., *The First Lady of Waikiki, A Pictorial History of the Sheraton Moana Surfrider*. Pictorial Histories, Missoula, Montana, 1995.

Daws, G., *The Shoals of Time: A History of the Hawaiian Islands*. New York, Macmillan, 1968.

Dole, S. B., *Memoirs of the Hawaiian Revolution*. Honolulu, Advertiser, 1936.

Forbes, D. W., *Hawaiian National Biography, 1780-1900*. Honolulu, University of Hawaii, 2003.

Gillis, J. A., *The Hawaiian Incident: An Examination of Mr. Cleveland's Attitude Toward the Revolution of 1893*. Freeport, NY, Books for Libraries, (reprint of 1898 original), 1970.

Irwin, B. P., *I Knew Queen Liliuokalani*. Honolulu, Native Books, 2000.

Kamae, L. K., *The Empty Throne: A Biography of Hawaii's Prince Cupid*. Honolulu, Topgallant, 1980.

Kuykendall, R. S., *The Hawaiian Kingdom, Vol. I, 1778-1854, Foundation and Transformation.* Honolulu, University of Hawaii, 1938.

Kuykendall, R. S., *The Hawaiian Kingdom, Vol. II, 1854-1874, Twenty Critical Years.* Honolulu, University of Hawaii, 1953.

Kuykendall, R. S., *The Hawaiian Kingdom, Vol. III, 1874-1893, The Kalakaua Dynasty.* Honolulu, University of Hawaii Press, 1967.

Liliuokalani, *Hawaii's Story, By Hawaii's Queen.* Honolulu, Mutual, 1990.

Linnea, S., *Princess Kaiulani, Hope of a Nation, Heart of a People.* Grand Rapids, MI, Eerdmans, 1999.

Malo, D., *Hawaiian Antiquities.* Honolulu, Bishop Museum, (reprint of 1898 edition), 1976.

McWilliams, T. S., *James H. Blount, the South, and Hawaiian Annexation.* San Francisco, University of California, 1988.

New Georgia Encyclopedia, The, 'James Blount.' Augusta, GA, Georgia Humanities Council and University of Georgia, 2005.

Olsson. M., *The Waterhouse Padman Family History.* Boolarong, Brisbane, 1987.

Osborne, T. J., *Empire Can Wait: American Opposition to Hawaiian Annexation, 1893-1898.* Kent, Ohio, Kent State University, 1981.

Parker, D. K., *Tales of Our Hawai'i.* Honolulu, Alu Like, 2007.

Proto, N.T., *The Rights of my People: Liliuokalani's Enduring Battle with the United States, 1893-1917.* New York, Algora, 2009.

Roosevelt, T., *The Letters of Theodore Roosevelt, Vol. 1, The Years of Preparation, 1868-1898.* Cambridge, Mass., Harvard University, 1951.

Sarhangi, S., *Honolulu Then and Now.* San Diego, Thunder Bay Press, 2007.

Seidlen, A., *The Hawaiian Monarchy.* Honolulu, Mutual, 2004.

Siddall, J. W. (editor), *Men of Hawaii: being a biographical reference library, complete and authentic, of the men of note and substantial achievement in the Hawaiian Islands, Vol.'s I-V.* Honolulu, *Honolulu Star-Bulletin,* 1917-1935.

Sobrero, G., *An Italian Baroness in Hawaii: The travel diary of Gina Sobrero, bride of Robert Wilcox, 1887,* (translated by E. C. Knowlton). Honolulu, Hawaiian Historical Society, 1991.

Tate, M., *Hawaii: Reciprocity or Annexation.* East Lansing, Michigan, Michigan State University, 1968.

Tate, M., *The United States and the Hawaiian Kingdom: A Political History.* New Haven, Conn., Yale University, 1965.

Thurston, L. A., *Hand-Book on the Annexation of Hawaii*. St Joseph, Michigan, Morse, 1897.

Thurston, L. A., *Memoirs of the Hawaiian Revolution*. Honolulu, Advertiser, 1936.

Towse, E., *The Rebellion of 1895*. Honolulu, *Hawaiian Star*, 1895.

Wisniewski, R. A., *The Rise and Fall of the Hawaiian Kingdom*. Honolulu, Pacific Basin Enterprises, 1979.

Young, L., *The Real Hawaii: Its History and Present Condition, Including the True Story of the Revolution*. New York, Doubleday & McClure, 1899.

JOURNAL ARTICLES

Devine, M. J., 'John W. Foster and the Struggle for the Annexation of Hawaii,' *The Pacific Historical Review*, Vol. 46, No. 1, Feb., 1977, University of California.

Hammett, H. B., 'The Cleveland Administration and Anglo-American Naval Friction in Hawaii, 1893-1894,' *Military Affairs*, Vol. 40, No. 1, Feb., 1976, Society for Military History.

Livingston-Little, D. E., 'A Scotsman Views Hawaii: An 1852 Log of a Cruise of the *Emily Bourne*.' *Journal of the West, Vol. IX, No. 2, April, 1970*.

Tate, M., 'Australasian Interest in the Commerce and the Sovereignty of Hawaii,' *Historical Studies, Australia & New Zealand*, Vol. 11, No. 44, April, 1965, Melbourne University.

NEWSPAPERS & JOURNALS

Boston Evening Transcript, 1893.
Boston Herald, 1893.
Chicago Evening Post, 1893.
Daily Bulletin, Honolulu, 1884-1895.
Daily Telegraph, London, 1893-1898.
Daily Telegraph, Sydney, 1893.
Evening Post, New York, 1895.
Evening Standard, London, 1893.
Friend, The, Honolulu, 1889-1893.
Herald, New York, 1891-1898.
Hobart Town Gazette, 1851.
Honolulu Star, 1893-1895.
Journal, New York, 1893.

Moniteur Universel, Paris, 1893.
New York Times, 1887-1898.
Pacific Commercial Advertiser, Honolulu, 1887-1917.
Pall Mall Gazette, London, 1893.
Sydney Morning Herald, Sydney, 1893.
Times of London, 1893-1898.
Tribune, New York, 1893.
Vossiche Zeitung, Berlin, 1893.

US CONGRESSIONAL REPORTS

Executive Documents of the House of Representatives for the
    Third Session of the Fifty-Third Congress, 1894-95, Foreign
    Relations of the United States, 1894, 'Affairs in Hawaii.'
    Includes the so-called 'the Blount Report.' Washington,
    Government Printing Office, 1895.
Hawaiian Islands: Report of the Committee on Foreign Relations,
    United States Senate, with accompanying testimony, and
    executive documents transmitted to Congress, from January
    1 1893, to March 10, 1894, a.k.a. 'The Morgan Report.'
    Washington, Government Printing Office, 1894.
United States Public Law 103-150, 103rd Congress Joint Resolution
    19, Nov. 23, 1993; contained within Congressional Record,
    Vol. 139. Washington, Government Printing Office, 1993.

DOCUMENTS IN HAWAII STATE ARCHIVES

Cleghorn Collection.
Foreign Office & Executive Papers, No. 39–1893, Executive &
    Advisory Councils Annexation.
Foreign Office & Executive Papers, No. 41, 1893.
Foreign Office & Executive Papers, No. 44–1895, Executive &
    Advisory Councils–Loyalty Reports: Government Employees.
Foreign Office & Executive Papers, No. 45–1895, Political Prisoners.
Foreign Office & Executive Papers, No. 46–1895, Rebellion.
Liliuokalani Diaries.
Rice Family Papers.

ABOUT THE AUTHOR

Australian-born novelist Stephen Dando-Collins trained as a graphic artist and worked as a designer, copywriter, and later senior executive with leading advertising agencies before serving as chief operating officer for Australia at a US market research group. He has been a full-time author, editor, and researcher since 1996, dealing mostly with historical subjects. His acclaimed work of American history, *Standing Bear Is a Person*, telling the true story of an 1879 Nebraska legal case, was published in 2004. The first in his series of definitive histories of the Roman legions, *Caesar's Legion*, based on more than thirty years of research, has found a broad audience around the world since it was published in 2002. The second in the series, *Nero's Killing Machine*, was published in 2005, followed by *Cleopatra's Kidnappers* in 2006 and *Mark Antony's Heroes* in 2007.

OPEN ROAD
INTEGRATED MEDIA

Open Road Integrated Media is a digital publisher and multimedia content company. Open Road creates connections between authors and their audiences by marketing its ebooks through a new proprietary online platform, which uses premium video content and social media.

22603906R00219

Made in the USA
San Bernardino, CA
13 July 2015